We're Everywhere,

Us:
Liverpool's 2014/15 season
told through the stories of fans and foes

We're Everywhere,
Us: Liverpool's 2014/15 season
told through the stories of fans and foes

Edited by Sachin Nakrani & Karl Coppack
Foreword by John Barnes

First published by Pitch Publishing, 2015

Pitch Publishing
A2 Yeoman Gate
Yeoman Way
Durrington
BN13 3QZ
www.pitchpublishing.co.uk

© 2015, Sachin Nakrani and Karl Coppack

A CIP catalogue record is available for this book
from the British Library.

ISBN 978 178531-042-3

Typesetting and origination by Pitch Publishing

Printed by Bell & Bain, Glasgow, Scotland

Contents

Foreword by John Barnes

I never minded whether we attacked the Kop in the first half or the second, it didn't bother me. But I know it did bother our opponents. You could see it in their faces, you still can, and it never surprises me when a visiting captain wins the toss at Anfield and switches Liverpool around.

The Kop is a psychological disadvantage for teams that come to Anfield. They don't like it, they fear it even, particularly during the era when I was a Liverpool player. Back then it was all-standing and the roar the 20,000 or so people in there made was incredible. It disturbed whoever we were facing and showed just how passionate Liverpool supporters were, and are, about their club.

Having lived in both halves of England I can say with confidence that people from the north of England are more passionate than those from the south, and that people from Liverpool are the most passionate of the lot. Scousers have a Latin-like temperament in that they are forthright and, occasionally, aggressive in how they speak to you, but they are also incredibly loving and loyal. In that sense Liverpool feels like a very un-English city, lacking the reserve that is common in many other parts of the country, and nowhere is that more obvious than at Anfield and the way in which the fans get behind the team. At its best it is loud, proud and colourful.

Liverpool has changed since I first arrived here in 1987 but at its heart it remains a working-class city where the people are down to earth and expect everyone else to be the same, including their footballers. It struck me the first time I met the Liverpool team during my time at Watford just how, well, normal they were. I remember playing at Anfield during the 1982/83 season, when Liverpool won the title and Watford finished second, and afterwards going for a drink in the players' lounge. I was suddenly in the company of the best team in the country, if not Europe, and yet there wasn't a single superstar in the room – they talked to me as if I was their equal, as if we were all friends having a beer at the local pub. I'd seen the same with England, when I came across the likes of Phil Neal, Alan Kennedy and Sammy Lee. This way of behaving no doubt had much to do with the city these guys were from and represented, and it was universal. Even the likes of Ian Rush and Kenny Dalglish didn't act like superstars, and they really were superstars.

I'd like to think that's why Liverpudlians also took to me. From the moment I arrived to now I have always been a normal person who does normal things, like go to Tesco and pick up the kids from school. In this city I have always been John Barnes the man and not John Barnes the footballer, and the people here appreciate that. More so, they demand it.

It hasn't always been easy and I remember there were a few supporters who didn't want me at Liverpool when I signed from Watford. The club had come in for me in January 1987 but I didn't move until the summer because Graham Taylor, Watford's manager at the time, made it clear that I would not be leaving mid-season. That, however, was never announced by Liverpool so when I didn't join in the January it was assumed that I had snubbed the club. I hadn't of course but that view stuck so there was a lot of resentment when I did eventually move; some fans said I had come reluctantly and that I actually wanted to join Arsenal. Some simply didn't want a black guy playing for their club.

My friend, who watched Liverpool a lot at the time, tells a story of being sat next to two old guys on my home debut, a 2-0 win against Oxford in September 1987, and hearing them moan about me straight from kick-off. I then scored with a free kick in the first half and one turned to the other and said, 'Well he's not as black as I first thought.'

Some people might find that story depressing but I've always been able to laugh about it. After all, it doesn't compare with having bananas thrown at you and monkey chants made in your direction, which was often the case in 1981, the year I made my debut for Watford. But even then I didn't need anyone's sympathy or support. Why should I? I'm an empowered human being, I always have been, and in no way would I ever allow the actions of an ignorant minority negatively affect me.

That first season at Liverpool was a great one for all involved, especially the fans who were clearly enjoying watching such an entertaining team perform week in, week out. I've always said that the 1977 and 1984 Liverpool sides are the best in the club's history, but there's no doubt the 1987/88 team that I played in was the most entertaining and, as one of the players, you could see just how much we meant to those who watched us by the noise they made, especially at home. It seemed to get louder every time we took to the pitch.

A relationship existed between the team and the fans and it's one that only strengthened after Hillsborough. That was a dark time but it brought people together and showed just how caring and supportive all Liverpudlians are, for it should never be forgotten that Evertonians also played their part in helping the city grieve and heal.

I went to as many funerals as I could and that's obviously something that still lives with me. I still see some of the families now and all of us have experienced much since 1989. We're all older yet that connection, that instant recognition, is still there. It will never leave us. In that sense there is something very deep and very personal about the bond that exists between Liverpool Football Club and its supporters. Together they have shared both joy and tragedy.

'You'll Never Walk Alone' unites everyone and while I don't have a favourite Liverpool song or chant that one is special, and personally so because it was played at my father's funeral. He loved 'You'll Never Walk Alone' but mainly because he was a big fan of *Carousel*, the musical that it came from. I never knew about those origins until my father died. Before that I thought it was just a football song, born and heard on the terraces.

Nowadays you hear 'You'll Never Walk Alone' not only at Anfield but across the world. Liverpool has become a truly international club and I am forever meeting new and different fans when I go to countries like China, South Africa and elsewhere. For them Liverpool is a unique club, like no other on the planet, with an identity that is both local and universal, traditional yet expansive. Whether a supporter has seen Liverpool play in the flesh or not, they feel they belong.

And when I meet a supporter, whether it is abroad or at home, they always ask me the same question, 'When are we going to win the league again?' Like most people I felt it was going to happen in 2014 only for that sadly not to prove the case. But I feel confident Liverpool can and will be champions in the future.

I for one will keep watching, keep supporting and keep hoping. And I'll do all those things from Liverpool itself, the city where I have spent some of my happiest years both personally and professionally, where my kids were born and where I'm sure I'll remain for a very long time.

Liverpool isn't just my club, it's also my home.

Introduction by Karl Coppack
Welcome to the 2014/15 season

I hope you've enjoyed the almost inevitable rise to Premier League victory/cup win/unbelievable Champions League campaign/ disappointment/scrape with relegation and are still celebrating/ recovering/slowly beginning to fight the urge to smash your head against a wall for several hours. It can't be good for you, that.

I write these words 11 days before the start of the season so you'll have to bear that in mind. Also, this introduction is somewhat suspect. I should have watched every nanosecond of the pre-season and scouted Emre Can, Lazar Markovic etc, but the truth is I haven't seen a thing. This bit has nothing to do with insight.

There are a number of reasons for this but the main one concerns football exhaustion. I'm still recovering from the madness of last season. Seriously, I'm a broken man. At Upton Park last season I found myself shaking an hour after the final whistle and that was a game we won. No, I needed time off before the madness reignites itself once more in the same way that heavy drinkers need a few days off before going at it again. I'll enjoy the next 11 days because, once again, life changes and the horrors and joy will return.

Liverpool are ready for me even if I'm not quite ready for us.

I've no idea what to expect this time. Not a single clue. Last year I predicted sixth place, 66 points and a runaway Chelsea league victory. I also said that we would take Andre Wisdom to our hearts and sing his names to the skies. Now here I am trying to predict the future again with a pretty awful track record in soothsaying.

I know what we should be doing, but that isn't quite the same thing. Liverpool should be targeting a league win. That's what should be happening. That may sound mad despite last season but I'm going gung-ho these days. I always hated it when Gerard Houllier would concede the title in August. Let's have some ambition, man! We start level after all.

Yes, we've lost Luis Suarez and half of the team haven't met, but if 2014 showed us one thing it's that unpredictable and poetic football is back. We could win the league or we could finish seventh, but where's the hope in setting the bar low. Shit or bust, that's what I say. I'm going for shit, if you see what I mean.

At the Cardiff game last year, when we were 2-1 down, my mate Andy said to me, 'We're going to need four goals here.' We got six. We destroyed Arsenal and Tottenham, beat Manchester United home and away, watched Suarez beat Norwich on his own and were only a penalty away from putting five past Everton. Me and my 66 points didn't see that coming. I'd like to think that anything is possible. I'm expecting everything. If a game is called off due to a meteorite storm I won't turn a hair. I like it like this.

Of course, we're without Suarez. Sachin will talk about him in a forthcoming chapter so, as he seems to be carrying some scars from his departure, I'll leave the whole farrago to him. But it's impossible to assess next season without considering the loss of a genius. The bites and his sulks aside, and wherever you are on the racist argument, he was simply the best striker I've seen since Kenny Dalglish. I thought we wouldn't see another Fernando Torres for another decade but he eclipsed even him in a matter of months.

It wasn't just the goals or the endeavour, it was the poetry, the romance of his performances and his sheer doggedness. My favourite goal last season was Daniel Sturridge's header keepy-ups at Stoke but following that it was the first Suarez header against West Brom. Shades of Steve Nicol at Highbury in 1988 maybe, but in some ways it wasn't even the goal itself that made it so glorious. It was the fact that he thought about doing it. No, it's more than that. It's that he expected no other outcome. If I just run at this full pelt it'll go in. The distance is irrelevant. I have willed it so and that's enough. It was the type of goal that you don't leap about to. You just stare at it and wonder if everyone else saw the same thing.

How do you replace that? Well, you can't. You've got the benefit of hindsight here and could be laughing at me in the future – 'This fool has no idea about Raheem Sterling's 70 league goals' – but he's not going to be Diet Suarez, nor is his mate Daniel. Suarez will be missed so Brendan Rodgers has to just find even more different ways to win. We did well last season when Suarez was on his ban so there's no need to panic just yet. Certainly not 11 days before the season starts. That's what I keep telling myself, anyway.

I know little of the new signings. This is deliberate as I don't want to pre-judge them. I'd rather the unnecessary fretting be put on hold for a while. I'd rather wait until Southampton before the rage/joy comes out. I hope they're good. Top insight there.

The day after the Newcastle game, the final fixture of the 2014 season, I was asked if I would take 84 points next season. Too hungover to form rational arguments, I waved a tired arm and said yes, even with Suarez in the team. I'd still take it now. I still think we could win the league and do it with that points total. I also think we'll be top at Christmas. Next season won't/can't be as mad as last season, but the foundations are there and the young players have tasted a title near-miss. Sometimes you have to go close and lose so you can win later.

Look at United in 1992 at Anfield, losing it at the worst possible place. Look at them losing it to Manchester City when they'd brought their ribbons all the way to Sunderland – they absolutely walked it the following season. That's the single-mindedness that should burn in Rodgers's men even at this early stage. Even if I'm not involved yet.

Then there's the captain. He's a year older and frustrated with the events of May. It wasn't his fault. From the second half at Norwich away we had nothing in the tank thanks to a squad that needed Victor Moses and Iago Aspas to relieve tired legs. He'll redouble his efforts. He'll be booed at more away grounds because of the World Cup debacle and he won't care. It could be his last complete season.

Actually, you can't blame anyone. You can look to Simon Mignolet for the City goal in December but he also won us the game against Stoke. You can blame Jordan Henderson for his sending-off but who got us the winner at Swansea? Football doesn't work like that. Liverpool will make mistakes next season. There's no such thing as a perfect season. It's what makes the game so great.

And finally Europe. Again, predictions are difficult. At this stage I'd be happy to just get out of the group stages, but then you think about 2005 and just wonder if the madness of 2014 can stretch to other stadia on the continent. Sod it, we'll win that too. Why not? I'm game.

I'm aware you're wincing or smiling from the future at these words. Liverpool could implode as much as explode. Great, isn't it?

This book is more about the fans rather than the games themselves. I wanted to find a scientist in Antarctica and hear how he/she is struggling to see or hear extra time in a League Cup game. I wanted to know about a Red who is crossing an ocean with little more than a crystal set and a rough idea about the kick-off time. This is everyone's story – not just those who can make it to the games. We're everywhere us, and it's not just the 90 minutes that unites us.

Thanks and enjoy. I hope it was quite a ride.

17 August 2014, Liverpool 2 Southampton 1

'My mum gave him a bacon butty. He still talks about it today'

By Karl Coppack

Well, here we are again. It's new season time and I'm more than up for it. It's been a long summer of World Cups and Commonwealth Games but that's all done now. That was merely the undercard. This is what we've been waiting for. The real fun is about to begin. This is it.

The day augurs well. Liverpool are already ahead of Manchester United before a ball has been kicked. Their 2-1 defeat to Swansea led to some pretty swift volte-faces on Radio 5 yesterday, from saviour to sally in one game, so we're already smirking. On Radio 5 Danny Mills was talking about how confident Louis Van Gaal looked and how David Moyes always looked a bit nervous. This is completely the opposite to what he said last season.

Spare a thought for Ashley Young, though. I wouldn't want to wish that on anyone.

Anyway, sod them. Today's all about Liverpool. It's about seeing my mates again and getting back into the matchday routine.

I'm looking forward to seeing one mate in particular. Today I'm going to the game with my mate Gerry. This is a big deal for the both of us. We're finally going to Anfield together. This is something that's been planned for 34 years. Let me explain.

In 1980, Gerry and I started at the Liverpool Institute. We arrived as milk-coloured first-years – all blazers and uncomfortable ties. We were both 11 years old and excited and petrified by the smells, the noises and the sheer grown-upness of a new school. Following years of junior school we had to start again – making new friends, fighting people for the sake of status and talking about 'break' instead of 'playtime'. Gerry and I became mates simply because our surnames fell close together in the register. Sometimes that coincidence is enough to begin a lifelong friendship.

The Liverpool Institute. It sounds grand, doesn't it? The Liverpool Institute. The Liverpool Institute High School for Boys, to be exact. You're probably picturing boaters and school songs along with hampers from home and pupils called Chaudley Minor. You'd be wrong. The name and history of the school were in stark contrast to the reality of what went on there in September 1980. The building fell into the L1 postcode bracket but if you crossed the road at the back of the schoolyard you'd stand in the shadow of the Anglican cathedral in L8 – Toxteth.

Us 'newts' (first-years) were thrown slap bang into the riots. It was the second year of an unwelcome Conservative government – a government that would soon discuss cutting the city off and allowing it to fall into 'a managed decline'. By the end of our first year the area went up in flames. That said, it wasn't all bad. We were made aware of the benefits of looting. There was an awful lot of stolen Mars Bars going around the yard back then.

Talk about growing up quickly. From *Willo the Wisp* and *Blue Peter* to petrol bombs and police cordons. This isn't what our parents wanted. This was the Institute. This was about possible Oxbridge entrance. Two Beatles went to the 'Inny'. Charles Dickens gave readings there. The headmaster wore a cloak at assembly. We did Latin. You could do Russian – Russian! – in the third year.

In reality, though, the place was falling to pieces around our ears. The teachers were, well, unusual. One had a car engine next to his desk. Another was about 300 years old and would let you walk out of the lesson and play football if you were bored. Our science teacher once told us that he fully expected to be dead by the end of the school year. We were 11 years old. This was far removed from *Goodbye Mr Chips*.

In 1985, my O Level year, the school closed down. Gerry had long since gone by then. He made it through a part of the opening term of our second year but just disappeared. One day our form teacher told us that he'd gone to Breckfield Comprehensive School. There was no farewell from him. No phone call. No nicety. School kids don't betray things like that. There must always be a cruel detachment. I was not to see him again for another 31 years.

I was disappointed. Our little gang was a man down but by then we were older and picking on the new intake of newts, so life moved on. Every now and then Gerry's name would come up but that was about it. Several years later I was on a bus when I saw him crossing Sheil Road, but didn't get off to say hello.

I would often go to his house when I made my way to school, travelling from Croxteth to Kensington. We'd walk through Edge Hill and the back of the hospital. For years I never made the connection between Gerry leaving school and the haunted look he threw over his shoulder at his dad and stepmother when he left the house. See, I was never invited into the house. He'd hurry out of the door and would gulp quietly, as if shaking off a demon or two. Then he turned into Gerry again – laughing, punching me in the arm for no reason other than that he could and just generally being an irritating pre-pubescent child. I just assumed that his family were as poor as mine and would rather not share stories. My dad had been made redundant from the Liverpool Docks and Harbour Company a year earlier and work was difficult to come by. I knew that Gerry's dad was working, but maybe he too was struggling. Maybe it had something to do with his stepmother. Gerry had hinted that his stepmother was a bit of a harridan, but he'd soon change the subject.

One thing we did have in common was football. Gerry could play. I could fake. He played for the school team and I could watch. Liverpool would end that season as European champions and all we wanted was to go to Anfield and see the Reds. Gerry had left before I was finally allowed to go to the match so we never shared that pleasure. Today, we're finally going to do just that. It only took 34 years. That glimpse of him from a bus was the last I saw of him until 2012.

One day I did a bit of online stalking and put his name into Facebook's search engine. There he was. The same russet red hair, albeit aged. Grown-up Gerry. I sent a friend request and within minutes he sent me a message asking if it was really me. How many Karl Coppacks from Liverpool did he know, I wondered. Over the next few hours he told me about what happened when he left the Institute. There was no Breckfield Comp.

One afternoon, in the winter of 1981, he went home and found his clothes shoved into Kwik Save bags. His dad threw them at him and told him that he was no longer welcome. Confused, Gerry asked him where he was supposed to go. 'Your mother's.' He hadn't seen his mother since he was four years old. She wasn't well and had been in hospital and care for years but he had no idea where. He might as well have been told to go and find the Golden Fleece.

His dad, not shy at showing his fists, didn't find it unusually cruel to put his son on to the streets in the dead of winter. Gerry didn't argue either, save for the confused questions of a child. He knew what would happen if he did. He would often come to school with the odd bruise or cut but 12-year-olds are always subject to the odd scrape so no one ever suggested anything might be wrong. Gerry was homeless and soon to be hungry.

For two days and nights he wandered the streets, trying in vain to bunk on the Isle of Man ferry. He then walked to Speke airport and back, sleeping rough in Sefton Park. He survived on stolen milk from doorsteps. He was settling in for a third night when two policemen approached him. He made up some cock-and-bull story as he didn't fancy another beating from home. They took him to the police station, fed him and tried to put him somewhere where he wasn't at risk.

There were no available foster homes or much of a social services system back then so he was placed in the only free place – a young offenders' institute. From one institute to another. Of course, he wasn't an offender but over time he became institutionalised and was treated the same as everyone else. A few weeks into his time in the facility he received a letter and a fiver from his dad asking why he hadn't been in touch. Some people aren't cut out to be parents. Some people aren't cut out to be decent human beings either. Some people should be in jail.

Again, the signs were there for me to see. One day, a few weeks before his life changed, he travelled across the city to visit me. My parents were less than pleased at the ten minutes' notice I'd given but were courteous when he arrived. My mum gave him a bacon butty. He still talks about it today. Ordinarily when he would come home his stepmother would feed her own children before him, and even when there was extra she would throw it on to the fire and send him to bed beaten and hungry. He was effectively being starved, so the simple episode of a mother feeding a child as mine did was an all too irregular occurrence. He never spoke of it and I never asked. I wasn't really into reality at that age. All I wanted to do was listen to The Beatles and talk about Ray Kennedy and *Doctor Who*. I had no idea that my mate was living in such appalling circumstances.

So today is Gerry's first Anfield game since the mid-1980s. He was allowed an escorted visit out at weekends so, with no family to visit, chose the ground of the European champions. Last season we went up to Hull to shout at Victor Moses, but today is all about an overdue day out at the place we always talked about.

In February we travelled up to Liverpool for a school reunion organised by our own George Sephton – himself an old boy. On the way I asked Gerry two questions. Firstly, why the hell did he book the Adelphi hotel (it was deemed posh when he lived in Liverpool) and secondly, how did he feel about going back home. He hadn't been home for years but saw the trip as a chance to exorcise some demons. We met some old mates and had a fantastic night. We even managed to get a guided tour of the school, now the Liverpool Institute of Performing Arts (LIPA) and no longer looking like a museum for fallen masonry. I kept an eye on Gerry for obvious reasons. He told me that seeing the lads and the school left him feeling cheated. Our school history didn't include him and it should have done.

My oldest mate Chee, also from Croxteth, was with us that night. I'd taken my first trip to Anfield with him in 1981 and shared many celebrations and disappointments over the years. That first game was also against Southampton. Gerry should have been with us back then. We're making amends today.

It's an early start. I like a 3pm Saturday kick-off but as today is a 1.30pm game I'm picked up at 7am. A few of the other lads are on their way up too but from different starting places in the capital. Simon and Tony are picking up Steven at Banbury. Mart and Richard are coming up from Haywards Heath while Sachin is on a coach somewhere, feeling all smug because he has his first ever season ticket. Ideally, we should all meet at a service station on the way up but we're not too good at this and Gerry and I end up getting to Liverpool hours before anyone else.

Liverpool is quiet. Very, very quiet. There's hardly any traffic. There was no queue at The Rocket. This is odd. We head for my mum's. This is a necessary visit.

Flashback 24 hours. My sister has left my tickets at my mum's so I call her to make sure that she'll be in. 'Do you want something to eat after the game?' She probably thinks Gerry is still a poor, starving waif rather than a grown man of 45 who now has his own building business and a degree from London Guildhall. I decline as we want to get back on the road once we've dropped the tickets off afterwards.

'Are you sure?'

'Yes, mum. Thanks though.'

'OK luv.'

The city awakes. Anfield is a great place to be before a match. There's laughter and moaning in equal measure and a riot of red and white. We visit my mates outside The Sandon and discuss the key points of the day – the inclusion of Lucas, crown green bowls and the character of Mother Teresa. Then we're in! Anfield! The greatest ground in the world! We're also in the worst seats in the ground.

There's even more ire coming. The club's mascot, Mighty Red, is now included in the on-pitch photos. Yes, I know it's harmless. Yes, I know it's for the kids and not for a curmudgeon like me, and yes, I know that a charity is involved somewhere. But please, can we have no more of this? Mascots on the pitch just bring us a step closer to celebration music at goals and half-time cheerleaders. I didn't need a mascot to make me feel part of the club when I was a kid. I had Kevin Keegan. This is a worrying development. Bolton have a man dressed as a six-foot lion who dances when they score. I've always been glad that we didn't do that. Liverpool doesn't need added razzamatazz.

I'm still not happy with us having a scoreboard in the Kemlyn stand. All a bit too futuristic for me.

And then there was the game. You know what happened. We got through despite a performance that was as flat as Norfolk. I like the look of Javi Manquillo and Jordan Henderson fills my heart with nothing but joy. But we're very, very rusty and in dire need of another striker. Dejan Lovren, a debutant today, looks suitably scary, which I'm convinced is half the job for centre-halves. He also likes to shout at Simon Mignolet, so we're already firm friends.

One thing that does have to change is Glen Johnson. I used to love Glen Johnson. Gifted, useful and integral at times, but when he's bad he stinks the place out. There were numerous occasions today when he was still strolling back from an attack, leaving Lovren to cover two players at once.

I'm also not convinced that Lucas and Steven Gerrard on the same pitch makes sense. Joe Allen gave us a lot more energy when he replaced the Brazilian so I'd like to see more of him. It's also OK to rest Steven from time to time. That may be seen as a heretical view in some quarters but it's something that should at least be considered.

Anyway, 2-1. Third in the league. Good.

After the match Gerry and I had some chips on the walk back to the car. I'm trying to eat more healthily these days and haven't eaten bad matchday food since the final game of last season. I felt a bit sick and very stuffed by these over-salted chips. They were a mistake. Bilious and sluggish, I rang the bell at my mum's house.

You're ahead of me, aren't you?

She'd prepared a full roast dinner. The works. The absolute works. You can't say no to your mother.

We could barely walk back to the car. And I still forgot to give her the tickets.

Day one and it has to get better.

25 August 2014, Manchester City 3 Liverpool 1

Well, that wasn't great. There was a slight worry about the rather laboured win against Southampton and to follow it up with a trip to the champions so early in the season was clearly a step too far. I'd hoped that there would be parallels with Manchester United's early visit to Anfield last season which set us up for a fearful run, but tonight we played a better team and it showed.

I couldn't be doing with a long post-match autopsy so trundled off to bed. It was then that I made a mistake. I went on to Twitter. Here be dragons.

Twitter is an odd thing. Being that you yourself control your timeline it's difficult to blame anyone when you read such extraordinary views. I keep my 'Following' number down to a manageable level and always make sure that the funny, the reasoned and informative get on there, so I was surprised at some of the arse gravy that flowed down the page. *£233,234*

It seems that I was alone in consigning the defeat as an 'oh, well' reverse. It seems that we won't win anything now. It seems that we've bought the wrong players. It seems that we've set them up incorrectly. It seems that we've blown it and it also seems that Glen Johnson is as close to being Satan without the necessary diabolical tattoos.

I can understand people being deflated, angry or just downright sulky when things don't go our way, but this is absurd. It's from times like this that prejudices form.

Don't get me wrong here. I like a moan. There are many people who throw my old sentences back at me to emphasise this point but this seems a little strong. And premature.

I suppose this is only to be expected. As far back as May a few of my mates were discussing whether 2013/14 was our only and final chance at the title. Compounded by an empty number seven shirt, there's an air of defeatism in certain quarters before a ball has been kicked. It took just one defeat against superior opposition before panic set in.

Fans are notoriously bipolar when it comes to expectation. My mate tells me of the day he sat next to an old boy at Anfield. This man had sat through titles, Europe, cups and some of the finest football ever seen. His response to the poor game they'd seen? 'Thirty years I've been watching this shite.'

I love that. I like a cantankerous curmudgeon, but it would be churlish indeed to write us off so soon. At least give us till Christmas. This game was our first away league defeat this calendar year. I'll take that.

Negativity is fine. Moaning is fine. I just hope that Brendan and his team aren't as down as some of our lot tonight. You learn from mistakes (Alberto Moreno) and from better players.

This was a defeat, not the final act of a tragedy.

I'm sleeping fine.

KC

31 August 2014, Tottenham 0 Liverpool 3

'These are a few of my favourite things'

By Martin Cloake

'Joey Ate The Frogs Legs Made The Swiss Roll Now Hes Munching Gladbach'. That banner in the Liverpool section at the 1977 European Cup Final is one of my earliest memories of football's terrace culture. I was 12, and the game was on the telly.

In those days clubs hadn't turned into brands and football wasn't up itself, so when an English team was in a European match we tended to get behind them. Liverpool were in quite a lot of European matches in those days, as well as frequent main features on *Match of the Day* or *The Big Match*. So they were one of the first teams other than Spurs that registered with me in any detail.

The players I remember in the red shirts were the exciting ones; John Toshack, Steve Heighway, Kevin Keegan, Kenny Dalglish. But for all the allure of those players, Liverpool's red machine was founded on the 1-0 win, the shutout, what the Spurs legend Danny Blanchflower would have called 'waiting for the other side to die of boredom'.

There was a bit of a myth that grew up around Liverpool as the media obsessed with their success, a myth tied in with the image of the chirpy Scouser, the wit and energy of a city with a rich cultural heritage. That, in turn, led to a growing resentment, something which grew around me as I began the journey from innocent pre-teen to streetwise teen. Stories of dodgy days out to Scouseland began to filter back as I began to mix with the lads and older fans who travelled. They told stories of kids with knives, kids who'd offer to 'watch yer car, mister' and then have it away with your hub caps, being 'taxed' for your trainers or a nice bit of clobber. And if you were a black Londoner, you got it especially bad.

In Liverpool and London, we were two tribes; thieving Scouse bastards, flash Cockney twats. And the tribes laid claim to leadership in fashion, music, humour, football…anything you could think of was turned into an example of why 'we' were better than 'you'. It was, as many of us came to realise, just a game; one-upmanship or, before the word became indistinguishable from 'being a prejudiced prick' – banter. It's what you did if you were a working-class male, you took the piss as a way of breaking the ice. The sociologists would call it the peacock strut, the male need to manoeuvre for position and influence. We called it getting over yourself – not being a dick, a divvy, a muppet, a soft lad.

And what all this meant was that, beneath it all, we were pretty much the same. We had the same values about loyalty and attachment, the same passion for our music and our clobber, and for our football clubs. That became more apparent as many of us got older, but at the time many of us were caught up in it. We were kids. But there are many ways to be shaped by the times we lived in, and growing up through the 1980s also meant that Liverpool was always in my field of vision.

Even at the time I knew Thatcher would be a disaster for the country, and I was right. My family was one of the few round our way not to be mesmerised by the Thatcherite revolution. It's hard to write convincingly of how divisive those times were but, even though I grew up in the London suburbs rather than an industrial town, it soon became clear that in the war that had been declared we had to take sides. So I did, becoming politicised at an early age and actively involved in a range of left-wing political movements. And if you were on the left in the 1980s, you knew about Liverpool and identified with it. It was a working-class city where solidarity was important, and so in the Thatcherite plan it had to be destroyed. Thatcher, the great patriot, ready to sacrifice the citizens of her country for multinational capital.

Toxteth went up, Brixton went up, local authority unions fought back, two labour movement strongholds fought tooth and nail to hold on to the things we had created, the values we had embedded. We got a kicking. Around me, people retreated into their ghettos – buying into the line peddled by the Tories that all our problems could be blamed on whatever 'other' they had decided needed persecuting.

Too many embraced the image of 'flash Cockney wankers', a shift demonstrated starkly by the adoption of Harry Enfield's satirical strike at working-class Toryism, 'Loadsamoney', as a cultural icon to be aspired to. Spurs fans, along with fans of other London clubs, took to waving tenners at visiting teams from the north, and Liverpool really had it stuck to them.

'Sign on, sign on, with a pen, in your hand, and you'll never work, again, you'll never work, again,' sang the terrace wits from a capital city in which urban deprivation and unemployment were also rocketing. Banter. One-upmanship. But now it seemed to be a little more.

And all the while the Liverpool FC media love-in seemed to continue. As the fanzine movement burgeoned, there was a fanzine called *Liverpool Are On The Telly Again*, produced by Norwich City fans. Liverpool were undoubtedly successful, but it was the apparently uncritical adulation in the media that rankled with many fans.

Some of that was, without doubt, the familiar backlash against anyone or anything that has been judged too successful. But we knew about the darker side of the Liverpool support too and it seemed that was never acknowledged. And that cocktail of resentment led to the afternoon at Plough Lane when Spurs and Wimbledon fans joined together to sing 'We hate Scousers and we hate Scousers' as news of deaths at the 1989 FA Cup semi-final at Hillsborough was announced on the half-time PA system. The announcement used the word 'riot' and the reaction on the terraces was 'here they go again'.

For all that, we resented the way all football fans were treated back in those days – as hooligans waiting to happen. At Spurs we were perhaps quicker to realise the truth. In 1981 it was nearly us caught in the tunnel and crushed in the pens at that very same ground. Eight years later the lessons still had not been learned but now 96 people were dead and they could not be ignored, as we had been.

When football resumed, Everton came to White Hart Lane. An impromptu delegation of Spurs fans took a wreath to the away end and presented it. In memory of your loss. Petty divisions were exposed for what they were. The gates at White Hart Lane had been particularly heavily festooned with scarves and banners and messages in the days after Hillsborough. And 20 years on, as the fight for justice continued – the passage of time itself a stark indication of the contempt in which the people of this country are held by those who consider themselves our rulers and betters – it was testimony from Spurs fans that played a part in forcing another look at what had unfolded and why.

History is shaped by those who tell it. So my view of Liverpool, which I've tried to set out here, is very much a personal take. But I have always had a soft spot for the place. I've spent relatively little time there, so I'll concede that what I like is an idea of the place as much as what I have found on my visits. And that the idea is possibly a little idealised. But I don't think it's rose-tinted. I know not everyone in Liverpool is a Scouse wit, a musical genius, a committed socialist. But I'm a city boy, and I like the energy and the mix of a city that's confident in itself.

I'm a Londoner through and through, but my reference points have a strong Scouse flavour running through them. Kevin Sampson and Peter Hooton writing in *The End* and *The Face* back in the early days; the Partizan media collective; Phil Thornton; the Head brothers; Echo and the Bunnymen; a fascination with Adidas trainers; terrace anthems; jangly-pop four-piece bands...these are a few of my favourite things.

But what, you may well ask, about the football? In the early 1980s, when the great Spurs team of Hoddle, Ardiles and Perryman and all the rest of the boys from White Hart Lane firmly hooked me on football, it was us and Liverpool. For three years we slugged it out to be the top dogs in English football. If you want to argue about who came out on top, you don't really understand anything I've written. Those were the days, my friends, and they were bloody brilliant.

There have been great times since, in particular the 1995 FA Cup quarter-final victory at Anfield. Two great goals from Jurgen Klinsmann and Teddy Sheringham and a fine performance that had the Kop applauding the Lilywhites off the pitch as one of the largest travelling contingents I'd ever been part of went wild in the Annie Road. In contrast, I remember a cold, strange night at a half-empty Anfield during which Spurs swept aside a Roy Evans side in the dying days of his tenure. We actually worried for Liverpool after that.

Games between Spurs and Liverpool have tended to be exciting, open affairs. And, in more recent years, the edge has come from two teams fighting to regain a little of what they once had, two sides on the brink but not quite able to cross into the promised land.

The football memories have been some of the best, and the trips to the city some of the best, too. Even when we got kicked out of a hotel on the Albert Dock with raging hangovers at about 4am after someone in the 40-strong hen party staying there had sparked up a ciggie in their room and set the alarms off.

One of the many things I think links the folk cultures of Liverpudlians and Londoners is the pleasure in having the craic, exchanging stories and chewing over the facts, so here's one of my favourite anecdotes. It's one which you'll get if you get it, if you know what I mean.

Quite a few seasons back, around the time of football's second summer of love, a few of us got the train up to Liverpool for the match. We took the early out of Euston, and there was a pretty large contingent of the Liverpool London Supporters' Club aboard. A few of the fellas were standing in the space between the carriages, having the odd spliff and a few cans, and so we shot the breeze with the through traffic.

It was all good natured, but inevitably there was some discussion about the stereotypes of Scousers and Cockneys – the cartoon characters we were often reduced to. There was a bit of friendly stick exchanged, but we all agreed that stereotyping any set of people was wrong.

Arriving at Lime Street, fresh from our philosophical discussions and display of liberal understanding – together, it must be said, with the spring in the step engendered by a few cheeky fresheners partaken on the train – we strode into the pub opposite Lime Street station. Most of us sat down at a table by the door having despatched two of our party to the bar with our order. Our bums had barely touched the vinyl seat covering when the door burst open and in walked a bloke with a bubble perm and a moustache, wearing a shellsuit and brandishing a tracksuit top which still had the security tag attached. 'Any of youse lads wanna buy some gear, like?' he asked. We pissed ourselves.

Sunday lunchtime kick-offs aren't right. Not enough time to do much before or after the game, so the day's written off. But football demands a lot these days on many levels. It takes me an hour to get to White Hart Lane, changing at Highbury and Islington where I believe some other side relocated to. That's another Liverpool memory; Michael Thomas's last-minute winner giving Arsenal the first title of their modern era of success. I was living in Edmonton at the time so I should have been safe, but waking into my local I was confronted by four suited-up Gooners taking their wives out to celebrate the title. Thanks a bunch ya Scouse muppets!

I like the early season games, seeing the familiar faces gather again – off the pitch at least – and catching up on everyone's summer over a few beers in the Irish Centre. As my mate Bruce says, it's the best of times, before reality has taken the edge off the hope.

In truth, we know it's going to be a test. We've beaten two poor sides in our previous two league games. But Liverpool haven't looked great either. So today's a test for both sides. And it's one that Spurs comprehensively fail.

Liverpool out-press us and also manage to find greater width in their diamond formation than we do in our 4-2-3-1. Mario Balotelli is making his debut and works harder than I've seen him work since he was driving his studs down into Scott Parker's head a few years ago at the Etihad. Raheem Sterling is on fire, Jordan Henderson running everywhere, and the old-stager Steven Gerrard is pulling the strings.

Defensive numbskullery leads to a first goal. And on it went, Liverpool chasing and running and squeezing and creating and Spurs leaderless and clueless. Still, it's only 1-0 at half-time and we have created a few chances – one lifted on to the roof of the net by Emmanuel Adebayor and one fired at the optimum saving height by Nacer Chadli after a neat through ball from Nabil Bentaleb.

The second half starts badly. Very badly. After the linesman misses a blatant offside, Joe Allen runs into the area and performs a physics-defying dive to get the softest penalty you'll ever see given after being brushed by Eric Dier's finger. After the game, the analysis from so-called football experts seems to conclude that Allen 'had the right to go down'. To not understand this is, apparently, to be naïve in the extreme. The 'right to go down', after being slightly brushed, in a contact sport. Ironic when you think of the assaults regularly perpetrated on Gareth Bale which got him labelled a diver by many, including our fine corps of professional referees and, on one occasion, an unusually gormless Anfield crowd who booed his every touch.

I'm not totally enamoured with everything the Red Scouse do, see.

Gerrard puts the penalty away, Spurs exude their familiar 'Well that's that then, what are you doing after work?' aura and it's game over even before Andros Townsend sets up Alberto Moreno for his debut goal just to make sure. It finishes 3-0. It's better than the 5-0 and 4-0 last season. And it's an improvement. If we keep improving the result at this rate we should be good for a draw towards the middle of 2016.

It's a reality check for Spurs, and cause for rueful reflection. Just a few seasons ago we'd overtaken Liverpool – more often favourites to win against them than not, securing higher finishes in the league, playing better, more attractive football. But after new owners moved in to stop the rot, a new manager was appointed and, importantly, the new board gave him the time if not at first the resources to do his job. And he stayed patient with his board, earning the right to greater backing.

This was his 100th game in charge, for the new Spurs manager – a cliché of modern football if ever there was one – it was the fifth. For Spurs fans the hope that we could learn a lesson from a club that seemed to have learned its lessons was all we had. We'll have better days than this, but it didn't make the lack of fight or guile any more palatable.

I was supposed to meet up with some of the Spirit of Shankly crew after the game. They're a decent bunch with a great campaigning spirit and a bright, shining humanity. Respect between them and the newly-revitalised Tottenham Hotspur Supporters' Trust was cemented when they unfurled a banner bearing the name of former Trust chairman Darren Alexander, who died tragically young, on the Kop at the end of last season. We know how valuable a symbol that is. But I didn't get the text until I was on the train home, and in truth it was probably best to leave them to the carousing. A few tweets I saw later that night suggested there was plenty of it.

So that was Liverpool at the Lane, Liverpool Football Club as yer actual Scousers so often say it. We've got a trip to their city to come midwinter. And the crew from the Irish are already booked up for the last game of the season – the title decider we're calling it – on Bank Holiday weekend, the weekend of Sound City. But that's against Everton.

13 September 2014, Liverpool 0 Aston Villa 1

'The animals openly mocked us'

By Sachin Nakrani

I f anybody wants proof of football's ability to turn optimism into hopelessness, the sublime into the ridiculous, grown adults into childlike souls, cold and desperate for home, then it was all there to see on the edge of the M6 on this autumn night. Keele services to be precise, where 21 men of varying ages found themselves under the glare of artificial light, eating pizza in the early hours and wondering precisely what they had done to deserve this fate.

Seriously, a Mancunian or Evertonian couldn't have scripted it. Here we were, a coachload of Liverpool supporters returning to London after seeing our team lose in dispiriting fashion against Aston Villa when the lights went out. Literally. The coach (or glorified minibus to be precise) descended into darkness not long after we had got on the motorway and soon our Bulgarian driver (he was really excited about coming back for Ludogorets on Tuesday) made it clear that we were in trouble. The power was going, first inside and now, slowly but surely, outside. Soon there would be no headlights and eventually no movement at all. We had to stop.

So we pulled into the nearest service station, which was Sandbach in Cheshire. En route, the driver (I really should know his name by now, he's taken us on enough trips) called his boss and told him about the problem. The boss, Jerry, told him to call him back as soon as he pulled in, which he did. Except now Jerry wasn't picking up his phone. It was a little before 9pm and we wouldn't hear from Jerry for close to an hour. In the meantime we discovered that our Bulgarian friend had no breakdown cover and, calling Jerry aside, no contingency plan to deal with such a situation. To say we were pissed off would be an understatement: there were swear words, demands for explanations and cries of illegal practice. Some even went inside and got a McDonald's.

Then it got mad. Shortly after a group of Villa fans pointed out that Liverpool had just been 'fucked up the arse', a huge lorry pulled up carrying crate upon crate of lambs. As the female driver (blonde, posh, clearly not interested in our plight) headed inside, the animals openly mocked us. OK, they were 'baahing', but these were no ordinary 'baahs' – they were laced with sarcasm and a distinct hint of piss-taking. Imagine a snotty teenager screaming 'aaah!' seconds after tripping you up on the pavement. It sounded just like that.

It was only after the cruel lambs had come and gone that Jerry finally made contact. He told Riyaz, the leader of our group, that the power shortage on the bus was an 'imaginary problem' – apparently the same thing had occurred a couple of weeks back and upon checking the coach in question, he discovered nothing wrong with it. Nevertheless, he was on his way.

In the meantime, and having decided never to use these charlatans again (or The Little Bus Company to be precise), Riyaz asked our Bulgarian friend to try the coach one more time. We all gave a helping hand – literally – and after a push-start the shitty little thing revved up with its lights on. Hooray! We were saved! London please driver and stop for no man.

We just about reached the next services before the power went again.

So here we were at Keele on an increasingly chilly night, fed up, stranded by the side of the road and with a minimum of two-and-a-half hours to wait until Jerry turned up with a new coach from his base in Stanmore, north London. We went inside and while some slept and others paced, many ordered grub from the 24-hour café. There was a wide range of food on offer, including sandwiches, yogurts, fruit, cakes, pies and burgers. Riyaz got in a job lot of Papa John pizzas and for the first time since Gabby Agbonlahor had struck at the Kop end, we were mildly content.

Having consumed a homemade sarnie and a Cadbury's Fruit & Nut bar on the coach moments before it went dark, I didn't have a pizza. Instead I sat on a plastic chair under piercing brightness and contemplated what was happening. In so many ways this was absolutely shit – my team had just been beaten at home by a side containing Philippe Senderos and Kieran Richardson and here I now was, waiting for some dickhead I'd never met to take me home and end this wretched day once and for all. So why was I smiling? Why, as the minutes ticked on and my eyelids became heavy, did all of this seem so ridiculously brilliant?

Because as much as being a football fan, and a fan of Liverpool in particular, is about the joy of winning and building genuine hope for even better times ahead, it is also about nights like this – nights which test your faith and rationale, your decision to spend time and increasingly large amounts of money on watching a group of strangers come up against another group of strangers in the battle to put a ball into a steel-framed net.

It's fucking mental and common sense suggests the hassle is not worth it, especially when you're at Keele services in the dead of night watching a middle-aged woman on minimum wage struggle with a packet of frozen pepperoni slices. But despite the bad times we keep going because we know the good times are worth it, and even if they are long into the future we have each other for company.

Certainly that was the feeling among the stranded 21 as we ate, laughed, cursed Jerry and wished Simon Mignolet would show some bloody decisiveness.

We members of the Hertfordshire Supporters' Club (11 years after joining, I'm still not sure why we're called that given we meet and depart from nowhere near Hertfordshire), had truly bonded – from herein, we would always have Villa 2014.

It was a little moving, a little *Stand By Me*, so it felt rather appropriate that the weekend had begun with me calling my dad to ask why he was a Liverpool fan. You might think it incredible that it had taken me until the age of 33, and having seen the Reds play countless times home, away and in Europe, to enquire over this matter. You might think it even more incredible that this was to be the first meaningful conversation the old man and I had engaged in for decades.

Don't misunderstand me, we have spoken plenty of times. But not since I was a pre-pubescent rascal who had to be told why it was wrong to keep nicking stuff from Woolworths had we entered into what could be considered a proper chat, an exchange marked by meaningful, personal messages, and something that stretched beyond, 'Pass me that hammer', 'You watching that?' and 'Tell mum I'm going out.'

Maybe it's a man thing, maybe it's an us thing. For sure neither dad nor I are great conversationalists. As he gets older, now past 60 and way past being the strapping tradesman who used to carry me up the stairs and seemed like the strongest, bravest man in the world, it worries me that I know so little about him.

What were his hopes as a child? How have they changed in adulthood? Is he happy? Does he have regrets? What, for fuck's sake, are his favourite crisps? I know none of these things and, at very best, have 30 years to find out.

Well I made a start on the Friday before the Villa game. As I said, neither of us are great talkers, and on top of that he has chronically bad hearing. I feared the worst.

'Hello?'

'Dad, it's me.'

'Oh hello.'

'Hi. Did mum tell you I was going to call?'

'Ah yes, she did. She said you were going to call tonight.'

'Can you talk now?'

'Yes, no problem. You OK?'

'I'm fine. I have a slightly strange question for you.'

'OK.'

'Why do you support Liverpool?'

'Why do I support Liverpool?'

'Yes, why do you support Liverpool?'

Shanti Nakrani was born and raised in Mombasa, Kenya, and around the age of 12 or 13, he began regularly watching a local team called Liverpool. They played in red and, as my dad soon found out, were named after a team in England managed by some guy called Bill Shankly. The old man became rather fond of this team (who if Google is anything to go by, no longer exist) and upon moving to this country with the rest of the Nakrani clan in 1971, decided to show loyalty by giving his support to the English Liverpool.

However, aged 19, living in London and focused on shoring up a job with Plessey, an electronics, defence and telecommunications company, he had neither the time, money nor inclination to watch Liverpool in the flesh. Indeed it wasn't until Wednesday 11 January 1995 that he made his first and still only trip to Anfield, taking my brother Shanil and I to see Liverpool beat Arsenal 1-0 in the Coca-Cola Cup. Rushie scored.

The chat went well. There were none of the usual 'can you say that again?' from him and frustrated replies from me. Instead we spoke calmly and with clarity; dad clearly happy to explain how and why he became a Red and me genuinely interested to hear his story. Maybe one day my daughter will make the same call and I can tell her that I became a Liverpool supporter because at the age of eight I got into football and did what most boys do at that juncture in their lives – ask their dads who they should support. I'm a Red because he's a Red. Simple.

My brother's child/children may one day ask him the same question, and as I observed him snoozing at Keele services, stretched across two chairs with a hoodie covering three-quarters of his face, I thought even deeper of this thing we do – traipsing up and down the motorway, losing hours of our lives and hundreds of our pounds to watch Liverpool on the basis that our dad sort of did the same thing with an amateur club that, if the internet is anything to go by, he's completely made up. But once again it's about more than that, and separated by distance and age these are the moments when my brother and I also get a chance to connect.

For us that Saturday it happened at the Flat Iron on Walton Breck Road, where we first went for a drink before the FA Cup tie against Oldham in January. Then it was freezing, now it was mild and warm, so we decided to drink our pints outside, resting our glasses on the boozer's large, black-painted windowsills.

We spoke about Liverpool, of the match to come, but we also spoke about our lives, and just like with my dad 24 hours earlier it felt good to share, to enrich and maintain a relationship with someone I've literally known all my life. What a shame that the game itself was dog shit.

Liverpool weren't actually that terrible, well I didn't think so anyway. But it was such a poor goal to give away, with the defence, an Achilles heel during the otherwise marvellous reign of Brendan Rodgers, malfunctioning again. Mamadou Sakho yet again looked like a basic upgrade of Djimi Traore as he let Agbonlahor win a corner which didn't look on, and from the preceding cross Mignolet again showed all the assurance of a drunk chimp on skates. There were more than a few 'we should have kept Reina' shouts among the 21 as we got back on the bus outside Stanley Park.

In attack, Mario Balotelli did a few decent things in between getting kicked by Senderos, but overall his performance was too still, too anonymous, and showed just how much we're going to miss Luis Suarez this season. That mad bastard would've won us this game, for sure.

Oh and then there was Mighty Red, the mascot Karl mentioned in chapter one and who nobody asked for and most fans don't want to see anywhere near the ground. MR made his/her/its first appearance at Anfield since the club went back on their word and said he/she/it would now be a regular pre-kick-off presence on matchdays (cheerleaders, goal music and massive foam hands anyone?). I actually wasn't as angry as I thought I would be upon spotting the winged tossbag by the Paddock just after 'You'll Never Walk Alone' had been sung, but I still wished he/she/it wasn't there. In fact, I blame him/her/whatever-the-hell-it-is for the subsequent defeat. There, I said it.

The journey home began in typically fraught and panicked mood. The same men who had been hailing the team on the northbound carriageway were calling practically every member of the squad useless on the way back south. One even expressed his 'fear for us in the Champions League'. We've got Ludogorets first up for fuck's sake.

Hindsight may prove me foolish but as I write this two days out from the match, I'm guessing we beat them comfortably.

I kept my counsel. Yes I was disappointed, but there was no panic here. We remain a good team and once that defence gets sorted out (which Rodgers has no choice but to do) and the new guys in attack play more games (alongside Balotelli, Lazar Markovic and Adam Lallana also made their home debuts), we'll get back to beating most sides in style.

The journey looked set to remain tetchy and blame-riddled all the way back to London, but then the blackout happened and soon Jerry was the new target of our frustrations. He eventually turned up at 1.22am and with us too tired to berate him, it became simply a case of getting on the new coach and heading home. The Bulgarian drove.

We eventually got back to Stanmore underground station, our regular pick-up and drop-off point, just after 4.30am. I live in Bromley, south London, and with it impossible to get there at that time, I jumped on the night bus with Shanil and headed back to the family home in nearby Kingsbury. When we got there dad was in the kitchen making his sandwiches ahead of another crack-of-dawn shift at the BT Tower, where he works as a security guard. I took a moment to watch him, this grey-haired man in a purple shirt and black trousers, cutting up slices of lettuce and tomato in half-darkness. Gone is the warrior of my youth and instead now stands a grandfather-of-one who looks every bit the part.

But there also stands a story, one which I am belatedly discovering. The bit I found out the previous Friday was genuinely lovely to hear and explains why I was in my family kitchen at 5am on an autumn Sunday, feeling tired and hungry. I wouldn't change any of it, it is all part of who I am; my past, present and future, and my strongest link to the man who made me.

'I'm off to bed dad, have a good day at work.'

'Yes, OK. Sleep well.'

And I did.

16 September 2014, Liverpool 2 Ludogorets 1

'He is the man from Milk Tray. He is Gabriel Clarke'

By Simon Hughes

When I was asked to write a chapter on Liverpool's first game back in the Champions League, I'm certain the fine editors of this book were hoping to read something flowing with positivity. Football, though. *Football.* Already, I'm worn out by it all. It has been a World Cup year. The season is two months old if you include all of the friendly matches. All of the tours. All of the flights. All of the cities. All of the games that don't matter but are portrayed as if they are. It's exhausting. It's boring. Can we just start over in August 2015 again? *Please.*

Then the real matches begin. The ones that have been lost. Liverpool are behind Chelsea and Manchester City already. I've seen both Chelsea and City play live – perform live. Chelsea and City look like teams of real men. Liverpool do not. Liverpool look like they are taking baby steps. It feels like two seasons ago all over again. And that is a concern. Brendan Rodgers has worked so hard to turn Liverpool from a bog-average outfit into the most entertaining side in the league. It might take another 18 months to build another team – possibly longer, and one without the naughty boy that is Luis Suarez. Does Rodgers have the patience, concentration and determination to do it all over again? I arrive home after the defeat to Aston Villa thinking about this.

I had reported on the defeat for the *Daily Telegraph* and, for the first time under Rodgers, Liverpool were lacking in ideas. I'm not talking about a Plan B, either. In England a Plan B is considered the opposite of Plan A. I've never understood the point in that. Why try and execute a tactic which contradicts a formula that is well drilled because the score isn't the one you want? Just be better at Plan A. Tweak the formation, perhaps – just as Rodgers did so brilliantly and seamlessly at times last season. Against Villa, this did not happen. As soon as Villa took the lead in the ninth minute, it felt inevitable that Liverpool would lose.

I open the front door. Does Rodgers have the patience, concentration and determination to do it all over again? We're having a takeaway. The First Lady is asking whether I want Chinese, Indian or pizza. But does Rodgers have the patience and determination to do it all over again? I go to sleep on a barrel-load of ale that eases the pain somewhat but not the memories. Does Rodgers really have the patience, concentration and determination to do it all over again? Do I, indeed? Do the majority of supporters?

Oh fuck off, it can't be that bad.

I have an ongoing battle with my inner monologue. So I will warn you now; if you are hoping for fluff about how great it is to be in Europe again, maybe read the chapter on Real Madrid at home. Or Real Madrid away. Or Ludogorets away. Or Basel at home. Just anything but this. You won't be following the Yellow Brick Road with me. I cannot see a better place.

On dark nights my girlfriend wonders why she finds me staring out of the window and into the middle distance. What she does not know is I am considering April and May time. Can't help it. *That* Gerrard slip, for which he has my sympathy. *Palace.* Two car crashes in one week. I cannot remember how it felt last time Liverpool won the league. I was too young. After Palace, I returned to my home for the evening in Angel at around 2am following a hellish journey across London's wastelands to find friend and fellow journalist Timothy Abraham sitting alone in front of the TV with a can of Stella in hand. He'd travelled down without a ticket and ended up staying in a pub. By this unholy hour, he was watching re-runs of the Champions League Final from 2005. 'This won't be happening again,' he kept telling me, pointing. 'Not in our lifetime,' pointing again.

His words followed me throughout the summer and into the autumn. Unlike the older fellas who go the game, I have not been raised on a rich diet of success. There is not much evidence that fortunes will change. I worry that Tim might be right.

By Tuesday my lugubrious mood has not lifted. I begin the day by taking a seat on a Merseyrail train from Crosby and Blundellsands at 7.41am, heading towards Moorfields. Merseyrail should have arrived at 7.37am. I am approached by a family acquaintance at the platform. He likes to talk at me about Liverpool. Especially after Liverpool have lost. Each word is spluttered from the side of his mouth. He's the type of fella you see at the penthouse of the Twelfth Man: teeth like a row of bombed houses, talks like he's been chewing tobacco for a decade and drinking Skol. Probably has.

He is a season ticket holder, one who has experienced too many disappointments to be optimistic. *Villa, Villa, Villa.* I was hoping to read a book and escape from football. But there is no escape. I am like Jason Bourne, looking for the exit routes. Yet the doors slide shut. I am encased in a vortex of *Villa* noise. This morning we shall only talk about *Villa,* and his frankly annoying success with a diet. He is middle-aged. He has lost two stone in as many months. He has not touched a drop of Skol. I find this quite depressing too.

Once at my desk, I read the morning's newspapers online as I do every day. Liverpool are back in the Champions League for the first time in five years. Yet it is a place they must remain. What happens if they don't make it next season? Oh, the financial implications. Can't we just enjoy the ride? Football tries its best not to let you enjoy the moment. There is always the future, laden with financial pressure. Whatever happened to just going to the match with your mates, escaping the realities of life?

Fuck off football. Why can't I leave you?

At lunchtime, I take a walk along Liverpool's waterfront. The sun is shining. I notice a shadowy-looking figure walking towards me. He is dressed all in black: polar neck, keks and loafers. There are also dark shades. He is the man from Milk Tray. He is Gabriel Clarke, presenter extraordinaire for ITV, the television company screening tonight's game live from Anfield.

Now I've always liked Clarke. Think he's underrated. In my opinion, Clarke is to documentaries about the inner workings of football clubs what David Attenborough is to wildlife shows. He can deliver wonderfully insightful interviews and has a voice that is cautiously brilliant. He does a lot of Champions League stuff and for some reason, this reminds me that Liverpool are back where they want to be. Spirits are raised.

I am at the match in a working capacity. I never forget just what a privilege this is, being able to enter through the front doors of Anfield – into the red carpeted foyer, which as a kid I likened to that scene from *Titanic* where Leonardo Di Caprio steps on to the grand staircase for the first time. How romantic.

I was 14 years old when in 1997 I was invited into the players' lounge after a game against Barnsley. The dad of a mate knew Joe Corrigan, Liverpool's goalkeeping coach. It was like the build-up to Christmas. The club conducted stadium tours but I was never interested in that.

Here, I was being allowed into the inner sanctum when it was active. On a matchday. Players. Managers. Milling.

For weeks, I dreamed of this wondrous place. That Ashley Ward scored a 35th-minute winner for Barnsley during an embarrassing 1-0 defeat for Liverpool did not even matter. Afterwards we were allowed down the tunnel. We touched the This Is Anfield sign. We sat in the dugouts. We visited the trophy room and even the changing rooms. They were small and basic. A medical table with ripped leather cushioning stood in the middle of the room. Shorts and jockstraps lay on the floor. There were empty bottles of Lucozade. The place reeked of liniment.

I passed Roy Evans and Danny Wilson chatting outside the new Boot Room, which had been relocated from its original position in order to create a press area. Evans was putting on a brave face. I wondered how he must deal with being a Liverpool supporter and leading the team towards defeat against dubious opposition like Barnsley. Does he just go home, turn the lights off and go to bed? Wilson, arms folded, could not stop smiling. He held the expression of a man who had sacked Rome.

I entered the players' lounge as if I somehow belonged there, acting all cool. I was not alone. The players – those that had just lost to Barnsley – were lounging around as if it was the after-show party. David James lay splayed on the couch with a bottle of Carlsberg in hand, the top button of his shirt undone and his tie all over the place. Paul Ince had not played and was wearing a crass-looking New York Yankees cap. He seemed to have a lot to say for himself. Jamie Redknapp was in there with his pop star girlfriend, Louise Nurding – I considered this an unexpected yet welcome bonus. Robbie Fowler and Steve McManaman stood joking. Michael Owen's attentions were on the only TV in the corner of the room. There was a racing event at Newmarket, Market Rasen or another place like that. He must have had a bet.

I thought this was all perfectly natural. Liverpool had played. Liverpool had lost. It did not seem to hurt too much. In the intoxicating microclimate of the players' lounge those around me eased my naïve teenage mind. I went home reasoning that matches come and go quickly in football. Focus must switch to the next challenge – which happened to be Arsenal away during a season where Arsenal would finish as champions. Somehow, Liverpool ended up winning that one. Typical.

Times have changed. Football in the 1990s was a brave new world. Now, it is a professional and clinical beast. Anfield tries to retain its humble values but struggles. On European nights like this, more people hang around – people trying to look very important, indeed. Hostesses in red dresses welcome you at the doorway, as if you are entering into a Bond villain's lair. Business types in club suits buzz annoyingly, all busy.

As Brendan Rodgers might say, *it is all part of the dance,* though it does not sit easily with me. I wonder what Bill Shankly and Bob Paisley would make of it all. The press room is packed and journalists are commenting on the size and price of the match programme. At A4 and £5 a pop, this is the added cost of Champions League football, where match tickets now stretch to £58 a seat. As it happens, I have ghost-written Steven Gerrard's captain's notes for the occasion. If only Liverpool had more players like him. I don't think people realise how much he cares. He wears a bad result on his face. He always shows up to interviews on time. He always answers his phone. He is the most professional of all the Liverpool players I've met both past and present.

That leads me conveniently to the enigma that is Mario Balotelli. He's the last on to the pitch when the teams are led out by the intriguingly named Slovenian referee Matej Jug, whose performance is in keeping with the match itself: stop-start and crap. Balotelli almost forgets the pre-match team line-up photograph while he fiddles with his shorts near the centre circle. He fiddles with his shorts quite often throughout the evening, does Mario. I wonder if he has a nervous tick.

The visiting supporters, decked in green and white, are in fine, audible form as you might imagine. This is the Bulgarians' first foray into the Champions League group stages and they are expected to lose every fixture. Yet Liverpool offer little and at half-time it feels appropriate that the scoreline should be 0-0. Worryingly, it reminds me of some of those European games in the final days of Gerard Houllier or Rafa Benitez. Olimpija Ljubljana, Levski Sofia, Unirea Urziceni. It must be an Eastern Bloc thing. I hope it's not a Brendan Rodgers thing.

Anyway Balotelli, whose movement has been comparable to a corpse for most of the night, jolts into life to volley Liverpool into a lead. He doesn't really celebrate. Just stands there in front of the Kop, as if we should have known he'd do this.

Ludogorets are surely beaten now. But they are not. An anonymous Spanish substitute named Dani hits post. *Oh no, here it comes. Surely not… and there you go* – the fucking equaliser.

They celebrate Dani's goal like it's the year 2000 and are celebrating still moments later when Serbian-born goalkeeper Milan Borjan emerges from his line like a bear that has been shot with a tranquilliser. So disorientated, he swipes at Javi Manquillo and surrenders a penalty, from which Gerrard seals Liverpool's victory – quite an achievement considering all seemed settled less than 60 seconds ago.

So there it is, Liverpool have beaten Ludogorets. This has been my story – a lot of it indulgent woe. I apologise for sulking. I want to change. West Ham next.

20 September 2014, West Ham 3 Liverpool 1

'It's mental, like something from a Mighty Boosh sketch'

By Sachin Nakrani

We hate journalists don't we? Of course we do. The lying, muck-rucking, soulless, grandmother-selling scumbags. Lock 'em up and throw away the key. Better still; herd 'em up like the stinking cattle they are, blast their ankles off with a sawn-off shotgun and after they've writhed around in pain for a bit, calling madly for their falsified taxi receipts, chuck 'em in the nearest burning van. Lock the doors and watch the pricks perish.

So anyway, I'm a journalist. No please, don't feel awkward, regain eye contact and believe me when I say it's OK, it's fine. Seriously, don't worry. I've heard it all before and I'm braced to hear more in the days, weeks and years to come.

I've learnt over the past 11 years, ever since I walked into the offices of the *Harrow Observer* as a raw but enthusiastic reporter, dressed head to toe in reasonably-priced clobber from Burton, that journalists are among the least liked and trusted people around. In fairness, us journos have hardly helped ourselves in terms of reputation-building. We all know about the dark arts of Fleet Street (on which, incidentally, there are now more Starbucks than there are newspaper offices), with a torch well and truly shone on the lowest of the low during the recent hacking trials and exposés surrounding practices at News International. Liverpool supporters have, of course, been aware of such loathsome behaviour for more than a quarter of a century – the lies behind 'The Truth' scaring the bereaved of Hillsborough and the city many of them hail from in a manner which beggars belief and betrays the lack of a moral compass among those responsible. Only in the last couple of years, and after the most incredible fights for justice, does the world know the real truth.

I work for the *Guardian*. Yes, I'm one of the good guys, or one of the less-bad guys if you prefer, an employee of a company more renowned for its grammatical errors than errors in judgement or taste. At the *Guardian* there is no hacking and obsession with celebrity, no blatant and intentional making-up of damaging, hurtful accusations, and certainly no class-driven, racist agenda. Saying that, upon joining the company in October 2007 I discovered my password for the internal computer system was 'token31'. I've been looking for the other 30 coloured members of staff ever since.

Joking aside, I've enjoyed my time at the *Guardian*, particularly having all but given up joining a national newspaper after more than four years at local level. I enjoyed all that too, and despite what most people think local journalism is not all about summer fetes and planning meetings. Yes, there are a fair few of both, but there is also a variety of important, community-centered stories for would-be hacks to cover each and every day and the entire experience provides all those who go down that route with the best, most complete grounding for the job. What I learnt as a reporter at the *Harrow Observer*, and as a news editor at the *Ealing Gazette*, has proved invaluable throughout my career, and it is a source of great sadness that so many local and regional papers are dying a slow death in this digital age. Once young journalists cut their teeth in actual newsrooms, learning off actual, hardened journalists, while interacting with actual, proper people; now most blog from their bedrooms and don't know what an off-diary story is, let alone try and get one in the pissing rain.

Sorry for sounding like a grumpy relic from a bygone age (or the noughties to be precise) but journalism is something I feel passionate about, and that is why the abuse and hatred stings from time to time. I know, it's part of the job – thick skin and all that – but most of us are not scumbags, and most of us have worked fucking hard to get where we are.

Sports journalists probably get it worst of all and that is perhaps not a surprise given we involve ourselves in areas which spark strong emotions among many people. The word you often hear is 'agenda' – the fella who writes a negative piece about Arsenal has an 'agenda' against Arsene Wenger, never mind that he's the same guy who praised Wenger a week ago. Oh did he now? Well he's a hypocrite then, say the same people. We can't win.

Don't get me wrong, journalists mess up – I certainly have from time to time – and there are those who do have personal gripes with certain clubs and certain people. But in any profession there are good people, bad people and people who fuck up – it's called life and a little more understanding wouldn't go astray.

But that seems unlikely, especially in the era of Twitter, where those who dare to write about sport, and football in particular, are hit with 140-character bile-bombs on a daily basis. I've certainly got my share. It got so dark, in fact, that I considered legal action before pulling back from the brink and deciding to block the bitter tosspots instead.

So things carry on and, believe me, I accept I'm a very lucky boy. I wake up every day and get to immerse myself in sport for a living. I've worked hard to get to this point, but I also recognise that some of this has got to do with chance and circumstance so there is a need to be grateful and simply accept some of the associated abuse, that which doesn't cross a line anyway.

To be specific, I work as a sports features editor at the *Guardian*, part of a two-man team – alongside the Tranmere-supporting Stephen McMillan – who are in charge of managing our non-football content. That means liaising with writers in regards to who covers what, what story is written when and, between myself and Steve, generating ideas. It's a fulfilling, enjoyable Monday-to-Friday job, but one that can also prove exhausting and time-consuming. The hours are so long, in fact, that I'm writing this chapter at 11.05pm on a Wednesday having got up at 6.30am and worked pretty much non-stop from when I entered the office up until I left shortly before 7pm.

It's also temporary; year-long maternity cover, and probably not something I want to do long-term. Not at this stage of my life anyway given I'm still relatively young and maintain the energy and enthusiasm to be out and about writing regularly. That's what I did when I joined the *Guardian* a little under seven years ago as part of its now-defunct trainee reporter scheme. They threw me straight in at the deep end and by the end of week two I was covering Premier League football (First match: Wigan 0 Portsmouth 2 at the DW stadium on 20 October 2007). After some early setbacks – specifically, I didn't know what I was doing – I grew into the role of full-time national sports reporter and did well enough for the then editor Ben Clissitt to keep me on after my year contract had ended. I was, however, employed as a full-time sub-editor (checking copy, writing headlines etc) and while I enjoyed that role, it was meant to lead back to reporting and writing regularly, particularly given that I continued to cover games in my free time (as well as doing the occasional feature, interview and news story) and performed well on practically each and every occasion.

'If I keep at this they're bound to give me a proper writing job,' I told my wife as I sacrificed yet another weekend with her, friends or family, to cover a game. And each time I returned home, often in darkness following a long round-trip to Bolton, Burnley or somewhere else in the north, the belief that my moment was around the corner grew. Yet here I am, many years later and now with a young, utterly wonderful child, still sacrificing my free time to write about football. The difference is I accept that regular reporting job won't be mine, not at the *Guardian* anyway. Instead this is now for the sheer pleasure of it all.

And it is a pleasure. Even after all this time, and with cynicism and a sense of professional injustice running though my veins, I still get a thrill from packing a notepad and laptop in my rucksack, heading down to the train station and making my way to whichever football stadium the *Guardian* wants me at. On the Saturday just gone, that happened to be Upton Park.

Liverpool were in town. This, then, was a bit of a perfect storm – combining watching Brendan's tricky Reds with doing the reporting gig. Saying that, there was a nervousness flowing through me as I stepped out of Upton Park tube station and walked to the stadium of the same name given Liverpool arrived in east London in less than fabulous shape having lost to Aston Villa a week ago and just about scraped past Ludogorets on Tuesday.

The scene was like every other I have witnessed when making this journey in the past; an intense frenzy of people on both sides of Green Street, moving in all directions, crowding every possible square inch of space. On matchdays there is always a lot of white faces in this maelstrom (white faces above claret shirts), but there remains a noticeable smattering of brown, too, visible proof of east London's ethnic mix and sizeable Asian community.

Once the crowds and seemingly endless parade of burger vans have been navigated, Upton Park smacks you in the face, a vast structure among a row of dilapidated shops, pubs and cafes and surely the only stadium in Britain shaped like a gigantic bouncy castle. The press entrance is to the far left as it stands and can only be reached via a side road whose name I have yet to take notice of.

With my press pass checked by the extremely friendly fella at the front counter it's time to enter the Upton Park press room and, not for the first time, be stunned by the sheer number of people inside. It's absolutely heaving, and as I look around it's impossible not to wonder what most are doing here. I spot some fellow newspaper journalists, and over there are some radio and TV folk; she could well be from West Ham's official website, and I'm pretty sure he's a Liverpool press officer. But the rest...

Again it is a sign of how journalism has changed; an ever-splintering sector with a multitude of obscure, web-based outlets, and as someone who believes passionately in the power of print there is the feeling that many members of the press room crowd are threats to the profession. Indeed the rise and rise of the internet has seen the *Guardian* and most other newspapers focus an increasing amount of attention on their online coverage, which is a bit of a gripe for us traditionalists.

I'm sounding grumpy again aren't I?

There are only a handful of seats left and one is by a table occupied by the *Daily Mirror*'s John Cross. Now I know Crossy (yes, I said Crossy) is not a favourite among many Liverpool fans following his reporting of the Luis Suarez-Arsenal-£40,000,001 saga of 2013, but I've always got on well with him and he's always been good to me, which given the chasm that exists between our respective statuses as football writers is no given. Once again he offers up a cheery hello and a friendly handshake as I take up the chair directly opposite where he is sat.

It's not long before our attention is taken by the large TV screens located on two of the press room walls. *Gillette Soccer Saturday* is on and Arsenal have scored three times in three minutes against Aston Villa. A grin creeps across Crossy's face and he instantly searches out Stan Collymore, who is sat on a table nearby. It's light-hearted stuff; an Arsenal fan looking to tease a Villa fan, but Stan, presumably here for talkSPORT, is having none of it and keeps his head down.

Soon I notice another former Red in close proximity. Jim Beglin is sat at a wall-side table to my right, dressed in a striped-blue shirt and grey trousers. He leans across, looks over my shoulder and checks out one of the two TVs. 'Blimey, 3-0,' says the former left-back before returning to his lunch.

Speaking of which…

It's a real perk of this job that you get fed practically everywhere you go. The quality of the spread varies from venue to venue, with, in my experience, none more spectacular than those served at the Emirates Stadium and Stamford Bridge. The cheese selection at Chelsea alone is enough to make you want to toss off the football and eat until it's time to clear off.

Anfield's spread is surprisingly sparse – usually one dish, and that served in a small room with a terrible phone signal. Five-times champions of Europe but no five-star treatment for hacks. Thank God for the staff, who I've always found to be lovely.

West Ham's offerings are usually decent – on Saturday the options were scampi and chips or lasagne and chips, with the lasagne option working out very tasty – which is somewhat surprising given the overall shit experience of covering games at Upton Park. Where to start?

Firstly the toilet facilities are a weird joke, amounting as they do to one urinal and one of the seated variety located in a very small room, with the urinal the one hidden behind a wall. Seriously, it's mental, like something from a *Mighty Boosh* sketch.

Then there's the ever terrible wi-fi signal, in both the press room and the press box, which is a major pain in the rear when you're filing a story to a tight deadline. And speaking of the press box, it's located at the very top of the Alpairi Stand and can only be accessed by climbing what feels like 83 flights of stairs and through a crowd of West Ham fans drinking away as us journos attempt to catch our breath. And once you finally make it your seat you remember it has the sort of legroom that would make a toddler rub their knees in discomfort.

I was reminded of this as I took my seat shortly after 4.45pm – A107, located on the front row and beside the *Sunday Times*'s chief sports writer David Walsh. I'd never sat beside him in a press box before so for a sports journalist-geek like myself this was a genuine thrill, if not a slightly curious outcome given he was separating me from my colleague Dominic Fifield, who was covering the game for our Sunday paper, the *Observer*. Normally when reporters from the same organisation are in attendance at a game they are sat together, but this is Upton Park so anything is possible. Just check out the toilets.

Kick-off was at 5.30pm and despite the lack of leg space and increasing chill in the air, I was buzzing. In a press box, sat next to David Walsh and watching my team play; it doesn't get much better than this, I thought. What a shame, then, that my state of contentment lasted for just 72 seconds and up until Liverpool gave away yet another goal from a set piece. This time it was Winston Reid scoring from a close-range header after Martin Skrtel decided to abandon all responsibility and Simon Mignolet flapped and fucked about all over again. I saw it all coming as soon as West Ham got a free kick at the far side.

It was 2-0 less than six minutes later and 3-1 at the final whistle, with Raheem Sterling's 26th-minute goal the only bright spot of a truly miserable evening. We were shocking and it's at moments like this when getting paid to watch Liverpool really loses its lustre. There I was, angry as fuck, and completely unable to express my emotions. Saying that, I did pump my fist when Sterling scored. Not the most professional thing to do, and not something I've done on the other occasions I've covered Liverpool, but who cares, we lost anyway.

As I made my way down the never-ending stairs, my mission was to get some answers from Brendan Rodgers. As is protocol, he was going to first do interviews with radio and TV, followed by a general press conference with the Sunday journalists (and the many other people in attendance) before finally spending some time with those of us writing considered, less match-focused pieces for Monday's papers. This was to be the moment when I found out why Liverpool cannot fucking clear a cross.

Sadly it didn't quite work out like that as the majority of the Monday mob wanted to ask Brendan if he felt Liverpool's involvement in the Champions League had played a part in this defeat. For me this was not the primary issue – the team's consistently poor defending, particularly on set pieces, was. But I was overruled, with my more nuanced knowledge of the team ignored in favour of the more obvious line of questioning.

Don't get me wrong, I understand why the likes of Matt Dunn from the *Daily Express* and Alyson Rudd from *The Times* wanted to go down this route – Liverpool had lost having played in the Champions League for the first time in five years and it is a widely-held view that recombining European and domestic football seriously disrupts sides. But for me the defence is the wider, more glaring concern.

Here is a transcript of the short and sharp Q&A session we had with Rodgers in the Upton Park press room corridor, a sliver of space located by the front entrance and the weird toilet, and where the manager was practically pinned up against a wall as a pack of hacks bayed for quotes:

Q: 'Will you accept Champions League involvement as an excuse from your players for this performance?'

BR: 'We have no excuses today. We made some changes to the team, which we're going to have to do along the way. But there is no excuse. We came here to win the game. It would be easy to stand here and say, "It was our first game, the emotion of the Champions League and all of that...."'

Q: 'They've got to be bigger and better than that don't they?'

BR: 'Listen, I don't want to criticise the players. I don't want a headline saying "I said this and I said that". This has been a great group to work with, we've added a number of players to that this season and we'll be better as the season goes on. We have no excuses today, we just weren't at our level.'

Q: 'Have you learnt anything from your first Champions League week?'

BR: 'Our priority is the Premier League, make no mistake about that. This is our bread and butter, we want to sustain that ability we've shown at the top-four end. But for that you've got to win games.'

Q: 'So you'll do things differently during the next Champions League week?'

BR: 'No, we'll continue to work how we've done. We just haven't been playing well enough, it's as simple as that. I can stand and give you excuses about the number of players, and injured players, but for us we just need to work together. When we win, lose, draw, there's no blame. We just have to focus on our performance level.'

Q: 'Is there a sense of inevitability that this season would be a backward step because of the extra distractions?'

BR: 'May well be, but I think for us our focus is just on the next game. We don't want to get carried away, the Champions League for us…there is a great history for the club in the competition, to be back at that level after so many years is great, but now the first game has gone we have to concentrate on the football. There is a big emotion with the competition but for us we have to focus on our next game. It's a tiring competition, one that is mentally draining, but we've earned the right to be in the competition and we have to also do well in the Premier League.'

Q: 'How is being in the Champions League tiring?'

BR: 'The preparation time, travel time, and then you need your players in recovery time. They need to recover after games in order to get ready for the next game. Of course there is a big emotion in it but that's something we all want because we want to be at the leading edge of the game.'

Q: 'Liverpool need to work on defending set pieces don't they?'

BR: 'We'll need to put extra work into it. We do a lot of preparation work on our organisation. We'll have to analyse it more, it's a disappointing goal to concede…the ball goes in and the defender ends up scoring it right in the middle of the six-yard box. So yes [we will work more on defending set pieces].'

Q: 'How have you found the dynamic of your first Champions League week?'

BR: 'You've got a lot less time working with the team; if you play on the Saturday, you've got Sunday/Monday for recovering, you've got the Tuesday game, and then the players who play are recovering Wednesday/Thursday. So you're doing your first tactical preparation on the Friday, and then you're travelling straight down to the game. But you can't complain about it, we're glad to be here, this is what we have to get used to. We just want and expect to be better.'

Spot my question? I couldn't resist.

Having spoken with Rodgers – and he was very polite if not understandably downcast – I left Upton Park still in a state of seething anger, a mood not helped by a journey home made tortuous by yet another bout of rail-replacement works. I remained the same way when I finally got through the front door just before 11pm, which was not cool given my daughter had stayed awake so she could see me before going to bed. I tried my best to be warm and loving but it was obvious to her and her mother that I wasn't in the mood.

I didn't sleep well that night either, with my mood only slightly better when I wrote my report the following morning, which given the nature of the quotes we had secured the previous evening had to largely focus on the whole Champions League involvement thing. To be fair, Rodgers said some pretty interesting stuff about all of that.

With my report emailed to the office, I took a moment to reflect. Saturday was another occasion when I chose a sixth successive day of work over spending time with my wife and daughter, and ultimately it was a hugely frustrating experience. Yes I would've felt the same way had I gone to the game as an away fan, but given it was a London fixture, I wouldn't have left home so soon, returned so late and seen my Sunday also disrupted. I would've also been able to have a pint.

Equally, however, I recognise what a fantastic thing it is to cover Premier League football for a national newspaper – there are thousands of people who would fall on their knees and beg for the chance to do the same, and so it would be ungrateful of me to moan too much. Besides, my wife understands how much this all means to me and is often the one encouraging me to keep at it and not get overly depressed that my free time is getting eaten up by something I feel should be my day job by now.

So I shall. Arsenal v Tottenham awaits next Saturday, after the small matter of a Merseyside derby. If we lose that game because of a set-piece goal then questions really will have to be asked of the manager.

23 September 2014, Liverpool 2 Middlesbrough 2
(aet; Liverpool win 14-13 on penalties)

'I've been breathing in some inconsiderate twat's match farts'

By Dave Usher

I'm not one of those who looks down their noses on the League Cup. Far from it in fact, I've always viewed it much the same way I do the FA Cup. One may have more prestige and history, but they're both cup competitions with a Wembley trip at the end of it, and winning one is as good as winning the other for me. And at least the League Cup doesn't hold semi-finals at Wembley.

So yeah, I quite like this competition, and I've enjoyed it immensely any time we've won it. That being said, I struggled massively to summon up any kind of enthusiasm for our game with Middlesbrough at Anfield. It was a combination of things really. I'm suffering a massive hangover from last season and I'm finding it difficult to come to terms with what's happened to us. If last year's team were a Hollywood movie character, it'd be Achilles (played by Brad Pitt) in *Troy*. An adonis destroying everything in it's path until eventually some little snide discovered our weak spot and that was that.

This year's team is more like Steve Martin in *Planes, Trains & Automobiles*, just lurching from one setback to the next. At the risk of coming across like some lovesick sap who can't get over being dumped by his stunning bird, the truth is I'm finding it hard to get over Luis and I'm not sure I ever will. I'm pining for him and that's not being made any easier looking at who we spent all his transfer fee on. Going from Suarez to Mario Balotelli is like being dumped by Kylie Minogue and

48

ending up with Pat Butcher. OK, that's a little over the top as Mario isn't that bad, but the point is that the drop-off from Suarez to almost any other striker is astronomical.

I'm worried where we are headed this year. I want us to be good in the league again, and all these midweek games are interfering with that. Brendan Rodgers needs time to work with all these new players, to integrate them into how he wants us to play and get everyone used to playing together. Suarez may have been the main reason we were so devastating last year, but he wasn't the only reason. There are a lot of talented players still here but last year we were playing once a week and Brendan spent the whole week preparing for that game. This year he hasn't been able to do that because of these midweek games, so this game with Middlesbrough was one I could really have done without. Nothing against the League Cup, I feel exactly the same way about this year's Champions League too.

I couldn't have been any less motivated for this game as I made my way to Anfield. It wasn't just me either, the lads I met before kick-off were of similar mindset. The news that young Jordan Rossiter was making his debut at least provided us with something to look forward to, but generally most of us couldn't be any less interested.

I didn't want to be there, and for most of the game I was wishing I'd saved the £30 and watched from the comfort and warmth of my living room. That kind of thought never used to occur to me no matter how shite we were, but I guess I'm getting older now.

But by the time I came out of Anfield at around 11pm, I'd changed my mind. I was glad I showed up. This is a game I'll remember for a long, long time.

The penalty shootout was one of the most bizarre things I can remember in all my years of going to Anfield. None of us could have predicted how that was going to unfold, especially after Boro missed their first kick. What went before was sadly easier to predict though.

It feels like every time we play a lower league side in the cups the game follows a similar pattern; we go ahead, then just meander through the game not doing a great deal and allowing the opposition to hang around and slowly grow in confidence. Then they either equalise or have us right under the cosh until we eventually scrape through with a huge sigh of relief. Northampton, Reading, Mansfield, Notts County, Oldham and Bournemouth all followed a similar pattern, and those are just off the top of my head; there are probably others.

This wasn't actually *that* bad a performance all things considered, and I can draw several positives from the game, or at least certain aspects of it. There were a couple of things that pissed me off though, namely the way we threw away the lead right at the death for the second home game in succession, and the fact that Raheem Sterling played for two hours in a fucking League Cup tie a few days before a Merseyside derby. His selection makes a mockery of the decision to rest him against Aston Villa a couple of weeks ago.

If Brendan trusted the other players more then he wouldn't have even entertained the idea of playing Sterling in this one. It's easy to see why he doesn't trust them though isn't it? Rickie Lambert is having a really tough time unfortunately, Lazar Markovic is faring little better and even Balotelli is still finding his feet and isn't the kind of player Rodgers can hang his hat on yet (if he ever will be).

Meanwhile Adam Lallana had looked sharper at the weekend but is 'still in pre-season' according to his manager, so the conclusion I'd draw is that he picked Sterling because he didn't believe we could win without him. The sad thing is he's probably right.

Sterling's inclusion aside, the rest of the line-up at kick-off makes perfect sense, although I would have found room for Suso myself (more on him shortly). Generally though, players who needed games are included and those who you'd want to rest are rested.

The inclusion of Rossiter in midfield is most welcome. He could easily have been handed his debut a year ago but circumstances always seemed to conspire against him (injury, international call-ups and tough draws in the cups). Still, here he is, making his first appearance at just 17 years old. And what a start he makes too, side-footing in from 30 yards after Lambert's effort had rebounded into his path. The keeper makes a right hash of it, but it's still a composed finish as Rossiter keeps his shot down and ensures he hits the target when he could easily have leathered it miles over the bar.

Lambert's not in the game at all though, his touch and passing are not at the level we've seen when he was playing for Southampton or England and it's looking as though it's all a bit too much for him at the moment. Having been granted his dream move he's desperately trying to convince people – perhaps even himself – that he belongs here and this is not just about sentiment. He probably wants it too much as he doesn't seem to be relaxed or confident, and the longer he goes without a goal the worse I fear it's going to get.

I feel bad for the fella. We can all relate to just how much this means to him and how much he wants to do well, but he's a passenger in this game and it comes as no surprise when he's eventually substituted. It feels like an act of kindness.

Speaking of painful...two things stand out about Boro's first equaliser. Firstly, Mamadou Sakho causes it by playing an underhit pass and then handling the cross. He does this kind of thing too often and it does my fucking head in because in between these lapses he often looks the part. Secondly, the defending of the set piece isn't good at all. Lambert ducks underneath it, Jose Enrique goes with his foot instead of his head and it's all too easy for the Boro player to nod it past Simon Mignolet.

It's irritating, not so much that we concede but more that we fail to build on the early goal and make the game safe. Last season we could get away with things like this because we were so lethal in attack, but now these defensive errors are killing us because we're a bit, dare I say, toothless.

At 1-1 it almost gets worse when a pass by their number ten takes four of our players out and a midfield runner bursts through and hits the post. We're wobbling and nothing's really happening in attack, despite the occasional flash from Sterling and the constant industry of Lallana.

Balotelli comes on for Lambert and has more shots in two minutes than Rickie managed in 70. Rodgers also takes Rossiter off and sends on Jordan Williams for a surprise debut. He wouldn't have been high on a list of Under-21 players who I'd have given a chance of being involved in this game, but he does well. For him to have been called up for this game suggests he must have been really impressing Rodgers in training, so he's one to keep an eye on in future.

The last thing I want is extra time. A whole 90 minutes of listening to Boro fans singing about Scouse unemployment and Steven Gerrard slipping over is bad enough, but to top it off I've been breathing in some inconsiderate twat's match farts since early in the first half. I've had enough, but now I have to sit through another half an hour of it. Fuck's sake Liverpool.

The introduction of Suso for the disappointing (and ridiculously shot-shy) Markovic raises my spirits slightly. I love Suso, he's ace. He's one of my favourite players, actually. It saddens and baffles me that Brendan doesn't seem to want him – I love watching the little fella and in a few years he could be one hell of a player. He's just never really had a chance with us and we don't seem to know where to play him.

His goal is a tidy right-footed finish after great play by Enrique and Lallana on the left. Boro have nothing left and it looks like we might even get another as we're suddenly looking more dangerous than at any point during the previous 105 minutes.

Suso nearly bags a second but the keeper makes a good save, and as time ticks away you can see we are just looking to see the game out and not over-commit. Then a sloppy ball from Sterling put us in trouble and just like that we are heading to penalties. Lots and lots of penalties.

It feels as if what happened last week against Ludogorets was foremost in Sterling's thoughts when he gave that ball away. Last week he ran forward and was dispossessed, resulting in a goal that should have been avoided. This time he had the option to carry it forward but instead checked and attempted to pass the ball back to Sakho, clearly thinking about doing the sensible thing. Unfortunately he picked out Danny Ayala, a former Red, who turned and played a pass through Sakho's legs (second time in three games he's been megged like that with a through ball) and Kolo Toure did the rest, racing over on the cover and needlessly clattering the onrushing forward, Patrick Bamford.

It mars an otherwise solid display from Toure. Some of his clearances were a little on the alehouse side, but if he doesn't give that pen away I'd probably be saying what a good game he'd had. Like Sakho though, that one costly error ruins everything good that went before or came after. It was just so stupid.

Bamford picks himself up to bury the penalty in the bottom corner. His celebration pisses me off – far too cocky. But then he's on loan from Chelsea so what do you expect?

All the momentum is with them going into the shootout so things don't look good. But when it comes to penalties it's foolish to ever bet against us. Balotelli converts to set us on our way and Bamford's cockiness turns to despair when his kick is saved by Mignolet. Everyone else then scores until it comes to kick number five; the decisive one that will send us through.

Up steps Sterling…SAVED!

It's up for grabs again.

With sudden death I'm always expecting it to be over any time the team that is up first converts their kick. We have that advantage, so every time one of our lads buries theirs I'm just waiting for Mignolet to make the winning save. And every time he fails to do so.

They say there's no pressure on keepers during shootouts, but in total Mignolet faces 16 penalties. There has to be some pressure to save a few, surely? As it is, 14 of them go in. He only stops one and that's basically because it's straight at him.

'NOW FUCKING SAVE ONE YOU, SOFT LAD! WE CAN'T KEEP DOING THIS ALL FUCKING NIGHT!' I see Lucas yelling at Mignolet. OK, maybe those aren't his exact words – he might actually be saying 'SIMON! COME ON! COME ON!' but we all know what he means.

But on it goes, and my big fear is that Sterling will have to step up again. Thankfully it doesn't get to him after the Boro lad puts his pen wide. Game over. We've won, finally.

The players don't know what to do. They start running towards Mignolet and then seem to realise, 'Hang on, he only saved one.' Mignolet himself is stood there looking all sheepish. He took a hell of a pen himself though, proper keeper's pen. Four-step run-up and then twat!

The whole thing is mad, hard to take in. It reached a point when every time Boro converted a pen there was an audible sigh around the stadium. It was like nothing else I've ever experienced, and the shootout alone made me glad I'd attended this one.

I'll remember this game for years to come. It's one to tell the grandkids about and when I'm telling the story I expect I'll have forgotten all about the small-time smog-monsters chanting about Gerrard and those rancid match farts from some stealth bomber in the Main Stand.

27 September 2014, Liverpool 1 Everton 1

'I've no idea how he got there, but he had the biggest smile on his face'

By David Downie

The Merseyside derby. The away Merseyside derby. In my 26 years as an Evertonian, even just the reading of this fixture has made my stomach knot and my head fill with dreams akin to a ten-year-old pretending he was his favourite player in the park with his mates. 'And that's the hat-trick for Rooney! The youngest ever goalscorer in a Merseyside derby!' So went the hopeless narrative in my head, well, for the last 15 years at least and the last time we actually did ourselves justice at Anfield.

Kevin Campbell netted early and we went on to snatch it 1-0. My abiding thought was how on earth we didn't score more with Steve Staunton in goal.

Being brutally honest, the derby always terrifies me. Each second we don't have the ball I'm in agony waiting for Liverpool to score. It's a perverse form of torture – you're desperate for it to be over but you never want it to end. It's that one chance to buzz off your Kopite mates properly. I know it's rich given my audience to have a preference given our record this millennium, but the away one always means so much more to me.

Of course these days are a far cry from when I first became immersed in this fixture in the mid-1990s, learning what it meant as a kid growing up in this city. My first memory is a beautiful one for any Evertonian – when big Duncan Ferguson announced himself on the derby scene with that bullet of a header on his debut. I sat watching my dad and his mates going crazy when he nodded home. I'd never really got football until that moment. I suppose at the age of seven it didn't really matter too much to me. All I knew was that I supported Everton and I was happy if they won but never too bothered if they lost. I'm sure all of us wish our emotions reflected that youthful optimism, but alas this was when I became hooked and set for a tormented life at the hands of Liverpool.

The 90s was a depressing time for Everton, which is why the derby became so important – for me at least. Even now I can't ever deter myself from the thought that this is the defining fixture of any season. As much I play it down over and over in my head, and try to convince myself it's just another three points up for grabs, I'm dragged back in to that torturous and relentless feeling that saves itself for this game. Every year there's always a few who, when asked what would be a good season for Everton, always reply, 'Beat the red shite in the derby and finish above them.' I've never been one for that, but when the game comes around and you see what an institution Liverpool are at first hand, you can't help but understand what they mean.

Most of my mates when I was young were Reds, so it was either a case of suffering the wrath of the mob or taking great pleasure in their misery for a few days. Luckily for me that was a period of relative derby joy for Everton. We went through an eight-year spell all the way up until I started senior school without losing one. Unfortunately the tables turned quite quickly as the new millennium dawned, which also coincided with everyone I knew becoming far more passionate about their team. You can imagine how difficult it was going through your entire secondary school experience without a win in a derby. I don't have to imagine because it was my reality.

Everyone used to call this 'the friendly derby' didn't they? You could probably see why up until a certain game at Goodison a few years back. In my opinion, there was an upturn in hostilities as soon as Gary McAllister stole 20 yards and pea-rolled a shot into the Park End net that Paul Gerrard had time to have taken a shower and got dressed before saving.

Horrible day, that. On the way home I remember seeing several kick-offs. I was 13 and probably the only sober person in the vicinity of Goodison. County Road was gridlocked and there was a nasty atmosphere around the place – you could sense it'd probably be breaking point for many under the influence who were either too happy or too angry. That was also only a few months before David Moyes took over. I think you'll agree his persona and approach did plenty in widening the gap between our two sets of fans. The proof is in how much of a renaissance there's been in that relationship since Roberto Martinez succeeded him.

Taking those extra few steps through the park in a direction that doesn't seem right is a peculiar feeling as you see Goodison becoming smaller when you look over your shoulder. The ground quickly appears behind the trees and then you get that tingle in your belly, that anticipation, excitement and nerves as you walk down Anfield Road. It has the same smell of overpriced burgers and hotdogs as we have at Goodison, yet although you're only up the road it still has that feel of a proper away game. That backs-against-the-wall mentality when you know you're in the minority but you want each and every person supporting the other team in that stadium to know who you are. That's what gives you the urge to bellow out your songs. You want these bastards to know you're here. On derby day at Anfield those feelings are multiplied ten-fold.

I've never had the pleasure of being there when we've won. My fondest memories comes from 2009 when we had that double in the FA Cup and league. Tim Cahill loved a goal at Anfield. I always felt we had half a chance as long as he was on the pitch in a derby. Many Blues will point to Graeme Sharp's volley or Kevin Sheedy's two-fingered salute as their favourite moments. Mine is the night Andrei Kanchelskis bagged two at the Kop, but in terms of being there when it happened, Cahill's stooping header in the 87th minute is my fondest Anfield memory.

I remember nearly passing out from screaming at Pepe Reina after he told a ball boy to take his time retrieving the ball when it had gone out for a goal-kick on 80 minutes. I was about ten rows back and level with the six-yard box so he definitely heard me. In my head he did anyway. I was praying it would come back to humiliate him, I was seething. It's the done thing to waste time when winning but Reina was the absolute worst for this at the time.

Next thing Yossi Benayoun unnecessarily snaps one of ours near the byline about halfway between the box and touchline, right in front of us. The Reds nearest to us in the Main Stand were fuming with Benayoun as he trudged into the area to defend the free kick. Everyone was on their feet on a Baltic Monday night and some kid, about eight, was on his dad's shoulders a couple of rows behind me. I couldn't help but think what would happen if we scored and it went off. Sure enough, Mikel Arteta belts a cross towards the near post and there he is. Tim fucking Cahill. I don't think I've ever celebrated a goal like it in my life. I definitely heard a few seats giving way to the sheer pandemonium as the team celebrated in front of us.

As it gradually calmed and the chants of 'Rafa's cracking up' erupted, I spotted that kid. He was now about six rows in front of us, clambering up through the seats back to his dad who was still going mental. I've no idea how he got there, but he had the biggest smile on his face. I know it was only a draw, but as goals come that was as good as it got for us under Moyes at Anfield.

I would never claim to hate Liverpool, but when it comes to these games I can't help but feel desperate to get one over on them. Again going back to when we were crap but somehow always turned up in derbies, it's that feeling of overcoming insurmountable odds. Winning is great, but it's so much more when it isn't expected. I think that's a big reason why we've been so poor at Anfield, and in any game against Liverpool generally, in recent years. The lengthening of years not winning there has become more of an issue for Everton than anything Liverpool have done to us in that time. I always come to the conclusion I'd take a draw in any derby.

At the start of the week I'm supremely confident and running the rule over how poor I think Liverpool are. It's a lengthy process but eventually I begin to look at the players who can hurt us and then, all of a sudden, I start thinking it'll be a cricket score. Judging by recent results, you'd be hard pushed to disagree and some players may think that too. Oh before I forget, one thing that really does piss me off about Liverpool is the way George Sephton takes so much joy in announcing our result when we've lost and the inevitable cheer that follows. Does my head in, that.

Anyway, in almost six years at Radio City I've only been privileged to see one derby win. The Hodgson one. For your consideration, I'll leave it at that…but it was lovely. In front of the new owners too. OK, OK, I'll stop.

Derby day at work usually means I'm confined to a studio in the Radio City tower with several other staff, the majority of whom are Reds. That's no different this year, only with the early kick-off it means our weekly show with Ian Snodin and Ian St John starts at three instead of its usual 12noon slot, and being in the company of a jubilant Liverpool legend for a few hours if the worst is to happen.

To be fair, Saint isn't the type to scream and shout unless something really gets to him. He's also very subtle in his piss-taking of Everton and, to his credit, he's never really done my head in when talking about us.

On hearing the line-ups my obvious concern is Tony Hibbert getting the nod at right-back. The lad's barely had a kick under Martinez and the worst stat is that he hasn't started a game for Everton in 666 days. An omen if ever there was one. I spend most of the build-up fearing how many times I'll be editing Raheem Sterling shots, runs, assists and goals as he is sure to rip dear Hibbo apart.

Martinez's selections have been very strange in almost every game so far this season but playing Hibbert proves the squad depth we supposedly have now is a myth. That being said, I'm happy with the rest of the team. It feels like a game of this magnitude is perfect for Mo Besic to cut his teeth in an Everton shirt – he'll be key to our midfield battle with Jordan Henderson.

I'm an admirer of Henderson. I remember interviewing him when he signed from Sunderland and my initial thoughts were that he would never last on Merseyside. He was very timid and looked like a kid who'd just started big school. For a while he played like that too, but I have a lot of respect for a player who can turn themselves around like he has, particularly considering the magnitude of that battle at a club like Liverpool.

As the game kicks off an unusual feeling overcomes me. It dawns on me that there is no Luis Suarez. No Daniel Sturridge either. Come to think of it, Steven Gerrard had been playing crap and is ageing, so what is there to fear from these? Defence as poor as ours and a keeper who competes with Tim Howard on a list of people you wouldn't trust to catch a beachball thrown at a medium pace. 'Hang on,' I think. 'We should do these here.'

I couldn't have judged it any worse. Opening 20 and it's up there with any of our poorest efforts during the past 15 years. Romelu Lukaku is being schooled by Alberto Moreno, Gareth Barry should've been sent off and the rest of our midfield can't find a blue shirt or get within the same time zone of the front two. I sit there waiting for the inevitable, screaming out loud how we need to change shape and pass the ball properly.

Like most Evertonians I love Martinez and what he's done in just over a year. But in the half a dozen games so far this season there have been some very concerning signs. There almost seems to be a defiance not to change things when they're clearly not working. Here Lukaku might as well have donned the Mighty Red costume and be parading down the Centenary giving out sweets such is his lack of threat. Still, we haven't conceded and Samuel Eto'o is on the bench to mix things up.

Second half doesn't go much better but to my surprise, Hibbo's doing alright. Next thing Balotelli snaps Barry and makes his way forward before hurling himself to the ground after minimal (if any) contact from Baines. 'Here we fucking go,' I think, praying Balotelli steps up because he's been terrible so far and no history of taking the piss in the derby. But no. No. No. No. No. No. It has to be *him* doesn't it?

I've never understood the barrage of abuse given to Gerrard. Many seem to save all that for the finest of players just to have it stuffed right down their throat. I don't like him because he's netted ten times against us and, like I said, he takes the piss. But as a player the lad is one of the best I've ever seen. And I'm not arsed what anyone says, even him, he's definitely a Blue. We've all seen the photo.

But surely this time, at 45 or however old he is, Gerrard won't pull it off again. As I hear the place erupt a voice inside my head shouts, 'Of course he fucking can Dave.'

I run to the nearest screen to see what he's done. It'll divide opinion but I reckon Howard should've saved that – he gets a full hand to the ball but, regardless, he knew what was coming. Never a good goalkeeper for me, but that's another argument.

After conceding I lose hope we'll get anything from this game and it should be two shortly after as Sterling jogs past Hibbert and Howard gets in the way of Mario's sitter. We're desperately poor and a complete refusal from either Martinez or Lukaku to shift his arse into the middle means there's nothing for us to play with in the Liverpool half.

It wouldn't have been the first sub I made but Hibbert is taken off for a new kid in Tyias Browning. Many would admire the rationale and relative calm of a such a bland substitution. It isn't attacking in the least.

I don't think I've ever seen an Everton game where so many simple passes go astray. We look petrified of Liverpool and no matter how many chances they waste or how much Martinez bellows instructions, there's no sign of that changing. It feels like Moyes, his stench still lingers in games like this. It was the same when we had the initiative when pushing Arsenal for a Champions League place last season; afraid of the unknown, too scared to dare at the thought of losing. It's not Martinez's fault – 11 years of pure containment will leave a mark on a group of players, certainly in a mental sense.

Into stoppage time I begin thinking of the fall-out, the inevitable text messages and social media piss-taking. Imagining two hours of radio with Saint and a load of pissed-up Reds ringing up to talk to him. Just get me home.

Next thing, and as I'm preparing a tweet reflecting on the scoreline, Steve Hothersall's voice goes higher by a few octaves before being drowned out by the unmistakable screams of, 'Goal! Goal! What a goal, haha!' from Sharp.

I jump up shaking, screaming so hard I fall to my knees. I run over to a lad covering the game on social media and kiss him. It's only an equaliser but Christ, what a goal. I calm down just enough to catch the replay. Fittingly Sharpy was the man who called it because that strike from Phil Jagielka is as immense as his volley in 1984. It's a thing of beauty. At the Kop, too.

No sooner has the final whistle gone than Saint comes bursting through the door. 'What a goal!' I croak to him with my vocal chords still reverberating. 'Shut up big man,' he snarls en route to a chair.

'It's unbelievable,' he adds, quietly. 'I haven't seen the goal, I was parking my car. I missed the second half as I was driving in here. What were we like?' 'Shite,' I reply with a laugh before filling him in with how appalling Everton were and how Liverpool should've won comfortably.

Snods follows about ten minutes later. 'Fucking get in!' he shouts upon shaking Saint's hand.

Reflecting on it, this is up there with the most mundane derby draws I've ever seen and it will now be at least 16 years without a win at Anfield. We were terrible, but to get away with it with a goal like that at the Kop end is about as sweet as it gets. For now anyway.

1 October 2014, Basel 1 Liverpool 0

I'm writing this a little under two months after this match was played and I can barely remember a thing about it. How shit-stained is that? Our first away game in the Champions League since 24 November 2009 (a 1-0 win at Debrecen in case you'd forgotten) and it's completely passed through my consciousness. Utterly forgettable, horribly regrettable.

I do remember that we lost, oh yes, I remember that. I also remember not being that surprised when the goal came; a scruffy, close-range shot from their captain Marco Streller on 52 minutes. It was from a set piece, and we are fucking woeful at dealing with those.

The goal was also not a huge shock given we'd been next to useless up until then. Our kit (yellow with red trim) looked ace, and the travelling Kopites were making a decent noise in the far corner of the ground. But the players, well they looked half-arsed as usual.

No one more so than Mario Balotelli. Jesus, he was terrible. This was the moment when I properly started worrying about him. Up until this match I was of the mind that all players need time to adapt, even those who don't run around a lot and, you know, look that bothered. But after Basel away, dark thoughts started entering my head.

I lost it in the second half when we were on the break and Balotelli had possession around the halfway line. A chance was on, especially with Jordan Henderson clear to his left. 'Play Hendo in Mario!' I screamed at the telly. 'Play him in, now!'

Balotelli duly lamped the ball towards goal and watched as it ballooned over the bar. Henderson was furious, as were the other players around him. I was pissed off, too, but it wasn't straight-out anger, more like that fearful disappointment you feel when you realise your firstborn is properly thick and probably won't get into university.

The final whistle almost came as a relief – thank fuck this dross is over. Sadly, and I didn't quite realise it at the time, there was more dross to come.

SN

4 October 2014, Liverpool 2 West Brom 1

'A full-out Scouse accent amused her no end'

By Karl Coppack

For the last few days I've been missing the bygone days of strong defences and clean sheets. We've had one this season. One. That came at Spurs in September, which is also the last game we won. So when I was asked what I wanted from this game I replied 'West Brom 0'. OK, I know that we conceded a joke of a penalty, so this could have ended that pierced run. But, alas, the quest continues.

However, today isn't about the game. For the first time in my match-going career I'm introducing a child to Anfield. Today I'm sort of a parent. This is new and terrifying territory.

Jessica is my girlfriend's 15-year-old niece. I've known her since she was three years old and used to eye me with a healthy distain from her aunt's lap. Despite that uneasy start we get on famously, mostly because we have a similar sense of humour, although hers has passed mine on its way to maturity in recent years.

I'm not really her uncle but she'll always be my niece. We're mates as much as anything. She makes me laugh a lot, she's clever and I'm ridiculously proud of her. She might read this one day so I'll stop embarrassing her now (do your homework).

She has little interest in football but is inquisitive enough to wonder what all the fuss is about. She nominally supports Chelsea but I'm hoping the bright lights of the Sandon wall, the LFC fan park (for the uninitiated, it's a car park with a bouncy castle) and the glamour of The Flattie might bring her to a better world.

It's an early start. She wants to see the city and, an overnight stay being impossible, I beep the horn outside her house at 8am. By 8.10am she emerges and we begin the trek. This should give us a couple of hours playing tourists before the game.

Although the traffic is relatively light, the journey can't be easy for her. As I say, her interest in the game is fleeting at best yet here she is, trapped in a car for four hours with a man who spends a quarter of that time talking about his love for Jordan Henderson. It's a good job she's been brought up well. She smiles politely and goes back to reading the airbag instructions on the dashboard. She will later exact her revenge by mishandling the car radio and inflicting all sorts of aural rubbish on to the M6.

We arrive early, though not as early as I'd like. My plan was to drive to the Albert Dock, walk to the Pier Head, stare at the Royal Liver Building for ten minutes while mouthing mutely and then take the ferry. Sadly, the thing I didn't bargain on was the teenage relationship with the weather. They don't like the cold. It's not for them. It rained on the way up and although Liverpool shines with a weak sun, it isn't enough to drag her from the car. October plus proximity to the river means I can't persuade her and we have to make do with driving around instead.

We cruise past the cathedrals, Chinatown, Lime Street and the classical quarter before heading south down Dale Street and straight on to the Liver birds. I wax lyrical for several minutes about the various legends; how one is male and the other female and how they face different directions so they cannot mate and fly away, leaving the city in rubble.

Nothing.

'Well?' I ask, as we sit under them.

'It's all right.'

'All right? It's the greatest building in the world!'

'OK.'

A minute later she's cooing over the Atlantic Tower Hotel – a building built in the style of a ship.

'That's amazing!'

I swear I will never understand children.

We head up to the ground, pleasingly passing the road where I spent my first non-maternity hospital years – Blackstock Street, L3. If she's fascinated she makes a good job of hiding it. We turn left on to Scotland Road and head up through Kirkdale. Finally there is an excited shout from the direction of the passenger seat. She's seen an Iceland on Breck Road.

They really are a mystery.

We park up and walk through the Anfield streets. I tell her that we have to meet a few of my mates first as I have to collect my tickets. I know she probably won't be doing anything like talking to them – she is quite shy after all – but they put her at ease all the same. I mean, she doesn't join in with our theory that Simon Mignolet is merely a petrified Shay Given but she doesn't sigh and tap her watch either. However, all this is an hour away and I've got to figure out how I can keep a child who is seemingly only interested in frozen goods shops entertained until kick-off. There is nothing to do near the ground if you can't go into a pub. It's also cold. Well, teenage cold.

I take her to the fan park. Not for the chance to see Mighty Red but for the toilets. Then we head to our meeting place on the wall opposite the Sandon. Yes, a wall. See, we used to meet in the pub but once the upstairs was closed in order to house corporates and their need to meet ex-players, we voted with our feet. Now we stand next to the garage wall opposite, regardless of the weather. Bearing in mind that I was still wearing a coat at the last game of the season back in May this can be a trial. Teenagers would stand no chance.

We pick up our tickets and it turns out that we're in Block 306 in the Kop and not 104, as I'd supposed. This is the singing section where standing throughout the game isn't deemed to be the heinous crime it is in other parts of the ground. I tell Jess that although West Brom at home will never make the ground shake, Block 306 might generate a bit more atmosphere.

In we go.

Now here's an odd thing. When you go into a ground you have to put your ticket into an electronic reader first. You'd think that would be the end of it. However, for this game we are met at the top of the stairs from the concourse and asked to both re-exhibit our ticket along with the stub showing our seat numbers. I suppose that could be to prevent any Kopite consumed by wanderlust to head up to the back for a better view and a bit of a singsong, but if you entered from the 306 concourse there is no other way you could have got into the ground without coming through the 306 turnstile. All very odd and it rankles me, particularly after a steward asks me (jokingly) why I am wearing a Road End T-shirt on the Kop. Fashion tips from a man wearing a luminous orange bubble coat.

This seems unusually heavy-handed. I usually like the stewards at Anfield, apart from when they're telling me to sit down. Going back to the civil war of the Tom Hicks and George Gillett era, I heard a few of them join in the protest songs about our malevolent overlords.

We're finally in our seats. My mate Stringer (he doesn't sell drugs on the mean streets of West Baltimore, it's his surname) is next to us, so we indulge in a brief tactical discussion while Jess looks around the old place. Like any good tour guide I show her who goes where and how that man down there really is Steven Gerrard – one of the three Liverpool players of whom she's heard. The others, Daniel Sturridge and Mario Balotelli, do not start. Sadly, there is also no starting place for young Danny Welbeck. She thought we'd signed him in the summer. I ask her not to repeat this accusation in mixed circles.

The players take five or so minutes to practise hitting the target from 18 yards. They miss every one. Every. Single. One. I offer her a weak smile and decide not to mention that the last two games I've seen have both ended 0-0.

So to the game.

I can finally see why we've bought Adam Lallana. I didn't think he had that much fight in him. Sort of Niko Kranjcar without the steel. His goal is beautiful. Henderson scores, too, and is impeccable in midfield, and even Gerrard is pushed up to have a go at a fairly average Albion side.

We celebrate the goals and she smiles throughout. I ask later what was her favourite part of the game.

'The man behind us.'

Ah, yes. Him.

There was nothing wrong with this man. He was vocal and I agreed with everything he said, even turning around to add further evidence to whatever his point was at the time. But he had an accent. Quite an accent.

I should explain that my own Scouse accent has been worn down from the harshest of guttural snorts to a softer, mumbling, more generic northern accent. Oh it's still there and clearly recognisable to the trained ear, but it's eroded to the point where I can now be understood by non-natives.

Jess isn't used to a full-out roaring Scouse accent and it amused her no end. She asked if he's angry. No, that's just how we talk. She then asked me why I don't talk like this. I could say it's because I left the city in 1988 to go to poly but a) I'd have to explain what a poly was and b) I was sulking. No one likes to be told that they're somehow different from the city's sons.

On the way home we listen to *606* before the inevitable request for teenage music pipes up. One of the debates concerns swearing at the game and whether it has become too much of a problem these days. I look to my left. 'No, it's football. People swear at football.' I then leap in with a follow-up, 'Would you have felt more engaged had there been a man dressed up as a six-foot dinosaur on the pitch before the game?' It's a tense moment. She's a bit old for Mighty Red but she might think it's cute or something.

'Why would I want that?!'

Have that, Mr Ayre!

I realise that in this car, unlike my old one, I am unable to control the volume of the radio from the steering wheel. That used to work so well. I used to tell her that the car itself was refusing to air Capital FM – that it much preferred *The Ramones Anthology* to Usher and Sean Paul, but she's on to that ruse.

The journey home feels longer. There are no stops so I can make it back for *Match of the Day*, which I'll gladly watch for once.

Some 14 hours after I'd picked her up Jess is back home.

'Did you enjoy it?'

'I really did.'

This is going to cost me.

19 October 2014, QPR 2 Liverpool 3

There are many categories of victory. Broadly speaking there's the hammering, the convincing, the tight, the lucky, the dour and the anti-climactic. This match provided us with a different incarnation – the furious.

It's not every club that can have you shout abuse at your team following an injury-time winner but today saw just that. I'm livid. Raging. Incandescent. Yes, I know it's three points and we showed character to grab victory from the jaws of an embarrassing draw, but I've also just seen Liverpool's back four be ravaged by Bobby Zamora, a heavily-injured man in his 30s, I've seen Mario Balotelli sky one from four yards and I've seen Jose Enrique break every rule in the full-back's handbook. Worst of all, I've seen our manager bested by Harry Redknapp; 21st-century philosophy undone by 1970s pragmatism.

I'm glad of the points but Brendan Rodgers got away with it, thanks to two own goals and a lot of luck. Now he can speak of a great team spirit when he should be explaining that first half performance.

Gerard Houllier once said, 'You take the performance, I'll take the result.' I understand that logic, even agree with it to some extent, but he was talking about strong Premier League and European sides rather than a side staring at relegation. QPR should have been quaking in their boots. Sure, they'd dominate the first 20 minutes, but then Liverpool should take over, yeah?

Nope. Nothing.

Dejan Lovren being turned constantly, the midfield lads offering the same open-door policy that was a feature of those early Rodgers games and a forward who plays like he's doing us a favour. A pitiful, meek and puny display but one with which we got away. Real Madrid may not be so accommodating.

KC

22 October 2014, Liverpool 0 Real Madrid 3

'Where was I in Istanbul? In bed at home'

By Jim Boardman

For any Liverpool fan growing up in the 1970s and 80s the European Cup was our cup. Rome, Wembley, Paris and then back to Rome. Four times in seven years.

Paris, in the Parc des Princes, was where Bob Paisley picked up his and Liverpool's third European Cup, a feat no other manager had achieved until 2014, and a feat he remains the only manager to have pulled off with one club. Paris was where Liverpool met Real Madrid for the first time in their history. Paris was a 1-0 win that brought to an end three years without 'Old Big Ears'. The two sides wouldn't meet again for 28 years.

The man who now shares that record of three European Cup wins as manager with Bob Paisley is Carlo Ancelotti. He won his first two with AC Milan, the second one after beating Liverpool in the final in Athens in 2007. He was the losing manager in the final two years earlier, also against Liverpool. He got his hat-trick in 2014, as manager of a Real side who began their defence of that tenth title as top seeds in a group including Liverpool. Football loves its coincidences.

European champions or not, Liverpool fans aren't scared of Real. They'd never beaten us. They'd never even scored against us. They had to play us at Anfield first. Did you see what we did last season, Carlo Ancelotti? Do you know how good we can be on our day, Gareth Bale? We're back in the big time and we're going to make you sweat, Cristiano Ronaldo.

Well, that was the plan anyway.

My own football memories start in 1977, the year Liverpool won their first European Cup in Rome. I do remember stuff before that, but it's all very disjointed. I remember being told about Bill Shankly retiring a few years earlier and not really understanding why it mattered. He didn't even play. I also remember Kevin Keegan being my favourite player and wondering who this Kenny Dalglish fella was and why we'd swapped our 'iconic number seven' for him.

I remember being gutted about us losing at Wembley to the Mancs. I remember being annoyed that they got to wear their home kit and we had to change. I remember people going on about how much bigger the prize a few days later would be and struggling to understand why. Of course we won that bigger prize and pretty soon I understood why.

I was annoyed with Bertie Vogts for stopping Keegan scoring a goal himself – our full-back took the penalties back then – but winning that great big massive trophy is probably the anchor that meant all the other memories have stayed so clear to this day. Not disjointed, not vague.

It was the first of many. We won it the next year, thanks to a winner from that Dalglish fella. Other clubs got in the way a bit – Villa and Forest, namely – but by 1984 we'd won it four times, and by then all that silverware (we won the league a lot, too) felt totally commonplace.

Of course the awful events in our last European Cup Final under its old name, at Heysel in 1985, meant we wouldn't be allowed near the competition for a while. By the time we were allowed near it again we couldn't get near it – we'd lost what we'd once had as a force in English football, let alone in Europe.

The last time Liverpool were league champions, in 1990, you had to be champions to get a shot at the European Cup. Champions of your own country or champions of Europe. The next time Liverpool got to play in it they weren't champions of anything. For some reason, someone somewhere decided to rename it the Champions League while removing the requirement to actually be champions. The things we get used to.

The only time Liverpool had been champions of anything in almost a quarter of a century was in 2005, when they became champions of Europe for a fifth time. But even that is starting to feel distant now, and that's because it is – ten whole years since Rafa Benitez masterminded that journey via Olympiakos and others to Milan in Istanbul.

That night against Olympiakos was probably when the belief really kicked in. We hadn't gone into that season thinking we would win the thing, we went into it delighted we were back on that stage. It would have been disappointing to be out before Christmas, but needing a two-goal win to progress, then being one down at half-time, it looked like the task was a too great for us. We needed to score three to go through. Never mind, there's always next season.

Except there was also that season. We came back out, fans hoping we could at least still win on the night even if we didn't go through, and went and scored the three that we needed. It is up there among Liverpool's best ever comebacks, but then came the comeback to end all comebacks six months later in Turkey.

'Where were you in Istanbul?' we like to sing to Michael Owen, who was probably with his horses. Where was I in Istanbul? In bed at home, unfortunately.

I was pretty ill at the time, undergoing all kinds of unpleasant tests and getting nowhere with any of them. Time and time again I was given the news that I'd not got that particular thing, which was good, because I wouldn't want to have that particular thing. But that was also bad because it meant they still hadn't worked out what was wrong with me and so couldn't give me medication or surgery to fix it.

Some days I'd sleep almost around the clock, 14 or 15 hours a day. I'd be in bed before 7pm some nights, sleeping through until 7am the next morning, up for a couple of hours before sleeping half the day.

Sleepiness was only part of the problem; there was also the tiredness. But tiredness doesn't really do it justice. I was too tired to hold a phone to my ear or to cut my food up to eat, while shaving became a battle of will.

Tired also means pain, and I had a lot of that. The kind of aches and pains you get with flu, bad flu, were there pretty much all of the time. Some nights the sleepy side of the tiredness battled the pain side of the tiredness leaving me in and out of sleep and waking the next morning feeling more tired than when I went to bed. My legs felt heavy. My arms felt heavy. Over time they actually did become heavy because the weight piled on.

Even before the weight gain the pain was soul-destroying, there was just no escape from it. It felt like I'd fallen down the stairs. I needed a wheelchair to go out, so I didn't really go out much.

Football kept me going. I started to get ill when Gerard Houllier was still the manager, my tiring state matching the club's. When Benitez arrived the club slowly got better, but I was slowly getting worse. By the end of that first season under Rafa I was struggling badly. I stayed up beyond my bedtime for the final, thinking back to all those nights when I'd stayed up beyond my bedtime for European Cup finals as a kid.

I went up to bed at half-time devastated. We'd lost, surely. We'd got carried away about how good we were but 3-0 down said we weren't as good as we thought. I stuck the telly on in the bedroom and hoped we could at least pull one back and end the night with a bit of pride. I hoped I'd be able to stay awake long enough to see it.

We did more than salvage pride, of course. We made history. We brought that European Cup home for keeps. I was too ill to go and see the trophy being paraded through the streets on the open-top bus, but I didn't let it get me down. I might be missing the party but I was glad we were finally able to have one. I also thought I'd be better in time for the next one.

I wasn't better in time for the FA Cup win the year after. I wasn't better in time for the Athens Champions League Final the year after that. I wasn't better in 2009, what turned out to be our last year in the Champions League for a while.

I was starting to see some improvements – I wasn't sleeping quite as much and I didn't need the wheelchair. I was far from back to normal, I'd just learned how to pace myself better or accept that I couldn't do certain things.

I still couldn't go to the match – the walk from the car to the ground would have finished me off before the game even started. What I could do was wait to get better. Fight to get better. Over time I had tests, treatment, surgery and all kinds of medication.

Liverpool had also been fighting. Fighting to get better. Then they took the wrong medicine, something called Hicks and Gillett, and by 2009 the medicine had started to have serious side effects. Little did we know that 2009 would be when it all started to go wrong again.

It didn't feel like it was going wrong in 2009. We beat Real 1-0 at their place and embarrassed them at ours, winning 4-0. We didn't quite feel invincible but we felt like we were a match for anyone.

Sadly that Hicks and Gillett stuff was about to kick in and make things worse, making 2009 the end of the Champions League era for Liverpool for a while and putting my hopes of going to any Champions League parties on hold for a while.

We didn't expect it to take five years. We didn't expect Benitez to be out of a job a year after beating Real 5-0 on aggregate and a year after finishing second in the league. Rafa had fought on and off the pitch and it turned out Hicks and Gillett weren't the only people meant to be on his side who were stabbing him in the back. The poison those people spread through the club is still there in little pockets, the damage never fixed, the will to truly fix it not there.

Time moves on. As I started to get better – without ever getting fully fixed – I saw my club go through more ups and downs. Never quite the ups of 2005, never quite the downs of 2010, but both good and bad.

By the time Dalglish returned as manager I was fit enough to go to the game if I pushed myself, paying for it over the days that followed. I managed to go to Wembley, twice, for finals that some people thought were beneath us, or not good enough for us.

In some ways they had a point. If we could pick one trophy to win in a season we'd not put the League Cup or FA Cup down as first choice. But you can only look down on those trophies if you've got something better to look down from. Liverpool have only won one trophy since 2006, and that was the League Cup.

Going into 2014/15, ten years on from the Istanbul season, Liverpool were in the Champions League. Liverpool had just finished second in the league. The good old days were finally back. Coincidentally, my own health has taken a massive step for the better. I have to manage it carefully, have regular injections, take loads of medication and have blood tests every month or so to keep an eye on it all. But it is all extremely manageable.

I also had a new job, and that new job means, like five years earlier, I couldn't go to see Liverpool play Real at Anfield. Part of me was disappointed to miss another opportunity to see my team play *Los Blancos*, but most of me was delighted that the reason I was missing out was such an improvement on last time. Then I was too ill with no sign of ever getting better. Now I was working late because I had to make a video call to someone in Spain. I didn't ask him about the match.

I was just pulling in at home as 'You'll Never Walk Alone' was being sung. I was in the house by the time it kicked off.

So, could we turn them over like before? For a spell it looked possible. Liverpool were in control if lacking an end product, but if we could keep this up and score a goal we could really unnerve them. But the spell didn't last long and after 23 minutes Real had scored first, through Ronaldo. Their first at Anfield. Their first ever against Liverpool. It wouldn't be their last.

Seven minutes later Karim Benzema made it 2-0. Four minutes before half-time he made it 3-0.

Before the game Brendan Rodgers had denied Liverpool were underdogs. To be 3-0 down at half-time suggests he was being a little bit over-confident. Some might say arrogant. Not so much the case in the second half when he seemed to decide damage limitation was the way forward. Mario Balotelli was substituted, replaced by Adam Lallana to leave Liverpool without a recognised striker on the pitch. It was soon obvious why.

Rodgers wasn't thinking about famous nights, like those in the 2004/05 season when in two separate Champions League games Liverpool needed three second-half goals to keep their dreams alive. Goal and dreams that they got. Instead it was all about keeping the score down for this manager. He seemed happy afterwards to have drawn the second half 0-0.

If he'd had a striker on the pitch maybe Liverpool would have scored. Instead the striker Rodgers had bought to replace Luis Suarez was getting changed. He'd already taken his shirt off as he went down the tunnel – and before long Rodgers had turned a 3-0 humiliation at home into a story about Balotelli swapping shirts.

'It's not something I stand for,' Rodgers said about the shirt, not about the three goals without reply. 'If you want to do that, do it at the end of the game. It is something I will deal with on Thursday. It's something that doesn't happen here and shouldn't happen here.' As some were taken in by what had gone on, others were more concerned about the score.

Much has been made about the loss of Suarez over the summer and the difference it has made to Liverpool's chances. What jumped out at me after this defeat was that it wasn't just his skill we were missing but also his determination. Can you imagine Suarez being a willing participant in tactics designed to keep the scoreline down to 'just' 3-0? Can you imagine him settling for any kind of defeat? Can you imagine the Steven Gerrard of old being a willing participant in that kind of approach? Has he changed or has his manager changed him?

In truth Liverpool won't be able to carry on like this much longer without the whole season being a write-off. They've won the last couple of games in the league – just about – but last time out it was relegation candidates QPR and it was a nearly thrown away 3-2 win. Not only will they write off this season if they continue in this manner but they'll write next season off too.

So Liverpool is a club that seems to be unwell, with those in a position to cure it distracted by tittle-tattle, or perhaps too arrogant to accept there is an illness that is slowly taking hold. What is it that they say? As some things change, some things also stay the same. Welcome back Real Madrid, welcome back the bad old days.

25 October 2014, Liverpool 0 Hull 0

'I've seen behind the curtain'

By James McKenna

Well this is rare, isn't it? In the grand scheme of things, and there are many, many 'things' at the minute when you mention Liverpool FC, it isn't much at all. Nonetheless, it is rare. Liverpool FC, at home, on a Saturday afternoon at the traditional kick-off time of 3pm. Not moved to cater for the television schedules. Not moved because of European excursions and exertions. Not shifted for no other reason than to just keep us on our toes. Nope, one of the things people long for from the distant past is here for us to enjoy. It will be one of only a few 3pm kick-off times we have, so let's savour it. Enjoy one of the little things, as so much of what we once had, or perceived we had, has now gone.

Going the match, it's mad how you remember the little things. I've forgotten loads of things and I would struggle with match-related observations and memories if asked to recall them. But I can remember some random things when I think back to going to various matches. Take Istanbul – I remember conversations word for word, buying programmes, the view from my seat, the need to fix my shoelaces when the score was 3-2 but being too scared to move, weird thoughts like that if I crossed my arms or didn't realign my watch and justice band that all hopes would come crashing down. But I'd really have to put my mind to it to remember any of the match events.

Or take one of the Celtic games at Anfield – I remember very little from the match apart from John Hartson dashing our dreams at what seemed like the very end of the game. But I can remember the queue for tickets at Anfield, asking my mum if I could go to school late while I got them and promising I would be in school by 9.30am. By 9.35am

I was still somewhere by Skerries Road. I remember the Celtic fan, in a kilt, by the Dixie Dean statue offering me and my mate £500 for our tickets.

Or my very first game, which I had to watch back when I was older as I had the order of goalscorers wrong. Yet I can remember so much of that day like it was yesterday.

It is 3 April 1996. Sometime during the breakfast show, Radio City has a competition to win a pair of tickets for the Liverpool v Newcastle match taking place that evening. There are two questions. I can't remember them. I didn't even answer them, my dad did. But he puts me on the phone. Caller 96 we are, so I (we) just have to get the answers right. My dad in the background, I repeat them correctly – Kenneth Wolsthenholme and Kevin Keegan. Now I'm excited and I've got school.

Get home from school and my mum has bought me a Fowler T-shirt. We get the 68 to the ground. I will never forget the view from the bottom of Stanley Park, looking up and seeing Anfield all lit up. We are in the posh seats, Upper Centenary. Padded seats. Seven goals later I'm screaming at my dad, a petrified nine-year-old as he lifts me up while celebrating Stan Collymore's winner, and all I can see is the drop to the Lower Centenary. There's the Newcastle fans on the 68 bus who were staying at a house in Bootle and wanted to drink somewhere. We sent them to the Mons.

The little things. What a game, though. No wonder I had to watch it again and remember the order of the goals.

I could fill this chapter with the little things. Once you are hooked – and let's face it, we are all hooked in this quasi-religious, cult-like following of football – it consumes us, dictates to us and becomes us in a lot of cases. The little stories, the little intricacies and the routines that we share or have. I am the first to admit I am hooked. It's taken huge parts of my time following and supporting Liverpool FC. I don't say that as a badge of honour. Nor do I think it is all one way – not many people have experienced or seen what we have as match-goers and supporters. This certainly gives back to us. Now try and explain this to someone who doesn't get 'it' and the things we like are probably the things they don't. Yet if you are reading this, you're probably a bit like me. It matters.

Once you start growing up and going the match more regularly, it really matters. The results. The crying if we lost, like in the 1996 FA Cup Final. The disappointment, the anger, the frustration versus the happiness, elation and outright delirium. Debates on Monday in school that grew in to debates at work on a Monday through to Friday. Which players to sign, which ones to sell.

I remember a long debate on 5 July 2005 as we accounted for the Steven Gerrard money and signed various players to make a team. I remember the relief and happiness when on 6 July we never had the Gerrard money.

Today, though, it's a bit different. There is still joy and happiness, and anger and sadness, and the emotions in between. But it's different. For some it's the change in our support. For others it's being priced out. For a few, it's just that it became time to give up, or it wasn't like it was in their day. For myself, the winds of change began on 6 February 2007. I just didn't realise it at the time.

When Tom Hicks and George Gillett took charge at Anfield, we were just the latest in a soon to be long line of English clubs owned by foreign 'investors'. It had happened at Chelsea to great fanfare and up the road at Manchester United to less fanfare and more fan frustration. Let's be honest, we all by and large welcomed it. We all wanted our share of the pie, an owner to kick us on and build on Istanbul. We had the promises to back the manager and put a spade in the ground for a new stadium, and to not burden the club with debt. It was great when just a few months later we swaggered our way through to our second European Cup Final in three years. Athens 2007.

Hindsight is a wonderful thing. I can look back on it now and see where it stopped being the same and where the winds of change began to blow a little stronger. There was the Athens ticket fiasco, when a woefully small allocation of tickets was made smaller by the disappearance of thousands of tickets to corporates, sponsors and hangers-on, and then the sudden reappearance of thousands of tickets just a few days before the final. For the first time we protested against club owners. What we imagined would be a one-off was to become a regular occurrence in the years that followed.

Now some of you might be wondering what all this has to do with a football match against a team called Hull City (not Tigers, definitely not Tigers, like their owner wanted to ludicrously call them despite the objection of thousands of supporters #AMF). Well for me, Saturday and a 3pm kick-off isn't the only thing happening. In the morning, it's the Spirit Of Shankly Annual General Meeting. A Liverpool supporters' union, nearly six years old, meeting to discuss all things supporters and the politics of football. The main topic of debate, aside from the voting in of our new committee and motions about Qatar and the 2022 World Cup, is ticket pricing. It's the big issue amongst supporters at Liverpool and across the UK.

For a couple of seasons, the Spion Kop 1906 group, who are responsible for the majority of flags and banners you see at Anfield pre-match, have worked with Spirit Of Shankly to highlight the growing expense of match tickets. It's reached a head at Anfield as ticket prices in parts of the ground have breached the £50 barrier. They announce that before the match, there will be none of the usual red flags supporting the team. Instead it is to be all black with ticket-price protest banners out in force.

Another thing we hear about is an initiative that Spirit Of Shankly have been involved in with the German Reds Supporters' Club. One of their members, Andreas Moller (or Paul as he calls himself), has for the last three seasons contacted us with match tickets that their members have bought at full adult price and subsequently donated to SOS to pass on to youngsters to experience Anfield, or parents to take their children. German Reds, recognising there is a problem and going out of their way to try and fix it.

As grateful as I am to help youngsters out and see the smile on their faces as they get the opportunity to see their heroes play, it's wrong. It's a perfect example of how football has changed and not for the better. That it requires an act of charity to give youngsters the opportunities that were freely available to many supporters in the past leaves you wondering about the disconnect that exists between the ageing generation of support inside Anfield and the youngsters locked out, looking enviably upon Anfield and the match-goers up and down Walton Breck Road. Is this really what we want?

I could talk about football politics for ages. I could probably write a book. Writing the Spirit Of Shankly story would be more like writing books of the Bible; very long and someone would always contest the accuracy. But no, now it's time for a bit of football, because on this day, once motions have been voted on, tickets for kids handed out and banners unfurled, it's all about the 90 minutes of football. Well, sort of.

We aren't very good at the minute. For things that have changed off the pitch see things that have changed on the pitch, too. From a title that slipped out of our fingers to all looking a bit lost. From beating Queens Park Rangers last weekend with energy to a 0-0 against Hull that only at times looked like bursting into anything. It was more like letting down a balloon. Slowly.

Our impression of looking lacklustre looks in danger of actually being lacklustre. I could try and be a pundit here and say Liverpool need to change this or that, that tweaking this little thing improves the overall. But I really don't know what the solution is short of building Luis Suarez II, or new muscles for Daniel Sturridge's legs, or new legs for Steven Gerrard, or a bit of courage for Simon Mignolet, or an actual defence.

Knowing I have to write about this match, I leave the Kop thinking, 'How do I put that into words?' Anyone who knows me, and even some of those who don't, know I am not short of an opinion or ten. But even I struggle, thinking there's not much I can say about that, even if I tried to describe the blow by (lack of) blow account. Instead I wander away from the ground, rushing between people to get back to the car. I people-watch as I do, hearing their opinions about the game, the players, the manager, the football in general, and I find myself wondering if they think like I do. Thinking that football has changed. Not just because of what takes place on the pitch but because of what takes place off it. Sometimes overshadowing, sometimes not, but just there, in the immediate vicinity.

This goes full circle to the post-Hicks and Gillett days. I remember the little things. I remember the excitement of talking about signing players. Of the talk in school and in work about the new season, fixture list release day, the dawn of a new season. Now we have news about club accounts, profit and loss, financing of clubs. The directors are no longer there to just sign the cheques, it appears.

When did all this change? In truth, it was gradual. Supporters got more switched on as owners like the Glazers and our own two decided they would be bold and mortgage football clubs up. No longer did I and others need to know formations and tactics but we did need to know about leveraged buyouts, high-level financing, contract amortisation and the politics that float around it. How under Hicks and Gillett, and even today, I just want to talk football. But it won't ever be the same again.

I've seen behind the curtain at the magic show and realised that it isn't quite magic after all.

And that sort of sums up where football is for me. I love Liverpool, being a Red and going the match. It's part of who I am. It's been great to me, but it isn't the same. The path it has taken for me isn't what my dad envisaged, or could have imagined, when he draped a Liverpool scarf around the neck of my few-hours-old body. It's that we love it so much, that it is a part of us so much, that the things that happen matter so much. And for me, what happened under Hicks and Gillett matters. It's altered football, Liverpool FC and our attitudes and behaviours as supporters.

Yet for all the downsides of the change in football there are positives we take from it. We now, as supporters, have a voice which when used collectively is important. I'm passionate about the idea that supporters are the most important 'stakeholders' in the game and it's why I spent the evening of my dad's 50th at the first Spirit Of Shankly meeting and spent the morning of my 21st birthday speaking at the second. For me, the match is no longer just diamond formations, players and trophies. It's become more – stadiums, ticketing, how supporters are treated and much more.

How does it make me feel? Well I just take it as it being one of those things. But I'll turn up at Anfield for the next match, and hope things have changed and we win.

And off the pitch, things need to change. We need to make football more affordable. More accessible. Pass on the traditions and our heritage, ensure there is a legacy. We need to ensure that what makes us famous as supporters carries on into the future for the next ten, 20, 100 years. And we need to make sure that people keep doing the things they love and enjoy. Whether that is going the match and moaning about a formation or moaning that the directors haven't got a clue. If we don't, football is in danger of just becoming a thing that some people do instead of it being our thing.

25 October 2014, Real Madrid 3 Barcelona 1

'Meatballs, chorizo, squid and potatoes'

By Sachin Nakrani

Exactly 12 months ago I met John Barnes for the first time. It was over breakfast at the Grosvenor Hotel in Park Lane and basically I was there to stare at him for as long as possible. I told John I wanted to speak to him about Liverpool's upcoming league match against Arsenal, a clash between two of the division's most in-form and eye-catching teams, but really he could have said anything or nothing and I would have been content.

Barnes is my childhood hero, you see. Like many Reds of my age I idolised him growing up, those swaggering hips, those dancing feet, that sense that here was a footballing genius who was too cool for school. Christ, Barnes was amazing, the closest thing this country has had to footballing perfection in my eyes. Pure poetry in motion.

The strange thing about my love of Barnes is that I never saw him at his very best – the 1987/88 season, his first at the club having arrived from Watford for £900,000. I was seven years old when he inspired Liverpool to a 17th league title and was rightly named double player of the year. It would be another 12 months until my interest in football really began, but I saw enough of 'Digger' growing up to know he was something else, doing that incredible thing of adapting his game so he could be both sublime winger and crucial holding midfielder for Liverpool up until his departure to Newcastle in 1997. He was my hero sure enough, and that hour or so I had with him on a wet October morning last year will live permanently in the memory.

Which brings me on to Luis Suarez. He wasn't born in Jamaica but he did make the crowd go bananas during his three-and-a-half-year stay at Liverpool, and there's no doubt that if I'd been born 20 years later it would have been his face that was instead plastered across my bedroom walls. With his beguiling brilliance and inspiring qualities Suarez is a modern-day Barnes, with the key difference being that the latter never broke Anfield's collective heart.

I'm not over Suarez's departure. It's been three months since he moved to Barcelona and I can't truly let go. I never loved him like I loved Barnes, how could I given I was a full-blown adult when he arrived from Ajax and way past that point in life when you form fresh idols (and wear colours to the match)? But no player post-Digger has thrilled my Kopite heart as much as Suarez, particularly last season when his goals, assists, menace and lung-busting desire to win led us agonisingly close to a first league title in 24 years.

And now he's gone. Some supporters have moved on, outwardly at least, but many like myself haven't, with the pain of loss acutely felt the longer Liverpool struggle during this campaign. Suarez couldn't have done anything about the defeats to Aston Villa, West Ham, Basel and Real Madrid, as well as the draw with Everton, even if he had remained at the club as he would have been suspended. But us fans could have at least come away from those results with a firm sense that things would improve once our genius of a number seven was able to play again.

Which would have been this weekend, against Hull at Anfield. Imagine the excitement around the place had the game been Luis's return – the smiles would have been that much wider, the roars that much throatier and the songs that much more Depeche Mode. But as Jay McKenna wrote, the afternoon was instead characterised by (fully justified) protests against ticket prices and a stale goalless draw. How bloody apt Liverpool should fail to score on the same day Suarez could have been back.

I didn't go to the match. I was planning to, and had not it been for this book I would have. But as part of the process of putting together a diary chronicling the 2014/15 season it was decided early on by Karl and myself (well, just me really) that there had to be a chapter dedicated solely to Suarez given his contribution to the last campaign and the gaping hole his exit has left in the side. The man is irreplaceable, irrepressible, and even though he's gone he cannot be forgotten.

Which is why instead of being at Anfield I spent this Saturday afternoon riding two buses through south London (the 136 and the 185 in case you're interested) before hopping off in Dulwich and heading to Barcelona Tapas, a restaurant/bar located on the corner of Lordship Lane and Melford Road, right next door to a florists.

Shanil came too and while keeping an eye on the score (or lack of it) from Anfield, we took up chairs by a table between a window and the bar, above which was a flat-screen TV that, as the owner had promised me during a phone conversation at the start of the week, was showing live coverage of El Clasico.

Yes, Suarez's return, his first competitive game for Barcelona, was against Real Madrid at the Bernabeu. Bet he was gutted to be missing Hull.

I'm a big fan of this fixture but no so much that I would miss watching Liverpool play and venture through shitty Catford to watch it. But, as said, this time it was different, *he* was involved. From the start, too, which came as a surprise as the talk had been that Luis Enrique, the Barcelona manager and one-time Championship Manager versatility king, would start Suarez on the bench given how long he'd been out having sunk his teeth into Giorgio Chiellini during the World Cup.

It's possible Shanil and I knew before you did that Suarez was starting given we were watching the game on Spanish TV, or Canal Liga to be precise. For we could see the build-up as well as the opening 15 minutes, none of which were available to those tuning in to Sky Sports due to British broadcasting rules that stipulate no live football can be shown in this country between 2.45pm and 5.15pm. This was seriously exciting, like being able to peek backstage prior to a Prodigy gig and see Keith Flint setting fire to a miniature doll of himself while banging his head against an oversized cheese grater. Not for the rest of you, this.

And what a 15-and-a-bit minutes they were. Let me run you though the highlights:

Suarez warming up – first shot is of him stretching alongside Dani Alves in a circle of Barcelona players.

A female presenter appears in a smaller, split screen. She's talking to a fella I don't recognise. Suddenly another fella I don't recognise comes into shot. He's got ice-white hair and is holding a glass of beer. He looks very pissed and very happy.

The camera cuts to the commentary box. Michael Robinson! Look, it's Michael Robinson! There, sitting there, with headphones on. Michael bloody Robinson!

Match starts.

GOAL! Neymar's only gone and scored after four minutes. You'll never bloody guess who set him up.

Karim Benzema shoots just wide. He then heads the ball against the bar before crashing the rebound against the post.

Some start, shame you're missing it Britain.

I looked around. Nice place this, what with the bundles of natural light pouring through the windows, the giant stone lizard draped across two pillars by the door and the group of tanned folk sat by the table near the toilets, muttering in Spanish and drinking coffee from strikingly small cups.

I'd been to a Barcelona Tapas in Liverpool Street five years ago and the original plan was to go there for this match. But it doesn't open at weekends, which is a shame given my cousin Rajan and I had a great time there. We went to watch Barca take on Manchester United in the 2009 Champions League Final. Me a Red, he a Gooner, the hope was that us being together in a Barcelona-supporting establishment would in some intangible way inspire the Spanish club to victory. As it transpired, Pep Guardiola's boys didn't need our help – they were simply too good for United, winning 2-0 thanks to goals in each half from Samuel Eto'o and Lionel Messi.

So anyway, I was in Dulwich instead of Liverpool Street watching Suarez's debut for Barcelona and it had started well for our former superstar. Kick-off in the Clasico came just under half an hour after the final whistle had blown at Anfield, and with every move Luis made I couldn't help thinking how different things could've been in L4 had he been wearing Liverpool red instead of Catalan stripes. Somewhat freakishly, it was as my mind mulled over this thought that I got a text from Archie Rhind-Tutt, the producer of LBC's live Saturday afternoon show, *Scores*. Presented by Ian Payne, it's basically *Gillette Soccer Saturday* for radio. In fact, it is *Gillette Soccer Saturday* for radio given Ian and his studio guest spend the afternoon watching the show and commenting on the goals, which they cannot see, as they go in. I know this because I've been the studio guest a few times.

It's actually a really enjoyable gig and more professional than I make out given Ian is an excellent host and there are detailed bulletins from reporters at the main Premier League games of the day. Archie is also a very good producer and a fine bloke.

On this Saturday he wanted to know if I'd been at the Hull game and, if so, would discuss it with Ian live on air. I pointed out that I hadn't and was instead in a bar with my kid brother sipping pints of Estrella and watching Barcelona lead Real. He then asked if I knew anybody who had been there. I took a second to think of someone, a person who could speak eloquently about Liverpool's current struggles.

I texted Martin Fitzgerald.

'Hi mate, it's Sachin. Were you at the game today?'

'Hi mate, yes I was.'

'Fancy talking about it on LBC? Producer of their live scores show wants to get a fan's verdict.'

'Can do. Just give me a call.'

'Can I pass your number on to him? His name's Archie. Nice fella.'

'Sure thing mate.'

'Ta boss.'

'No probs, thanks for asking.'

'No probs. Were we shite?'

'Very stale 70 followed by a chaotic kitchen sink last 20.'

'Meanwhile Suarez has set up Neymar for the first goal in the Clasico.'

'Ha, course he did. That's all Twitter needs.'

Before long he had also put a chance on a plate for Messi. Some debut this, not only given the amount of time Suarez has been out for and the quality of the opposition, but also because he was starting in a wide-right position.

I watched on and noticed my mood change. From being begrudgingly happy for Suarez I suddenly felt a surge of bitterness course through my body. 'You should be doing this for us Luis. We've drawn 0-0 with Hull for fuck's sake, you should've been there, doing this for us!'

Imagine my delight, then, when Cristiano Ronaldo equalised with a penalty ten minutes before half-time.

I'm no fan of Real, far from it actually, and given the torment they put Liverpool through a few days earlier it wasn't easy cheering a goal by those smug bastards in white. But as I said, I was feeling bitter.

'Vamos Los Blancos!'

With the first half over, Shanil and I got stuck into the tapas – meatballs, chorizo, squid and potatoes, all washed down with another pint of Estrella. It was all pretty marvellous and became even more so when Pepe made it 2-1 to Real five minutes after the break. He scored with a bullet of a header, no doubt inspired by the shirt he'd got off Mario Balotelli on Wednesday night.

Just prior to that goal came a moment of classic Suarez; a wriggling turn under pressure and then a burst right through the heart of the opposition, with Luka Modric forced into making a desperate tackle in order to halt his momentum. Now if this was Liverpool, Suarez would have been over the subsequent free kick, stood with hands on hips, panting gently as he eyed the keeper and decided just how he was going to make a mug out of the bastard. But here he was nowhere to be seen, with Messi and Xavi around the ball instead.

'This is your lot now Luis, third fiddle at best. Third fucking fiddle!'

Suarez eventually went off on 69 minutes, by which stage Real had made it 3-1 thanks to a fine Benzema goal. Game over, job done.

'Take that Barcelona, you superstar-stealing bastards!'

Our bill came to £40.22 and my brother paid it, which on a rather tense afternoon was a much-welcomed highlight. Not only because it saved me a few quid but also because it was, as far as I could remember, the first time he'd done that. This baby boy of ours was now a man, with a full-time job and a debit card.

He even flirted with the waitress, at which point I was seriously close to welling up.

Back on the 185, my thoughts turned back to Luis and what I would say to him if we ever had breakfast together at a posh hotel in Park Lane. I'd ask him if he knew just how much we loved him, that his presence on the pitch, whether it was at Anfield or elsewhere, made the match the only place any of us wanted to be. We came to see Liverpool but we also came to see him. That hunger, that magic, it overwhelmed us, and just when we thought we had seen everything there came more.

That first game against United.

That goal at Sunderland.

That dive in front of Moyes.

That moment of perfection against Newcastle.

Norwich, over and over again.

Last season, every single fucking minute of it.

I'd tell him the love also meant pain because we stood by him when we shouldn't have. Racism, bite, dives, Arsenal, bite again; we forgave it all because we adored him like a battered wife adores her drunk, feckless husband.

'I can change him, I know I can,' we told our friends as they rolled their eyes and said he was no good, that we deserved better. And in the end they were able to say 'I told you so' because he left without saying goodbye. Not properly anyway.

We could have won the league if he stayed, I honestly believe that. But now, no chance, not when you're drawing at home to Hull and looking as likely to rip a side apart as Rolf Harris does of appearing in panto. It's over. The title dream is over.

I'd tell Luis all of that and more, much more. I'd tell him that I'm struggling to cope without him, that I fear I may never move on. That however hard I try, I just can't get enough.

28 October 2014, Liverpool 2 Swansea 1

Look, it's only the League Cup. No one cares about that. Oh, we won? Oh that's different. In that case it's a good opportunity to get to Wembley and get us on the trophy gravy train.

I like the League Cup and can remember the blue members of my household singing about how they were going to win it before Liverpool did back in 1977. We Reds scoffed. As it turned out they lost thanks to Terry Darracott jumping over a cross, and we were Brian Greenhoff's spawny deflection away from a treble of real cups.

Winning four in a row in the early 1980s meant something. Firstly, it was all done and dusted by March so we didn't have to worry about congestion at the business end of the season. It gave us a sense of achievement, too. Plus it was silverware which is, y'know, the point of it all.

Most clubs blow it off so there's a chance of us progressing, and it's never a bad thing to get your team used to Wembley and medals. I'd like us to get used to that.

It's also the last thing we won in 2012 and as I sat in the stadium that day, guts torn to pieces by recalcitrant food poisoning, I didn't give a damn about player tiredness or Mickey Mouse cups.

Liverpool exist to win trophies so well done to Dejan Lovren for putting us through. It's Bournemouth next so we should, should, at least have a semi-final to look forward to.

Even if it goes tits up, it's only the League Cup.

KC

1 November 2014, Newcastle 1 Liverpool 0

'A wave of the hand, a smile and an intense examination of his boots'

By Karl Coppack

Ah, my favourite away game. I love this game. Always have. I don't know if it's because of its badge of honour status given the distance travelled or the propensity for both defences to simply give up and just leave it to the other lads, but this has long been a favourite. I've seen us win and lose there. I've seen a man fall down the stairs and I've seen much of the surrounding counties as the elevated away end rivals Kilimanjaro in its miles above sea level.

And yet I'm not there.

I haven't been since 2009. I'm less fond of that. I've just been unlucky, being stymied by early or late kick-offs, work commitments or something equally mundane. Today is no different and it's digging into my ribs. It's work again.

Later tonight I'm attending a fireworks display as part of my normal job. I'm a guest, as is Denise Pearson – the chanteuse of 1980s band Five Star. I doubt Denise will be perturbed at missing out on the game. Maybe she went. I don't know.

Liverpool have a fine tradition with the North East. Bob Paisley has a memorial plaque dedicated to him at his birthplace of Hetton-le-Hole while Terry McDermott, Kevin Keegan, Peter Beardsley and Alan Kennedy all wore those stripes against us more than once. Sunderland also have links with the club as Jordan Henderson – the focus of many a love song within these four walls – was once a Black Cat. Best not to mention Bolo Zenden here.

There's another reason I love going to the North East too. I get to see Ray Kennedy.

Oh, that was subtle. That's just about the worst, most clanking name drop you can ever come across. I was softening the ground up with my Denise Pearson news earlier and, I've got to warn you, there's another sizeable one coming soon.

Let's do a bit of time-travelling. It is 1979. I am in my final year of junior school in Croxteth, Liverpool. I am, as Derek Trotter once observed, full of snot and Marmite. The only things that dominate my fledgling thoughts are guitars (my dad played so we had a few in the house), Madness (I also liked 'Reunited' by Peaches and Herb, but kept that quiet), chess (I was pretty good before puberty struck) and the man with a big number five on his back.

Liverpool were easy then. We always won. It was rare to come into school with a cob on after a Liverpool defeat as they just didn't happen. I remember sitting on the school wall the morning after we lost the 1978 League Cup Final with a lad called Michael Bligh. We'd never been so angry at a defeat. The ref was bent. I still believe that now. Michael roared at the sheer indignity of not winning a game.

But it was more than that. Liverpool FC were literally Liverpool. As a child of the city it meant something that many of the league and European champions were from the same area as us. Phil Thompson and the aforementioned Terry Mac hailed from Kirkby, a mere bus ride down the East Lancs Road from Gillmoss. Jimmy Case was from Allerton in the south end. You could watch them train over the wall at Melwood from the upstairs of the 12C bus if you had to go to Cantril Farm, where my nan lived. These were local lads who ran the best midfield in our history. Of course we had Graeme Souness too, who was just freakishly great and deliciously violent, but for me it was all about the man on the left.

We all loved Kenny – how could we not – but Ray Kennedy fascinated me. He was enormous and never backed down from any confrontation, but he also had a simple grace to his play. He would glide down the left flank and cut inside as his right foot matched his left. Capable of a delicate through ball or a thunderous shot, he had the lot, the absolute lot. But it wasn't this that led the fascination. It was his calmness.

Look at the goal celebrations from the 7-0 win over Tottenham. David Johnson does a little dance, Kenny goes absolutely berserk and Ray...well, Ray just smiles and claps before dropping his head in embarrassment. You want more but that's all you're getting – a wave of the hand, a smile and an intense examination of his boots.

Look at what he does when the ref gives the penalty in Rome, 1977. 2-1 up, a few minutes to go and we get a penalty. You'd go mad, wouldn't you? You'd leg it over to Kevin Keegan and shake him with joy. So, what does he do? He looks nonchalantly across to the referee and claps. 'You saw that, did you? Good.' No histrionics, no dramas, no screaming at the cameras. Good.

There's a word for that and although it's one I dislike, it sums him up – cool. Ray Kennedy was cool. Fonz cool. Leather jackets were the thing in my primary school before the Mod Revival kicked in, as *Grease* and *Happy Days* were still in the culture, and if there was such a thing as a footballing Fonz it was the man from Seaton Delaval. He wasn't a Scouser, but he was really. He even had the curly hair. He played for Liverpool, the best side in the world, and he still didn't react. *That* was cool.

Let's leave 1979 there and move on to 2006. By this time I'd dropped all interest in chess and early Madness albums but my love of guitars and Ray Kennedy hadn't waned. I was now living in London, working in media sales. I took to writing quarterly articles for the LFC fanzine *Through the Wind and Rain*, along with the odd letter. A few years earlier I'd written a double page spread on Patrik Berger (must be a left-sided midfielder thing) and it had gone well. However, in 2006 I had a problem. I didn't have the first idea what to write about. Everyone was talking about Istanbul and Rafa and Steven Gerrard and Carra and whatever, but I wanted something else. I know, I thought. I'll write about my favourite player.

It started well. I banged on about 1979 and his famous goal in Munich in 1981, but I needed more. Ray's story ended in 1991 when he left the Highbury pitch following his testimonial. Back then his fight against Parkinson's disease, diagnosed as far back as 1984, was mentioned in the press from time to time but once the floodlights went out he disappeared back to the North East. He was seldom heard of again, save for an interview with the *Daily Mirror* in 2001 when his old sides met in the FA Cup Final.

I'm a blogger more than an investigative journalist and the last thing I wanted to do was to impinge on his private life, but I wanted to know what happened next. I'd just re-read Dr Andrew Lee's biography *Ray of Hope* for about the tenth time and figured that if the good doctor was on Google I'd at least be able to speak to the man who speaks to the man. And yes, there he was – Professor of Neurology at the National Hospital for Neurology and Neurosurgery in London. There was even an e-mail address. What the hell? In for a penny.

A few hours later I received a reply. I can still remember it word for word:

'Dear Karl,
I can't say too much thanks to doctor–patient privilege but
suffice to say Ray is fighting his illness as he fought on the
Anfield pitch.
Regards,
A Lees
PS. I once wrote a piece on McManaman for TTWAR. Say
hello to Steve.'

Perfect. That could go into the last paragraph. Not exactly a scoop but
not bad for a 1,000-word love letter.

Hang on, another e-mail:

'Spoke to Ray. He's happy for you to call him if you want
to extend your article.'

What?!

I didn't ask for it but suddenly there was an opportunity to actually
speak to Ray Kennedy. From decades earlier a snotty little kid threw a
packet of Spangles at me and accused me of being a jammy sod. I was a
wreck for the rest of the day. I was about to ring Ray and speak to him.
This time I'd have to communicate in everyday language rather than
shouting at the telly on Saturday nights.

I borrowed a Dictaphone from a mate and called him the minute
I got in. It was the most surreal experience I've ever had. I said hello
to this shaky voice and somehow got through the interview, although,
thanks to his exhaustion, it took three goes across four days for me to
complete it. We got on well though and I asked if I could stay in touch.
The poor sod didn't know what he was letting himself in for.

I've met him a few times since then. The first was electrifying in
as much as it was Ray Kennedy – Ray Kennedy! – offering me and my
mates a cup of tea and chatting amiably about the traffic, but at the same
time it was a tough hour. He's still mentally sharp but Parkinson's disease
has taken its toll over the years. A mixture of the illness and medication
has left him with slurred speech. Add to that a very pronounced Geordie
accent…well, we needed his son, Dale, to help out.

In 2009, after a brief dalliance as a patient of Dr Lees myself, a few
of us organised for Ray and his son to watch the 4-4 draw with Arsenal
at Anfield. We arranged it with the club and just needed to get him
there. That was a hell of a day. His last trip was five years earlier when
he was forced to leave at half-time due to ill health. That, too, was
against Newcastle. We also arranged two mosaics at either end of the

ground – one enormous '5' to represent his Liverpool days and a '10' for the Arsenal end. The plan was a simple one. Have someone drive him to the ground, give him a seat in the directors' box, win the game/ title, let him meet some of his old mates and then drive him back to a hotel in Manchester. Nice and easy.

Except it wasn't. The day was fraught with worry. There was every chance that he could be tired out en route and we'd have to turn the car around. We looked at our phones every ten seconds or so. 'No news from the car' became the most quoted sentence of the day.

Second name drop. Sorry.

I'd met Jimmy Case a couple of times as a consequence of knowing Ray. We saw him park up in the Sandon car park so I went over and told him who the guest of honour was for the day. I also told him that Ray was worried that no one would remember him. Jimmy laughed and shook his head. 'He doesn't realise, does he?'

Phil Neal wandered over (look, I promise to stop doing this. Just allow me one more. Think of it as a competition. Try to work out who it will be before I get there. It will save you from murderous thoughts. I'll even give you a clue. He played for both clubs) and Jimmy told him about the visit. He gets a bad press does Phil, thanks largely to his autobiography and that Graham Taylor documentary, but I've never seen anyone happier than that in my life. He was ecstatic. He hadn't seen Ray for years and, as he was in the Main Stand, he'd be able to make amends later. The 1979 me would be throwing a paddy at this point.

Then Dale called. Ray was still in the car and was heading up Queens Drive. He would be there any minute. We legged it to the car park to greet him. We made no specific plans to see him other than those seconds from the car to the door.

Of course he got mobbed. It was great to see him climb out of the car and stroll across that tarmac. Most of us can picture the Ray Kennedy smile but to see it again and see it there was something special. We shook hands and he disappeared inside. He to a nice restaurant meal, us to the Golden Dragon on Utting Avenue.

Dale had told us that his dad had no plans to walk on the pitch. Yes, he was concerned that people would shrug their shoulders at his name, but there were more physical concerns. Ray's balance isn't always the best and the prospect of falling over in front of 44,000 people was a very real one, so he'd decided to wave from his seat if it were needed.

Then he saw the mosaics and felt he had to say thank you. We didn't know that. We had no way of knowing, being in the Kop rather than the directors' lounge. That season I was low to the right of the Kop goal and would wander over to Block 104 at half-time to see my mates, Steve and Matt. As I struggled through the concourse the stadium announcer welcomed a very special guest on to the pitch. I started to jog.

The next day I spoke to Ray's daughter. She'd been watching the game at home and was amazed to see her dad casually stroll out in front of all those people. 'He barely leaves the house!' Yes, that was a good day.

The last time I saw him was when Spurs tonked us 4-0. I was in the North East as my girlfriend was competing in the Great North Run and I wasn't expected to stand around in the rain for hours, waiting for her to finish. I'd been invited for Sunday dinner so again had the surreal feeling of, 'How the hell did I get here?' It was very pleasant but the game was about to start in the other room. I politely coughed and looked at my watch. Ray got the hint and wolfed down his food so he could watch every second. It reminded me of being a kid and asking my mum if I could watch *Match of the Day* if I cleaned my plate. Yes, even three-time European Cup winners do that.

We were useless at White Hart Lane but talk about having your very own pundit on hand. This is a man who won every single honour in the game so I kept my mouth shut when he talked. See, I'd learned a valuable lesson a few years earlier at St James' Park when I was on a rare corporate visit. Most clubs ask an ex-player to move from box to box and say hello and give the moneyed men a sense of inclusion. I've only done this twice and it's not for me, really. I missed being with my mates. Anyway, on this occasion it was Peter Beardsley (and there it is).

Newcastle were being Allardyced and were a goal down thanks to Gerrard's free kick from roughly 40 miles out. My hosts – an insurance company who advertised with us – were not happy at what looked like another home defeat. They hadn't told me that Beardsley would be popping in as it would be a treat for me. A treat? No throat has ever dried up so quickly. They shoved me at him and we shook hands. We got talking and became so involved that we were unaware that the game had re-started. I'd been trying to convince him that Dirk Kuyt was never going to play the number ten role behind Fernando Torres. Peter disagreed. Then two things happened. Firstly, a small voice creaked in my head, reminding me that Peter Beardsley was the archetypal number ten in the 1980s and 90s and would probably know a little more about that role and, secondly, Kuyt was scoring behind me. Sometimes it's best to just shut up and listen, which was precisely what I did upon my last visit to Ray's house.

From such happy memories then to such dull times now. Liverpool were awful today. Absolutely abysmal. A 1-0 defeat (a defensive error, naturally) and a trip to Madrid to come midweek. Maybe it was a good thing that I didn't go. After all, what would I have said to Denise?

4 November 2014, Real Madrid 1 Liverpool 0

'What the fuck are you on about, soft lad?'

By Andy Campbell

Geoff has lived in Madrid for a few years. He's friendly with a few Real lads and they are telling him about how it kicked off the last time Liverpool had come to town. 'Yeah I know mate, I was there,' I interrupt with a laugh, remembering the handbags in the lower tier opposite us after Yossi Benayoun had slammed the ball home to deliver us another memorable night in the Rafa Benitez era. Madrid ending up at each other's throats was fairly ironic given the Liverpool away support had gone into meltdown earlier that afternoon with rumours that Rafa was about to resign. Fifteen months later, Benitez was indeed shoved out by a board composed of card-carrying Tories and leverage louts, and it's 'only' taken a further four years for Liverpool to get back to playing the likes of Real.

It's 72 hours until kick-off and we're sat in a backstreet off Sol Square easing our way in with the first few pints of the trip. Wives and girlfriends have waved us off at airports with orders not to hit the ale too hard (and in one case, not to return home with an STD), and, all genial faux smiles and sincerity, we tell them what we think they need to hear.

It's all arrant nonsense and lies of course, because it's Liverpool in Europe and we've got a full three days to enjoy one of the best cities in the world and get right on it.

Let's be clear, this isn't about wanting to behave in a drunken Englishman abroad anti-social way – it's about doing what Scousers do best in Europe. Watching the Reds on foreign soil with your mates is as good as it gets, and for us that means embracing the local culture, celebrating all things Red and having the best time possible. Everyone's got their own definition of following Liverpool, but – and trust me on this – our way is the best.

About an hour before we sat down in this pub, we were wandering across the Plaza Mayor and a group of Scouse lads in their late teens and early 20s, all stripy polos and dark coats, shuffled past doing their best to look as moody as possible to no one in particular. You want to go over and just say, 'Lads, sorry, but you're just trying way too hard here. Not everything in life is Man U away.' So just relax, go native, start with a friendly smile to the barman and fire the ale in.

Most of the lads are arriving tomorrow, so for tonight it's just me, Geoff, his brother and, to my particular delight, my old fella. They're a dying breed, Shankly's original Kopites, and it's great that he can join us on this now he's retired after years of giving to other people in his teaching career. Games like Real Madrid away are for the fans like him who've put decades of hard graft in. Not for some newcomer who steps off a Thomas Cook one-day flight with a half-and-half scarf.

And you don't spend 50 years around Anfield without seriously knowing what you're on about. Joe was calling Jamie Carragher as a natural centre-half as early as 1998, several years before the penny dropped with Gerard Houllier. Me and my brother (AWOL on this one due to recent fatherhood) count ourselves enormously lucky that we have a dad who's not only passed us a lifelong love of Liverpool but also given us the time and care to take us the match every week. It's good to be able to give him this trip back, and so he's here, enjoying it every bit as much as us, and we gamely get stuck in.

Having a mate who lives locally and knows where to go is a massive bonus on these trips as it means you don't end up gravitating towards the main square, or, for example, going to a Champions League tie in the wine capital of Europe and spending 36 hours in an Irish bar. This is Geoff's local, and he does the honours, boxing us off with plates of tortillas, Manchego and the biggest plate of meat you'll ever see. It comes to nine Euros each for nine dead animals. Seems a reasonable deal. As one of the lads puts it, in footballing terms, it's a vegetarian's Michael Thomas 1989.

In the interests of polite society, and the fact there's Manchester United fans present, we keep the conversation at a high level for the first hour or so – there was fault on both sides in the Evra–Suarez saga; Fergie is a fascinating and complex personality really and Cristiano Ronaldo is indeed a hell of a player. Needless to say, within a few hours and several more tapas bars navigated later, the evening descends into drunken farce. A conversation on best away-end celebrations gives mention to Fernando Torres's winner at Portsmouth in 2009, which in turn allows me to try and articulate one of my long-held theories to the lads – that of the very important goal celebration as the male orgasm. It sounds tangential – and it is – but hear me out.

There are several stages. The first is the build up of pressure and anticipation as Liverpool turn the screw (potentially involving several woodwork shots and world-class saves over a 20-minute period). Then, there's *the* moment – the white light and utter bliss as the ball hits the net. That is followed by several seconds of detachment when you genuinely don't know where you are before one, two, three, you're back in the room, hugging and embracing your willing participant, euphoric but conscious, talking all kinds of broken biscuits before the process ends in one final, loving contented hug and you bounce out the away end ready to face the rest of the day with a smile on your face. And you see – that's *exactly* what Torres did at Portsmouth on that cold February night. He gently massaged and energised just the right part of the away end, carefully peeling back the layers of skin before delicately tucking the ball into the top corner with all the precision and timing of a master love-maker.

And I'm back in the room.

Joe clocks me with one of those looks which only your arl fella can give and which says, neatly, 'What the fuck are you on about, soft lad?' It's definitely time for bed. There are two and a half days to go and it's going to be a long road to the flight home on Wednesday afternoon.

'S'appenin lad?' Early Monday evening and as Madrid commuters scramble round, the broadest Scouse accent we'll hear all week greets us from across the square. Thing is, its owner is Norwegian. Oystein has been coming to Anfield since the 1980s and despite being from Oslo, is as Scouse as anyone we go the match with. He gets over several times a season, always staying at the same guest house in Knotty Ash that he has done for nearly 30 years. These things matter.

Tonight we're heading down to Rayo Vallecano to watch them play the Basque newcomers to La Liga, Eibar. Earlier in the day we'd taken the short journey down to Vallecas to pick up the tickets and, as a few doors were open, we decided to have a wander around. There's a fair amount of people about as during the day the stadium opens up as a communal sports and boxing club for Rayo members to use. We were also able to go down on the pitch and take a few photos.

Ticket prices have been slashed for tonight as well – as cheap as five Euros – to allow the unemployed and pensioners to get to the game. It's heartening to see that a football club with a sense of accessibility and closeness to its fans still exists in a top-flight league. I'd read before we flew out that Rayo fans have actually sung about us for years – one of their chants containing the line that 'one day we dream of playing at Anfield', so with this nice little cultural overlap in mind, we're looking forward to this one.

We step off the Metro and dive into a bar for a quick pre-match pint. There's a lovely working-class buzz and sense of anticipation about the place that you just don't get at Anfield anymore. The rickety concrete stadium and drizzling rain in the low floodlights reinforces what we all say – this is like going the match 20 years ago.

The game itself is an absolute belter; Eibar going two up before Rayo pull it back with two goals in a minute prior to a late Basque winner. The best thing about the evening, though, is the Rayo fans' co-ordinated protest against the game being screened on a Monday night. Before kick-off, the main Rayo end is empty in the middle other than a couch which contains four of their Ultras dressed as characters from *The Simpsons* mock fighting with each other. At the front, more Ultras hold up a banner which translated reads 'Until the day we go to Anfield, we protest anew against commercial football'. For the next 20 minutes they rotate a series of banners, all with *Simpsons* characters and all with an anti-modern-football message. There's one with Ralph Wiggum saying 'I like Monday night football – I'm special' and another with Fat Tony saying something about football mafiosos. Soon the Rayo fans pile back in and reclaim their end with a single, massive banner – 'NO EL FUTBOL LOS LUNES'. It's the most impressive, co-ordinated show of fan solidarity and protest we've ever seen inside a ground.

We're slightly jealous that such a thing could never happen at Anfield. Recently the Spion Kop 1906 lads (who do a great job by the way) downed the colours and held up black flags in protest against prices. But Anfield is so big, and the support so mixed, that the message gets diluted and it's not the same as Rayo pulling it together with 1,500 like-minded lads. Sadly, short of getting Purple Aki to bring everyone into line and co-ordinate matters (or perhaps to mischievously steward the away end) I'm not sure that a great deal can be done about it.

The evening ends with a few more bevvies and plates of meat back at HQ. We've had a brilliant night, there's still a day to go and we're happy to swerve the increasingly belligerent group of Liverpool in the Irish bar round the corner who want to start a fight with the riot police, who in turn are showing remarkable restraint. So sorry, but we'll have to pass on the kind offer to 'lad, get round the back with us and steam them, lad'. Still, we've all got our way of getting through the world.

It's matchday and we've now got a full turnout as 20 of us settle down to round three at HQ. The consensus is that finding this place off the beaten track was a good call as rumours are drifting around that a number of Liverpool aren't exactly covering themselves in glory in other parts of the city centre.

Now this is one of my long-standing bugbears in the post-Istanbul years – the decline of the European away. Because 2005 was so special and so glorious everyone wants a piece of it now, and there's a new breed, Scouse and out-of-town, who basically don't have a clue how to conduct themselves in someone else's city. I suppose we've all got our definition of following Liverpool but the issue is that because Liverpool in Europe, especially post-Istanbul, has such mythology around it the newcomers turn up thinking that it's all one big party in Taksim Square and that within that, there's a certain way you *have* to behave.

The traditional Scouse approach is get on it with the locals, make mates and embrace the culture of wherever you are – not the new vogue of piling into the main square, booting footballs round and acting like a load of bottle-throwing divvies from Division Two.

It's a weird example of football culture eating itself and is exactly what happened with Everton in Lille a few weeks ago, when (according to my bluenose mates who were there) a handful of divvies gave the police the minimum reason for a massive overreaction. You just know this particular scenario is never going to end well, and as such is to be avoided at all costs. I'm not sure I've explained all that very clearly, but if you get what I mean then you're probably on the same level as me.

Anyway, that's what we're hearing is going on elsewhere and we're glad to be well out of the way. At heart we're just friendly, peaceful people, big kids with an enduring love of all things LFC. And despite playing it down, all of us are desperate to get in and see the Reds do the biz tonight.

We can all be too cool for school at times but from father to son, the bottom line is we're all mad about Liverpool FC and it's those ties of family and friendship that keep us coming back year in, year out. Outsiders will never get it but this city, and this club, lends itself to a strange, weird breed of passionate obsessive. The type of personality who could do a line off a supermodel's arse cheek and contemplate Joe Allen throughout.

Tony and the rest of the lads wander in, more plates of meat get piled up and for the next few hours we proceed to drink Rioja like we fucking invented it. Everyone's relaxed and with tickets in hand we're having a boss afternoon, being looked after royally by the owners. Before too long, it's time to head up to the ground.

As tempting as it is to go find another bar, years of doing these trips teaches us that it's a smart move to get in early. We're not wrong as outside the away end we're greeted by dozens of riot police funnelling fans through a one-way system. It's a pain, but as Joe says if proper crowd management had been in place in 1989 then 96 people wouldn't have lost their lives. As usual your old fella is right on such matters, and after about seven different checkpoints we get in.

As Liverpool fans we have to accept that safety comes before a bit of inconvenience. But seriously – what is a dozen attack dogs with muzzles doing at a football match? If something serious did happen would the Spanish police be stupid enough to let a German shepherd loose in a crowded concourse? Sadly, the answer is probably yes.

It's hard not to be impressed by the Bernabeu, and despite my misgivings of football tourism it seems right to take a few photos with Joe. Even this high up it's an incredibly impressive stadium. What's less impressive, however, is the make-up of their crowd. I know Anfield is bad but there's thousands of Liverpool dotted about and the whole ground seems dominated by tourists, with the fighting Ultras moved four tiers up in a single block under the legend 'FANS RMCF'. It's a pretty powerful visual message as to where the hardcore support ranks in the new football pecking order.

As kick-off nears their Ultras unfurl a banner, 'Great teams have great supporters – welcome Liverpool'. A nice touch but sorry lads, you don't: 10,000 Vallecano made more noise the previous evening and by being relegated fours tier up, the joke's on you. The sad part is you don't even realise it and the only noise is the endless music being piped through.

Then for a few brief seconds as kick-off approaches, the speakers fall silent and YNWA booms out from the away end. The Santiago Bernabeu belongs to Liverpool. It's a genuinely beautiful moment against the backdrop of a corporate environment.

The game is the game and the result is the result. All things considered we did as well as could be reasonably expected, and given the performance I don't think it's fair to say Brendan Rodgers threw in the towel. You hate to see us lose any match, and moral victories are all a bit too Everton-in-the-derby for me, but at the same time it's also OK to lose a game to a better team fair and square. Kolo Toure gave us a few moments dancing down the wing and we worked it well into a few positions, but we didn't have enough up front to cause them problems. The bottom line is that Real were better, stronger and quicker than us all over the pitch and probably had another gear if they had needed it.

There were 50-odd goals in our attack last season which at least gave us a puncher's chance. I'm not sure we need to analyse the current problems much beyond that.

A half-hour lock-in and a few choice songs at Adrian Chiles later, the Spanish police kindly allow us to leave. The show of force we saw on the way in is absent on the way out as 3,600 people exit via one stairwell with zero stewarding or policing on show. This gives lie to why the police were so visible this afternoon – it's got nothing to do with crowd safety and everything to do with deploying police resources. Because like any organisation the police have got a budget to spend and overtime to allocate, and if the budget doesn't get spent it gets cut. So what better way to show how a budget can best be spent than overpolicing a 'risk' fixture with those English hooligans? Tomorrow someone will get to write up a report hailing the operation as a complete success. Not that it was ever going to be anything else.

So that's pretty much it for Real Madrid 2014, and I do hope our paths cross again sooner rather than later. Footy's boss when you win. It's a bit less good when you don't, but even the shit times are a great laugh with your mates, and Real Madrid v Liverpool? We wouldn't have been anywhere else. It's been an absolute belter of a trip, up there with the best.

We last a few more hours round the backstreets drinking and singing the night away, but it gradually turns into one of those evenings where someone goes for a piss or a ciggie outside and never returns. We melt off into the night, to start the journey home, livers battered and bruised but pride intact and still with an outside chance of going through. And the next day we all return home safe and, best of all, with no STDs that anyone's aware of. Still, there's always Bulgaria to see to that.

8 November 2014, Liverpool 1 Chelsea 2

'Dave said he was 18; like Paul Ince, Barnes and Roy Keane rolled into one'

By Kevin Sampson

Let's have this right: Steven Gerrard is the greatest player I've ever seen in the Liverpool jersey. One of the consolations of turning 50 is that, when it comes to football, you've had an absolute surfeit of magical moments. You've seen some unbelievable talent run out on that hallowed pasture in Liverpool 4, and the memories that don't even make your top 100 are more majestic than, say, a Stoke fan's best five ever. If you've been a Liverpool fan since the 1960s, it's been some ride.

My first game was against West Ham in August 1966. England had just won the World Cup and people were cheering Bobby Moore and Geoff Hurst, but I couldn't have cared less about them. I wasn't even that bothered about Sir Roger. Waiting outside the ground with my dad, I only had eyes for one player. The Saint. I think that, in my four-year-old's imagination, I expected him to appear out of the players' entrance (the players' entrance! A fantasy portal where only giants trod) like John Wayne, perhaps even wearing a polo neck jumper. I was a bit surprised that he smiled, all bashful, like a startled racoon, but I loved him unreservedly. He was the Saint – the man who won the cup for Liverpool.

Over the years I had many more heroes; Alun Evans, Jack Whitham, the Mighty Emlyn, Peter Cormack. All these exquisite talents who never even get a mention when we begin compiling our greatest ever LFC squads. Cally – a legend. Played about 10,000 games without ever getting booked. Peter Thompson – a genius. Steve Heighway – a maestro. Kevin Keegan – a little fella with the same name as me, who always scored important goals. An orange football fizzing into a red net. It was brilliant, but we never won anything. From when I started going in August 1966 we didn't win a thing until May 1973. Maybe if Stevie Peplow had played more...

But after that double-winning season in 1973 kicked off the 'new era' (when the UEFA Cup, which had been the Fairs Cup, was still the UEFA Cup,) the list of Liverpool magicians rolls off the tongue. Just the local lads alone would make most peoples' all-time greats squad – Phil Thompson, Jimmy Case, John Aldridge, Steve McManaman, Robbie Fowler. And that's before you get into your Ray Clemence, Alan Hansen, Graeme Souness, Ronnie Whelan, Ian Rush, Peter Beardsley, Michael Owen, Mark Lawrenson, Jan Molby, Fernando Torres debates. Kenny Dalglish, of course, warrants a list of his own, and, even though we only had him a year or two, I'll say with no hesitation that Luis Suarez is as good as the King.

Here's the thing, though – up until Gerrard arrived on the scene, I still didn't believe King Kenny was the greatest. For me, without doubt, the most spontaneous, outrageous, natural talent I'd witnessed week in, week out for the mighty Reds was John Barnes, especially those first three seasons. If anyone was ever going to oust Barnes as my own personal Jesus he was going to have to be, realistically, Superman.

Come in number 28.

The first time I ever heard mention of Gerrard was in August 1998. *The Echo* invited three wise fanzine editors – John Mackin of *Red All Over The Land*, Dave Usher of *The Liverpool Way* and Steve Kelly of *Through The Wind And The Rain* – to give their new-season predictions. We'd gone the entire 1990s without a midfield enforcer but Dave Usher said he had seen our future. Dave said that, if we got the new kid, Steven Gerrard, into the team we could realistically challenge for the title. This was the season after Owen had torn Argentina apart in the World Cup. McManaman had hit his peak and Jamie Redknapp was, at last, starting to live up to his early promise. So, who was this Gerrard kid, and where was he going to fit in? Dave said he was 18; like Paul Ince, Barnes and Roy Keane rolled into one and, for his money, he'd have Gerrard in the team over any of his elders and betters tomorrow. I thought I'd keep an eye out for this young whippersnapper.

Got to be honest, I didn't see it at first. Get this – I thought he had a funny gait.

He came on for Vegard Heggem, if memory serves, and ran around pointing. Then the game ended. He was in and out after that, had a string of games later that season but, compared to the other relative newcomers, he didn't really catch the eye. It was hard to see what all the fuss was about.

Much as Jordan Henderson seems to play better when Stevie isn't there to dominate him, Gerrard started showing signs of his relentless drive and penetration once Ince moved on to Middlesbrough the following season, 1999/2000, and he first really made a name for himself in a short-lived derby debut.

Having come on as a substitute after Sander Westerveld was red-carded for swatting Franny Jeffers, Gerrard nailed his colours to the flagpole by getting sent off himself following a thigh-high challenge on record label boss Kevin Campbell. It was Stevie's first derby, his first sending-off, but it set the tone for a talismanic run of games, goals and wins against Everton. He's been tormenting Everton for 15 years now, Gerrard, and there's hardly been a derby where he hasn't been the main story. Goals, sendings-off, decisive tackles, clearances off the line – from spats with Wayne Rooney to showing Ross Barkley who's the daddy, Steven Gerrard has set the agenda for the Merseyside derby right from his first game.

The goals, though – the goals! Penalties aside, every score Stevie has notched against the Blues has been a belter. They light up your memories and roll off your tongue; the shaven-headed number 17 (by now), cupping his ear and grinning madly following his rasper at Goodison in September 2001; the daisy-cutter at their place that left Nigel Martyn standing there like a gormless gibbon; the one he passed into the Kop net in 2005 when Didi rolled the free kick to him. There was the hat-trick under the floodlights a couple of seasons ago, when Stevie showed that the baby was his by shoving the ball under his shirt and winking at the heartbroken Bluenoses. The stonking great header that opened the floodgates for the 4-0 in January 2014. Make us dream…

But on the basis of his first season, not even Dave Usher would have dreamt what was to come. Stevie was in and out of the reckoning, seemingly under the surgeon's knife every few months for persistent groin problems. He scored an absolute stunner against Sheffield Wednesday – a slalom run (what we used to call a 'dribble') that took him past three or four Wednesday players for his first ever Liverpool goal (looking at his 170-odd goals, though, none of them have been stuffy. Seriously, try and name a Gerrard goal that wasn't beautifully executed. None of them – not even the penalties – are a tap-in). But he was stop-start. Injuries, an irrational growing spurt, stage fright, personal issues…these were all obstacles he had to overcome in those early years.

For me, Stevie really announced himself in 2001. He'd overcome a fair degree of turbulence by then – not just the injuries and operations, but the almost inevitable reports of hijinx and after-hours incidents with soap stars and colourful local businessmen. With Fowler before him, being such a friend of the night, and never quite living up to the full magnitude of his brilliance as a result, it was starting to look as though Gerrard might go the same way, too. But he just seemed to click. All that ability, strength, energy, exuberance, that magnificent technique.

On 31 March 2001, about 15 minutes into the game against Manchester United, it all seemed to come together. Gerrard received the ball just inside the United half. Their entire team backed off ten yards. He advanced and advanced, and still the United defence retreated. So he let fly – and with that one raging thunderbolt of a drive that just flew past the gaping Fabien Barthez all the various component parts of Steven George Gerrard came together. That goal was the making of him.

It wasn't just that goal, though. Gerrard was starting to get some seriously good advice from some outstanding mentors. Phil Thompson came back to the club as Gerard Houllier's number two. No one understood better than Big Phil the pressures that come with being a local lad on the verge of great things with the club you love. Dietmar Hamann helped Stevie work out when to surge and when to stick; but it was another cool old head, I think, who really helped the kid become a man. Step forward Gary McAllister, who arrived in the summer of 2000 and, more than anyone, showed Gerrard how and when to influence a game of football.

After the United screamer, Stevie's goals came thick and fast. Having been reluctant to try his luck he began to send them arrowing in regularly from 20, 25, 30 yards, every one a scorcher. He was phenomenal. In that run that took Liverpool to Cardiff for the League Cup and FA Cup, to Dortmund for the UEFA Cup, our third, by the way – to Charlton for Champions League qualification, and to Monaco to blitz Bayern Munich for the Super Cup, Gerrard was magnificent throughout.

Many Liverpool fans say they're not that arsed about England, but when Liverpool players are in the team I want them to do well. Gerrard carried his Liverpool form into the national team, scoring yet more corkers and memorably double-nutmegging his LFC godfather Hamann in a 5-1 demolition of Germany in Munich. Were all the England goals scored by Liverpool players that night? I think they were.

He replaced Sami Hyypia as captain in 2003 and grew another six feet. The team struggled but the Gerrard Moments lit up a disappointing anti-climax to the Houllier Years. We have a lot to thank Monsieur H for – he, more than anyone, dragged the club belatedly into the modern age and his new captain, Steven Gerrard, has more to thank him for than anyone. Crucially, Houllier gave Gerrard his trust. If you listen to Barnes or Ray Houghton or any of the great 1987/88 Liverpool team speak about Dalglish's tactical talks, the consensus is that his message went something like, 'You're all great players. You don't need me to tell you what to do. You're better than them. Go and smash them!'

It's difficult to imagine the urbane Houllier putting it in quite those words, but he entrusted Gerrard with the freedom to surge when he saw fit. In an era when £20m was an absolute fortune, it's a pity GH's swansong was a doomed gamble on Diao, Diouf and Cheyrou. Perhaps a concerted effort to find another Gary Mac to liberate Stevie G from his Superman burden might have led us to the promised land. Zinedine Zidane turned 30 in June 2002 and you can only wonder how he and Stevie might have gelled if all the talk that summer became real. But the following year Roman Abramovich arrived to change the face of English football forever and Houllier was on his way.

Abramovich's first move was to get rid of popular, rapid-blinking tinker-man Claudio Ranieri and bring in lisping narcissist Jose Mourinho. Mourinho had let it be known via his agent, Jorge Mendes, that he very much fancied the Liverpool job after Houllier left, but Liverpool had other ideas. A smiling Spaniard called Rafael Benitez rolled into Liverpool in the summer of 2004 and promised his Benitles would shake the world. Mourinho went to Chelsea and pledged he would only sign the best. The charm offensive began. Chelsea wanted Gerrard and they'd keep on flattering, scheming and tapping him up until they got him. Gerrard for Chelsea? Unthinkable. We turned them down flat.

Rafa's first season limped out of the starting blocks, literally. That first season saw Gerrard, Xabi Alonso, Hyypia, John Arne Riise, Carragher, Djibril Cisse – just about all his senior professionals, in fact – forced out of action through injury for significant lengths of time. LFC stumbled through their Champions League campaign with, at various stages, Scott Carson, Djimi Traore, Stephen Warnock, David Raven, Neil Mellor, Darren Potter, Anthony Le Tallec, Josemi, Antonio Nunez, John Welsh, Florent Sinama Pongolle, David Mannix and the redoubtable Salif Diao himself as our standard bearers. They did us proud, all of them. They kept us in the competition.

Then to 8 December 2004. It's engraved on our psyche, now. We had to beat Olympiakos by two clear goals to make it through to the knockout stages. No one seriously expected us to win the thing, but it would be nice to prolong our stay into the new year. It was what commentators like to call one of 'those special European nights at

Anfield', with the crowd well and truly up for it and Liverpool charging out of the blocks like men possessed.

Everyone knows what happened – Rivaldo scored from a free kick, and looked a bit sorry. We thought that was that, but then Pongolle equalised and Mellor toe-poked us into the lead. Time was all but up. A punt…a clever, cushioned chest-down by Mellor…Gerrard runs on to it…

Here's a question for you: when you watch and re-watch Gerrard's most important goal ever – the one I'm talking about here where he crashes an unstoppable monster of a strike into the Olympiakos net – does Andy Gray's squealing commentary make it or break it for you? His voice shatters the squeakometer as he gasps, 'Ohhh, ya beauty! What a hit!'

For me it's become part of the folklore of that goal. I was at the game, I lived the moment, I fell ten, 12 rows, enmeshed in one delirious, deranged, disbelieving and joyous mass celebration. It was in! We were through! But, when I watch the goal again, there's something equally deranged and spontaneous about Gray's shrieking commentary that completely fits what that moment was all about. It was Steven Gerrard, Superman, against all possibility and beyond even the most extreme remit of human ability, taking our team by the scruff of its scraggy net and shouting, 'Come 'ead! We're going in!'

And we were. We were going through. We were going in. We were going to play Chelsea and knocking them into last week.

But we had to play them at Cardiff, first. Mourinho had become a complete dickhead by this time – February 2005. On New Year's Day that year Frank Lampard had deliberately, with malice aforethought, maimed Alonso. On 30 minutes he stamped on Xabi and broke his ankle. Mike Riley didn't send him off, and our crowd had voiced its displeasure. Just after that, we had an absolutely blatant penalty waved away by Riley. He seemed to give it, then changed his mind.

It looked nailed on for 0-0, when Joe Cole – JFC – scored in the last minute with a stuffy, jammy, deflected shot. Mourinho went berserk on the touchline, running to the cameras beating his chest. If he hadn't always been then, by now he was a nailed on, transparent, indefensible blert. He was always going on about other teams, he was always slating referees, managers, fixture computers – and he was always hinting at his admiration for Gerrard. Our crowd sent him home with 'fuck off Mourinho' ringing in his ears.

So when Liverpool took the lead against Chelsea in the League Cup Final of 2005, the jubilant Red hordes let Mourinho know. Gerrard's most vengeful gremlin couldn't have contrived what happened next.

He decided to head clear a decent but overhit cross. It skimmed off the top of Stevie's scalp, into the net for 1-1. Mourinho ran the length of the touchline to bait the Liverpool support, shushing them with his forefinger pressed to his lips. He later claimed that he was silencing the English media, who were all against him. The prick.

Revenge is sweet, however. After Alonso broke his ankle, he came back for the first leg of the Champions League semi-final at Stamford Bridge. Xabi was booked for reacting to a trip by Eidur Gudjohnsen, who stood over him, sly and smirking, reminding Xabi he'd now be banned for the second leg. Afterwards Mourinho criticised Liverpool for their negative tactics, so Anfield was always going to be lively for the return game, never mind it being the eliminator for a place in the Champions League Final.

Lively? I have never known an atmosphere like it. I was in the crowd for great European occasions like the 1976 UEFA Cup Final against Bruges, where we came back from 2-0 down to win 3-2. The entire ground was shaking; the first time I'd heard the Main Stand and Kop join in with the singing. I was in the Kop for the fabled St Etienne game in March 1977 and still had the scintillating scream of white noise drilling through my ears in school the next day. But this semi-final second leg against Chelsea in 2005 was something else.

Coming so long after we had last been in the running for one of the major prizes, the sense of occasion, the sense of destiny, fate and impending greatness was overpowering. The feeling in the pubs and streets around the ground was akin to nothing I had ever experienced in 40 years supporting the Reds. An hour before kick-off the Kop was rocking – literally, visibly vibrating as the entire ground let Chelsea know what they were in for. There's an apocryphal story that Abramovich turned to his chief executive of the day, Paul Smith, and asked him why the noise at Stamford Bridge wasn't like this. Smith probably sealed his own fate when he told Abramovich that there were some things you just can't buy. He was out of a job by the start of the following season.

Liverpool knocked Chelsea out of Europe that night. We beat them in the FA Cup semi-final the following season, too. We beat them in the Champions League semi-final in 2007. Mourinho was on the pitch after all three games, but not to shush the Liverpool supporters. He was there to pick up the distraught John Terry, not for the first time crumpled on the turf, sobbing his guts out.

The 2005 win over Chelsea got us to the Champions League Final. We won it. Steven Gerrard was a colossus. His header set up the most incredible fightback in the competition's history – surely the greatest final, ever? The sight of Gerrard, European Cup aloft, his wild grin lighting up the Istanbul sky is one of the greatest moments of my life; yours too, no doubt. Steven gave us that. He gave us so much, and he gave fucking Chelsea what for.

The 2006 FA Cup semi-final win over them sent us to a final against West Ham. I think we all felt the hard part had been done when we blitzed Chelsea so emphatically at Old Trafford. In the final West Ham were exceptional. Their crowd were right behind them, making giants out of journeymen. With seconds remaining and West Ham 2-1 up, Liverpool's tired legs pushed forward one last time. Gerrard was in a similar position to that definitive goal against United. He advanced. They backed off. He advanced. PFK made a half-hearted, bum-first shuffle to close him down. Gerrard shifted the ball to his right. He was still 35 yards out.

'Not from there, Stevie – not from fucking there...'

Stevie didn't hear me. Stevie let fly. The ball made bright red streaky scorch marks in mid-air as it flashed into the net. I went down under a demented piley-on that left me with livid bruises well into the summer of 2006: seat scars – the new silk scarves.

Another impossible, spectacular, last-minute goal, then. This was what we came to expect of Gerrard. In 2009, the year that Rafa nearly pulled it off, Gerrard and Torres were unbelievable. Each and every goal was either critical, decisive, outlandishly brilliant or all of the above. Again and again, he pulled us out of the fire. From the last-minute winner against Boro in our first home game of the season to the 4-1 stadium-emptier at Old Trafford, Stevie was at the heart of every victory. We came so, so close.

But not as close as the Make Us Dream season. Jesus.

Gerrard's most vengeful gremlin couldn't have contrived this one, either. The drama of the Manchester City game; 2-0 up. 2-2 in the blink of an eye. Then 3-2. Ecstasy. Nirvana. This is it. Stevie had his men in a huddle – the Huddle of Destiny. 'This does not slip!' he told them. This does not slip. The nervy win at Norwich. Seven points needed from three games and the title is ours. Chelsea, of all teams, next up. It would have to be Chelsea, wouldn't it? Mourinho. Let's show this whopper once and for all – you're fucking history, Jose.

Mourinho, of course, knows all about history. He remembers when Chelsea were strong and Liverpool were underdogs. He remembers Benitez's Liverpool coming to Stamford Bridge in the Champions League semi-final for a draw. He says he isn't interested in this April 2014 game, where Liverpool can effectively seal the title. But he's interested, all right. He's obsessed. He parks the bus. He has no shame, no humility. He instructs his Chelsea team to frustrate, to waste time, to get the crowd angry. But this is fine. It may well take time for Liverpool to break Chelsea down. We may, perish the thought, have to settle for a draw. But Chelsea are not even pretending to attack. They will never score. There can only be one winner. This does not slip.

So here we are, then – Liverpool versus Chelsea, 8 November 2014. After all the history between them, after Chelsea's repeated attempts to sign Liverpool's talismanic captain right through to Stevie's Slip when the league was all but won, this game was always going to be about Steven Gerrard; and so it turned out to be. In the run-up to the game the radio phone-ins and social media were full of how many hilarious songs those renowned Chelsea wits had made up. They couldn't wait to rub it in. But maybe, just maybe, Steven would have the last laugh.

I'm writing this only hours after the game. Steven did not have the last laugh so let me just get this over with. I have only this left to say and I'll try to be unemotional about it, I'll try to just stick to the facts. Steven Gerrard is the greatest player I have ever seen in a Liverpool jersey, but it's over, now. It's over. He'll drive the team on when we make hard work of things at Bournemouth. He'll slot home a penalty to make the game safe, just as Leicester look like they might get back into it. But he won't drive deep into the United half and unleash another piledriver to break their hearts. He won't drag his raggle-taggle troops to another European Cup. Today's game against Chelsea was just numbingly sad.

We took the lead against them with a strangely Gerrard-like strike from distance by young pretender Emre Can. Can Can become a player for us? Quite possibly. But at no point did it look or feel like we'd hold on to that lead, let alone build on it. The game kicked off at 12.45pm; By 1pm each of Cesc Fabregas, Oscar, Nemanja Matic and Eden Hazard had breezed past Stevie in the heart of our midfield. They didn't even have to exert themselves, they just eased past him. It wasn't that he was having a bad game, it was beyond his powers of influence to have a good game. You couldn't help but think that in Brendan Rodgers's shoes, either Rafa or Mourinho would have taken Steven off right there, right then.

He's too iconic a player, too great a leader, too powerful a symbol and too lasting a legend of our club for me to micro-analyse the fault lines and flaws that have emerged. But by 3pm on 8 November 2014, I knew for sure what I'd feared for a while; everyone has to go sometime. Thanks a million for everything, Stevie, it's been some journey. No, scratch that – it's been absolutely fucking brilliant.

23 November 2014, Crystal Palace 3 Liverpool 1

'History has been written by the losers'

By Martin Fitzgerald

Post-traumatic stress. People have been sold post-traumatic stress. Brendan, committees, players, fans, owners. Queuing up for it they were.

They've bought all the post-traumatic stress that's going. There has been a run on post-traumatic stress and now it's sold out. No spares, no black market, no more demand. Everyone has post-traumatic stress, everyone demanded it.

The trauma of Selhurst Park on 5 May 2014. The trauma of Crystal Palace 3 v Liverpool 3.

With thousand-yard stares and the quotes of dead men, people pilloried the madness of that day. People turned their back on everything that came before and what may come again. They turned their back and they opted for trauma. They opted for 'wisdom'. They opted for 'I told you so'. They named names. My word, they named names.

'A good defence is the bedrock…' Finish the quote in your heads. I don't have the empathy to write it.

You're told history is written by the victors. But this history hasn't been. It's been written by the losers. Written over and over again, joylessly, by the losers.

Any attempt at celebration has been decried, any attempt at turning that and what came before into a victory has been ridiculed. Any attempt to dream has had a rude awakening.

Trying to win a game of football 10-0 to win the league has become 'losing'. A shot every three to four minutes, away from home, has become 'losing'. That moment on 55 minutes, that moment when Luis Suarez carried the ball out of the back of the net, that moment when

10-0 seemed possible, that moment when everything seemed possible, that moment has become 'losing'.

Then they turned that 11 minutes into trauma. And it's never been the same since.

A total demolition of what came before, a complete betrayal of what came before. All for 11 minutes in south-east London. Catharsis. All the talk since has been of catharsis.

How that 11 minutes must have been studied. How that trauma must have been embraced. Resolved for it never to happen again. Determined for it to never afflict us again. What plans have been hatched? What money has been spent? What lessons have been learnt?

They're sure about the lesson, they're sure we need to learn.

But who grieves for the previous 78 minutes? Who grieves for everything that came before? Who's embracing that? What lessons are to be learnt from that?

Dissenting voices. Dreamers.

History has been written by the losers.

And now here we are, back at the scene of the trauma. Exposure therapy for those that way inclined. They're confronting fears – heights, spiders and poor defending at Selhurst Park. How brave they are. How wise they are.

And look at our new team. Look at how grown-up we've become. Look at how we're shed our naivety and immaturity. Look at our poise, our consideration, our patience. We've signed for a major label, we can play our own instruments, we're getting calls from the best producers. I'm so so proud. The big time at last.

Thank God we've bought defenders, thank God we've bought depth. Look at that bench, what a lovely bench that is. I can't wait for us to rotate, different teams for different tournaments and that. You need that. They're always saying that, they're always going on about all the competing on all the different fronts. They're so very wise.

Oh and how wise the money men have been. Let's never forget them. How wise of them to spread the funds generated by one player. How wise of them not to buy goals. Look at all those bargains. Look at all that potential for resale value. It doesn't matter if they don't work out because we didn't spend that much on them in the first place. It really is very clever, to not spend over £30m on one person. How we've learnt from our previous trauma in that respect. The Carroll lesson.

How we've all become empathetic with the business. How we now see it from their side. How we love to calculate the net spend. How we second guess, how we influence. How we make this sensible yet more difficult at the same time.

A golfer tried to win The Open by getting a hole in one on the par three 18th. The ball hit the pin, ricocheted into the water and the golfer made a five. Everyone laughed at the golfer and now the golfer has got a new swing. And now the golfer is missing the cut.

But do you know the worst part? Worse than the new swing? Worse than no win in five, worse than 18 points behind Chelsea in November? Rickie Lambert scores after two minutes and he didn't even bother to get the ball out of the back of the net and run to the halfway line.

How sensible, how very sensible.

All for 11 minutes in south-east London.

26 November 2014, Ludogorets 2 Liverpool 2

If Liverpool had to write an essay on where they are at the moment this would have been it. Firstly, there's the how. How are Liverpool in Bulgaria? Answer: because we were very, very good last season. When the final whistle went at Carrow Road many Kopites' thoughts turned to the Bernabeu or Camp Nou, while others flew to quaint Czech villages with pints of firewater for 7p.

Other, more hardy folk, pictured inaccessible Russian towns where cars only work at -21 degrees. Liverpool's draw sort of had all three.

Next up, why aren't Liverpool doing well? Answer: the defence. Simon Mignolet has to come out and claim the ball more. He came out tonight. Came out in three minutes. And yes, our clean sheet lasted three minutes. But then Liverpool are good. Rickie Lambert scores and then Jordan Henderson, with his Desperate Dan jaw, put us into the lead.

Sadly, question two has yet to be fully answered as it comes in two parts: 2ii – Why can't we hold leads? Answer: we are useless at defending set pieces. With two minutes to go, and with the points in the bag, we concede a stupid goal and somehow we move from comfortable to uneasy.

Basel must be conquered at Anfield. I think this sounds easy enough but then I remember the answers to those questions. We can concede, we can't defend and our goalkeeper can stop things but not catch them.

Like Han Solo, I've got a bad feeling about this.

It's still in our hands. Anfield will be a cauldron. We play well on nights like these. Liverpool and only Liverpool can escape from a group with three defeats and a draw, so why not?

Well, yes, it's possible, but there's a nagging itch I just can't scratch. I love Liverpool but Liverpool, this Liverpool, concern me.

KC

29 November 2014, Liverpool 1 Stoke 0

I'm not a big hugger. Don't get me wrong, my daughter can have as many as she wants, and there's always one for the wife so long as she's not calling me a clumsy, crumb-spilling, good-for-nothing sod (really stings, that). But otherwise...no. A handshake's the best you'll get from me. Except at the match. Then, and in the immediate aftermath of a Liverpool goal, I'm liberal as fuck with my hugs. I'm practically giving them away to whoever wants and doesn't want them. As was the case again on Saturday.

Christ that Glen Johnson goal was a relief, and the source of some humour given those around me had been shouting all sorts of abuse at him prior to what may be the bravest thing I've ever seen a Liverpool player do. Well definitely the bravest thing I've ever seen Johnson too; a lazy-so-and-so who suddenly adopted the heart of a lion. What a header son, what a header.

As the ball nestled in the net I swung around, looked at the lads behind me and shouted 'yeeeessss!' before grabbing the pair of them in one go. I then looked at my 'mate' to my left (more on him later) and shouted, 'You're not slagging Johno off now are ya?!' before grabbing him, too. Finally I glanced at the woman to my right, realised we'd made eye contact and decided, 'Ah, what the fuck, you can have a cuddle too.'

She was properly mad that one, what with her furry ice-white coat, bizarre hand dance during 'You'll Never Walk Alone' and the moment just after the players ran out for the second half when she asked me, 'Where's Steven Gerrard?'

'On the bench,' I replied, at which point she wailed, 'Oh no!' The captain wasn't playing and it had taken her the best part of an hour to realise. As I said...mad. Anyway, we'd won, so who cares – she could have been wearing a straight-jacket and predicting an invasion of Mancunian aliens and I still would've hugged her. The three points meant that much given our current struggles and despite Mark Hughes's best attempt at revisionism, we deserved it.

SN

2 December 2014, Leicester 1 Liverpool 3

'The chart belonged to a 70-year-old Muslim man called Mohammed'

By Karen and Paul Pitchford

Karen

My first live game, other than going to see Everton with my dad when I was really little, and a Besiktas versus Galatasaray match in 1995 (which is worth a whole other chapter on its own) was in January 2007, at the ripe old age of 37. When I was growing up, women in our family did not go to the footy – we stayed at home and made the tea and butties for when the men and boys came home. We were not a shining light for feminism. I had a school friend, Fiona, who did attend all Liverpool games and I always found the notion of that somewhat exotic, but also fairly strange – she was the only girl in our class, that I knew of, who did that. I, on the other hand, followed the team from the couch, or various chairs in pubs and clubs.

Paul

I'm from the old school where if your dad was an Everton supporter you were a Liverpool supporter. I first started going to the match when I was a little kid, in the 1970s. In those days if you had a season ticket you got to go to the reserves games for free, and one of my mates could use his dad's reserves ticket so I went along to those games with him. There were no shiny silver cards back then but instead a book of real tickets, one for each game in the season that were ripped out at the turnstile. Me and my mate would look through the booklet to see what was coming up – great games against Nottingham Forest and Man United. We would get to Anfield for about 12 o'clock and stand at the railings at the front of the paddock. That's where all the kids went. The reserves in those days had their own league and this was often a proving ground for new players, or players returning from injury, so we got to see some greats. I remember Steve Ogrizovic always being the goalkeeper.

This adventure lasted for several years until I was a bit older and was taken to see real First Division football by my stepfather. I was there for Sammy Lee's debut, when he was subbed on for David Johnson. Ironically the game was against Leicester City. We won 3-2. This was pre-Hillsborough, so standing was the norm. In the Kop there were barriers strategically placed around the stand so as to stop the pushing forward of the crowd. Being behind a barrier wasn't the wisest move because if the crowd did surge you would be pushed on to it, so I used to go to one of the barriers at the side of a walkway and stand in front of it with one arm behind it so as to keep me in place.

I stopped going the match after a game against Man United. I would like to say we won but I honestly can't remember. What I do remember was the carnage rising from the fights and vicious attacks by both sets of fans. People had darts and circular saw-blades sticking out of their heads – this wasn't what I was there for then and still isn't now. I want to see a great game where if they score two we score three. However, at that time, violence was synonymous with football. From then on I only watched Liverpool from my armchair for rare televised matches, like the FA Cup Final. For everything else, there was *Match of the Day*.

At the time of both disasters I worked for Liverpool City Council and knew people involved in both. One of my work colleagues went to Heysel and told me of the Italian fans throwing bags of urine at the Liverpool fans and the Liverpool fans retaliating and charging, leading to the wall collapse and needless deaths. He also told me that some of the Liverpool fans were not the usual match-going crowd but instead were clearly there to seek trouble. Meanwhile, I watched Hillsborough unfold via news reports on TV. Another acquaintance from work was killed that day.

Life went on. I was made redundant, went to university, met Karen and we moved to a Leicestershire village where we settled in quickly and made new friends. We carried on watching Liverpool on the box, and watched the 2005 final with a load of mates in a local club in the village.

In January 2006 one of those friends, a lifelong Gooner, got tickets for a game up at Anfield and asked me if I wanted to go. My first live match in over 20 years – you bet I wanted to go! The tickets became available because this was a night-time match on Valentine's Day. The original owner of the tickets knew there was no way they'd be allowed to go but me and my mate, Ron, Karen and Ron's wife Jen, made the pilgrimage to God's own city – me and Ron for the match and Karen and Jen for a romantic meal for three with Karen's mum. They got some funny looks in the restaurant. It was brilliant to be back. We were in the Annie Road so saw the Kop in all its glory. Ron, who always tells us how much he hates Liverpool because they used to win everything when he was a lad, said the hairs on the back of his neck stood on end when we sang YNWA. On the way to the ground, a bloke was hanging off some railings and he immediately clocked Ron as an outsider. He is a Cockney, so maybe he just looked a bit funny. The other thing that sticks in the mind was that despite us all being searched on the way in, Ron found he had a waiter's friend in his sleeve pocket – not sure how he would have explained that to the stewards, it wasn't like we were going to share a nice bottle of Malbec at half-time.

Anyway, the upshot from that game was that Luis Garcia was subbed on in the 84th minute and scored three minutes later. Liverpool 1 Arsenal 0. Me hooked all over again.

Karen – 9 December 2006
I was doing a locum pharmacist stint in the local village pharmacy. The pre-Christmas rush was hotting up (every patient thinks the NHS shuts for a month at Christmas) and there were colds and flu aplenty to respond to, so it was a busy morning. I considered ignoring my mobile when it rang before deciding to pick up. It was my mum, ringing to tell me that my brother Karl had been admitted to hospital; he'd had a seizure and had been vomiting. It was OK, my mum said, because it was to be blamed on a lunch he'd had where he had been using a shisha pipe; since he didn't smoke this had made him ill. You see, she went on, when people get a bug and get a fever they can have fits, just like you see in kids.

Sometimes knowing a bit about healthcare can be a curse since I knew that grown men did not have epileptic seizures from a bit of food poisoning or a funny reaction to some shisha smoke. If Karl was vomiting and having seizures I knew he was very ill, indeed. I stood in the stockroom, crying and trying to calm down. We're not talking dignified weeping here but full-on snot and panic. One of the counter assistants wanted me to go and see a man with a cold, but I couldn't. Closing time couldn't come quickly enough.

Karl's girlfriend rang to say I shouldn't come down as Karl was OK, so I stayed put, and even went to Paul's Christmas works do. We had somebody in to decorate a couple of rooms in the house so were moving furniture when the phone went the following day. It was Ruth again, but this time the news was that Karl wasn't OK – he had 'bleeding into his brain'. Ruth said she couldn't face telling my mum so I was the one to ring her. It was me who'd told my mum that my dad had died ten years earlier and I'd honestly thought that was the worst thing I'd ever had to do – turns out I was wrong.

I was on the earliest train to London that I could catch the next morning, with mum in hot pursuit from Liverpool. At the hospital we found Karl had been moved to the stroke ward and it took a lot of calming from me to persuade mum and Ruth that this was only because it had a free bed – the name of the ward meant nothing. Sadly it did mean something, namely terrible levels of care delivered to the old and vulnerable. Karl was the youngest in the room by a good 40 years.

My brother looked terrible. He was groggy but conscious and acknowledged our presence ('I can hear the sister' – he often refers to me as 'the sister'). Karl was on hourly 'obs' (where they check blood pressure, temperature etc) so I thought I'd take a look at his chart to see what that was saying. My first thought was that the hospital had been presumptuous in recording him as being married – until I realised that the chart in my hands belonged to a 70-year-old Muslim man called Mohammed. Karl's chart was nowhere to be found.

We received a visit from an occupational therapist who helpfully told Karl he'd had a stroke – cue tears from both mum and Karl and again a long period of soothing from me. My objections to this diagnosis unsettled him so he thought he'd check the chart, which obviously wasn't a lot of use to anyone. The OT said that Karl could pull the cord by the bed if he needed anything and demonstrated, resulting in the cord coming away in his hands. The OT then decided to cut his losses. I guess most patients on that ward couldn't really question anything and most seemed to have no one to do the questioning for them.

We sat with Karl for a long time and at one point he said he needed to use the toilet. It's funny how some incidents stick in your head.

I was too scared to get him up myself so went to ask the staff, who said they'd be with me soon. Twenty minutes later and another 'yeah, be right there'. Eventually I went up to a huddle to ask again, only to be castigated by the senior nurse for interrupting a staff briefing. I politely asked for help again, and was told that Karl could just go on his own. I don't often lose my temper and it's not a pretty sight when I do.

I suggested to them that asking a man who had a recent acute brain injury to toddle off alone down the corridor was perhaps not the brightest idea they'd ever had. An auxiliary was despatched to get Karl up. She was, I'd guess, in her late 50s, with electric blue eye-shadow stretching up to her unfeasibly high drawn-on eyebrows and a smear of pink lipstick that didn't seem to see the point of staying within the lip line. She patronised my brother with baby talk but did get him to the toilet, which probably saved her from getting a clout from me.

As time went on Karl's condition seemed to be deteriorating. His words were becoming more slurred and he seemed more confused. I asked the nurses to do his 'obs' – his oxygen saturation was in his boots. There followed panic from the staff until I saw that his nasal oxygen cannula had slipped out. Re-fixing that perked him up no end. It was evident that he really needed to be on the oxygen.

The next thing was that the hospital decided they did not have the correct facilities to test or look after Karl (or perhaps his relatives were too troublesome), so he was to be moved to a specialist unit. I'd never heard of Queen's Square before but I now know them to be the National Hospital for Neurology and Neurosurgery and I can not thank them enough for all they did for my brother.

The senior nurse (she of the earlier telling-off) told me that a taxi would be called so I should go and get some things for Karl, while my mum accompanied him to the new hospital. Foolishly I thought 'taxi' was the colloquial term they were using for an ambulance.

Sadly it was not, so Karl was transported in a hackney cab, with only a blanket and my mum to keep him upright and warm on the journey. I'm assuming the cabbie didn't have a spare oxygen cylinder tucked in next to his A-Z, or the requisite neurological training should Karl have had another fit, but he did practically carry Karl up the steps into the new hospital where a porter rushed to grab him and stick him in a wheelchair.

Karl told me afterwards that he was convinced on that journey that he was actually dead and 'they' were cleverly keeping him occupied so he didn't freak out at his untimely demise.

Anyway, Queen's Square was like an alternative reality compared to the first hospital – 15-minute 'obs', staff who spent time talking to patients and really caring for them. The place was spotless and the care first-rate. After several scans (some of which I'd never heard of before) Karl was diagnosed with an intra-cerebral haemorrhage. It was idiopathic, meaning that the cause was unknown.

Paul

Before all of this happened with Karen's brother, we secured tickets to our next game. This time Karen was coming with me. It was the glamour fixture of Liverpool versus Bolton on New Year's Day 2007. We booked into a hotel for New Year's Eve, had the tickets secured through Ron's mate and were all ready to go.

Karen

I was a bit apprehensive about going to the game – as I say, women in our family did not go to the footy – but also a bit excited. Anyway, we beat Bolton 3-0 and it was brilliant, miles better than watching it on the telly. I was hooked there and then and our adventures as match-going Reds started that day. Karl was still far too unwell to join us at the time.

We spent a long time taking spares from people whenever we could, keeping their loyalty going and exploiting their membership of the PTS (remember that?). Then we progressed to building our own loyalty up, little by little. I remember the palaver of the postal applications where you sent off your hard copy form to the club, stating the games and preferred stands, and, if you were lucky, the ticket office would send you back some paper tickets in the post. By this time the internet had been around for a couple of decades so the club was slightly behind the times, I feel.

God bless Roy Hodgson because in those dark months when a lot of people stopped going, we were able to snap up tickets and build our own loyalty. We now have the magic number of credits to be able to buy for any home league game. We've got to know some brilliant people and through them have also been to a lot of away matches. We haven't managed to make it to a European away yet but that's on our agenda as soon as we can sort it.

Paul

When Leicester were promoted back to the Premier League in 2014 we celebrated the chance to go to an away game on our doorstop. As soon as the fixtures were announced we started to scout about for tickets and thankfully a good friend of ours obliged. The game was on a Tuesday night so all of our plans of getting everyone down for the weekend were scuppered. Instead we arranged to meet everyone in a pub close to Karen's work (she works right by Leicester's ground).

Karen

What a brilliant night. There were about 15 of us in the pub and we met more at the ground. The London-based Red contingent (ex-Liverpool and Wirral) were wary of what to expect of a Midlands pub, but it was fantastic. Great food, fab jukebox and a good laugh. I also met Gerry again (see Karl's chapter on Southampton) for the first time in over 30 years.

It was great to be with my brother at the match. We've been to many matches together but have only stood next to each other twice – once at Anfield and once at Upton Park. He escaped the haemorrhage with no after-effects, save for resultant epilepsy, but even that's controlled by medication. I probably see him more at matches than at family occasions now. When we won at Craven Cottage in the 2009 run-in we didn't even know that we were both at the ground, so it was great when we bumped into each other during the hour-long singalong after the game.

Not everybody agrees but I like the King Power stadium (or the Walkers Crisp Bowl as I like to call it). We've been to a couple of Leicester games (on weekends when Liverpool were not playing) and I've always enjoyed the 'match-going experience' as the suits like to call it. This time, of course, we were in the away end – second row from the back, so a very long way up and in need of an oxygen tent by the time we got up there. The Liverpool crowd were brilliant – in full voice and making our presence known. It was Steven Gerrard's return from a short period of 'rest' and we welcomed him back with gusto.

Leicester scored first, or rather we did with a Simon Mignolet own goal that would have been hilarious if any other team had done it. Adam Lallana equalised, followed by Gerrard's second-half strike. Jordan Henderson finished it off to make it three.

Some of the Leicester fans were pretty upset on the way out – I saw one trying to kick a street sign off its posts just outside the ground. We've got quite a few mates who are Leicester fans who reacted a wee bit better to the defeat.

Karen and Paul
So there you have it – a tale of a match-going Red who stopped and then went back, taking his wife with him. We've had some brilliant days out following this team and also some heart-crushing ones too. Importantly we've made some great friends along the way and thanks to those hospital visits in 2006, I've come to meet Karl's match-going friends and been welcomed into a whole new community.

These Reds are now part of our social fabric – we've been to their weddings, birthday parties and celebrated the births of their children. We are part of the Liverpool family and long may that continue.

6 December 2014, Liverpool 0 Sunderland 0

This is the tale of an East End pub, a Danish internet stream (featuring Jan Molby actually talking Danish), a double birthday weekend and my mate Dev staring at his lap for much of the game through bloodshot eyes.

Dev 'attended a social function', as Bertie Wooster euphemistically puts it, a handful of hours earlier and was feeling a little polluted. I asked where he had been. The question left him perplexed, but one thing's for certain – Liverpool were an inconvenience to him today.

Not for me, though. I was up with the lark. I'd already attended a taekwondo grading and spent a couple of hours getting over to Dev's local. Having been to Leicester in midweek I was giddy with thoughts of three consecutive wins and a little bit of optimism. Chelsea surrendered their unbeaten run in the early kick-off and Arsenal were a goal down at Stoke in nanoseconds so, suddenly, the league table was interesting again.

Dev accepted a birthday bottle of Becks with a grimace and thanked me with the almost sibilant use of the word 'Christ'.

Alas, the Reds failed to trouble the scorers, the fans, the pub volume or Dev's siesta. Beige from start to finish. In injury time, Simon Mignolet, Kolo Toure and Martin Skrtel passed the ball between them with the urgency of Dylan from *The Magic Roundabout*. Later, the manager wrote off Mario Balotelli. Balotelli didn't play.

This game was beyond poor. At least poor is interesting.

We moved pubs and discussed what alcoholic drink you would have when you didn't really want any but had to. Guinness is too heavy, lager too gassy. We settled on Bloody Marys as they're more of a soup than a drink. Slowly the night awoke and only the deep bass of sitting through that shite took the edge off it.

This has to improve, but if seven points from nine and one (mad) goal conceded involve dull games, maybe it's a small price to pay. Maybe.

KC

9 December 2014, Liverpool 1 Basel 1

'It was just me, sitting alone in my pyjamas, eating a burrito'

By Danielle Warren

I t wasn't supposed to end like this. We are supposed to triumph in the face of adversity, rise just as we are all but knocked out. This is what Liverpool do. This is who Liverpool are. And with a signature whip of the ball into the top corner of the goal from, who else, Steven Gerrard, it felt like another game in a long line of games where we snatched the improbable win that belonged to us. A win that was our right as Liverpool Football Club to hold aloft to the world and shout, 'See? This is Liverpool. We will always win in the end!'

As I scrutinised the game from my couch in New York, rain lashing against the window, I was thankful to have had the opportunity to at least watch the game live. Being five hours behind the UK, that isn't always an option.

Unfortunately for me, not long before the game kicked off I was struck down with a dreadful headache. It became so bad that I had trouble moving toward the end of the game and found myself merely raising my fists and letting out a screechy yell when Gerrard plundered his equaliser. Normally after a goal, I jump up from the couch and scream and clap and yell and run around the room like an idiot. I was suddenly overcome with worry that I wouldn't be able to celebrate properly like this, like an idiot, *when* we found the unlikely winner, which we were undoubtedly going to find.

We had to. The season depended on it. Liverpool had done this time and again and they would do it again today. But after a paltry four minutes of injury time, the whistle blew. It was almost as if time froze. The game couldn't be over. We hadn't won yet. But it was. And over the silence of the distraught Liverpool players – epitomised by, who else, Gerrard – crouching on the Anfield turf, the Swiss champions celebrated.

With their measly tally of five points from 18 in the group, Liverpool are currently a team devoid of ideas, creativity, confidence and leaders. We needed a win and the game finished 1-1. It just wasn't good enough.

As an American Liverpool fan (and a woman to boot), I often get asked how and why I support LFC. Growing up in a suburb of Los Angeles in southern California, I couldn't be farther away from the city and the culture of football. So how, you ask, did I end up here, watching Liverpool slump to a draw to Basel on a frosty December afternoon in New York?

It began on another frosty December day in the early 1980s, when I was born. A strange thing began to happen in suburbs across the US. Kids, a vast majority of them girls, began to play soccer (football). Teams and leagues were everywhere, so much so that a new breed of overprotective and supportive mother was born, affectionately known as the 'Soccer Mom'.

For a country that has historically had very little interest in the biggest and most popular sport in the world, this was a peculiar anomaly. But even with this new generation of children playing the game, no one watched professional games on TV. There were no local teams to see play at the weekend, unless of course you included your own kid's team.

From the age of four and throughout most of my adolescence, I played soccer. I used to spend hours at the park, or on the grass in front of my house, running drills and practising juggling. This sport spoke to me, and I happened to be pretty good at it.

I would find through trial and error over the years that I wasn't terribly good at pretty much every other sport, especially ones where you had to use your hands, but I was incredibly athletic growing up and I always wanted to be doing something active outside. Whether that was soccer, softball, basketball, running, skateboarding, rollerblading, surfing or boogie boarding, there I was, outside, playing to my heart's content.

Growing up in the suburban enclaves of West Hills and Calabasas in the San Fernando Valley in southern California, it's easy to enjoy all kinds of outdoor sports and activities all year round, especially living so close to the ocean. On the rare days it rained, I would juggle my soccerball in the living room, hoping my parents wouldn't catch me.

I had a real affinity for soccer and yet I probably never watched a professional game on TV until I was ten years old, during the World

Cup in 1994. Even then I really didn't understand the game or know what I was watching. I just knew that I loved it.

But while I played soccer in the local leagues and made the junior varsity team when I entered high school, I also grappled with the limitations of my body. I had double knee surgery when I was 12 for a lingering problem that caused both my kneecaps to be pulled too tightly to the sides. It was arthroscopic and routine, but I was forced to rest and it took a while to get back into shape, even at that age.

When I eventually started playing again, I began to over-think everything and a lack of confidence enveloped me. I was too focused on not making mistakes and anxious that I couldn't keep up with the running involved. For the first time in my life, the enjoyment that I took from playing the game I loved so dearly slowly evaporated. My sophomore year in high school, after I turned 16, would be the last time I played soccer competitively.

I was disappointed, but as is normal for that period of one's life, other things interested me more than soccer. Some legal, others less so. I fell in love for the first time, began to DJ after becoming engrossed in electronic music and found myself among a crowd of friends who were all at least a couple years older than me, if not more. And we definitely didn't spend our time playing sports. Not when there were raves and parties to attend.

But prior to all this adolescent merriment and experimentation, I often felt alone. My interests and sensibilities were ahead of my time. The films and TV shows I watched, the music I listened to, the boys I had crushes on, they were all very different to my peers. I was most certainly an odd duck.

When I was around nine, my friends and I were celebrating a birthday party at the local roller-skating rink. Instead of choosing a popular track from someone like New Kids On The Block to play over the next skating session, I chose a song by Soundgarden. Riding the bus to and from school with my cassette player, I was chided for listening to the Alice In Chains album *Dirt* rather than whatever was currently popular at the time.

On top of this, I was obsessed with everything British. The accents, the culture, the comedy; I was hooked. Not many of my friends understood or thought this was cool. So it made sense that I would eventually gravitate towards actual British people, and even find an Englishman to date. Perhaps it was with the English that I truly belonged.

In the summer of 2004 I met a lovely man named Brye. We met at a bar and got on from the start. He was originally from Liverpool but had lived in Los Angeles for quite a long time.

One of the lasting memories I have from when we began to date was being at his apartment one night as he looked at the sports news on his computer. I didn't know much about English football (or football at all beyond my limited experience playing the game), but he was showing me news of his team, Liverpool Football Club, buying two young Spanish players named Xabi Alonso and Luis Garcia. I remember him showing me the picture of the manager, Rafa Benitez, standing between the two Spaniards. Brye was excited and began explaining to me who these guys were and what it all meant. It was interesting, but I honestly had no idea what he was talking about.

We continued to date, and as the summer ended and throughout the fall of 2004 I found myself watching Liverpool and Premier League games with him. Before I knew it, I was watching games on my own at home. I began watching more games than Brye. I became obsessed and fell in love with football almost immediately and watched as many games as I could. And because of his passion for Liverpool, I became a Liverpool fan. He would tell me about the history of the club, the great players, the traditions, the trophies. It all felt so right. Plus, I quite liked The Beatles. So in my mind this all made sense. I didn't choose a team to become a fan of, it chose me.

As far as I was concerned, Liverpool was the best club in the world. And they were also involved in the biggest club competition in the world, the Champions League. Like with European football in general, I didn't truly understand the weight and significance of this tournament. I remember Brye being over the moon when Liverpool beat a Greek team called Olympiakos. He enthusiastically showed me the goal that would send Liverpool through the group stages at the death, scored by, who else, Steven Gerrard. It was a great goal, but I had no clue what the big deal was. It didn't take long to find out.

The final was on a Wednesday afternoon, with kick-off at 11.45am. Brye and I went to the local British pub near his apartment called The Fox and Hounds, on Ventura Boulevard in Studio City. I remember being sandwiched in among the crowds in the corner of the bar where the Liverpool fans were congregated. The other side of the bar was where the AC Milan fans were standing.

We were distraught watching the scenes unfold on the TV above the bar in front of us. At half-time we walked out the back door to the parking lot and many a disgruntled Liverpool fan lit a cigarette. The smoke, like the gloom surrounding the game, engulfed us all. Everyone looked like their favourite pet just got put to sleep.

Yet somehow – and to this day I still don't know why – I was positive. I told them all this wasn't that bad and there was a whole second half of football to be played. In between the inhales around me, I enthused that we shouldn't give up, because you never know. I had a strange belief that we would find a way to come back. They looked at me like I was slightly unhinged.

One of the benefits of having no idea just how big a game this was is that I wasn't overly emotional. I really didn't know enough about the sport and the players on each team to know just how inferior Liverpool were and how they had no right whatsoever to think they could come back against such a strong Milan team, especially from 3-0 down. I saw two teams playing a game that was only half-over and somehow believed all was not lost.

I can still smell the beer that splashed and spilled all over us after that first goal went in. There was hope. And when there's hope, everyone starts to believe.

The second goal went in and there was a huge shift in energy from Milan supporters to Liverpool supporters in the bar. They looked like they had just got punched in the gut and glared at the screen hoping that somehow everything would make sense.

The score went to 3-3 and we proceeded to go bananas. We screamed, we yelled, we high-fived, I jumped up and down. The rush was incredible. I remember peering over at the Milan fans. They looked incredulous. They couldn't understand what had just happened.

After the final whistle, the Liverpool fans erupted. Some fans were crying. We went back to Brye's place after the game finished and it was only about three o'clock in the afternoon. We lay down on the bed and watched Sky Sports News showing live reactions after the game. It was incredible. I had never felt anything like it. This was my first and only season of being a Liverpool fan and it was great.

In the years that followed I religiously watched Liverpool, and as much football as I could. I graduated college in 2007 and began my working life. Brye and I broke up around the same time, but my love of Liverpool never faltered and I will forever be grateful to him for having introduced something to me that would change my life forever.

But I again felt alone. I was 6,000 miles from the actual home of the football team I loved and had almost no one to share that passion with. None of my close friends were interested and my work colleagues were much more into American sports. I only ever heard pathetic criticisms and was teased for my love of something that was still seen as very much an outside sport in the US.

I almost always watched games by myself at home. With the games being on so early in the day (eight hours behind the UK), it was not really practical to watch them at a bar. And since LA is so big, having to drive to a bar that shows the game was always difficult anyway. The occasional Champions League game aside, I watched the majority of football in my house, often delayed after recording it on the DVR.

It would have been nice to talk to other people who loved the game and the club as much as I did. Instead it was just me, sitting alone in my pyjamas, eating a burrito and watching this football club that at once felt so familiar yet couldn't be more foreign.

In 2008, I finally got the chance to see Liverpool in the flesh. I planned a two-week trip to the UK, partially to explore potential work options as it had always been my dream to live there, but also to visit friends, and most importantly, to see my team play.

I paid a ridiculous amount of money to secure a ticket to the game they played against Chelsea at Stamford Bridge at the end of October. It was brilliant. The game was on a Sunday and I remember getting the Tube to the ground. I was in complete awe. Seeing the fans milling around and walking up to the stadium, the cops on horses (I still can't believe that's a real thing), and the rumbling din of football conversation all around me. It was genuinely a dream come true.

Not knowing what to expect and being there on my own, I wore a grey T-shirt rather than a Liverpool top, just to be on the safe side. I was in the away end on the second level, just behind the goal. I had a camera and settled into my seat, taking loads of pictures.

Very early in the match, Alonso struck a sweet shot and scored in the goal I was sitting behind. I was ecstatic. I never thought we would hold out long enough to win, but we did, 1-0, simultaneously breaking Chelsea's 86-game home unbeaten record. I couldn't believe my luck.

So this is what people in England get to experience so often. I paid a small fortune for my ticket (as well as my plane ticket and hotel rooms) and would happily do the same again. It was one of the best experiences of my life.

The following year I ended up moving to New York. The first weekend I was in NYC I went to the Liverpool supporters' club at the 11th Street Bar in Manhattan's East Village. We played West Ham away and won 3-2. I met a nice group of guys there and became friends with them. One of them, James, became my boyfriend, whom I have been with ever since.

After spending years watching football matches at home in my pyjamas, things changed when I got to NY. For one, there was a place where loads of Liverpool fans gathered for every game, crazed fans just like me. And alcohol was included, even at 7am.

Suddenly I had people to share my love of the game with. It was wonderful. We watched games, sang songs, drank lots and lots of beers and would celebrate and commiserate as one. I was no longer alone. Especially because I found someone to share my life with who also loved the same team I did.

My first season as a Liverpool fan was not an accurate representation of what following this club would be like. The fortunes of the club since I moved to NYC have swung from dire to exquisite, culminating in the thrilling end to the 2013/14 season. But I am here for the long haul, and as down as I can get watching the team I get the equal and opposite amount of joy as well. More importantly, without this football club I would have never met my amazing boyfriend, met some of my most cherished friends and had some of the greatest moments of my life.

In May of this year James and I had planned a trip to Madrid for our friends' wedding. I was insistent on including a trip to the UK to visit his family (who live in Nottingham) as well as seeing a Liverpool game at Anfield, something I had yet to do up until that point. A decade after my journey with Liverpool began, I was lucky enough to see them play at Anfield as we managed to get tickets for the last game of the season, against Newcastle.

My first game at Anfield also included Liverpool's best chance of winning the title since they last won it in 1990. Unfortunately for us, it was Manchester City who won the title that day. But we didn't let that disappointment bring us down. We had a brilliant day and night in the city, where I got to see many new friends, some of whom I had met previously in New York and others whom I conversed with on social media and was meeting in the flesh for the first time.

Despite the fact I was born 6,000 miles away and had never seen Anfield until I was 30 years old, this club feels like home. And as I sit in my apartment in New York and watch Liverpool fall at the hurdle that is Basel in the Champions League, I am reminded about how I used to feel so alone in my love for this football club.

But there's a lot to be said about a sports team that has the power to bring people from differing backgrounds, cultures and birthplaces together. It might sound cheesy, but the anthem is true. When it comes to Liverpool Football Club, you'll truly never walk alone. And as long as I have this football team, I know I never will.

14 December 2014, Manchester United 3 Liverpool 0

I didn't want to get up. The alarm clock went and I didn't want to get up. This is not normal matchday behaviour for me. Even if I'm shattered, or cold, or both, I get out of bed with pep running through my bones. The match awaits, there's no time to waste.

But this time around, I didn't want to get up. I wanted the alarm to shut the fuck up and let me get back to sleep.

Being a Liverpool fan you go into every game with hope. You might be playing shite and the opposition may be in decent form, but you always believe the Reds can get a result. We're Liverpool for fuck's sake, of course we can win. But I didn't feel like that when the alarm went off on this icy December morning. I knew only heartbreak awaited. I didn't want to get up.

Even in the car with a few lads from the supporters' club, I felt a deep sense of dread. We were talking up our chances, the optimism based largely on rumours from the previous night that Brendan was going to change the system in order to give us more attacking threat. The keeper was changing too, with Brad Jones coming in for Simon Mignolet. OK, Jones is shit, but at least it was a bold move. Anything to end this never-ending sense of despair that had by now drained me of hope. All hope.

But it was no good, I knew we were going to lose. And to them. Christ, that was really going to sting. I'd been at Old Trafford last season when we won 3-0. We were fucking awesome and that match remains my favourite ever away. To go there and play them off the park, well … it doesn't get any sweeter than that.

Our end was like one long party, lads bouncing all around me, me bouncing higher than everyone else, staring straight at the dumbfounded Mancs and giving it loads, 'Po-etry in mo-tion, tr-la, la, la, la la, Po-etry in mo-tion, tr-la, la, la, la la!'

I didn't know then that the next time I travelled to Old Trafford it would be to see a definite defeat. I felt pig sick all the way to Salford.

And so it was – a defeat. In fairness, we played pretty well in Brendan's funky new 3-4-2-1 formation and had it not been for our poor finishing and David de Gea being brilliant for them, we could easily have drawn. Or won. Well perhaps not won given the crap performance Jones put in. He's a professional goalkeeper apparently.

Leaving Castle Grayskull I didn't feel as bad as I had in the morning; there were some definite green shoots there. Oh and I bumped into Martin Fitz in the concourse before kick-off. Which was nice.

SN

17 December 2014, Bournemouth 1 Liverpool 3

'Don't get me started on 'Strange Town''

By Karl Coppack

So we're in the quarter-finals of the League Cup and we're playing a side we can beat. Even us. And we're fairly awful at the moment. There's another reason why I'm happy to be here. AFC Bournemouth is a new ground for me and is my second in as many weeks. Dean Court, and it *is* Dean Court (not whatever some sponsor has chosen to temporarily call it), follows Leicester City's ground (not actually Filbert Street but it remains so to these tired eyes) as another tick in the 'Grounds Done' column.

It's lovely, too. Four stands of almost equal height with the corners not filled in. My favourite type of stadia, in fact. Tonight it will house just over 11,000, with the Liverpool supporters running alongside the side of the pitch in the East Stand. Along with Brunton Park and Griffin Park it's already a hit with me.

But the day does not begin here. It begins with a lorry on the North Circular. I'm driving from my flat to Dev's in Hackney. Dev has recovered from his hangover (see Sunderland match) and has probably fought off a few since, it being the festive season. There are only two of us today as Tony has no holiday left while Si is volunteering for a charity and got his dates mixed up. But we're meeting Mick, an exiled Wirralite, later, along with our mate Ben.

The lads are few on the ground tonight as many are prioritising Arsenal on Sunday and using that fixture as a chance to have a pre-Christmas gutful. I won't be there – I'm working on Sunday – so this is my chance to cross off a ground and see the Reds before the end of the year. But I can't do that while there's a lorry in the way. He's playing 'hide the Nissan' and won't let me pass. As I try to change lanes, so does he. He too leads down the North Circular, through the A1 and on to Highgate and the Seven Sisters Road. For a brief, surreal moment I wonder if he's giving me a personal motorcade.

And 2pm becomes 2.15pm becomes 2.30pm.

Dev has his own problems. His wife has somehow contrived to leave the car window open all night and a storm has saturated the driver's seat. He will spend the journey sitting on a towel with a wet arse. I think he's relieved when I turn up late as a few droplets may have evaporated in that time. After all, you don't really want to go to a night game in December with a wet arse.

We set off. I expect him to take the Euston Road followed by the A40, the M25 and M3 but am surprised when he heads to the North Circular. Yep, he's chosen the same route I've just taken. He could have just picked me up at the bottom of my road. But it's a matchday and I'm with my mate and this is what the day is about, so we join in that curiously male bonding ritual of shouting at traffic and singing loudly to his MP3 player. As we approach Hangar Lane I frown at him as a Girls Aloud song comes on. He has his eyes on the road but notices my silence. 'It came free with something.' I let it slide. I'm the guest here.

This is often the best part of a matchday. Sitting in traffic and talking shite with your mates. Thanks to social media and smartphones I can also bring in other people if we seek clarification on some points. Later today we will discuss Lucas Leiva goals. I'm fairly sure he scored in the 4-4 European Cup game against Chelsea but Dev can't picture it. This leads me to wonder if Ryan Babel claimed it. A few keystrokes later and we know the answer. He scored with a deflection.

We think that, between us, we have seen every Lucas Leiva goal in the flesh. This leads to further discussion. Important male stuff.

I've always liked Bournemouth but am not so keen on the weather. It's hammering down and I've brought a hoodless coat. The windscreen wipers are on their highest setting and the constant stop-start motion on the M3 isn't helping. All in all it takes over three hours, door to door.

One thing we don't discuss is team news. Much of it is already known. Liverpool are starting with three at the back with two defensive midfielders, no strikers and Brad Jones, as revealed on Twitter last night. Our approach seems to be to create chances but have no one to finish them off. Mario Balotelli is out too and I have more chance of making the starting XI than Fabio Borini. We could be resting people for the Arsenal game but I'm not sure what represents the first team and which the squad these days.

I'm looking forward to seeing Lazar Markovic, though. I like players who run with the ball at their feet. I'm yet to see him in the flesh so this is a good thing. We park up and go meet Mick. He's with another Mick, our mate Andy's uncle (see Real Madrid away), and has holed up in a curry house near Boscombe. I'm starving but am in two minds. See, I don't always get on with curries. I'm strictly an onion bhaji and biryani man but even that mild strength can wipe me out for a couple of days.

It's a mystery to me just how many people want to actively fight their meal rather than enjoy it. Food shouldn't be a war of attrition, and there's absolutely no way you should go to a football match with spices and ghee in your guts. I fight the urge to find a chippy and settle down to a king prawn biryani. Pleasingly, there's little sauce on it so I'm fine for a bit. I really should admit defeat with curries, though. I've no idea why I stick with them.

So to the match. I like Raheem Sterling's haircut, our kit and the fact we've scored. Bournemouth dropped six players, which is strange as they'd be a match for us with a strong team. I've been following the Championship this season and they're currently league leaders. They've ex-Blue Dan Gosling and former Stoke and Southampton keeper Artur Boruc in goal, so they've got some pedigree. I don't know why they've gone in so weak. Haven't they been watching us?

Today's gripe: Liverpool don't seem to tackle anymore. We press but seldom get a foot in. Our entire defensive strategy seems to revolve around hoping the opposition give the ball away. Fortunately, Bournemouth do. A lot. We deserve our lead.

There are some larks at half-time. Like most clubs, Bournemouth grant requests from the crowd and acknowledge birthdays etc. But they also have a 'crossbar challenge' competition, where locals win a prize if they can hit the bar from the 18-yard line. Three lads, all Bournemouth fans, have a go to various 'oohs' and 'aahs' as they narrowly miss the bar or are miles out. The away end isn't really interested and are either on the concourse or vainly trying to find a signal on their phones.

So, we come to the last contestant. The link man with the microphone takes over:

'And now, a Liverpool fan!'

Boos from the home fans. A collective raised head from our section.

'Think you can do it?'

'Yeah, I think so.'

'That doesn't sound like a Liverpool accent. Where are you from?'

'Bournemouth.'

Oh, they don't like that. The lads in the North Stand give us a lively rendition of 'we support our local team'. We give him a round of applause. There's a little war to be had here.

'Off you go, then.'

He doesn't take a run-up. He offers little in the way of backlift. He simply belts the ball without looking up. It thumps the middle of the crossbar. He could not have hit it any sweeter. Our end celebrates for the third time of the night.

I love moments like that. Sometimes fate can be your friend.

After the game we head back to the car and bump into Ste, another mate. It always amazes me how you see the same people at the match and never say hello to them for years. There's a lad in front of me tonight who seems to be following me around the country. I always seem to be sat directly behind him. I wonder if he was the lorry driver from earlier. Weird.

Same with bumping into Ste now. There are two to three thousand Liverpool fans here tonight and I knew he'd be there, and I was in absolutely no doubt that I'd see him. Nothing arranged, you understand, just knew I'd run into him. And, yes, there he is – strolling over the iron bridge on the way back into town.

I had something similar in 2003 when we played Crystal Palace in the third round of the FA Cup at Selhurst Park. Two of my closest mates had managed to get tickets and I was very late in getting mine as I was in two minds about going. I'd just started seeing a girl and was invited to meet her parents at her birthday lunch a few hours before kick-off. I went along and smiled and ate with my mouth closed but I was aware that I wouldn't be able to see Matt and Ben before kick-off and they both had to shoot off at the final whistle.

I left when it was polite to and legged it to the ground. No phone reception then so I grimaced at the lost opportunity of a pint and a chat. I got to my seat with a cob on. Matt and Ben were standing next to me. We'd bought our tickets from different sources. We couldn't have planned it better. Strange.

The journey home is much simpler and we manage it in two hours. To pass the time we discuss the veracity of The Jam's lyrics as their compilation album *Snap* noisily fills the car. First up is 'A Bomb In Wardour Street'. Strictly speaking that's 'A' as in 'atomic' but presumably that didn't scan too well.

Our first bone of contention is the title itself. Atomic bombs don't explode at ground level, so to claim that it is centralised in one Soho street is bogus at best. But no, the lads are adamant that they are standing 'on the Vortex floor' – this being a 1970s punk club in the named thoroughfare.

This place is hardy indeed as it's somehow managed to survive the bomb. It also contains '15 geezers' who have the narrator's girlfriend 'pinned to the door'. Not only have they too survived but they've been overcome with a potent sexual desire. I had no idea atomic warfare had such aphrodisiacal qualities.

Then there's their classic 'Down in the Tube Station at Midnight' from the same album, *All Mod Cons*. Jesus. The song tells of a gruesome mugging of a man who has bought a takeaway curry to take home to his wife who has a bottle of wine ready. It's a fantastic song but comes with some unusual assertions.

Firstly, this man has chosen to buy his curry *before* starting his Tube journey. Who would do that? How hot, in terms of temperature rather than spiciness, is this curry going to be once he's a) travelled on the Tube and b) walked home upon arrival at his station? Wouldn't it make more sense to buy the food once you're there so he and his poor wife can enjoy something better than a lukewarm ruby?

I suppose it's midnight and he may not have a nice one near to hand, but all the same. Anyway, he gets mugged and while he's getting several shades kicked out of him he becomes concerned as to his wife's safety as 'they took the keys and she'll think it's me'. Sorry? How will they know where he lives? Are they just trying doors until they get lucky? Surely he hasn't written his address on the fob. He can't be that stupid. Even if he did, the muggers aren't going to visit the house of their victim after he's been assaulted and the police have been called.

But then there comes the most damning line of all. I still wince every time I hear it, 'The wine will be flat and the curry's gone cold.'

I mean, really.

Well, the curry will already be cold as the idiot has elected to buy it miles away from his house and reheating it might cause some sort of health scare, but 'the wine will be flat'? Flat? He's drinking sparkling wine with a curry? Wine with a curry is bad enough, but sparkling wine?

Given my own curry confession earlier you can guess how that would sit with me. I'm even worse with sparkling wine. It's putrid stuff. This isn't a mugging; this is a cultural punishment and I'm firmly with the thugs on this one.

The things you discuss on long journeys. Don't get me started on 'Strange Town'. Been there three weeks and he still hasn't settled?

And so home and to bed. It's just after 1am and I have an all-day meeting starting at 10am the next day. I know I won't sleep either thanks to that curry but the Reds won and another ground is scratched off. It'll be my last one this season unless we get a lower league team in the cup.

I won't be going to Chelsea, who we've predictably drawn in the semis. I think every Liverpool fan has been there at least a dozen times by now and I can't stand that place.

'I imagine he still has nightmares of the 83rd minute and beyond'

By Melissa Reddy

L ook left: 5-1. Look right: 5-1. Even the EverPool burger shack is decorated with talk of the scoreline from 8 February 2014. What of the Family Park? No difference. There are vivid re-enactments of Martin Skrtel's header and shirt-over-head celebration in the single-digit, dull weather conditions. Luis Suarez gets a mention, too. He always gets a mention. Yes, Arsenal are back in L4 on this bitter December day, and it's now impossible to speak of the north Londoners without referencing that mentally magnificent thrashing at Anfield last season. For all the games to miss in 2013/14; I'm still ugly crying.

I annoyingly, despite enjoying the opportunity to indulge in some sunshine and sea, had to fly back to South Africa to fetch my work permit. If you've ever had to go through such a process, especially to enter the United Kingdom, you'll have an understanding of how hopeless the Gunners felt as they were mocked by Liverpool's mesmerising attacking aggression in that match. To summarise the work permit procedure: you fill in countless forms and stack up several supporting documents to show why you should be allowed the right to ply your trade in the country. You take tests, both health and skill-related, to further enhance your odds of acceptance. You cough up money that you don't really have to pay for something you aren't really guaranteed. And you wait. Wonder. And wait. In my case, you also miss the best football match of the season.

Why did I endure this self-inflicted torture? Well, Liverpool Football Club is the easy and honest answer. For as long as Raheem Sterling has existed I've been tied to the Reds. But not for any geographical or paternal reason, so why then? Well you can blame much of it on John Barnes and how he drew defenders in only to gleefully and gracefully wave them bye-bye while gliding away. His cerebral brilliance and effortless application was utterly enchanting. My friends were playing with Miami Barbie while I was playing the role of 'Digger' on an imaginary pitch.

Robbie Fowler is at fault too, toying with the opposition in his playground and scoring for fun. Have you seen someone enjoy themselves so much in four minutes and 33 seconds? Hi again, Arsenal.

As a South African, my first experiences of English football were via the limited highlights packages on television. In the early 1990s we'd get a summary of top-flight games and the treat of the FA Cup Final, live. As the years rolled on the exposure expanded, and suddenly I could teleport myself from my couch to Premier League stadiums.

My affinity to Liverpool emerged around the age of eight, and it was a choice in opposition to the rest of my household. My dad – bless him – supports Manchester United, and my two younger brothers brainlessly followed suit. Of all teams, them. Why them? Well, during the days of apartheid Gary Bailey bravely ignored the rules on zero integration to coach at my father's school and that was him sold on being a Red Devil. Coming from a politically charged, freedom-fighting family I understand his decision, no matter how much it does my head in.

My granddad and uncle, meanwhile, threw their weight behind Tottenham – inspired, in part, by their status as one of the first English sides to hand a debut to a black player (William Tull in 1909) and the stellar, victorious European Cup Winners' Cup squad which toured South Africa in 1963.

My affiliation towards the Merseysiders, as you can ascertain, was thus self-harnessed under conditions of constant and cunning jibes from my relatives. My love for the club grew just as I did. I taught myself everything: the rules of the game, the history of the side, the chants…I read and researched and lived Liverpool. It was my release, but also my addiction.

I remember standing on the coffee table much to my mom's irritation when Michael Owen broke through against Argentina in 1998. It sounds stupid now, but it felt like me urging the 18-year-old on as he finished expertly in that World Cup last-16 clash.

We're no longer allowed to say it out loud but, holy hell, Owen was some player for us. As I watch Arsene Wenger get off the team coach in his easy-zip Puma coat, I imagine he still has nightmares of the 83rd minute and beyond of that 2001 FA Cup Final. He could finish until he was finished, Owen. And God, how we miss those decisive Sami Hyypiä interventions, too.

Liverpool became part of my routine. I never missed a game, a book, an article. DVDs, magazines, scarves and such formed part of a shrine in my bedroom, which was practically wallpapered with articles on Steven Gerrard. My friends were annoyed by my religious intake of the club, and I'm sure they still are even though I'm no longer in the country. I'd miss lunches, parties, launches and just about anything if it clashed with the fixture list. By the time I was in high school I wanted to either be a sport reporter or the Minister of Foreign Affairs.

Don't judge me, I was (still am) a history nerd and politics fascinated me for a short spell. After university and odd jobs of PR and the like, I was convinced: I had to be a journalist. Fast forward and I've been a football writer/editor/broadcaster/analyst for eight years now.

In September 2013 I finally made the trip to Anfield during a working holiday, and Daniel Sturridge headed in the winner against United on his birthday to hand me an unforgettable gift. After that splendid 1-0 victory, which began with a stirring Bill Shankly mosaic to salute what would have been the great man's 100th birthday, I was a sponge to the sights and sounds of the city centre. I decided it was where I needed to be and so I embraced the unconventional and set off on a bold, exciting course (which unfortunately consisted of a lot of pain-in-my-arse admin). Two months later I was trading in my dream car and trading continents while waiting for the final bit of my work permit to be pushed through.

I left everything behind for LFC.

So this Arsenal game. Pre-stuffing my face with Christmas turkey and cranberry sauce, it marks a year of me living exactly where I want to be, doing exactly what I want to be doing. Here I am now, just outside the club shop entrance waiting for a rare treat – a visit off a mate from South Africa. Daniel, an Arsenal supporter whom I've known and worked with since 2007, was visiting family in London and travelled to be in the away end for the encounter. He admitted it felt like someone had kicked his 'dingley-danglies' consistently for 90 minutes during the 5-1, in between our moans about the depressing weather (SA basks in glorious sunshine in December) and the ridiculous rand–pound exchange rate. It was good to have a piece of home during the festive period, even if it was from behind enemy lines.

I usher him towards the away fans' entrance and pace towards turnstile V to take my seat in the Main Stand. It is still weird experiencing a game purely as a supporter every so often as I've spent the last eight years working on matches. It's markedly different to being in the press box, where emotion is evil and your reactions are automatically robotic.

I start to gather my thoughts as the players warm up. What am I expecting? I rewind to Brendan Rodgers's pre-match presser, which was a fiery four-minutes-30-seconds exchange and, as bizarre as it may sound, I derive some confidence from his cold shoulder.

Being fortunate enough to interview the manager and engage in conversations about a variety of subjects, I've gained insight that I would have never imagined possible while in South Africa. That assertive show from the gaffer, bucking his usual trend of playing the good cop, told me that he was being bold again. Brave again. While listening to fans behind me dissect the disadvantages of Brad Jones and Simon Mignolet, I figure it to be a turning point and predict the aggression will rub off on the team. Lazar Markovic, Raheem Sterling, Adam Lallana and Phil Coutinho prove me right. Liverpool are on the front foot. This makes me happy. Very happy. They pour forward so fluidly and fluently that 'defensive screen' Mathieu Flamini looks as moronic as Harry and Marv in *Home Alone*. 'Shit' was the succinct text I received from my mate. He had no fear before 4pm but he was certainly shitting himself during our swarms of attacks.

Then Coutinho happens. Clever, creative, calculating. I would bathe in the Brazilian's through balls and flicks if I could. Drink his sharp turns every morning instead of coffee. Sturridge told me Coutinho makes his job easier, Mario Balotelli sings the 'Coutini-oh-oh-oh' song, Suarez said he is the difference. Off the pitch he is shy and reserved and so well mannered, always stopping to sign autographs or agree to picture requests.

But before I can send a smug message back to my mate, or even blink, Arsenal are level. Defensive shambles strikes again. There football goes, taking me from ecstasy to agony in a matter of seconds. It's mad how 11 men running around after a ball can alter your mood, make your day or ruin your weekend. It's mental but marvellous that you get to share these conflicting emotions with millions worldwide.

I remember when Andrey Arshavin ruined my Tuesday night and my entire week. In my cranky state I cancelled plans and kept my headphones on for a good few days in the office to swerve the sea of mockery. And here is Olivier Giroud on 64 minutes, trying to take me back to that unhappy place. Arsenal didn't deserve to be level, let alone 2-1 up.

But seven minutes in to stoppage time, there's that switch again. This time from agony to ecstasy as Skrtel's head gets the better of the Gunners again. It's 2-2.

GET IN!

In the whirlwind of emotion Fabio Borini's two yellow cards are a distant memory. I hug the women of 50-plus sitting next to me, and who spent much of the game swooning over Lallana's ability to shift out of tight spaces still in possession. High-fives go around with all those in close proximity.

It's brilliant how you don't need to know someone's name or story to share in this kind of exhilaration. Whenever I'm at the stadium, I take it all in because I'm still in disbelief that I'm at Anfield for every home game – that what I imagined 20 years ago is now an actuality. I love interacting with supporters to assess how their opinions differ to mine. I also spend time chatting with the stewards to hear of their experiences, predications and just about anything else. It intrigues me to know how the game has been played from all these different points of view.

Liverpudlians are such an amazing bunch – incredibly friendly and welcoming. From my first day in the city to now, I have been shown such warmth and friendship on Merseyside. It's that old idea of 'it's not where you are, but who you're with that counts' and I'm blessed to be in such fine company. Do I miss my friends and family back home? Of course. But Liverpool has gifted me more friends and another family.

Christmas is the hardest time of year to be separated from loved ones, and while I longingly throwback to festive cocktails by the pool and my aunt's fantastic trifle I'm made up that I'll be spending a second 25 December in Liverpool.

Post-match, my mate asks me what it will be like. 'Lots of mulled wine, board games, bad jokes and brilliant people,' I reply. I must confess, I get really caught up in all the elaborate decorations and extra effort that's put into Christmas over here. In South Africa it's the exception rather than the rule that houses boast lights and such outside. There's the standard Christmas tree and interior decorations, but here – wow!

Walking in the city centre with my mate, who cannot believe Arsenal departed Anfield with a draw, and even he is enchanted by the music and holographic projection outside Marks & Spencer. I leave him at Lime Street and begin the short walk home. The lads in front of me are discussing Liverpool's lack of team spirit before delving into the dimensions of Rodgers's personality. It's weird for me to be on the inside and outside. I often hear or read things that are as off as that Iago Aspas corner, especially when the cuckoo land of the transfer window comes around.

For the benefit of those lads on the steps, there is great camaraderie at Liverpool, not only between the players but also the staff. Skrtel, for instance, is planning his 30th birthday party and has invited everyone that works at Melwood – from the kitchen crew to those at reception – to his evening out. The team has also bought Christmas presents for the kids of all staff and they've paid for a special lunch for everyone at the training complex.

Rodgers is always working, too. Always. From 7am to 7pm, and even when he leaves to go home, he never stops. Watching, plotting, fidgeting, fixing…you don't have to agree with his team selections but he is a great manager and a great man. When one of the club journalists had a kidney operation in the summer, the manager called him before the surgery to offer his support and have a general conversation. Dean Furman, who Rodgers coached in Chelsea's youth team, has been given the armband for South Africa and the boss requested that I send his best wishes to the midfielder. He pays attention, he deals in the details. I don't always agree with him but I appreciate that the club I love has a good character in charge, who's committed to doing the best for them.

Gerrard passes up his seat on the plane if someone else needs it. Markovic refused to travel first-class while the pregnant player liaison representative was in economy. He insisted she have his seat. I'm proud that beneath the tra-la-la-la-la-ing or torture of an unfavourable result, these are the kind of people that I'm so passionately entwined to.

Let me stop being mushy and get back to the match. The Reds went in to last Christmas as league leaders, now we'll be under the mistletoe kissing tenth spot. Markovic is starting to truly dazzle, Coutinho is running games, Lallana's balance is becoming more breathtaking, Mamadou Sakho gets his chance to state his case, Sterling's movement is encouraging, the system is working, the swagger is back…a game we should have won ends 2-2, but there's a confidence and familiarity about this side now.

League position aside, competing with Europe's elite or not, and even through those face-rubbing days under you-know-who, it's never a bad time to be a Liverpool supporter because we're in such great company.

All I want for Christmas is this.

26 December 2014, Burnley 0 Liverpool 1

It can't be fair to have to work on Christmas Day. Having to say goodbye to your kids on Christmas Eve and not see them until late on Boxing Day, and even then only if you're lucky to have a local game. People are quick to lambast players with their pampered lifestyles and access to strong hair products, but no one thinks of the sacrifices they make for us, the public, year in, year out.

Tough.

I love Boxing Day games. Either red-eyed meetings with your mates if you're going or sat on a couch with the equivalent of a Kerry Katona buffet inside you – it's a great way to say goodbye to Christmas. All goodwill ends and we get to shout at people we don't know again. Marvellous.

You may have forgotten this game. If so, it was the one where we replaced Brad Jones with Simon Mignolet after 16 minutes and Philippe Coutinho and Raheem Sterling combined for a rare moment of verve to secure both a win and a clean sheet. Other than that it was grim.

There's a disconnect in our support when Liverpool win. Some think they've got one over on the group who endlessly criticise, while the glass-half-empty lads point out that it's against a Burnley side desperate to be put out of their misery. I'm somewhere in between. I like it when we win, but I also recognise that this had all the beauty of a lettuce exhibition. In the rain. On a Tuesday. With Piers Morgan in attendance.

For the record I am too full of cheese, mini bhajis, gin, lager, red cabbage, pickled onions and cake to care. It's also snowing outside. It's beautiful but some of us have to drive in the morning. I'd rather do that with three points, so I'm smiling at least. Although that could be wind.

KC

29 December 2014, Liverpool 4 Swansea 1

I really wanted to go to this one. Not because we were playing Swansea, or because it was our last game of 2014, or because I hadn't been to Anfield since the draw with Basel. No, I really wanted to go because for the first time in ages I had a reason to buy the programme.

There's a fella who sells them outside Stanley Park, where the coaches park up, and I used to give him £3 for one as a matter of course for years. Regardless of who we were playing, I brought a programme. Simple. It was part of the ritual.

And then I stopped, instantly. Well I say instantly, it was actually after seeing a pile of them at my parents' house and realising I hadn't looked at any in ages, and had no desire to do so. Don't get me wrong, there are some absolute classics in there that I wouldn't dare chuck out, but ultimately they've become dust collectors.

But I would've got the one for this game. Why? Because I wrote a piece for it. Yes, little old me, in the official Liverpool matchday programme. To say I'm chuffed would be an understatement.

I have Simon Hughes to thank. He works on the programme and e-mailed me at the start of the month to see if I wanted to write something for the Swansea fixture. Given it was the last of the year, perhaps a review. I immediately said yes and got to work. And then about halfway through I stopped having done 500 words on how crap it's been being a Red during the past few months. No fan wants to read that on their way to the ground. So instead I did a piece on Steven Gerrard, paying tribute to the captain and calling on all fans to cherish him as, more than likely, 2015 will be the final calendar year in which he plays for the club.

I was happy with it. What a massive pain in the balls, then, that Gerrard didn't start this game.

At least we won. And some win it was, too. Our best performance since Tottenham away. Adam Lallana scored twice – the first slightly fortunate, the second utterly brilliant – while Alberto Moreno got the opener (he only scores when we play well, it transpires) and Jonjo Shelvey the last with a funny own goal.

It was cracking stuff. I was gutted to have missed it but had no choice because of work. The bastards.

Simon's sending me a copy of the programme. Another one for the pile, and another one that isn't going anywhere.

SN

1 January 2015, Liverpool 2 Leicester 2

'Once you've got it, you can't un-get it'

By Paul Tomkins

Filing down Oakfield Road in the driving rain, darkness descending; drifting away from another underwhelming home encounter with Leicester City – a pattern that stretches back decades. Festive lights reflect on the pavement, at odds with the glum mood. Two points thrown away. Happy New Year indeed.

I would be making the exact same journey home as the away fans: I've been living in Leicester since 1999. It's not the most interesting place in the country but it's second-to-none when it comes to finding hunchbacked kings under car parks.

Going to the game used to feel like my raison d'etre, but then real life got in the way. Before you have a family, face mortality with a parent dying, and experience challenges like ill health and unemployment, football seems vital.

You build it up in your mind, to sometimes ludicrous levels. In many ways it's up to you how important you make it, as long as you don't expect everyone else to feel the same way.

At times we are all fanatics, but it becomes less sustainable with age. It can become something we hold tighter to in tough times, but often it's something that has to give.

Twenty years ago I couldn't imagine life without going to the game, but then again I wasn't middle-aged and wearied by Premier League hype, or the realisation of just how closely money and success correlate (something that has admittedly become far more pronounced since Roman Abramovich bought Chelsea) and the competitive balance of the league skewed towards the richest. Back then I wasn't older than all of the players, or old enough to be the father of half of them. I'm even older than the manager now. You stop idolising the stars, start merely respecting them.

New Year's Day represented another chance to go to Anfield. I still go when I can but it's no longer the be-all and end-all of my existence. Writing about the club for a living (which led to invitations from Rafa Benítez to spend time at Melwood and from John Henry to meet for lunch, among many other things) has in some ways left me jaded. I got to see behind the curtain, demystifying the club in the process. And for my troubles I've encountered a lot of hate and rage, and experienced just about every argument imaginable about football to the point where I can see how it goes round in circles. The magic has worn off somewhat, although every few years there's something that brings back the childlike sense of wonder.

And there have been plenty of players worth paying to see. The best of these – Steven Gerrard – scored two expertly-taken penalties in this strange, hungover kind of game. The Leicester supporters, like those of every other club, mocked the Liverpool captain for happening to fall over in a big game that had nothing to do with them (which, to me, is like distilling Zidane's career down to a headbutt), but even putting the Reds 2-0 up didn't seem to please him. Maybe he knew that his team were not playing well, or perhaps he'd already decided that he was going to announce his departure from the club later in the evening. The first day of 2015, he was now free to speak to other clubs, and, it turned out, he would be doing just that, with a move to America set for the summer.

Despite those two penalties Leicester fought back for a deserved draw, but the bigger story, breaking on the way home, was the announcement of the end of an era. There's nothing like the retirement of a player whose fresh-faced debut you witnessed to make you feel old.

Born at the start of the 1970s I knew only of Liverpool success until my late teens, and yet despite some utterly horrible seasons in the past two decades – and no league title – there have also been some quite incredible highs, the like of which fans of most other clubs would feel sated by. Let's face it, no Kopite was blasé about success when Istanbul unfolded, and that, of course, made it all the better.

I've been able to regularly see the calibre of player that fans of most clubs would only witness twice a season. Take Newcastle United, for instance, whose fans dream of winning the League Cup; a trophy they can't get close to lifting despite most other entrants seeing it as an impediment. Leeds United fans look up at the Premier League, their bubble having burst a decade ago; the Icarus of modern English football (they did, however, have the best fish tanks in any football HQ). Nottingham Forest, European champions twice in my lifetime, are nowhere. Liverpool may no longer be the greatest, but they still matter.

We got to see Gerrard play on a weekly basis. For a while he was part of 'the best midfield in the world' with Xabi Alonso and Javier Mascherano. And the club has had so many great strikers. So many, in fact, that Michael Owen, European Footballer of the Year, feels like one of the less remarkable talents. Even now I'd take peak-years Robbie Fowler, Luis Suarez and Fernando Torres (and maybe Daniel Sturridge, too) over Owen at his best.

While my love of Liverpool FC began during a west London childhood (Kenny Dalglish leaping the advertising hoardings at Wembley is, I believe, my earliest football memory) my match-going life began in October 1990, at Anfield, just months after the Reds last won the title. Yes, my timing is impeccable.

My first away game was against Derby, a city in which I briefly studied design. Liverpool ran out 7-1 winners, their biggest league win away from Anfield since 1896. Even though King Kenny had by this point stepped down, the title was still within reach. But this was the end of the empire. For the next three years I went to games at places like Selhurst Park and Craven Cottage to see Paul Stewart amble around uselessly, but also witnessed Fowler bursting on to the scene. A decade later I'd be at Filbert Street – again the Leicester connection – when God scored his last goals for the Reds with a fine hat-trick. Or rather they would have been his last goals had he not made a surprise return to the club when admittedly far past his best.

If I'd been a glory-hunting child who gravitated to Liverpool via a television set and a Panini sticker album (and I was) I also endured the fallow years of the 1990s first-hand. John Barnes had slowed down and widened in girth, Ian Rush was ageing, and a collection of misfits, no-hopers and Weight Watchers rejects paraded around what was once the most feared stadium in the world. The coltish Steve McManaman sprinted around, perhaps out of the fear that some of his team-mates might try and eat him.

Although I've gone to games with a wide variety of people over the years, there are two friends with whom my Liverpool story is inextricably linked. In 1994 I met a fellow Red, Adie, at a football club I played for and began using his dad's season ticket, two years before I got my own. We travelled up to Anfield for every home game, stopping in at his nan's in Litherland to be generously force-fed tea and biscuits, and did most of the aways in the south and the Midlands.

This included Leicester in 1996, when a certain Patrik Berger announced himself on the Premier League scene with two obscene goals, and two equally obscene cheekbones. I left Filbert Street that day thinking I'd seen the next big star, which didn't quite prove to be the case. But it remains a memorable match thanks to a Czech explosion.

In 1997, after a spell as a semi-pro – during which time I still went to all non-Saturday Liverpool games – I joined a new Sunday league team and met another Liverpool fan, Matt. Before long Adie, Matt and I were travelling to games together. Within a few years we'd all be married (not to each other, I hasten to add), and in my case that's what took me to Leicester. By the early 2000s we all had kids. I had recently been diagnosed with M.E., which meant I had to give up my job, and as a result of little money and even less energy, was no longer able to regularly make the pilgrimage up north.

Divorce followed soon after but I stayed in Leicester to regularly see my son, and the day of the week I happened to be assigned was Saturday. He was more important to me than football, which also happened to be something he didn't like very much, partly due to seeing his father come unhinged whilst watching or listening to a game.

It was Matt who gave me a lift to Liverpool on New Year's Day, this time with the third ticket taken by his nine-year-old son Henry, who is already on the books of a top Championship side and has had offers from Premier League academies. We used to discuss the relative merits of Emile Heskey, but now I get to hear about the Machiavellian methods some academies use to intimidate the opposition at under-10 level.

Our lives have changed but in my old season ticket seat I still enjoyed watching the footwork of Philippe Coutinho up close, much in the way that I marvelled at the Baseball Ground 23 years earlier when, just in front of me on the touchline, Barnes took a high pass on his chest with more aplomb than most players took a pass to feet. He stung it dead, tamed in an instant, and Coutinho, while not as effective overall, has some of that skill. I was there to see Liverpool win, of course, but there's plenty of other things to take away.

Back in 1991, as the Reds put seven past Derby just before my 20th birthday, I was still in denial, locked in the belief that Liverpool reigned supreme. Year after year it was 'just a matter of time'. But ever since the mid-90s Liverpool have been unable to get close to the British transfer record; the £35m they paid for Andy Carroll in 2011 only possible because Chelsea were first handing over £50m for Torres. Liverpool had fallen behind the rest of the pack in the 90s and were unable to catch up.

The sale of Torres came shortly after enduring a spell with Roy Hodgson as manager and after the cowboy owners had been forced out of town. Football was now about courtroom battles and roubles raided from the Russian state. In FSG it seemed that Liverpool had found smarter owners who'd transformed the fortunes of the Boston Red Sox, but they were not oligarchs or sheikhs. There would be no magic investment bullet, and anyway, Financial Fair Play was looming. Typically, only after Chelsea and Manchester City had got in under the wire to build their clubs sky-high.

As ever, the timing was all wrong. Liverpool were the best when it didn't pay at all well to be the best; the influx of money to the game coincided with Manchester United's long-overdue success. And by the time the rules were changed to work against billionaire benefactors, two 'unfashionable' clubs had usurped Liverpool as commercial entities, while Manchester United had expanded both Old Trafford and their global empire, and Arsenal had built a money-making stadium without slipping out of the top four. It seemed that Liverpool's shovels were merely for digging their own holes.

When more recent managers were getting slaughtered for not winning the league, I felt I needed a better understanding of why the Reds were falling short. Context is everything. I became obsessed with knowing why Liverpool couldn't compete, despite having good managers and some top players.

In 2010, along with Graeme Riley, I began work on a project called the Transfer Price Index, which after we calculated football-specific inflation (based on every transfer of each season), allowed us to convert all Premier League transfer costs to, say, '2014 money', and make comparisons across the years that were not possible before (football didn't begin in 1992, but it was more practical to focus on the new era when dealing with thousands of data points).

Our studies highlighted many things, plenty of which seemed highly pertinent to Liverpool's plight, things I'd been suspecting since 2005 but for which I only now had the full data.

It showed that, on average, the team with the most expensive XI over all 38 games will finish first; there will be differences from year to year, but that is the overall trend. Equally, the second-most expensive XI will, on average, finish second and the third-most expensive will finish third. This carries on right the way down to mid-table, and since 2004 no team with an average cost lower than £210m – that's the average cost of the XI over 38 games after inflation is applied – has won the league.

In 2009 and 2014, Liverpool's figure was roughly £143m each time. In other words, those sides, despite containing hardly any of the same players after five years, stood at only two-thirds of the minimum cost of what it takes to win the league, and yet on both occasions the Reds ran a richer Manchester club close. As such, both of those seasons were clear cases of overachievement (for the record, the average cost for clubs finishing second is £180m).

While I don't want to kill the romance of the game, once you know these facts it's hard to go back to thinking of football as a pure sport, where the best win; once you've got it, you can't un-get it. Liverpool have to be utterly remarkable to win the league, and what was so refreshing about 2009 and 2014 was that, in different ways, they were almost just that. They would have been league titles won against the odds, not bought. These were unsustainable seasons; marathons run as hard as possible, following which collapse was almost inevitable. To me it was important to appreciate them for what they were and to take the joy from that, rather than expect titles just because of the name 'Liverpool'.

There's another reason I feel jaded as my mid-40s approach, and it happened ten years ago, in 2005. Istanbul – we know it simply by the name of the city – was as good as match-going gets. The drama, the world-class opposition, the exotic location, the overcoming of the steepest odds, the half-time rendition of 'You'll Never Walk Alone', the logic-defying saves, the penalty shootout, Djimi Traore, it had it all. Even though the richest clubs tend to win the cups too, this again proved that the one-off game provides a greater chance of a miracle than the slog of the league.

I was sat with strangers in another part of the Atatürk and after the game my desire was to share in the moment with my two mates – it didn't quite seem complete until, crazed with adrenaline, we'd jumped in celebration upon rendezvousing outside the stadium. All those years spent winning next-to-nothing (and even when we did win something it was mostly the League Cup) were suddenly worth it. All those trips up and down the motorway, stuck on the M6 or looking for an alternate route on the B-roads of North Wales; every home game a journey that took hours, just like every away game. It was all worth it.

In May 2005 I was close to finishing writing my first Liverpool FC book – on the season that was unfolding – and flat broke. Matt, whose company had grown successful and for whom I designed the logo, very generously paid for me to go to Istanbul, and in its way the whole experience felt like another end of an era. Football could never be as good again.

And yet, as with all endings, it was also the start of a new era: I'd finally found a way to make a living after several years spent on benefits. I was no longer a fan but a writer, an analyst.

A few years later I was running my own football site, which introduced me to a whole new Liverpool FC community, young and old, spread far and wide. As I find it harder and harder to get to games, due to the time it takes to recover, I now share my experiences with these people online and only see Matt and Adie a few times each season. I also try to share my experiences on Twitter but this, it must be said, is often like walking up and down the corridors of an insane asylum which unwittingly provokes those most mentally unstable to fling their faecal matter in your direction.

Football is about community, but in different ways to different people. It's about joining together, with friends and family, to share in the spectacle and rejoice, or commiserate, together. This can be before or after the match, in the Sandon or Flat Iron, around the TV in a bar in Singapore or on an online forum. If you care about it, then it means something.

But what it means to you may not be what it means to me.

5 January 2015, AFC Wimbledon 1 Liverpool 2

'It's all getting a bit serious isn't it lads?'

By Sam Long

Selhurst Park is a dump. An eyesore, an absolute dive; windy, drab and dull. The place oozes the 1960s, just like the rest of the Croydon skyline which it protrudes from. It's a location that few players would have dreamt of gracing during their formative years, for there is no glitz or glamour to be seen. Set deep within the suburbs it's a nightmare to get to and, in truth, most would rather get as far away from South Norwood as possible.

Yet what it lacks in accessibility, appearance and prestige it more than makes up for with, well, a Sainsbury's. And a bloody good one at that. Being able to do a spot of pre-match grocery shopping is an added bonus no man should turn his nose up at.

The south London ground may well have been the butt of many a joke during the 1990s, but I was proud to call it home. The location will be remembered as little more than a temporary solution to an older generation of Wimbledon fans who had known the terraces of Plough Lane, but for me the Holmesdale Stand was where I first gazed upon the beautiful game. Only it wasn't an oil painting.

We didn't tickle everyone's fancy. We were direct. We were tough. We had a sprinkling of skill but we played to our strengths. When I hear people label Wimbledon as the 'original Stoke' I realise what utter wankers everyone must have thought we were.

We loved being the little guy capable of ruffling the feathers of those who looked down their beaks at us. It was on such an occasion that I first encountered Liverpool Football Club, and one striker in particular. The era of dominance was over but the once mighty Anfield outfit remained a sizeable scalp.

It was early May 1997 and the Dons' hopes of a sixth-place Premier League finish had stuttered following a run of just one win in six. The Merseysiders, meanwhile, needed all three points to thwart Manchester United's surge towards yet more silverware and keep their own hopes of a maiden title in the modern era alive. Had you told me on that day that they would still be waiting for it to arrive I would have laughed you all the way out of London.

As my two brothers and I climbed the hill towards the ground from Selhurst station, my dad, as ever, ran through the names of the players we were about to see in the flesh. Steve McManaman, Stan Collymore, Jamie Redknapp and Patrik Berger, the Czech magician who represented the calibre of signing outside the realms of possibility for us. But the man I yearned to witness above all others was Robbie Fowler, but he was suspended. Sod's law.

Without the hometown hero leading the visitors' line, Roy Evans's boys wilted. Headers (what else?) from Jason Euell and Dean Holdsworth put us in a comfortable position, which proved to be just about enough, despite a late rally.

Yet the consolation goal is the one that will always be remembered. For a 17-year-old Michael Owen needed just a matter of minutes to tuck his debut Premier League strike past a helpless Neil Sullivan. (Let's not allow the fact that we were a man light because our criminally-overlooked centre-back Chris Perry had picked up a knock get in the way of a good story, eh?)

The teenager's pace was electric. His finish calm and composed. I was left mesmerised, and a little over a year later he would enthral the entire globe with a stunning individual goal against Argentina in St Etienne.

During the 1997/98 campaign, when Liverpool returned to Selhurst, Owen rescued a point from the penalty spot after Marcus Gayle's opener. But in December of 1998 the underdogs bit once again following Robbie Earle's strike, which secured a 1-0 victory at 'our place' (I featured alongside the Jamaica international's son Otis during a summer community football camp). Meanwhile, routine victory after routine victory, along with the odd draw, was claimed by Liverpool in front of the safety blanket of the Kop.

But despite our diminishing stature Wimbledon had Liverpool's number, and it doesn't take a genius to pinpoint the day when the Scousers' digits were noted down by the boys in royal blue. The finest moment in Wimbledon's history; the 1988 FA Cup Final.

Billed as one of the biggest shocks in the competition's history, there were actually only six league places separating the two teams on that Wembley day. Nevertheless, the gulf in class was clear and Kenny Dalglish's men could have been excused if they had expected the showpiece to be little more than a procession at the venue dubbed 'Anfield South'. The cheek of it.

The stories surrounding, and within, the game are ones I know well. The pre-match trip to the pub on the eve of the game, orchestrated by manager Bobby Gould. The early yet bruising tackle by Vinnie Jones. The header from Lawrie Sanchez. The superb save by Dave Beasant. But stories are all they are as I could not attend the game itself. Considering I hadn't even been conceived when said events unfolded and, whisper it, my family traditionally supported Fulham, I never stood a chance.

It seems there is plenty of ill feeling towards Liverpool down here. Anything but the people's choice in 1988, the club is still widely disliked in some quarters. Success breeds envy and such an emotion was compounded by the decades of dominance that were enjoyed by your lot before the Premier League's inception. There is scant room in the heart of a capital dweller for the Reds' cause. That's just basic tribalism, folks.

But I'm not among that number. For me, Liverpool are one of a mere handful of clubs to have retained an identity during the modern era of new money and so deserve respect. After all, they're not Chelsea are they?

Maybe my soft spot for Liverpool goes back to Owen and seeing him burst into life at Selhurst. For sure that was a great time to be a Wimbledon fan, with the seasons either side of the 1996/97 campaign our pomp, our prime. An eighth-place finish and pair of cup semi-finals – it couldn't get much better than that, could it? No, it could not. Rather, it was the beginning of the end.

We were relegated on the final day of the 1999/2000 season, 12 years after our FA Cup triumph, while Bradford City survived by the skin of their teeth. How? A shock 1-0 win over Liverpool. Soon after, the slimy Peter Winkelman got his wish and an independent FA commission were convinced: Wimbledon were to move 60 miles north to Buckinghamshire. Milton Keynes. Look it up on 'how to rip the soul out of a football club'. It's right there, on page one.

That was it. Cross the i's and dot the t's. Game over. Well it should have been, but a group of fans refused to let their team die and a phoenix club immediately rose from the ashes. In the ninth level of the football pyramid.

I owe plenty to those select few who were determined enough to start from the bottom up, for I was entering my teenage years when Wimbledon were displaced (or rather, stolen) and had drifted out of the loop, the pull of the Premier League proving too strong to ignore. I became a neutral, for a brief time.

But the first time I laid eyes on AFC Wimbledon, my passion, like the club itself, was reborn.

Those early years were special. The unity, the feeling of belonging once again. Sometimes I think those who support teams in the upper echelons of English football don't know what they're missing. The modern game has sucked so much life out of the sport. Matchday ticket, travel, programme, a few beers; you're looking at well over £100 and, over time, feeling increasingly disenchanted and disconnected.

On our way up through the divisions it was so much more human. Our players were normal chaps; after the game they'd come and have a drink in the bar. A bit unprofessional you might think, but that's because we weren't professional. I can still recall the sheer enormity of the club's decision to go full-time. Training every day? It's all getting a bit serious isn't it lads?

By then the promised land was in reach. The Isthmian League had been navigated, courtesy of the play-offs, at the third time of asking. Likewise the Conference South, but with the title in tow. We'd had a bit of a wobble during the run in but Jon Main popped up to spark chaos at Hampton & Richmond. That boy could finish.

Then we were in with the big fish. A national league. Away trips further north than Watford became a bit more frequent. But it wasn't all smiles and rainbows. We made our enemies, such as Bromley, who forgot that it's common courtesy to return the ball from a throw-in when an opposition player goes down injured, and Crawley Town, 'The Manchester City of Non League'. Their manager at the time, Steve Evans, shouldn't be allowed anywhere near a football club.

Annoyingly, Crawley cruised to the Conference title in 2010/11 and we had to settle for the play-offs, again, as runners-up. A trip to Highbury (not that one) to face Fleetwood Town in the semis awaited.

It was barren. There was a chip shop, and a pub that I daren't risk. A local place for local people that was stuck in the 1930s. We grabbed a 2-0 win and scarpered. But I didn't care a jot a few days later when we duffed them up 6-1 in the return fixture. We were on our way to Wembley for a date with destiny.

Oh, wait, scrap that. The FA wanted to make sure their hallowed turf was in pristine condition for the Champions League Final. So which prestigious, historical ground would we be playing at? The Etihad Stadium. Well, that's just swell.

Luton Town weren't best pleased either, I imagine. But we made a weekend of it, as you do.

I can't tell you much about the game itself, but those 90 minutes were the longest of my life. Stalemate. Extra time flashed past in the blink of an eye and then penalties; the cruellest way to lose, the ultimate way to win. The wave of euphoria I felt when Danny Kedwell's spot-kick hit the back of the net took days to subside.

The spontaneous chant that echoed around the Etihad is now a regular chorus. 'Nine years! It only took nine years, it only took nine years.' The Football League. No more playing in God-forsaken places on awful pitches, right? Wrong. That's what League 2 is all about. And I wouldn't change it for the world.

Monday night. The first one of the year. No one should be going to an FA Cup third round tie on a bloody Monday night. But no, the powers that be reckon it makes sense (just think of all those extra viewing figures – ching, ching). So I whizz out of work and nip down to Waterloo. It's absolutely rammed. Typical.

I squeeze myself on to the train and manage to read a couple of pages of someone else's discarded *Evening Standard* while a fellow commuter breathes down the back of my neck. I do believe they've forgotten to brush. Lovely.

Our goalkeeper, James Shea, once of Arsenal, is plastered across the sport section, admitting for some reason that he has never seen that Dave Beasant save. Still, any publicity is good publicity. It's nice to get some column inches.

My carriage isn't packed with expectant fans dreaming of FA Cup glory. Far from it. There's a few yellow and blue scarves dotted around, but the majority of my fellow travellers are bleary-eyed office workers heading home after their first day back chiselling away at the grindstone while simultaneously attempting to dig themselves out of a turkey coma. Ah, the magic of the FA Cup.

I meet my brother at Norbiton station and wander down to the ground. 'How are you mate?' All I get in response is a grunt. The January blues have clearly kicked in right on cue.

We have enough time for a quick pint outside the ground. We always do. Terry Brown, the manager who guided us back into the Football League three years ago, is ahead of me in the queue grabbing himself a swift half. Jon Main, the same Jon Main, is third in line at the burger van. Who can blame him? They're delicious.

We take up our usual spot on the terraces in plenty of time but each staggered step is already packed to the rafters. I can just about make out Alan Shearer's balding bonce and Gary Lineker's enormous ears perched atop the hastily assembled gantry. I don't have as much luck with the Liverpool players.

Unfortunately the tiny spikes that stop the pigeons from doing their business all over the crowd have not been replaced over Christmas, so I spend most of the warm-up trying to avoid a nervous bird dropping its guts on my head as I aim to pick out famous faces.

I check the teams on my phone. The Dons' is standard procedure; it picks itself. Liverpool's is a tad more complex and contains several surprises. Brendan Rodgers clearly isn't mucking about and one name in particularly stands out: Steven Gerrard.

Before I know it the teams are out. The roar is the loudest I've heard at Kingsmeadow, or for sponsorship reasons, the Cherry Red Records Fans Stadium. Every member of the 4,784-strong crowd are on their feet.

Kick-off. With a pink match ball? Honestly.

'Keep it tight for the first ten,' I think to myself. 'Don't do anything stupid.' A chant of 'get into 'em, fuck 'em up!' is belted out; we can't let Liverpool find their rhythm. But they do. The 3-5-2 formation has us all over the place.

The opening goal is inevitable, as is the scorer. Gerrard arrives at the perfect time to place a stooping header past a helpless Shea. The midfielder rises to his feet and places one finger on his lips as he wheels away to celebrate – a cutting response to a fan who had treated him to a one-fingered gesture of his own seconds earlier.

'Go and play some soccerball Stevie, you're shit!' shouts one man, with the irony of such a comment clearly not lost on him. Gerrard's just scored, pal. He's really rather good, even if he is going to the MLS.

That should be it, Liverpool should control proceedings from here on in. Naturally I fear the worst. Thoughts turn to a cricket scoreline. But somehow, Wimbledon grow into the game. The handbrake is off and we go at it full pelt.

Doubts creep back into Liverpool's defence, all of whom cut the appearance of a new-born foal. Matt Tubbs pulls an effort wide and Simon Mignolet's papier mache wrists prove they also contain bone when he tips a fizzing effort from Sean Rigg just over the bar. Suddenly the crowd sense that the tide has turned; we are playing as equals.

Well no one can be equal to Adebayo Akinfenwa. The 16-stone lump is not the quickest of cats but he reacts faster than anyone to poke home from close range. Mignolet flapped, defenders dithered, and the Beast pounced.

I can't make out who has delivered the telling touch, but it doesn't matter. Jack Midson's penalty against Fleetwood Town, which guaranteed league survival, was the last time I'd celebrated a goal like this. Pure and utter joy.

Half-time comes too soon. Another five minutes and we surely would have gone in ahead. The anxiety from the nigh-on silent away crowd speaks volumes. Rodgers may well be 45 minutes away from the sack.

As Mignolet emerges from the tunnel and jogs over to his goal, the taunts begin. 'Simon, Simon, Simon.' It is going to be a long half for the Belgian and he's soon caught in no man's land with Adam Barrett's header destined for the top corner. Gerrard nods it off the line and away to safety. Is there anything he can't do? The midfielder is carrying his team, which is no mean feat considering human manatee Rickie Lambert is on the pitch.

Momentum continues to build as the Beast bullies Martin Skrtel but it is ruthlessly snubbed out on the hour mark by Gerrard, the man of the hour, as he curls home a trademark free kick into the top corner. A deathly silence falls over the Chemflow End. I knew before he even hit it. I just knew. Delivering during moments of adversity is what he does.

A response to the setback ensues but as Wimbledon press, Liverpool swarm and the closing minutes ebb away. And when Mignolet manages to collect a corner cleanly I know Lady Luck has turned her back on us.

We've still got the moral high ground to fall back on, though, 'We own our club, we own our own club, you Yankee bastards! We own our club.'

Disappointed, I trudge out of the ground contemplating a full week of work rather than a night drowning my sorrows. Liverpool's pristine team coach has pulled up outside the players' entrance, waiting for its occupants to board. I catch a glimpse of Gerrard's face as he conducts a post-match interview on one of the television screens that adorn every seat of the luxury vehicle.

He is all smiles, a stark contrast to the discomfort that had been etched on his face earlier in the evening. I don't think his replacement will ever be found.

As for us; it was nice to see AFC Wimbledon's name up in lights. But it's about time we got a bit of bread and butter back on our plate. Next up? Stevenage away. Perfect.

10 January 2015, Sunderland 0 Liverpool 1

This is a story about shit broadband. The type of broadband that makes you slap an iPad in disgust and look upon an endlessly spinning wheel as the work of the devil. It is a very modern tale and, for that reason, rather pointless. Well not completely pointless as it explains why I didn't see a second of this match live.

Let me explain. One of the first things we did upon moving into our current house in October 2011 is set up the essentials; Sky TV and the internet. I sorted the first and my wife the latter – she chose BT and for months it was good, nay, great. Super-fast connections every day of the week. I was like a browsing pig in shit.

Last year there came an added bonus – all BT broadband customers could subscribe to BT Sport for free, which I jumped at given the channel had just secured rights to live Premier League games. More pig, more shit.

Then, however, things started to turn. The broadband got increasingly slow and unreliable, some days not working at all, and the more this happened the more I got pissed off. Less pig, less shit.

At the same time I found that having BT Sport was not as great as I thought it would be. Its main live match is the lunchtime one on Saturday, a part of the day when I'm normally on my way to watch the Reds play, on my way to watch some other teams play for work or simply out and about. So the decision was taken at the end of the season to ditch both.

But here's the strange thing – while I no longer have BT Sport I still have BT broadband. It's like a drunk guest who refuses to leave.

What actually happened is that my wife called up to cancel and, during the process, got sweet-talked by the guy at the other end to keep the broadband on the basis he could make it work. In fairness, it's been pretty reliable ever since. There's still the odd moment when the wheel keeps on turning and turning, spinning me into a proper fucking rage, but it's less often now.

So the broadband's still around but BT Sport's gone and, as is the law of the sod, Liverpool have been on the channel loads this season – against Everton, Newcastle, Chelsea, Leicester away and now, Sunderland.

I could've gone to the pub to watch it but there aren't many decent ones around me. Also, I couldn't stray too far from home as I had to leave for Selhurst Park straight after the final whistle in order to get to Crystal Palace v Tottenham, which I was covering for the *Guardian*. So instead I followed the game through a combination of Twitter and *Gillette Soccer Saturday*, and from what I read and saw we pretty much bossed it. The first half certainly, during which Lazar Markovic scored the winner and did some sort of Karate Kid shot-thing which smashed the bar.

Villa away next. I'm going to that one with Shanil, on the train. Bye-bye broadband, hello beer.

SN

PERFECT START: Daniel Sturridge scores the winning goal in the opening day 2-1 victory over Southampton at Anfield

BACK IN THE BIG TIME: The Kop gears up for Liverpool's first match in the Champions League for five years, the 2-1 win over Ludogorets

GOALS GALORE: Simon Mignolet is mobbed by his team-mates following the extraordinary 14-13 penalty shootout victory over Middlesbrough in the Capital One Cup

BOLT FROM THE BLUE: Phil Jagielka stuns Anfield with a thunderous injury-time equaliser for Everton in September's Merseyside derby

LOOK WHO'S BACK: Cristiano Ronaldo is in full peacock mode on his return to Anfield for Real Madrid's Champions League group match there in October

ENOUGH IS ENOUGH: The Kop makes clear its feelings over rising ticket prices ahead of the goalless draw with Hull

PAIN IN THE RAIN: Brendan Rodgers looks drenched and drained following Liverpool's 3-1 defeat to Crystal Palace at Selhurst Park

HEAD BOY: Martin Skrtel celebrates his late equaliser in Liverpool's 2-2 draw with Arsenal just before Christmas

GET IN: Liverpool players and fans rejoice together following Rickie Lambert's goal in the 2-0 victory at Villa Park in January

GOODBYE GOODISON: Steven Gerrard walks off the pitch after his last ever Merseyside derby

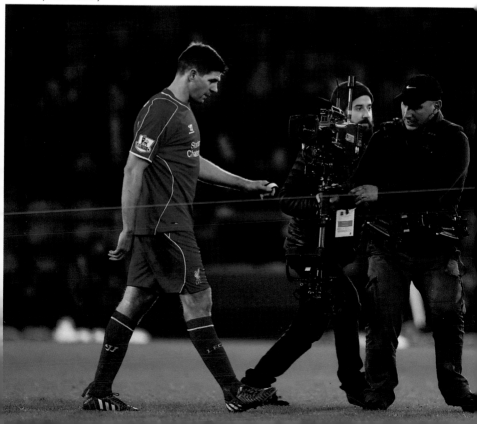

SAMBA STAR: Philippe Coutinho celebrates after scoring a stunning goal against Southampton in February. The Brazilian was rightly named Liverpool's player of the season

HELLISH WELCOME: Besiktas supporters offer a less than warm welcome to their visitors from Merseyside ahead of the Europa League tie at the Ataturk Stadium

NEVER FORGET: Liverpool remember the 96 during a minute's silence to mark the 26th anniversary of Hillsborough

WEMBLEY WOE: Mario Balotelli and Jordan Henderson in distraught mood following Liverpool's 2-1 FA Cup semi-final defeat to Aston Villa

HULL OF A PRICE: A travelling Kopite shows his £50 ticket ahead of Liverpool's defeat to Hull in April. Many fans boycotted the match in protest at the price

FATHER'S DAY: Steven Gerrard leads his daughters around the pitch and in front of an appreciative Kop during his final match at Anfield

17 January 2015, Aston Villa 0 Liverpool 2

'We ended up ploughing over the cattle grids of Woburn Safari Park'

By Steven Scragg

'Aston Villa, they're like Nottingham Forest, except with fans.' I can't remember who said it, but it is a one-liner that has always stuck in my mind.

I don't always remember things.

My name is Steven and I have brain damage. To be more precise I have a slight abnormality of the temporal lobe. Slight abnormalities of the temporal lobe are a heady combination of the confusing, frightening and disruptive when the effects are in the far extreme, yet upon the more *je ne sais quoi* days can be wildly entertaining. If I take a walk to the local shop for a few items that total more than three in number then I require a shopping list. If I go to the shop with a shopping list there is still no guarantee I will return home with all the items on that list. You can tell me a secret and be safe in the knowledge that within 27 minutes, I'm likely to have forgotten it.

Think of all those unforgettable Luis Suarez goals and game-changing moments. I can count on one hand how many I can readily bring up. I've already lost the vast majority of them, just as the exploits of Fernando Torres have largely long since slipped my mind. The goals of Michael Owen and Robbie Fowler have been refreshed on a regular basis thanks to the repetitive nature of LFC TV programming, yet now that I'm expected to pay for LFC TV and indeed won't be paying for LFC TV, the memory of goals by Owen and Fowler are slowly being eroded by a memory that struggles to retain basic day to day occurrences.

161

I'll also never get the chance to see that David Speedie interview I intended to watch.

Aston Villa away and January 2015 in general marks a personal milestone for me. I've now lived for longer as an amnesiac than I have as a 'norm'.

My life changed irredeemably on Saturday 10 September 1994. I still don't know exactly what happened as there are no known witnesses. I ended Saturday 10 September 1994 in hospital with a head injury and a stubborn belief it was 1992. Two years' worth of my memory was taken away from me in one fell swoop and my brain waves didn't settle down again until mid-1996. Much of September 1994 to mid-1996 is also lost to the ether. Everything else since is a bit hit or miss. I own a very good memory that happens to be a little bit broken. I can recall goals from the 1987/88 season in fine detail, but ask me to recall the latest goal Liverpool have scored and I will struggle.

My main recollection of late 1994 is of going into a giant Polo mint for a brain scan and being told not to follow the camera, only to spend half an hour or so following the camera until they managed to get the shots they needed. The other one is of me producing a litre of urine in a bottle from the inside pocket of my coat (very much in the style of someone selling stolen watches) as a 'sample', much to the amusement of a startled NHS employee.

I consciously resurfaced for a short while in the summer of 1995 only to disappear again until a year later. Everything has been a bit crazy paving since then. It's only over the course of the last five years through the help of my partner Beverley that I've been able to find some sort of order to the chaos my brain was left to deal with.

Amnesia is nothing like it is when it's being sold by Jason Bourne. I'm pretty certain I've never rendered any eastern European police officers unconscious on a cold and snowy night with an outburst of unexpected martial arts, and neither do I know of any safety deposit boxes stuffed with an array of different currencies and a variety of passports under a litany of different pseudonyms. I've never once surprised myself by conversing in fluent Russian, while the Hollywood interpretation of 'flashbacks' are complete and utter bollocks. The real deal is infinitely more mundane, pretty bewildering, but mundane all the same. I actually quite like the Bourne movies and I can't deny that I've got designs on being able to one day use the iconic line, 'Get some rest Pam, you look tired.' It is aesthetically bollocks, though.

Football can be therapeutic. I've shared some of the best days of my life watching Liverpool Football Club with a small band of people to whom for the best part of two decades I didn't once mention I am an amnesiac. Sue, Andy, Alan and Phil have unwittingly done more for me than they could ever possibly know. I can't remember when I first met any of them. One day I didn't know them and the next they were just sort of there.

By and large this was a set of people that didn't know the singular biggest thing about me. The thing that defines and even excuses the way I am sometimes. I quite liked it that way if I'm honest, to not have that sympathetic tilt of the head which I tend to be on the receiving end of from those 'in the know' on days when my brain basically stalls. For someone who feels a bit detached from day to day life, as if watching it from arm's length or though a shop window, it is invaluable to feel a bit 'normal'.

I possess an episodic memory. I only remember things in snapshot images, rather than in any flowing manner. Some days my memory won't retain a single thing, some days I'm classed as being 'away with the unicorns', while on other days I'm fine. There was no real follow-up care from the NHS 20 years ago and I was never told what to expect in the future. I used to get massively frustrated when the mist of brain damage descended, but now I understand it better and, in the main, I can cope with it. I can also see the humour in it.

Snapshot images are better than having no images at all. Snapshot images allow me to remember a trip to Chelsea when, in a bid to find a way around a major traffic accident at the foot of the M1, we ended up ploughing over the cattle grids of Woburn Safari Park on what was a dark winter night, with a convoy of other road users who'd followed us under the mistaken impression that we knew where we were going.

Snapshot images allow me to remember being stood at the side of a mountainous road answering the very loud call of nature on the outskirts of Istanbul, only to look over my shoulder to see that the green bus I'd climbed off was slowly starting to disappear up the steep incline of a deserted road in the middle of nowhere, leaving me on the cusp of Asia without money, passport and, more importantly, my match ticket.

From being stranded I managed to beat the bus and my travelling companions to the Ataturk Stadium thanks to a very enthusiastic and highly amused taxi driver who'd seen all this unfold. The others eventually stumbled off the bus in a vague panic, phones glued to ears in a bid to get through to me, only to confusingly find me sat on a stone wall at the side of the road asking what had kept them.

Snapshot images allow me to remember other occasions I'd hate to have forgotten. I'm allowed the memory of Alan vaulting over the advertising hoardings at Barnsley in a bright yellow coat to celebrate Steve McManaman's winning goal while his son (who was probably under the age of seven at the time) enquired as to the whereabouts of his dad as the police subsequently chased him back into the stands.

No amount of brain damage can also delete the image of Andy running over John Pearman's foot as we picked him up on the way to Charlton Athletic one season. The esteemed editor of *Red All Over The Land* just seemed to vanish from the back of the car in the blink of an eye before he'd had the chance to shut the door, or even get his trailing leg into the car. With Andy having lifted his foot off the brake pedal and not applied the handbrake, a degree of unexpected forward momentum was achieved, which left John flat on his back at the side of the A50 with only his ego bruised.

I can also recall ambitiously crowbarring Hayley, one of my very best friends, through the White Hart Lane turnstiles while she was eight months pregnant. The football often seemed incidental to the entertainment of getting to and from games in one piece.

Football has been therapeutic but it isn't necessarily the football that has done the healing. Since my head injury, Liverpool have been a pale shadow of the club I spent my childhood and adolescence obsessing over. When I 'awoke' the club had regressed to the point that it was almost as if I came to in a bizarre parallel universe, one where Liverpool were a mediocre mid-table side. My brain and memory was spirited back to a time when a goalkeeper could still pick up a backpass. You do realise Liverpool haven't won a league title since the backpass rule was changed? I don't believe this is a coincidence.

The game as a whole has changed dramatically. More accurately, what surrounds the game has changed dramatically. I don't feel an attachment to multi-millionaire football players, I don't need to watch an endless loop of Sky Sports News to keep me updated on the trans-mundane of the 'rumour mill'. I don't need well-paid ex-players sat in hi-tech studios to form my opinions for me and I don't expect footballers to be role models for my children. Football and the circus which orbits it is a strange, strange place.

It wasn't preordained that I had to be a Liverpool fan. I'm the youngest of my parents' three children and as my dad and my older brother supported the team in all red, a team that seemed to lift big shiny trophies on a regular basis despite an inordinate amount of bubble perms per head, I was more than happy to follow suit.

I was taken to Anfield for the first time almost a year before I even started school. The game was Kevin Keegan's return to Liverpool in a Hamburg shirt for the second leg of the European Super Cup. Liverpool won 6-0 and Terry McDermott ran a masterclass of a performance. I don't remember much about the game itself and the main recollections

I can summon up revolve around how small I felt amidst the crowds of people outside the ground, of being 'treated' to some dubious looking black peas in a polystyrene cup and being struck by just how bright the rectangular patch of grass seemed once we were in the ground.

If my mind's eye has it right, we were sat up in the Main Stand, with the Kop just below us. I've always hated those uncomfortable wooden seats in the Main Stand, but I was pretty much hooked on Liverpool from the word go. Liverpool gave me a sense of belonging.

A sense of belonging. Since September 1994 I haven't felt like I've 'belonged' very often. I've been loved by family and friends and I've loved them back, but they've struggled to tune in to my distorted wavelength. My mind might be playing tricks on me but I feel I'm either awkward with people or I make people feel awkward themselves.

For a while I felt I belonged with Liverpool again and also with Sue, Andy, Alan and Phil. We were a little family unit and given we at one stage went to every single game the club played, I would see them more often than I would some members of my actual family.

Life happens to everyone, however, and an eclectic mix of relationship break-ups, career changes, illness, parenthood, the death of loved ones, depression and escalating ticket prices means my little footballing family doesn't congregate for every game anymore. We all pick and choose our games in a manner that would have been deemed ridiculous a few years back. Missing a game just wasn't the done thing, but now there are sage and understanding nods from the others whenever any of us say we're not going to this or that game. That highly valued sense of belonging has faded a bit and that's not the unacceptable prospect it might once have been because I have all the sense of belonging I need at home with my soul-mate Beverley and our three children.

As far as my little football family is concerned, other aspects of life were happening for all but myself and Sue on Saturday. Aston Villa is my favourite away day and it was just the two of us that made the journey to the city of Birmingham for this one.

There's something brilliant about Villa Park. Of course, the fact we often come away from the place with all three points is a big plus, but it's more than that. Villa Park is a proper football ground, with four separate and individual stands. There is a history and character there that you just don't get at the soulless Meccano identikit grounds. I like football grounds that are temporal anomalies, football grounds that have countless stories to tell. Places where you can almost see the ghosts of the past flicker on the pitch. At Villa Park they just need to take the giant TV screens down and it would be perfect.

Villa Park ticks the right boxes geographically, too. It's far enough in distance to feel like an away game, but one that doesn't completely wipe out the rest of the day. Anything north and inclusive of Stoke, to the west side of the country at least, never feels like an away trip to me.

In an entirely grown up and respectable manner, we were back handy enough to be able to take Sue out for her *tea (*northern vernacular in use: tea is an early-evening meal) before she set off for home.

Liverpool's main rivals for trophies during the formative years of my football-watching existence weren't local ones. They didn't emanate from London, either. The Midlands was where the challenge sprang from. Nottingham Forest rose impressively and annoyingly in equal measure to win some serious silverware in the late 1970s, putting Liverpool noses out of joint in the process. Once Forest fell by the wayside it was Aston Villa who seized the day, taking the title in 1980/81 and adding the European Cup in 1982.

The Forest phenomenon was just before I fully embraced football, although I was under no illusions that they and their manager Brian Clough were not to be liked or trusted. In contrast, early-80s Aston Villa were an acceptable foe. We were out of the running when they won that title in 1981, and we'd gone out of the European Cup in the quarter-finals when they went on to win it in 82. Villa didn't directly wrong us when they won those trophies and then had the presence of mind to go into a marked decline that eventually took them to relegation in 1987.

Villa were far more respectful than Forest had been before them and we even won a trophy at Villa Park when we beat West Ham in the League Cup Final replay in 81.

Villa Park has been kind to me. Villa Park has been kind to Liverpool. So it proved to be once again and I was happy to take my allotted number of snapshot images from the game. Whether my memory will be able to develop this season's snapshot images from Villa Park into lasting ones is another matter altogether. They already seem set to evaporate a mere 48 hours after the event. I write to remember, but sometimes I can't write soon enough to record my faltering memories, and the fact I couldn't remember who scored our first goal in this 2-0 win without looking it up doesn't bode well.

That celebration for the second goal by Rickie Lambert won't be dislodged too easily, though.

There is something beautifully conductive about Villa Park when it comes to going nuts in celebration of a goal, especially when you're in the lower section of the Doug Ellis Stand. It has nothing to do with the inoffensive opposition; I think it's the seemingly shallow profile the stand has there. As Lambert turned to celebrate his goal the look on his face matched the look on our faces in the crowd, and it was the most natural thing in the world for the two entities to embrace. Lambert was essentially booked for the crowd going into him, rather than him going into the crowd. It reminded me of a similar celebration there for a late Torres winner in the snow a few years back.

Bouncing up and down while clutched within the bear hug of the three people in front of me, none of whom I'd ever seen before in my life, left me with a sense of something familiar but often elusive.

A sense of belonging.

'Perhaps they're lacking something'

By Sachin Nakrani

Born in L'Hospitalet de Llobregat in August 1978, Enrique de Lucas, or 'Quique' to his friends, made his name at his local club Espanyol as a pacey attacking midfielder. He earned caps at both Under-16 and Under-21 level for Spain but was never good enough to make the step up to the senior ranks. He was no Xavi or Andres Iniesta, which became particularly evident during a loan spell at Paris Saint-Germain in 2001.

The following year de Lucas's contract at Espanyol expired and with the La Liga club not overly desperate to keep him, he became available on a Bosman. PSG didn't want him back, so he ended up moving to Chelsea. De Lucas was their biggest arrival of that summer, and he cost nothing.

'Whoa there Sach,' I can hear the kids wailing, 'you're seriously telling me that Chelsea's standout signing before the start of a new season was an average Spanish midfielder on a free transfer? Are you absolutely sure? Chelsea, moneybags Chelsea, one of the biggest, most powerful clubs in Europe, signing a nobody for nothing? That can't be right, you've lost your fucking mind.'

Far from it young readers; I'm sane and speaking the truth. In 2002, a mere 13 years ago, Chelsea spent piss all on fuck all. Why? Because they were piss all and fuck all, a club on its knees financially and with no status or heritage to speak off. If you don't believe me, ask your dad, he'll remember, remember a time when Chelsea meant nothing. In particular to Liverpool supporters, bar being the place where Kenny sealed the title with a gorgeous volley in 1986. Rivals? You must be joking. For decades, Chelsea were to Liverpool what diarrhoea is to most people; an irritant that ultimately passes without much fuss.

But then 'it' happened and everything changed, for football as a whole and Liverpool in particular. No one envisaged 'it' when de Lucas rocked up at Chelsea, yet 12 months on there 'it' was. A Russian takeover. Roman Abramovich. The mother of all game-changers.

Before I go on, let me deal with the frothing outrage coming from any Chelsea fans who may be reading this by acknowledging that Chelsea finished above Liverpool at the end of the 2002/03 season, snatching fourth from us with victory in a final-day encounter that doubled as a straight shootout for the final Champions League qualifying place. Sami Hyypia gave the visitors to Stamford Bridge the lead on 11 minutes before Marcel Desailly equalised three minutes later and Jesper Gronkjaer scored what proved to be the winner for the hosts soon after.

In other words, Chelsea had a very good team before Abramovich's arrival. But it was one coming to the end of a cycle fuelled by the millions poured into the club by former vice-chairman and lifelong fan Matthew Harding prior to his sudden death in 1996. They'd been on the brink financially in 2002, hence the lack of summer spending, and celebrated Champions League qualification a year later largely because it would help clear the £80m-plus debts piled up by chairman and mouthy tosspot Ken Bates. Make no mistake, Chelsea were in a state, an ageing team with little to fall back on. As ever they looked set to pass without much fuss. Diarrhoea FC.

But then came Abramovich, landing in west London in his gold-plated helicopter (I might have made that up), and buying Chelsea for £140m, then the biggest takeover in British football history. I remember hearing about it on the news; it was the lead story that July night. 'So what?' I thought. 'It's still Chelsea, they're still fuck all.' Well the Russian with the dopey grin soon showed me.

That summer Chelsea spent £147.4m on 11 players, the following year they spent £142.5m on another ten, hired some Portuguese fella from Porto to be their new manager and, hey presto, became champions. The rest has been consistently painful history, with the latest punch in the nuts coming with this victory in the Capital One Cup semi-finals. Jose's on his way to Wembley and boy, didn't he celebrate.

I wasn't there to see it. I wanted a ticket but couldn't get one and instead watched Mourinho high-fiving everyone in sight from my sofa. Off went the television as soon as I could manage it and into the kitchen I trudged to clean the dishes. I couldn't even bear to put the radio on, just in case I heard his smug voice.

Has a single man caused Liverpool so much pain in such a short space of time? Brian Clough in the 1970s perhaps, and then of course there was Fergie. But his reign of terror lasted decades and, in fairness, hurt everybody. No, Mourinho seems to exist purely to annoy us. That's how it's beginning to feel anyway.

In just over a decade, and across two different spells, he's fucked us in a Carling Cup Final, a Capital One Cup semi-final and, most awfully, stopped us winning the title last season. And even when we get one over him, he still can't help chucking in a spoiler. Ghost goal? Oh do fuck off you smarmy prick.

Mourinho and modern Chelsea really are the perfect fit, one feeding the other until both are bloated on their own sense of self-satisfaction. The thing is, I can just about stomach Jose because for all his faults (and there are plenty) the guy is a fantastic manager, a serial winner who could get the job done with one arm tied behind his back. Loathed him as much as you want but deep down all Reds know that if he'd become Liverpool manager we'd have won the title again by now.

This Chelsea, though; no, I can't and won't accept. Other clubs have struck instant financial gold – most notably in recent times, Blackburn and Manchester City – but none have, how can I put this…become so cuntish on the back of it. From Peter Kenyon declaring the club's desire to 'turn the world blue', to their supporters waving banknotes at the nearest television camera, to ticket prices at Stamford Bridge shooting through the roof so now it's almost cheaper to go on holiday than it is to watch a match there, Chelsea have well and truly embraced their status among the nouveau riche. Whenever I go to the Bridge I still expect to see a pair of stone lions and a water fountain outside the directors' entrance.

I grew up in London but never in my formative years came across a Chelsea fan. Not one. There were none among the lads I hung around with at school – primary or secondary – or at AZ, the Sunday league team I used to play for (yes, that was their actual name). Perhaps if I'd met just one as a kid that would've made a difference to how I feel about them now, which largely is that they're a bunch of thugs and spivs who won the football lottery.

The resentment/hatred began pre-Abramovich, on 24 March 2002 to be precise. That was the day I first took Shanil to a Liverpool match on my own. We got the train from Euston, sat in the Kop and watched Vladimir Smicer score with a 90th-minute volley which temporarily put us top of the league. We were buzzing, elated beyond measure.. right up until getting on the train home at Lime Street and discovering our carriage was packed full of Chelsea fans.

Boozed-up, lairy and highly intimidating, they spent the vast majority of the journey back down south singing songs about how much they hate 'Scaaasers' and 'Yids'. Occasionally those sat at our table would glance at me and Shanil, and despite our lack of colours I could tell they knew we were Liverpool fans. 'This is going to kick off any second,' I remember thinking. 'Two brown-skinned Reds, we don't stand a chance.'

I was 21 at the time and felt deeply responsible for my 12-year-old brother, who was clearly terrified. Thankfully nothing happened and we arrived at Euston in one piece. But the experience still darkens the memory and, in relation to my subsequent encounters with Chelsea fans, proved to be the norm rather than the exception.

Whether it's been upon leaving Stamford Bridge after a Liverpool game there, or during the supporters' club's stops at Norton Canes services, I haven't come across a group of that club's followers who haven't pissed me off. Smug, snide, forever banging on about Steven Gerrard (he rejected you, get over it), it's difficult not to be left with the impression that these are people who despite all the wealth and success that has come Chelsea's way in recent years, simply cannot find contentment. Perhaps they're lacking something, something to make them feel whole. Something like…a history.

Ah, the history chant.

Now I know there are some Reds who don't like the chant, who feel it does us no favours and should be laid to rest, but I love it. In fact, I'd go as far as saying it's one of my favourite Liverpool songs; spot on rhythmically and lyrically, with the words not only cutting Chelsea in two but also celebrating our achievements loud, proud and gloriously.

'Fuck off Chelsea F-C, you ain't got no his-tory. Five European Cups and 18 leagues, that's what we call his-tory!'

I remember hearing it for the first time on my first visit to Stamford Bridge, the 1-0 defeat there in October 2004. Looking on from the away end (which back then was in the far corner of the East Stand) I could tell it stung those in the home seats because they knew that for all the money that had come their way, and the trophies which were bound to follow, they indeed had no history, no soul. This, after all, is a club who pre-2005 had been relegated more recently then they'd won the league title and were more closely associated with the National Front then they were with success.

Their fans claim the history chant is bollocks, that it is another example of 'Scaaasers' living in the past. But if that's true then how come Stamford Bridge has become awash with banners referring to Chelsea's supposed long-standing identity in the years since we started singing it there so prominently? 'Born Is The King', 'Matthew Harding's Blue & White Army', a vague one about the London Underground; Chelsea, we are being told by the club and their followers, has a history after all. Yeah, like fuck you do.

Don't get me wrong, I know not all Chelsea fans are dickheads. For instance, Rebecca Knight, the author of a chapter to come in this book, is a lovely person, as is Chris Taylor, a fella I used to work with at the *Guardian*. Then there's David Baddiel, who I've never met but like enormously, and the late Richard Attenborough, who seemed nice enough. But then there's also Tim Lovejoy, Jeremy Clarkson and all the twats I've come across in the past decade and a bit. So excuse me if, all in all, I think blue is far from being the colour.

I shouldn't let Chelsea get to me so much but it's hard to keep the emotions in check when my experiences of them have proved so emotional – from that train journey in 2002 and subsequent meetings with west London's 'finest', to the vast number of significant matches we've played against them in recent years, most of which I've been at. There have been extreme highs, such as the Champions League semi-finals of 2005 and 2007, and extreme lows, such as the 2005 Carling Cup Final and last season's title-slipping league encounter. I've shed tears of joy and pain, jumped up in ecstasy and sunk down in agony, and on each occasion seen Chelsea fans, players and staff in front of me. After that it's hard to feel indifferent.

And don't get me started on Fernando Torres and the way they treated Rafa. Seriously, I'll go all Michael Douglas in *Falling Down*.

So anyway, they've done us again. In truth I'm not as upset as I could be given the opposition and circumstances. After all, Liverpool played really well in both legs and while we may not be going to Wembley there's no doubt the team has rediscovered its confidence and sense of identity after those dreadful displays prior to Christmas.

At Anfield in particular we were great, reacting to Eden Hazard's first-half penalty with a proper chest-out performance. Raheem Sterling's goal was a peach and if one of Gerrard or Adam Lallana's very good efforts had gone in, we'd have headed to Stamford Bridge in pole position. As it was we desperately needed a goal, and despite bossing large chunks of the game simply couldn't get it. Instead they did via Branislav Ivanovic's header from Willian's free kick in extra time.

Liverpool conceding from a set piece. Well there's a surprise.

The following morning I e-mailed Martin Fitzgerald to find out what the atmosphere had been like at the ground. Watching on telly, our lot sounded in good voice while theirs could again be heard endlessly singing about Gerrard.

'They still have the staff waving flags at the side of the pitch,' wrote Martin. 'It's really weird.'

It is weird, but it's also very Chelsea. They may have the money, the manager and a team heading for the title, but deep down they remain the club of old; soulless and classless, fantastic but plastic. And on the back of another emotion-sapping encounter with the boys in blue, that is rather assuring.

31 January 2015, Liverpool 2 West Ham 0

'It was the first time I'd seen lads drink lager tops'

By Tony Hennessy

So on Thursday I celebrated my 36th birthday. On reflection, I find it fucking frightening that when my parents were my age I was sitting my GCSEs. That's really made me think. I'm now closer to my 50th birthday than my 21st, therefore I now intend on cherishing every day. Especially Tuesdays.

For non-football people, Tuesday is often ranked seventh in their hierarchy-of-days table, as whatever enthusiasm they had for the week ahead has been battered out of them by Monday. Not so for footy fans, though. For us, Tuesday can be a day which you can look forward to with a sense of excitement and anticipation. They can even end up being momentous occasions. For instance, I've witnessed Liverpool qualify for two European Cup finals, win in the San Siro and come back from three down against the Mancs on a Tuesday.

It's factors like this that make lads like me tolerate contemporary football beyond all matters of principle. This is why we continue to donate irrational amounts of spare time and disposable income to the game.

All this despite horrendous examples of corporate TV people stepping in and messing the average fan around. For example, Sky Sports producers think it acceptable to expect Middlesbrough fans to travel all the way down to west London for a lunchtime kick-off on a freezing cold January morning for their promotion six-pointer. They have absolutely no problem with making someone else get up at 4am. Sky's head office is just a stone's throw from Brentford's ground, for fuck's sake. It's all right for them.

Players such as Emmanuel Adebayor sulk around the pitch for £170,000 a week when a high proportion of hard-working people can't afford the extortionately high ticket prices to take themselves, let alone their kids, to the match. These people are forced out of the game and we have to now instead share our addiction with contemporaries who enjoy the humourless 'bants' of Tim Lovejoy and the sour bigotry of Jeremy Clarkson. It's despicable, really.

It was all very different on Friday 17 May 1985, the day Liverpool defeated Watford 4-3 in a cracker just a couple of weeks before that year's ill-fated European Cup Final and when my old man (a labourer from Corpy) first took me to Anfield. I was dead excited to be going the game that day, so much so that my ma let me have the Friday off school. This was a full-on dead rubber, but to a six-year-old going to watch his team play for the first time that didn't matter one iota.

That morning I fantasised about the game while kicking a ball around by myself, using the frames of the backyard toilet door for goalposts, emulating the heroes of the day. Not surprisingly it was one such hero, Ian Rush, who got my first ever live goal, in the 52nd minute, pulling one back for the Reds who, at that point, were two down. One of my few vivid memories of that night was a beautiful John Barnes free kick that made it 3-2 to Watford. Ironically, he would go on to become one of my other backyard heroes in seasons to come.

It's 2015 and for a single lad in his 30s living on a professional wage in London, you can get up to all manner of things. But going to matches with like-minded people who become part of a wonderful extended family has become a drug for me, a source of sheer and unrivalled hedonism. Like the time Emile Heskey smashed in the second at Elland Road in the fourth round of the FA Cup in 2001. That feeling was as strong as any orgasm, narcotic or amphetamine, or indeed any sense of fulfilment you may gather in your place of work. It's the closest feeling I have experienced to ecstasy. Moreover, for a lad exiled in west London who left Merseyside to study at 18, moments like that are the strongest connection I have to home and my working-class roots.

In a year when I've eaten Swedish caviar and supped pink champagne on my mate Si's lawn before the Epsom Derby, and dined in Il Forno on Duke Street before the Merseyside derby, maintaining a working-class identity is harder to achieve than it sounds. Looking around the Greater Anglia train on the way to Norwich last season while Liverpool were balls deep in the title race, trying to calm the nerves and saviour the occasion, I looked around and noticed we were all drinking fine wine and eating M&S chargrilled squid with lime and coriander. 'Fuck me,' I thought. 'This is not atypical behaviour at the match.' Working-class lads with bourgeois tastes? It's all a long way from my late nan's cornbeef hash. Guess you've just got to keep those Adidas Gazelles grounded.

As Pablo states in one of my favourite films, the Argentinean *The Secret is in their Eyes,* 'Every guy will have something that they cannot change. Not you, not me, not anybody and that's their passion.' I wholeheartedly agree with these sentiments and when I piece this all together I'm left with one overriding conclusion: that LFC and going the match with my mates is my passion.

I enjoy name-checking Pablo as his life consists of drinking with his pals to the destruction of a promising career, marriage and ultimately his life. As we've established, Liverpool Football Club is my passion and recreational drinking with pals is second, so going to the match is a match made in heaven. Days such as today are ideal for both purposes, and to make things even better I've got a retro 3pm kick-off against my favourite top-flight London club to look forward to.

Why are West Ham my favourite top-flight London club? Well, let me explain.

Firstly there is one Michael Anthony Palmer – a larger than life character who was brought up in a Dagenham council house. The son of a handyman called Raz – who, would you believe, was one-time British grass track motor cycling champion – Micky was my house-mate and one of my leading drinking partners during my time studying in Newcastle upon Tyne (1997–2001). The man adores his family, but his overriding passion is most definitely West Ham. Indeed his son is called Julian, after Dicks.

When visiting Micky in Dagenham not only did I gain knowledge of the local boozers of Daggers, Romford, Ilford et al (The Admiral Vernon in Dagenham Heathway is one of only three bars in the world I have entered the minute it opened and lasted in till chucking-out time), I also got to meet his pals. A lot of these lads, like Rivers, Del and Marshy, hadn't gone to uni like us. They'd started off as filing clerks in the City and have since climbed the ranks of some of the world's largest financial institutions. But back then it struck me that these West Ham lads were a bit like me. Lads from a tough urban area with a shitload of social issues, yet they only had pride and good things to say about the place and, to the surprise of a 19-year-old Scouser down '*sarf*' in the summer of 1999, they were very welcoming.

Despite the harsh economic reality of their area, no one felt sorry for themselves. They were just down-to-earth, working-class lads full of the spirit of aspirational socialism and trying to get on and make the most of their lives. They spoke about the Irons with the same enthusiastic pride and passion as my mates back home did about

Liverpool and Everton. These lads also loved having a grin, getting on the ale, chasing birds, having a bet and going for a 'ruby'. It was the first time I'd seen lads drink lager tops, mind. (At first I thought them soft shandy-supping southern bastards until I realised they put the top in so they could drink quicker).

So I see West Ham akin to us in many ways. I don't sense that with the other London clubs. Chelsea feels like they are in a parallel universe to us, with a completely different set of values and sense of humour. As for Arsenal and Tottenham, I'll defer to my great Uncle Frank, who you'll see in any Liverpool away end in both England and mainland Europe. In the mid-to-late-80s he moved to north London for a spell to run the Red Lion pub in Highgate, which back then was frequented on a regular basis by supporters of both clubs. He would tell me with a gasp of exasperation, 'You just can't talk to them about football, Tony.'

Incidentally, I read this year that the Red Lion won a Best Fireside Winter Gastropub award. Fucking hell, when Frank ran it the only gastronomy going off in there was the salted roasties he put on top of the bar.

It feels like Arsenal and Chelsea have lost a great part of their identity as many of their traditional fanbase have drifted away from the club. Priced out of football and, in some cases, their own city. They reek of nouveau fans, but when we go to Upton Park you don't feel that nearly as much. It's still 'our game' there.

The 1985/86 season was the first season I can fully remember. This was about as good a league campaign as it got for the 'Scousers of London'. The team of Phil Parkes, Ray Stewart, Alvin Martin, Alan Devonshire and the legendary strike partnership of Tony Cottee and Frank McAvennie would have played in a title decider against Everton on the final day of the season if King Kenny hadn't volleyed in the winner at Stamford Bridge.

One great game that season for the Irons was a 4-0 win at Chelsea, who Micky and his mates detest. I watched it on *The Big Match* highlights show and my abiding memory was a lovely curling shot from Devonshire and a breakaway team goal by Cottee. I've had a soft spot for them since then.

I also like that they had a song for their ex-keeper Ludek Miklosko and used the natural rhyme of his surname to make the line, 'He comes from near Moscow.' He doesn't, like. He comes from Prostejov in the Czech Republic – just over 1,000 miles away. I think Plaistow might be nearer.

I enjoyed watching West Ham back in those days as they played attractive football and, when under the lights on *Midweek Sports Special*, the atmosphere seemed wonderful. Today, unfortunately, they are managed by Big Sam, who doesn't quite follow the traditions of the club, set by John Lyall and Billy Bonds. This isn't the only change. They will be leaving Upton Park in the 2016/17 season.

Being my birthday, I've had a busy week. The cup defeat and multiple pints either side of the game on Tuesday, a night out with the footy lads in Shoreditch on Thursday, and last night my birthday meal in the Sherry Bar on Northcoate Road, which I believe does the best tapas in northern Europe. Discipline was required as getting picked up at Park Royal at 9am meant a 7.45 wake-up call.

Last night I had people around the table from as far afield as Addis Ababa, Valencia and Brighton, and today we've got Dev, a very good driver, (an explanation here from editor Karl: this all started the night before Fulham away under Kenny. We were all in an Italian restaurant in Battersea as Andy's dad Joe, and his brother John, were down for the game, so there was a gang of us out. Tony has a habit of extolling the virtues of those gathered, hence this speech, 'It's great, this…Joe's been home and away for over 40 years, Andy and John go home and away everywhere, Pete's a bit of a philosopher, Karl's a good writer and Dev's…Dev's a good driver'), my brother who, like me, is originally from Seacombe but now lives in Ealing, and Pete from Wallasey Village, who now lives in Luxembourg City.

Me, Dev and another mate, Armo, had a ball visiting Pete during the World Cup. Luxo is like a university town with the only difference being the majority of people are 30-somethings earning Brewsters rather than late teens scraping by on loans and grant cheques.

Pete was meant to get the train back to Limey from Euston last night but his flight was delayed so he kipped at Dev's, meaning we have the bonus of his company today. Pete might have missed his train but there was no way I was missing my lift for West Ham, so I got the last train home from Clapham Junction post a great nosh-up, wine and merriment.

When I found out Pete was in attendance I knew 9am on Park Royal was going to become 9.15am to 9.30am. Pete is a great lad but this man does nothing in a hurry. And given Pete never got home last night, today's journey is M6 on to the M53 to pick up Pete's season ticket from his parents, then on to The Sandon Wall for a bevy and doing the necessary admin surrounding ticket exchanges ahead of the game.

Four and a half hours in a Peugeot 306 means lots of chat. Today's topics include Walsall Football Club – with everybody in the car agreeing that it's the ground they've driven past the most without actually being inside – skiing, favourite WHU games and, somewhat randomly, women's tennis.

This conversation topic features as the Aussie Open Final between Maria Sharapova and Venus Williams is going off. I have to confess to not being an avid tennis fan but, like the other lads in the car, probably know enough to prolong some chat. After getting beyond our childhood crushes for Chris Evert, we discuss how the petite pixie Justine Henin managed to compete with and sometimes even beat the Williams sisters. Then we inevitably touch on Anna Kournikova, who Dev rightfully points out, 'Could have been good if she wasn't so interested in being a fucking dolly bird.'

On the subject of famous West Ham games, I'm keen to point out that in the 1989 5-1 game which relegated West Ham and had Liverpool on the verge of the title, Allen McKnight, the Irons' goalkeeper, actually had a decent game and had we won 6-1 there was no way Arsenal were winning by three goals at Anfield three days later. Mention is also made of the day Cottee was sent off for trying to inflict further damage on Rob Jones's already fragile shins, and the 2-0 in 2005 when Micky and Marshy stayed in Liverpool for the weekend.

My memories of that game, as well as a rare Bolo Zenden goal, was the Cockney lads being astounded that Wetherspoons was packed at 9am, the owner of the B&B they were staying in chauffeuring them into town on both the Friday and the Saturday, and Marshy downing a White Russian despite being lactose intolerant. This meant not only had he seen his side lose but his Saturday night in town met a premature ending on a khazi.

Inevitably we also discuss the Cardiff weekend and speculate that a West Ham final and a repeat of Steven Gerrard's greatest ever domestic game could be on again this season.

Our stop-off is Frankley services, which we affectionately call 'Mr Shankly' after The Smiths track. On this bitter Saturday I notice Frankley now has a Greggs and remember that at the home leg of the Chelsea semi, I'd been persuaded to go for a pie in Homebaked – the new Co-operative bakery located on the site of the old Mitchells Bakery, which closed in 2010. Now that was a magnificent Scouse pie – made by hand, not machine, by salt-of-the-earth lasses. We also witnessed them chopping up food for an elderly gent with badly disabled hands. In essence, a wonderful and worthy new addition to my matchday staple, alongside four cans of Red Stripe on the wall before and curry and chips from Sing Fong afterwards.

Today I'm sat next to 'Wise' Joe Campbell, which means some solid insights into the game and a chance to quiz him on how he thinks this side has been progressing after the defeat at Old Trafford. As it's below zero you'd think we'd be grateful that the large flags are covering us in Block 207 for much of the build-up, but we know better. At the Chelsea game last season, where we were stood close enough to Iago Aspas to give him some for the worst corner in the club's history, Karl pointed out that the enormous flag – the one that cover most of the Kop – absolutely reeks. Campbell Sr agrees that it needs a good wash.

The first half is marked by a low-key atmosphere despite West Ham selling their full allocation of tickets for the fixture. There's some great approach play in the middle third and some wonderful invention from Phil Coutinho, but it's not until Lazar Markovic misses a sitter just before half-time that Liverpool really look like scoring.

At half-time it's a scrum across from 207 to 203 to see my old man, his Welsh mate, my brother, and my pal from school, Lynchie, who has bought my godson's brother, another Pete, along to the match. Generally the consensus is that if we can finish we'll win this, and Daniel Sturridge should make his long-awaited comeback if it stays 0-0.

So it all transpires as Sturridge comes off the bench to make it 2-0 following a goal from Raheem Sterling on the back of good link-up play with Coutinho. Given that we look more solid at the back and the approach play in the second half is backed up by a genuine goal threat, I conclude to 'Wise' Joe that this is our best home league game of the season, to which he nods.

So as I take a run over to Sing Fong to be warmed up by their radioactive curry sauce, I'm thinking there is some cause to be properly optimistic. I articulate this on the wall, adding that given the lows of the first half of the season, if Brendan can win some silverware and keep the fight for fourth interesting until late in the season, it will, in some ways, be a bigger achievement than last season's title charge.

Once back in Dev's motor, Kev requests that we get the foot down as we're keen to get back to London to see Kevin Mitchell, one of the East End's other favourite sporting institutions, in his big fight. Talk idly wanders on to the logistical arrangements for LFC games ahead of the Easter break. Once we get on to Southampton I suggest we stop off for beers and a ruby in Winchester, something I've lobbied for every year since they've come back into the league.

I guess it's back to that passion thing. Some people want to climb Everest, walk from pole to pole, or be Prime Minister. Not me. At 7pm in late January, post my 36th birthday, I'm perfectly content with a Reds win and a plan to stop off in a medieval English town on the way to the Saints in mid-March.

4 February 2015, Bolton 1 Liverpool 2
(replay; 0-0 in original tie)

'A bum with one cheek is never as saucy'

By Roy Henderson

Bolton. Bolton in the FA Cup fourth round. The thought of Bolton for some reason brings a whole torrent of modern toss to mind. Like *Phoenix Nights*. My old boss had its theme tune on his mobile, and he was a cock. Max and Paddy. That's Paddy McGuinness. Let the bacon see the eggs. It's all Peter Kay's doing, actually. The insufferable little fella who's doing those Fray Bentos ads on syndicated radio – he's off *Phoenix Nights* an' all. Specifically though, Dave Spikey comes to mind, adapting the words of Patrice Rushen's 'Forget Me Not' to sell bin bags in a local supermarket. Modern toss.

'Come and get your black bin bags, they're long and black and slender. Heavy duty black bin bags, no matter what your gender.' *Dave Spikey, Phoenix Nights.*

Yet somehow, despite all that, Bolton still brings happy thoughts to mind. Our mate Elli – she's from Bolton, and Shaun Keaveny. I like Shaun Keaveny. Somehow it feels like he's on 6 Music each morning as a kind of diddy daddy proxy for me and everyone else my age, cracking the jokes that are running through our minds, doing the bad impressions we do to ourselves in our cars.

So Bolton's not all bad. It's Danny Boyle and Badly Drawn Boy. It's not all Peter Kay and Paddy McGuinness. It's Jay Jay Okocha and Youri Djorkaeff. It's not all John McGinlay and Andy Walker.

It's also Mixu Paatelainen.

That's the one redeeming feature about *Phoenix Nights*, the fact they name-checked Mixu Paatelainen. He played for Dundee United in the late 1980s, and we loved Big Mixu back then. Big Mixu, the Finnish Hulk Hogan, all chunk and middleweight presence, tearing up divots on the turf of my beloved Tannadice Park.

I'm a Dundee United fan, you see. Born in Glasgow in 1974, my family moved to Dundee shortly afterwards and my dad, being football obsessed, started to attend whatever game was on at the weekend. He'd go to see Dundee FC one week and Dundee United the next – he wasn't fussed at that point, he just loved football, and his first love on that front was a few hundred miles south, in Liverpool.

Both cities were on the cusp of witnessing football the like of which they'll maybe never see again. Teams born of hard graft, organisation and selfless work, pressing from the front, yet content when needed to sit deep and dig it out on the counter, or even just grind out what was needed to do the job. Each team capable of the sublime, of the rapier sharp, of flair and verve and collective movement and pace. Of genuine magic. We were spoiled.

My dad wasn't daft. He started to take me and my sister to Tannadice and Jim McLean's side didn't disappoint. They won the club's first silverware in 1979, then another cup the year after, and the only league title the club has ever won in 1983, when I was nine, going on to reach the semi-final of the European Cup the following year, cheated out of a final against no less than Liverpool in Rome by the corrupt machinery of *that* Roman club.

That Liverpool won the final and their fourth European Cup against them in their backyard was testament to the club's enduring greatness, but it was a heartbreak for me and my father at the time. You see, when Dundee United hosted the Romans at Tannadice we were down at Anfield watching Sammy Lee score the only goal in the first leg of the other semi-final. My dad loved Liverpool and Anfield, and that week was my first experience of the place. Aged ten, the experience consigned me to a lifetime of footballing bigamy, the early years of which were festooned with silvery glee.

My dad could scarcely have planned things better. Yet even in leaner times, my brainwashing hadn't gone too badly. With Dundee United riding high in the SPL and soon to face a League Cup semi of their own, Liverpool hosted Bolton at teatime.

At quarter to five, while driving, I said to myself, 'This is massive. Massive.' There was no shaking it. Bradford's impressive ouster of Chelsea at Stamford Bridge, Middlesbrough having done the same at the Etihad, Leicester having stillettoed Spurs...massive. Suddenly this was massive. An FA Cup fourth round tie against Bolton, on a chilly January night under the floodlights. Massive.

In the car, my son Jonathan said, 'Dad, if Chelsea aren't in it any more, and if Man City aren't in it any more, and if Spurs aren't in it any more, does that mean Liverpool will win it?'

I said, 'Well son, it means they have a good chance.'

My son Oliver said, 'But Steven Gerrard isn't with us any more, is he dad?'

I said, 'He's still here until the end of the season, son. And guess what?'

Oliver said, 'What?'

I said, 'The final's on his birthday. I bet you he wins it. It'll be the best day of his life.'

Oliver said, 'I hope he does.'

I said, 'I hope so too, son.'

It'd be massive. Massive.

In my mind, by 5pm, Liverpool had ribbons on the cup already. The feeling lurched into the pit of my gut as news of Jose Mourinho conceding the game early and sashaying down the tunnel hit 5 Live. So I was becoming unusually uptight as kick-off approached because, massive or not, we knew what to expect from the visitors.

Following Liverpool and Dundee United through the 1980s reaped a footballing tutelage that was rich and varied, peppered with lessons in both the effective and the cavalier – the pragmatic and the sensational.

In the early part of the decade, if either of my teams faced a tricky draw away in a cup it was only natural they'd sit deep, stay disciplined, defend for their lives, and hit with pace and quality on the break if they could muster it. That was how a tricky away tie in the cup worked, wasn't it dad? And when you needed to break a padlock you fielded the locksmiths, ideally ones who doubled up as playground bullies, didn't you dad?

So Bolton. Bolton in the fourth round of the FA Cup. We knew what to expect, didn't we? This was only compounded by the involvement of Neil Lennon, journeyman midfield dynamo when playing south of the border who grew into something of a General under Martin O'Neill's tutelage. He embodied the obdurate directness of his manager's approach to the game, and eventually graduated to the dugout.

Of course, Ra Selleck had a good spell under Gordon Strachan after O'Neill's departure, but their fans never took to him. Not *really*. That always got on my tits, because as a child I'd met Strachan and despite him having played for Aberdeen and later Man United and Leeds, I always remember how bloody nice he'd been.

Stories abound of this everywhere around my manor – Strachan is a good egg, despite the persona he sometimes projects in the media.

A genuine, kind-hearted, cheeky wee chappy. And during *his* time there it was that little bit harder to loathe Ra Selleck, albeit never quite impossible because while never as loathsome as Ra Rangers, the embodiment of establishment grotesque, they were always there, propping Ra Rangers up, being largely as objectionable and self-serving.

It was odd to feel less inclined to loathe them for a while. But that all changed when Neil Lennon took the helm. You see as manager of Ra Selleck, Lennon was the embodiment of everything about them that was loathsome. The permanent scowl of disdain, the sudden transmission of that sensibility to his squad of players, the needless bellicosity at every turn – needless that was until Ally McCoist took the helm at Ra Rangers, when the picture was once again complete; two loathsome cheeks of the same loathsome bum, clapping furiously upon each other as the Old Firm's gyratory twerking resumed in earnest. The two men squaring up to each other on the touchline, goading officials and opposing coaches, and just being typically *them*. Horrible twats, the lot of them.

But you had to concede that Lennon, bless his little heart, had an ability when facing a tricky draw away in a cup, facing wealthier and more sophisticated opponents, to sit deep, stay disciplined, and coax his team into defending for their lives. He'd even manage to occasionally hit with pace and quality on the break from time to time. So much so that Lennon even established himself a managerial pedigree on the Champions League stage, along with three back-to-back title wins, albeit in diminished Sevconian circumstances as the extent of the Ibrox tomfoolery became all too clear shortly into his reign. And Celtic, in the absence of *them*, weren't as sexy as they might have been – a bum with one cheek is never as saucy – and with Lennon hot property, and with the permanent subliminal hum of sectarian menace in the background, he made the perhaps sensible decision to leave them, determined to prove his mettle in England once more.

Stints in the media followed, with the formerly divisive figure cutting a reasonable, even personable figure on screen and radio, with insightful, measured comment when called upon. It was a mind fuck. The man appeared and sounded almost likeable at times.

But when Bolton came calling, off he popped. He started well. Too well, from a Liverpudlian perspective. And when Bolton arrived at Anfield for the late kick-off under the floodlights in the FA Cup, we knew what to expect. Bolton with a twist of Lennon. A little more obdurate and organised, but still Bolton, surely. Still a mid-table Championship side with Eidur Gudjohnsen and Big Ivanhoe up front, both pushing 40. They'd be a sight for sore eyes.

The sight of referee Kevin 'No Friend Of Mine' Friend only compounded this fear. Friend looking for all the world like a pantomime dame, with eyebrows that screamed Jared Leto in *Dallas Buyers Club*, or Terence Stamp in *Priscilla Queen Of The Desert*. The man looked like Jame Gumb and evoked the same dread, his eyebrows, straight from kick-off, proving a horrendous distraction. He wanted to be the story, Kevin Friend, rather than the unseen man in black – the man with the prompt cards, only stepping in to use them when absolutely necessary.

Bolton started in typical Lennon style, pressing the Reds deep into their own half, but there seemed no way they could sustain that into the longer reaches of the game with their two old men up front. No way they could cope with the relentless stamina and pace and movement of the Tricky Reds, so they'd surely retreat when the time came. So in time-honoured tradition, we'd see them settle into their shape, and throw everything at set pieces. We were, of course, born again capable when defending set pieces, but the wounds of early season were still fresh, still tender. A few frights might lie in wait, because the game was massive. Suddenly massive.

Shortly thereafter the pantomime dame set about turning the game into a pantomime, somehow failing to intervene when a beleaguered Matt Mills, singularly incapable of dealing with Raheem Sterling's movement, rugby tackled him. We'd seen John Terry pin the kid to the floor with a wrestling move the Tuesday before, but this was new – an actual 'dip the shoulder and go through your man' Mickey Skinner-style rugby tackle. If you're on the end of that every game at what point does it become acceptable to use the hand-off? And with the incident still fresh in the mind, Joe Allen got the same treatment from Carlos Vela. But by then we knew what to expect from Bolton, and we knew what to expect from Friend.

To be fair, Bolton showed some nice touches. Darren Pratley, who played under Brendan Rodgers at Swansea, showed some craft, and some crafty gamesmanship from time to time. But they still had that Bolton whiff about them, that physicality that lingers in the nostrils – Eau De Allardyce. And soon afterwards, with the Chelsea second leg looming large, Phil Coutinho seemed to pull up holding his hamstring. I thought to myself, 'Just get him off.' But then a second or so later it dawned on me, 'Oh no, this is massive. Let's just see.'

And they waited and saw, and Coutinho was fine. Along with Sterling, both twisting and turning and stretching their backline. We were comfortable, with Emre Can mopping up whatever Pratley and the two septuagenarians could throw at us up the other end.

On the half hour, the Bolton end sang 'Steve Gerrard, Gerrard, he slipped on his fucking arse' and another little piece of me died inside. Of course, that's the way things work nowadays – that's how people express their admiration for the greats. The last time the River Plate fans saw Juan Riquelme play, they broke into applause. These days in Britain we know only the snide. The ridiculous.

And the game died an inevitable death. We tried to play, and in fact played quite well, but the issues this squad will face in the second half of the season were there for all to see. We need cover for Daniel Sturridge – effective cover. We need to be sure our goalkeepers won't stand aside when balls are directed at their goal, flap at corners and free kicks, and make a general arse of things with the ball at their feet. But we know the men in the suits won't do a bloody thing about it. Perhaps it's some kind of Lenten fast in footballing terms. Who knows. All I know is it stinks. This side is a hop and a skip from being something scary. The Bolton game was yet more evidence of that.

After the game, Rodgers was asked about Mario Balotelli and replied by giving him short shrift. The Twitter crowd reacted as expected. In my mind's eye, behind the scenes, Ian Ayre danced round his front room in his Dunkin' Donuts onesie to 'Stuck In The Middle With You', a lovelorn finger squeaking a dewy gap in the mist of the window, his new Harley 'Jolene' stood proudly, seductively outside, tastefully lit in late evening moonlight. Or so I imagined it. I know for damn sure he wasn't out buying his manager a striker.

Fast forward what, ten days? And somehow, inexplicably, the world is a brighter place. We hammered Chelsea 0-0 at Stamford Bridge, somehow managing to leave Branislav Ivanovic unmarked in extra time, and were hailed from all corners as the better side on the night. And then Sturridge was reborn, his injection into the fray against WHAM! (sorry, I enjoy referring to them that way) made such an immediate, penetrative difference it all but brought a tear to the eye. In the two intervening games, Liverpool looked for all the world like the team they were in the preceding season.

At some point in recent weeks, it seemed Simon Mignolet had also been hypnotised into believing he was a functional goalkeeper. The fingers had snapped, Mongo had come to, and pulling on his gloves he wandered on to the park and started commanding his box, punching with purpose, looking like he knew what he wanted to do when the ball arrived at his feet. He is never going to be Hugo Lloris but here he is, playing his own game.

It was just as well. The intervening period had also seen the transfer window draw to a close with acute frustration on my part. Anyone with a brain could see that this squad needed a keeper and a striker that complemented the way our manager wanted to play football. At that point we were still in all three cups with a top-four finish looking increasingly possible. You'd have thought we'd have wanted to bolster our chances.

Regardless, the actual team on the actual park was resurgent, despite missing out on the League Cup Final, and I began to *almost* enjoy the anticipation of Liverpool games, home and away.

Can was the big story. Yes, Sturridge was increasingly fit, and yes, Mignolet was benefiting from the 'wake him up and tell him he's Clem' hypnosis routine, but Can's emergence has been a joy to behold. You get the feeling that wherever you fielded this manchild, he'd look like the best player on the park by a distance.

So we travelled to the Macron with high hopes. Compounding this was the fact Bolton were unable to field their superhero goalie. And with Ivanhoe missing for the return leg, they were forced to play Micky Skin…sorry, Matt Mills, up front. You remember him – the big fella who should have had a three-game ban off the back of his rugby tackling exploits in the first game? He proved to be a mild pain in the shorts but Liverpool dominated proceedings in the first half, playing at tempo, penning the Bolton players in to their own defensive third.

Coutinho was a joy – an actual joy – to watch throughout. He'd signed the mother of all contract extensions, evidently to pour balm on the transfer inactivity, and here he was looking a world beater – again. Sterling too, who hit the post with a moment of pure quality on the half hour.

It would surely come…again. But come it didn't and the Reds trotted back in for the half-time oranges at 0-0…again.

After the break Liverpool continued to play at tempo, with some beautiful lengthy passages of wonderful passing football, movement and incision. But Bolton were resolute, and while we just couldn't seem to finish – the woodwork rattling like Evelyn Glennie's xylophone as player after player came inches from a worldie – Martin Skrtel lunged in on the impressive Zach Clough as he scampered into the box and hey presto, Bolton had the spot-kick and the lead.

But the team kept playing, and playing, and playing. Shortly after the goal, Neil Danns made a second overexuberant challenge on Allen and was rightly dismissed. So would the tide turn? Rodgers swapped Allen for Sturridge, and hopes rose again.

But it wasn't until Can decided he wanted to make things different that lo and behold things started to look genuinely different. Our Emre demanded possession and cheekily dinked the ball over the seemingly

50-strong Bolton backline and into the path of the onrushing Sterling, whose eye triangulated it in the floodlit sky, and whose left instep struck it cleanly on the drop and through the advancing keeper's legs to equalise.

Mein Gott! What a moment! Maybe we shouldn't have been surprised when the decisive moment came. But what a moment...again.

Coutinho dropped a shoulder, made space to swing his right foot at the ball and clipped a dipping strike that looked as if it had taken a deflection off his marker en route to goal, looping over the keeper's head and shaving a few microns of paint off the underside of the bar as it bulged the roof of the net. A moment of sublime, decisive footballing beauty, lighting the fuse upon an enormous bed of adrenalin and tension. Safe to say my brain arrived at its happy place.

To football! To Mixu! But mostly to Gerrard and the happiest of birthdays.

This is going to be massive. Massive.

7 February 2015, Everton 0 Liverpool 0

'Ifithadnerbeenforheysel'

By Mike Nevin

Oh, Jesus. Here it is again. Right on bloody cue. Derby fucking Belly. Not one for the general practitioner, this. No, this is a peculiar malaise that strikes at the core of every Liverpudlian twice a year. Generally on a Thursday afternoon. There is no cure.

The build-up to Merseyside's 'family feud' fosters light-headedness and eats away at the stomach, but where a decent Alka-Seltzer can tame the worst of hangovers, you're stuck with this bastard for at least another 48 hours.

If there are complications, symptoms can linger for weeks, if not months. If surgery, in the form of revenge, is required (which can seem the only option in defeat) the afflicted in this country will be familiar with six-to-nine-month waiting lists.

In layman's terms you're shit-scared of getting beat; more so than in any other game. The derby, laced with the terrifying potential of the pub-office-bus stop-school-betting shop-aftermath, still outstrips our Manchester United grudge match in this respect. Needy Evertonians will be as horny as a sex-starved rhino at that admission. Any giddy excitement resulting from good form is tempered by the awful prospect of defeat.

It's the same as ever this week, and once Bolton in the FA Cup is negotiated, butterflies nagging away since Monday morph into a full-blown attack on my nervous and gastric constitution.

For me it wasn't always thus, although admittedly it's a long time since Derby Belly didn't rival acid reflux as the complaint which most interferes with my sleep. As it stands, at the age of 47, my aversion to Everton and Evertonians is on a par with...er, well nothing actually.

Growing up in the late 1970s, when Bob Paisley followed Bill Shankly in guiding the Reds to domestic and European dominance, Everton sat in the shade of a Mersey penumbra cast by Liverpool. Rather than the lame Blues, my adolescent bias was targeted at authentic title rivals; Leeds, Nottingham Forest and the darlings of the press, Manchester United.

The 1970s Blues, under Billy Bingham and latterly Gordon Lee, became vaguely comical having declined hurriedly from their reputation as football's 'School of Science' a decade before. A passionate but cordial rivalry between Shankly's embryonic Liverpool and the refined Everton of the Harry Catterick era was a distant memory. Long gone was the 'Holy Trinity' of Howard Kendall, Colin Harvey and Alan Ball, as was the zenith of the financial backing of the Moores family drawn from the wealth of Littlewoods Pools. A hackneyed, lame joke of the era spoke of a man whose dog turned summersaults when Liverpool won a derby, begging the question, 'What trick does he perform if Everton win?' The punchline? 'I don't know. I've only had him ten years.'

In the midst of this period came the infamous Clive Thomas 'incident'. Overwhelming favourites in the 1977 FA Cup semi-final, Liverpool had underperformed on a bog of a pitch at a rain-lashed Maine Road so that with minutes to go, the game was on a knife edge at 2-2. I listened to the radio commentary at my Evertonian granddad's house and can still hear his mocking cheers from the kitchen as Bryan Hamilton glanced home what sounded like a shock Everton winner.

But hang on granddad Sam, wait a minute…referee Thomas, perhaps in a moment of suspended disbelief, has disallowed the goal for an unlikely handball. Or was it offside?

The Welsh official, with a penchant for last-minute hullabaloo, didn't seem entirely clear on the matter afterwards, much to the chagrin of the Blues. The prototype for decades of Evertonian wailing over refereeing decisions was firmly in place, none more so than in the big derbies. Step forward 'you Redshite bastards in the black', Alan Robinson, Graham Poll, Mark Clattenburg and Martin Atkinson *et al.*

While the Reds swept all before them, Everton's woes continued into the early 1980s. The derby match nadir for the Blues came in November 1982 when Ian Rush's four-goal salvo condemned them to a chastening 5-0 home defeat. Strangely, I recall little overt bitterness from the Blue half of the city while we crowed over our growing local supremacy. Such was the performance gap between the clubs that acceptance of Liverpool's domination had become part of the Goodison psyche; venom reserved for manager Howard Kendall and the board of directors. Everton fans voted with their feet and stayed away in their thousands as attendances in Walton routinely dipped below 20,000.

Suddenly, though, and without warning, Evertonian fortunes were dramatically revived. From the brink of the sack, Kendall survived a Milk Cup tie watched by just 9,080 hardy Blue souls against Coventry in November 1983 with two late goals. A resurgence in confidence and the emergence of young players Neville Southall, Trevor Steven and Graeme Sharp, allied to the rebirth of the battle-scarred signings Peter Reid and Andy Gray, saw them to Wembley and a first cup final meeting with Liverpool. In hindsight, it was a remarkable managerial feat for Kendall to transform a team of tyros and virtual crocks into a potent force in the blink of an eye.

At a time of political strife caused by central government policy which wrought shared hardship for all but the few on Merseyside, the inaugural mass outing to Wembley in March 1984 was dubbed the 'Friendly Final' and treated as a weekend of release from the pressures of unemployment and domestic financial gloom by Red and Blue alike. Everton's revival and unexpected presence on the big stage was a relatively novel experience for Liverpudlians growing tired of a league where the strongest challenge in the early 80s came from the likes of Ipswich, Watford and Southampton.

Fans travelled together to London united in solidarity and determined to make a positive impression on a nation which increasingly lapped up negative, media-driven Scouse stereotypes. The occasion passed off in fine style, with mutual chanting of 'Merseyside' before and after a goalless draw notable only for relentless rain and the blue fume over Alan Hansen's goal line handball which went unnoticed by the referee. Predictably, the Reds prevailed in the replay to claim the first leg of a unique treble, but Everton's growing revival continued apace with a return visit to Wembley for the FA Cup Final and a first trophy in 14 years courtesy of 2-0 win over Watford.

The city of Liverpool had abruptly become the capital of English football, fostering a healthy, good-natured rivalry reminiscent of that which underpinned the healthy competition of the preceding generation.

For much of the following season, Liverpool toiled while Everton surpassed even their own supporters' expectations by romping to the First Division title and a virgin European triumph in the 1985 Cup Winners' Cup. Both teams excelled in the FA Cup, too, and the Reds gathered themselves sufficiently to reach a fifth European Cup Final in Brussels – ample compensation for losing our domestic crown to the neighbours.

At the age of 17 it just felt like a lot of fun. We would come into school on a Monday morning and swap stories of our away trips, our football special train journeys to the outposts of the country, and in some cases our escapades abroad. There was intense rivalry and much piss-taking, but it seldom got out of hand. In the Red corner there were genuine concerns that Everton, for the first time in a generation, were superior – as evidenced by the league table.

Then came Heysel and over the years that followed the dynamic of the rivalry changed. In the wake of the ban on English clubs from European competition, Everton were denied the opportunity to test their mettle in the European Cup, but on the home front things carried on as normal. The 1985/86 season, in which Liverpool pipped the Blues to the league and FA Cup to land a first domestic double, must have been hard to take for Evertonians. However, the second all-Merseyside excursion to Wembley for the FA Cup Final was another proud day, unsullied by any trouble despite so much being at stake. Everton fans were naturally downhearted but melted away into the night while the Reds partied.

Gradually over the remainder of the decade, Liverpool under the talismanic management of Kenny Dalglish reasserted their supremacy while Everton – although champions again in 1987 – lost Kendall to a new challenge in Spain with Athletic Bilbao. In turn, key players like Steven and Gary Stevens jumped ship for the lure of European football – and no doubt a fat pay packet – with Glasgow Rangers as the Blues entered a slow decline.

Hillsborough saw Everton and their supporters offer unconditional support and sympathy for their friends and neighbours; symbolised by a chain of scarves which stretched from Goodison to Anfield in the wake of the tragedy. The FA Cup Final of that year was a fitting tribute; Liverpool again the victors, although in hindsight the notion of attending a competitive match so soon after the heartbreak of Sheffield is harder to rationalise now than it was at the time.

Generally speaking, save for the sporadic actions of an unthinking minority, such empathy from Everton has persisted to the present day, and in the aftermath of the Hillsborough Independent Panel report in September 2012 the indelible image of the two children walking on to the Goodison Park pitch hand in hand, combining the numbers '9' and '6' on the back of their respective Red and Blue shirts, did much for the understanding that football rivalry of any depth should never usurp matters of life and death.

Everton chairman Bill Kenwright, a decent man with football in his heart, deserves great credit.

Overall, though, the last 20 years has undoubtedly seen a growing nastiness between the two sets of supporters as a new generation has taken to the sport.

The 1990s was a largely barren decade, seeing sharp decline for both clubs, albeit on a different scale. While Liverpool, bolstered by enduringly strong funds off the back of a world-renowned name, tried and consistently failed to match the new might of Man United, Everton, suffering the consequences of woeful boardroom stewardship and steadily imploding finances, twice flirted with relegation. How we laughed as the Blues threatened to lose their proud top-flight status dating back to 1954, and how we mourned their barely credible escapes from the trapdoor in 1994 and 1997.

With little more to look forward to than the perennial scrap to avoid the drop, Evertonians' hopes for each season appeared to rest solely with denying Liverpool six derby points in the Reds' admittedly flimsy, annual mission to reclaim a place among the elite.

I have a disturbing recollection of a frenzied Bluenose leering into a TV camera after one of Everton's last-day escapes and screaming into the lens, 'Ha, ha, ha – fuck off Liverpool – we're back to haunt yers!' The whole Evertonian raison d'être had reduced to an insular pleasure at the failings of Liverpool.

And, during this time, they developed a defensive 'no blame' culture bordering on propaganda, so well-versed were their consistent claims during the increasingly common and petty alehouse disputes with their Red counterparts. 'We've got no money' was the most well-worn of the clichés, which conveniently ignored the longevity of their own mismanagement in the dressing room and boardroom.

Evertonians appeared to revel in their lowly status, but were also slowly rotting in their own bile; apparently happy as long as the Redshite remained in the shadows of United and Arsenal. Suffice to say, Gary McAllister's last minute free kick winner in the 2001 Goodison derby, as Gerard Houllier's Liverpool chased a treble and Champions League football, didn't go down well amid a thoroughly poisonous Good Friday atmosphere.

By the dawn of the new millennium it had become tiresome to engage in a football discussion with your average Evertonian, and if it remained civil for more than a few minutes the topic of conversation would seldom be about goings-on at Goodison. The Blues had become experts on the Reds; a whole city now obsessed over the fortunes of one club – and it wasn't Everton.

Sadly Heysel, a decade and a half after the ban which impacted on Everton and Liverpool too, was often cited as the sole reason why

Everton couldn't compete. A new generation of increasingly bitter Blues lapped this up, as the word 'Ifithadnerbeenforheysel' seeped into the Mersey football lexicon.

Then, in 2002, along came David Moyes. Arriving from Preston North End to stem the tide of yet another relegation battle, the Glaswegian instantly curried favour with his new public. During his unveiling at an opening press conference he claimed, 'I am from a city that is not unlike Liverpool. I am joining the people's football club. The majority of people you meet on the street are Everton fans.'

There's no doubt Liverpool cast a wider net when drawing support from outside the city. The club's enduring ability to compete with the nouveau riche and established powers of the Premier League is built on a worldwide following that boosts the Anfield coffers. However, the notion that Liverpool is a city awash with Evertonians is the classic urban myth. If Moyes ever cast a glance across the playing fields of Merseyside he would have been at a loss to explain the overwhelming majority of red shirts adorning the Steven Gerrards and Robbie Fowlers of the future. In fact, of late, the lonely Everton shirts are often outnumbered by those of Barcelona and Real Madrid.

The now since-departed Moyesiah enjoyed his best season in 2005 when Everton claimed a Champions League qualification spot by finishing fourth; above Liverpool in the league for the first time in 18 years. Liverpool somewhat outdid his achievement in Istanbul a few weeks later, making a mockery of his champagne celebration when he invited the Sky TV cameras into his home to film him slurping the bubbles while wearing a very silly cardigan.

Of course such derision all sounds a trifle bitter on our part, and let's be honest – we too love a gloat when we come out on top. But an endless stream of clever little Moyes digs referencing Liverpool's superior spending power, while always refreshing his standing among Evertonians, did little for the ever more tense relationship between the clubs' supporters.

Blues might argue Rafa Benitez did likewise by referring to Everton as one of the 'smaller teams' after their cynical approach to an Anfield derby in February 2007, but if Benitez was unpopular among Evertonians it was largely due to his tactical acumen, supremacy over Moyes and restoration of the sworn Red enemy to European repute.

On balance, Moyes did a solid job of improving Everton's average position in the upper reaches of the table and, in his final two Goodison seasons, capitalised on Liverpool's inconsistency to finish above the Reds. Nevertheless, it's hard to imagine that a decade-long tenure devoid of silverware – and defeat in the 2012 Merseyside FA Cup semi-final when the Blues had much in their favour – would have earned him such Evertonian kudos without his continuous, thinly-veiled sniping at Liverpool.

After Moyes departed for Old Trafford in came the urbane, classy Roberto Martinez. Through the emergence of Ross Barkley, the shrewd signing of James McCarthy and loan acquisitions Romelu Lukaku and Gareth Barry, 'The Ev' looked a distinctly dangerous proposition during his first season, just falling short of the top four.

Evertonians initially warmed to his cultured passing style, never more evident than in last season's epic 3-3 at Goodison, and were sufficiently aroused by the prospect of Champions League football to overlook the abhorrent, concurrent prospect of a Liverpool title win. As it turned out, both clubs fell just short of their goals, but respectively strong seasons saw a minor thaw in the ever more frosty relationship between Red and Blue.

If the Goodison faithful were all into Bobby M's blue suit and brown brogue look last season, they've well and truly reverted to unsophisticated type this year as 'The Ev' have struggled big-time. Most Evertonians have reprised their honeymoon view of Martinez and the boos have wobbled the wooden boards of the old Goodison stands. The Blues have left behind their flirtation with the cavalier and reverted to default roundhead mode.

Last weekend's spawny 1-0 win at Crystal Palace has, for now, staved off growing fears of the drop. But Martinez's stock remains low. From the outside looking in, it appears the cooling of the Everton crowd towards Martinez goes both ways. Flat Goodison atmospheres at most games, which rival Anfield at its corporate worst, are one thing, but the parochial mindset and gleeful response of the Everton crowd to last season's 3-2 home defeat by Manchester City was also a massive eye-opener for Martinez. For rabid Blues, it was the most convenient of defeats.

Running parallel with Everton's pre- and post-Christmas plunge has been the Reds' healing from the trauma of our Premier League near miss in May. The travails of autumn have given way to a new spring in Brendan Rodgers's Liverpool step. As we enter February the Anfield patient is in recovery, with the extra-time reverse at Chelsea in the Capital One Cup semi-final the only blemish in 13 games. The summer scars are healing.

Rodgers's Reds are sitting up in the hospital bed, and it is Lucas Leiva who has brought the grapes. The return of the much-maligned Brazilian's pragmatic midfield presence has provided a base for the renewed fluidity and attacking play brought by the 3-4-3 system

Rodgers has engineered to cast off the torpor of autumn. So, Derby Belly notwithstanding, we're favourites today to continue the renewed push for a second consecutive season in the Champions League.

I wake at 6.40am and go for a run to soothe the collywobbles, but there are still hours to kill before the match. Unusually Sky TV is showing the game in the early evening, which has caused an almighty hoo-ha in the week before the match, with Merseyside Police taking the city council to court over the proposed 5.30pm kick-off. It seems the local constabulary, at odds with the sentiments of match-goers, don't trust the local football fraternity to behave itself under the cover of darkness and with the potential for afternoon drinking. Normal police presence at Goodison will be tripled and overtime paid in abundance to ensure the occasion passes off without incident at the ground and in the city centre. It is hardly the best message to convey on the citizens of Liverpool while the Hillsborough inquests continue in Warrington.

I've been lucky enough to source a ticket – and in our end, too. No sitting on my hands, gagged for self-preservation, in the enemy territory of the Main Stand, or worse, the Gwladys Street or Park End.

I watch a bit of the early afternoon racing on Channel 4, but it's no good. I've got to get out of the house. With apologies to the boys in blue – the ones with the helmets – I need an early drink.

I arrange to meet up with my Anfield Wrap cohorts Rob Gutmann and Neil Atkinson. These lads love their food and they're heading to Amalia, a little Italian place near Duke Street in town. It will not just be about the food – I've already eaten a simple stomach-settling egg and beans combo – and I anticipate arriving to a table full of ale. I'm not disappointed. I order a large bottle of Peroni at a cost of £6.10. On the one hand, it's a fucking ridiculous price when I can get three of these for a fiver in Booze Buster to accompany watching the darts on a Thursday night, but on the other it's effectively the same amount of ale that would come in two standard-size Peroni bottles at £3.05 a throw. So fair play.

Time is scuttling on now and I'm not remotely pissed enough for the trauma ahead, so I buy into Rob and Neil's round, which has moved on from beer to wine, soaked up by anything edible that accompanies the ubiquitous avocado.

We're joined by the sturdy presence of my mates Chris Maguire and Johnny Milburn, who are representing the ticketless thousands. They're watching the game in the safe haven – the exclusion zone, if you like – of the Liverpool Supporters' Club up near our ground.

At 4.30pm it's time to go. As darkness falls Neil and I share a cab, dropping off Johnny and Chris, while Rob taxis up with his lad, Danny, plus friends Paul and Giulio. There's plenty of animated chat on the way up but it's all tinged with those unpleasant nerves.

Neil and I get out the cab just as the police are shepherding a throng of Liverpudlians, who have been boozing near Anfield, along the last few hundred yards of the walk past Stanley Park round to the away section of the Upper Bullens Stand. We melt into the Liverpool escort and enjoy the tribalism of the moment. There's a bit of minor to-ing and fro-ing between some of our young lads and a few game Evertonians, but nothing to justify the suffocating police presence. For the umpteenth time I marvel at how our local force engage in the Movember concept all year round. Establishment dickheads.

Inside the ground there's time for two rapid pints with Neil before we take our seats. Under the lights, Goodison is a stunning vista – a kaleidoscope of colour majoring on the green of the playing surface and its clash with blood red and royal blue. This is one of the most beautiful sights in English football. It's much easier on the eye than on the nerves.

The game then kicks off and, well, nothing happens.

The atmosphere, buoyant at the start, is crushed by an appallingly dull first half. Everton, clearly targeting a point, stifle, smother and suppress. Liverpool can't get going, although Jordon Ibe, recalled from a loan spell at Derby County, cuts in from the right to unleash a left-footer which collides with the outside post at the Gwladys Street.

Half-time is upon us. Downstairs I see my old mate Billy Harrop, a veteran of the away games, and hear the unmistakable, exaggerated Scouse strains of another Billy, Billy the Farmer, a notorious, loyal, bat-crazy Liverpudlian. Meanwhile Neil and I have another pint, which we carve up with Martin Fitzgerald. The real beauty of football is right there; friends old and new brought together by the match, sharing a half-time bevvy and a gab. Nervous as a litter of kittens we are, but we're all smiles on the outside. If there is a sadness it's that thousands of Merseysiders have already been priced out of this weekly camaraderie.

The second half is only marginally better. The big moment nearly arrives when Steven Gerrard, a hitherto peripheral figure in his final derby, has a spectacularly athletic overhead kick deflected over at the Park End.

Liverpool continue to press and probe, but with Lucas off injured and Phil Coutinho also looking lame, we don't really trouble Joel Robles in the Everton goal. Barkley then comes off the Everton bench and frees Seamus Coleman, who forces Simon Mignolet into the reaction save of the match.

As the minutes tick away, I just want it to be over; the acute fear of defeat outweighing any lingering desire for the three points. The ref blows and that's it – a goalless draw to rival any of the mind-numbing derby stalemates I grew up watching in the 1970s.

Any ideas of going back into town to celebrate have long since been despatched. I shun the idea of a taxi and head for Bank Hall station – a walk which takes me back to my formative years going to the match.

As I near the station, walking along a sadly depressed, poverty stricken Stanley Road, I realise I'm starving. My Derby Belly has well and truly worn off, probably until next season, although we could still meet again this year in the Europa League. I wander into an off-licence and buy a bag of Hula Hoops for a quid. These are no ordinary Hula Hoops. They're massive, verging on the mutant, both bag and hoops, and I scoff them while waiting for the train home. They're a significantly tastier affair than the 224th Merseyside derby.

'We'll meet you by the wall after the match'

By Ian Salmon

For Robert Salmon. Bob. Dad

L ife is an accumulation of small moments reflected through memory and perspective. I see things differently now; literally and figuratively.

I'm sitting at a screen on Valentine's Day. A Saturday this year; a day when, no matter how much £5bn media deals distort the structure of our game, tradition dictates that you think about the match. And at half-past five I'll think about the match. I'll think about Crystal Palace in the FA Cup and that will lead to thinking about Crystal Palace in the semi-final in 1990 because there's no way the TV coverage will allow us not to. And in turn, that will lead to thinking about a 'beat bobby' in Birmingham casually saying, as we ran past him to that game, 'They never learn these Scousers do they?' Shocking then, shocking now.

No moment exists purely to itself, everything links to everything else. So I'm sitting on this Saturday thinking about Spurs last Tuesday, but then Spurs last Tuesday leads to so much more.

Mydad's birthday is next Friday. Friday is my dad's 80th birthday. Friday would have been my dad's 80th birthday. Sentences you never want to write.

I sit in the Main Stand now. I think I may have become a grown-up. I'm 51 and I think I've finally become a grown-up (my wife will probably dispute that theory). The season ticket that I was going to buy in 1986 on the back of the double (tumbling backwards down the Wembley steps, holding on to Fleety and screaming, 'We've done the fucking double!') – the season ticket that I didn't buy because I got a job that involved working Saturdays – looks like it's finally arrived. Anfield are being really good about it. The transfer is slow but it's happening.

All the scare stories about having to hand it back so a Norwegian tourist could get the benefit of a ticket that my dad held for nearly 60 years? No need to worry about them; the ticket's mine. My Kop days are over. I watch games from my dad's seat now and as long as I'm there – probably until they move us all for the redevelopment – it's my dad's seat. It always will be. The guys who sit around me are and always will be 'the blokes that sit by my dad'.

That hits you at times. It hit me during the Chelsea League Cup game; in the first half, that glorious first half under the Anfield lights that we've stood under on so many cold midweek nights, with the chill in the air and the warmth in your comrades. The snow which had started as I parked up became heavier, began to drift. We were attacking the Anfield Road end. In the snow and the lights, and looking like a Liverpool side – like a real Liverpool side, not a pallid shadow, not the early-season version, not the last version that my dad saw play. Like an actual, honest to God, legendary, glorious Liverpool side. I looked at all this and I thought, 'My dad should be seeing this.'

And the tears came. Briefly and unnoticed, but they came. It's the moments. Those moments. They're the ones that get you. Moments when I feel very aware that, although my brothers are watching from their seats in the Kop and knowing that our dad isn't in his seat, I'm watching from where he would be, where he should be, and I'm seeing exactly what he would see. I'm watching the game for him.

There was another moment, a much more terrible moment, when our dad watched from another stand for two of his sons. I'll come to that, I can't avoid coming to that.

I stood and I watched this wonderful display against Chelsea and I tried to figure out why I couldn't think of a single moment of losing to them in the league at Anfield. And then I remembered.

As we walked back across Stanley Park after this game, after another glorious performance, after another Liverpool performance, our Kev (youngest brother – middle brother Keith lives on the Isle of Man now, gets over as often as he can, coming over with his son Charlie for the Manchester City game) and I, aware that I was writing this, tried to pull together the moments as we recalled them. Tried to shape them.

Rituals change. What we did these last few years was this: Kev (Fazakerley-based) and I (Netherton) would meet at mum and dad's (Walton/Aintree) and me, him and dad would head to the match in one car. For an 8pm kick-off, Kev would arrange to meet at 7pm. I'd turn up at ten past. It's not deliberate. Not all the time. It's just what I do. We don't do this now. Generally we just go straight to the match. No need to all meet up anymore. Rituals change.

After the game we used to meet up by the wall at the corner where the Kop and the Main Stand meet. Dad from the Main Stand, us from the Kop, or wherever I'd managed to get a ticket for. The wall went a few years ago, but even when it became a mesh fence housing TV vans we would still 'meet by the wall'. The fence went. Replaced, quite poetically, by a wall. A big wooden wall to hide the digging behind it for the new Main Stand.

Dad always said that he wouldn't see the new ground built or the old one extended. 'Oh behave yourself, don't be so bloody miserable!' we'd reply. Always maintained that he wanted Spike Milligan's epigram 'Told you I was ill' on his gravestone. Part of me feels he'll be laughing about the fact he was right.

The wall's gone. That's important. Remember the wall.

Rituals change. The walk across the park remains constant, though. The walk that became harder for dad in the last few years. The walk that became virtually impossible at the beginning of this season. The walk that becomes the analysis of the match. The important bit, the bit where we talk football, where we talk glory and disappointment, and heroes and villains, and chances spurned and victory seized. Where we talk Suarez and Gerrard, and Torres and Fowler, and McManaman and Dalglish, and Rush (and that's where the tears come, 1,000 words in, three months on and that's where the tears come, the moments that surprise you, sneak up and grab you) and Keegan and Toshack, and St John and Hunt, and Clemence and Callaghan. And before us, Liddell. And Shankly and Paisley, and Fagan and Souness, and Evo, and Kenny and Ronnie Moran, and Rafa and (God help us) Hodgson. And now Brendan.

So Kev and I talked about the might of Emre Can and the speed of Jordon Ibe, and the way that Lazar Markovic can be fantastic when he's facing play but can't turn 180 degrees, and argued about Steven Gerrard and I maintained that this game had been Gerrard's best all season; argued that he'd been commanding, measured, cleaned up everything, linked everything. Thought Jordan Henderson had a dog of a game though; every decision he could make was the wrong one, the game passed him by, he added nothing. Until Steven went off. After Steven went off, Jordan grew. As he tends to. Loves a bit of responsibility, that lad. Wrong sub I'd thought, though. Pull Henderson, push Can forward, let him rampage to his heart's content. Kev thought the complete opposite; thought Steven had been woeful. We argued the point, agreed on Emre though. Everybody agrees on Emre.

We talked about Mario Balotelli and whether this was the start of something or a cameo that might take us to the end of the season and give us an alternative, and about the outpouring of joy, relief and hilarity that greeted his long, long, long overdue first league (and match-winning) goal. Dad didn't see Mario come good. Didn't see much of Adam Lallana, either. He knew nothing of the glory of Can and all the man love that's following him round. Didn't see Markovic emerge, Mamadou Sakho return, Daniel Sturridge come back. Didn't see the 3-4-3. So much that he didn't get to see in such a short time. It's not even three months since we lost him (I have real trouble with using the phrase 'he died') and so much has changed already. We're seeing a rebirth of Liverpool, of a Liverpool that he'd recognise; new but old. Still obviously Liverpool but the next Liverpool. The next one to bring the glory back.

Part of the disappointment of not winning the league last season – and this is just for me, I don't think I've even spoken about this to the lads – is that deep down I knew it would be the last chance for my dad to see one more title. He'd seen so much, though. Born in 1935, heading to Anfield from the late 1940s, early 50s. Seen some rubbish in the Second Division but saw Shanks arrive. Saw the start of everything we love, saw the start of everything we were given. Saw Shanks build his team. Saw Ian St John arrive, saw Roger Hunt arrive. He was at the final in 1965, the first FA Cup win. At the semi before that. Pictured in the *Echo* as part of the joyous pitch invasion, the invasion that felt the glory coming. A young man among young men, feeling what we felt last season. The same as us, the same as every other Red. Every one of us, the same person deep down. The same love for the thing, the wonderful thing, that we were brought up on, that they, that generation that invented fandom (they did you know, they did, singing on the BBC, 'She Loves You' and all that). The generation that gave us our anthem. Never forget. They did that, it's their song. We inherited it.

Wembley 1971 – the heartbreak of Charlie George. Wembley 74 – the glory of Kevin Keegan, the demolishment of 'Supermac'. Three European Cup finals – 1977, 78, 81. The glory that was Rome, three days (apparently) sober in the Eternal City so that he wouldn't miss a second. Gutted to find that when he ordered spaghetti it wasn't the same as the version you get in tins. Never allowed to forget the fact. A bloke out at the match with his mates behaving the way blokes out at the match with their mates behave. No different to your dad. All the same. All the same as us. It's the same story told from different perspectives in different memories.

And then there was that other stand (the tears are back). That stand that you can't avoid coming back to. Sitting in the stand at Hillsborough watching bodies being stretchered out of the end where his sons were. Where my brothers were. As I listened to the tragedy unfold on a radio in work, my dad watched and waited for Keith or Kev to be the next person carried out. They weren't. We were lucky. Keith and Kev had gone by car, dad by coach. The coach was kept waiting as one of the passengers hadn't returned. One of the 96. We never knew who. I don't know how dad got the news later that evening but I know it was the first time that I ever saw my father cry.

Four years earlier he'd waited for the phone call to tell him that Keith had safely returned to his hotel after another final. You don't expect to be lucky twice but we were.

So Kev and I walked across the park, analysis done and the possibility of the top four back on the table, and we tried to piece the moments together. The last game that dad had walked back from was the derby. I didn't walk back with them that day, I had a performance of a play on in town. I headed straight to town. Dad had seen the play the week before. Already ill, we already knew what was happening, but he came to see my play. Knew I was doing what I'd always wanted to do in life. Couldn't hear most of it but was happy, was proud. I hope you have the chance to know how that feels. He was proud of us. We were proud of him.

His last game was West Brom. Kev dropped us at the back of the Anfield Road and I walked with dad to the Main Stand. We stopped a lot. It was getting too much. Afterwards we had to get the car to him; the other way round was unthinkable, impossible. I don't remember anything about the game.

We tried for other games. Kev spoke to Anfield about using a wheelchair to get him into the stand for the Real Madrid game, stowing the wheelchair somewhere, giving him one last glorious European night. We knew by now that we were looking at last things. The club were fantastic. Couldn't be more helpful. But the weather was foul, it was freezing and he just wasn't strong enough to do it.

We thought about the Chelsea league game. Thought we could get a more portable version of the oxygen that he was on at home and use that at the ground. We didn't even get to ask the question. Dad went into hospital on the Sunday before and didn't come back out. By the time Liverpool kicked off on that Saturday lunchtime, we were simply waiting for the moment that he was ready to give up the fight. The game was unimportant.

The end was both quick and slow. The 'six months or less' that I'd been told about in October became a matter of weeks and then, far too rapidly, less than 24 hours. He wasn't having that, though. He refused to be beaten, refused to let go. There were 17 of us around his bed and he was told that he was loved. God, he was loved. I've never been in a room where there was so much love. He fought. I've never seen anybody with so much fight, but in the end – as our Keith so beautifully put it, in print and in church – 'On a sunny Sunday Liverpool afternoon, at two minutes past two, our father and best mate passed away.'

Two minutes past two on Sunday 9 November. My son's 2pm kick-off delayed by two minutes for the Remembrance Day silence. I don't know what you believe in life but I know this: I know that, as my son kicked off on his 14th birthday, my dad went to watch his grandson play football.

As I walked to the Spurs game, I fell in behind a father with his son. The lad looked about ten. Talking about the game, excited about the game. I don't get to do that with my lads; my eldest isn't interested in football, my youngest is a Blue, a very passionate Blue. Just like my wife. We don't go to the game together; I'm going to have to wait for the grandkids before I do that. Rituals change. Rites of passage change.

I was a bookish child and teenager, didn't really get the beauty of the game until my later teens, more interested in comics and books and music. Keith and Kev, though? They got it immediately, they grew up at the game with dad. Did the homes and aways with their mates as he'd done them with his. Carried it all on. The torch doesn't pass on, it co-exists for so long.

You find out more about your parents as you get older. As you become a parent yourself. I found out a few years ago that my dad had wanted more than anything to be a sports journalist. The fact that the *Daily Mirror* was the paper of choice in our house was due to his love of the boxing coverage. His love of boxing due to sitting at the stadium between Bessie Braddock and Hogan 'Kid' Bassey as a young lad sent on errands by his father, my love of Ali given to me by my dad. Dad wanted to be a sports journalist and by some bizarre series of accidents I've somehow managed to fulfil some of his dream. Connections and moments, it's all connections and moments.

The moment that I rocked up at Anfield last season, on one of those nights when you could actually pay on the door and managed out of 40,000 people to get a ticket on the same row as my dad. Both equally delighted. Dad almost as delighted as the night that my wife and I came over from Leeds – where we were exiled for four years – to surprise him and mum in a pub on the Dock Road. Me armed with a copy of Muhammad Ali's autobiography pre-signed but dedicated carefully in Ali's own hand 'To Bob'. Yes, I'd met Ali (it's a long story). Dad spent weeks telling his mates that he'd 'shook the hand that shook the hand that shook the world'. That, my friends, is a moment. That's one of the important ones.

The most important moments, though? They're the football moments. Not the Liverpool moments, glorious as they were. Not the moments at Anfield or the afternoons in a darkened social club watching Liverpool fail to capitalise on easy Newcastle aways, or at the pub where I caught up with dad for the second half of the Chelsea away game that Christmas. The moments on a cold, windswept Buckley Hill touchline watching my son, his grandson, play football. Together. Should you ever feel the need to define the term 'quality time', it's that. A very definite shared love.

My dad took Matt to his first soccer school, back when he still nominally supported both mine and my wife's teams; an Everton soccer school. Three days on a half-term touchline in Maghull in 2006(ish) watching his grandson show promise, medals awarded at the end by Leon Osman. My dad, a man who grew up watching Liverpool one Saturday and Everton the next – as they did when he was a lad – a man with a pretty encyclopaedic knowledge of football, had no idea who Leon Osman was. That one came up in conversation pretty often, too. True happiness comes in the smallest moments.

Then there are the moments that you expect to break you. Hearing 'You'll Never Walk Alone' again. We played it to him in his hospital bed, told him that from now on that was for him, that every time we sung it now it would be for him. Carried him out of the church and into the crematorium to that anthem that pulls all together, that supports us when we need it. I expected the tears to come when I next heard it, to come every time I sang it. They didn't. Writing about it, though? That's a different matter altogether. I dreaded telling the lads (lads? They're mostly my dad's age) who sit by him. They knew, they'd guessed. Knew he wasn't well, knew when the seat was empty for the Chelsea match that something was up. Independently of each other they all said one thing, 'Your dad was a gentleman.'

The wall. I told you that the wall was important, told you that you needed to remember it. The wall that we used to meet at after the game. The 'we' wasn't just the four of us, it was also my granddad and my uncle Len – my dad's best mates. They went before him but he's with them again now.

I knew for about a day before he went what my last words to my dad would be, knew the message I wanted him to have as he left, to know that nothing ends – it just changes and that we would all meet again.

'We'll meet you by the wall after the match.'

And we will.

There's one thing left to tell. I only discovered this a few weeks ago. Dad wasn't going to renew his season ticket this year. The walking to and from the ground was too tiring for him, his eyesight was failing. My mum told him to renew it, told him, 'Ian will have it.' It'd been what he'd wanted, and it happened. My dad's last gift to me. Passing it all on, part of the endless series of linked moments.

I sit in my father's place now. I see things differently.

14 February 2015, Crystal Palace 1 Liverpool 2

Christ, tonight's episode of *Casualty* was dark. There was this old woman, must have been in her late 70s/early 80s, who'd killed four children. She was properly evil, and a mum of one of the dead kids had rammed her car into the police van she was in – hence the old biddy being in hospital. The mum was in hospital too having suffered injuries in the crash and she was hell bent on confronting the mad pensioner and demanding she revealed where she'd buried her daughter. The whole thing was bloody terrifying. Not what I expected at all.

What's that you're asking, 'Why is this fucking idiot telling us about *Casualty*?' Well, because I can. Liverpool's match at Crystal Palace finished around 7.30pm and *Casualty* started just after nine – and I was home in time to watch it.

Yes, that's right, from ground to front door in less than two hours. Otherwise known as the perfect 'away' trip.

I'd wanted to make this journey ever since I moved to south London in 2009 and discovered Palace were the closest team to where we lived. Back then they were in the Championship so league visits were out of the question, and we didn't get them in either of the cups. It was a case of sitting tight and waiting, with the moment to rejoice finally arriving in May 2013 when Palace were promoted to the Premier League via the play-offs. I was happy for Ron and Marion, my neighbours and long-standing Selhurst Park season ticket holders, and I was really happy for myself.

As it turned out, I failed to get a ticket for Liverpool's 2013/14 league game there, which proved a blessing given it turned out to be *that* 3-3 draw. I then also missed out on this season's game, another blessing given it turned out to be *that* 3-1 loss. But once we got them in the FA Cup, there was to be no stopping me – I was going. Simple.

Rob Gutmann sorted me with a ticket, so there I was on a nippy Saturday afternoon stood outside a stadium I'm able to reach via two short bus rides. Bloody delighted I was. And even more so after the Reds had come from a goal behind to win 2-1. Fully deserved, too – we were excellent from start to finish.

As were our lot in what is possibly the strangest away end I've ever been in. You get no sense from watching on telly just how deep that part of the Arthur Wait stand is; like a battered Tardis painted in red and blue. Anyway, we filled it and made one hell of a noise, with an afternoon's worth of ale no doubt helping those in attendance belt out our songs that much longer and louder.

Watching the match with Rob was great, as was bumping into 'Barca John', a mate of a mate from Willesden who I'd gone to Barcelona with in 2007 to watch us win 2-1 at the Nou Camp (the Craig Bellamy game for those who've forgotten).

A top outing then, only spoilt by the fact I saw none of the three goals properly due to a badly-placed pillar. I didn't even know Alberto Moreno had done the Sturridge dance until I got home and watched *Match of the Day*, which incidentally followed the 10pm news, which incidentally followed *Casualty*.

Speaking of *Casualty*, did I mention I was home in time to watch it?
SN

22 February 2015, Southampton 0 Liverpool 2

This game made me think about *The Shawshank Redemption*. You may remember the lead character, Andy Dufresne, has to crawl through miles of shit to reach his promised land, both literally and metaphorically. When he climbs out of the sewage pipe and emerges into a small river outside the walls of the prison, he kneels, turns his careworn face to the skies and shouts something at God. God is watching and sends down a lightening strike to further invigorate the momentous moment.

Andy wasn't at St Mary's but Martin Skrtel was, and come the final whistle he looked like he'd been through a similar time in similar conditions. Where Andy D was ripped off by the governor, Martin had Emre Can and Dejan Lovren making his life hell. A silly tackle from one and a handball from the other while our hero blocked, jockeyed and dug in; Skrtel lived to tell the tale and somehow emerge into his own swamp with his clean sheet tucked under his shirt. I'm not sure how. I can't even imagine, or maybe I just don't want to. Skrtel crawled through a river of shit and came out clean on the other side.

Maybe this is it. Maybe we've arrived now. The season is open. Tottenham dropped points, Man Utd lost to Swansea and the quiet Reds have just turned over Spurs and Southampton in the quest for third spot. I hope so. I want nothing more than a trophy and a top-four spot.

As Andy Dufresne writes to Red – hope is a good thing, maybe the best of things, and no good thing ever dies.

KC

26 February 2015, Besiktas 1 Liverpool 0
(agg: 1-1. Besiktas win 5-4 on penalties)

'I shared a bear hug with Ronnie Moran'

By James Pearce

At first I thought the heavens had opened. Then I feared an attack from an Istanbul pigeon. But as Liverpool increasingly lost their way at the scene of the club's greatest triumph a decade earlier, the reality dawned on me.

It was raining Turkish phlegm at the Ataturk Stadium.

My laptop was getting pelted. When I looked up from the press seats towards the upper tier, 12 feet or so above, the perpetrators were only too happy to own up. 'Fuck you, mother fucker, fuck you,' bellowed one manic fella in his 20s, who had a Besiktas scarf wrapped around his neck and was dangling precariously over the edge to the delight of his equally deranged-looking pals.

I caught the eye of a nearby steward who simply shrugged his shoulders and gave me that look which in any language translates as, 'I'm not arsed, you deal with it.' I battled on, pausing at regular intervals to mop up when those above hit their target. Their accuracy was impressive, with the 'S' key in particular taking a battering.

Time was of the essence. I had to e-mail across to the *Echo* desk in Liverpool a 1,000-word analysis piece on the game within half an hour of the match finishing. A player interview from the mixed zone also had to be filed before boarding the flight home. We had already been warned by the suits from Thomas Cook that whatever the outcome, Brendan Rodgers's squad would be heading to the airport within 45 minutes of the final whistle and those journalists on the official trip needed to be in tow.

It was deep into the second half and Liverpool's performance was turning out to be as grim as the matter splattering against my keyboard. Once Tolgay Arslan's stunning 20-yarder had cancelled out the Reds' slender lead from the first leg, Rodgers's men were clinging on for extra time. Backs were firmly against the wall.

It shouldn't have come to this. During the opening 45 minutes, a depleted Liverpool side had gilt-edged chances to bag the precious away goal which would have silenced the white-hot atmosphere and effectively booked their passage to the last 16 of the Europa League. However, both Daniel Sturridge and Raheem Sterling were wasteful, with composure in the final third conspicuous by its absence. After the interval the Reds' attacking threat dwindled.

How they missed the creative talents of Philippe Coutinho, who had been left on Merseyside to put his feet up ahead of the weekend clash with Manchester City. And the energy and athleticism of Jordan Henderson, who was nursing an ankle injury and had also been spared the trip with one eye on Liverpool's pursuit of a top-four spot.

It was a pragmatic selection by Rodgers as he prioritised the visit of the Premier League champions. Yes, the Europa League offered both silverware and a place in the Champions League for the winners, but the Northern Irishman knew the more achievable route into Europe's elite was through their domestic rather than continental exploits. The scheduling had also done Liverpool no favours. With the Sky cameras at Anfield for a noon Sunday showdown with City, there were just 55 hours between touching down at John Lennon Airport and facing Manuel Pellegrini's side.

Rodgers had put his faith in youth, and to their credit the likes of Jordon Ibe and Alberto Moreno rose to the challenge in the most hostile of environments. They don't do prawn sandwiches or half-and-half scarves in Turkey. Fans don't turn up with selfie sticks or sit there in silence expecting to be entertained. At least a third of the 60,000-strong crowd had been in place more than two hours before kick-off – the fanatical Besiktas fans whipped into a frenzy by the cheerleader on the PA system. Liverpool had entered the lion's den.

As the players took a pre-match wander on the turf, deafening catcalls tumbled down from the stands. A wide-eyed Rickie Lambert filmed it on his mobile phone – you don't get that kind of reception on a wet Tuesday night at Rochdale.

The noise in the opening stages was at fever pitch, with fury unleashed from the stands every time Liverpool had the temerity to be in possession. The soundtrack was all the more impressive considering that the Ataturk – with its two open ends and a running track around the pitch – isn't particularly atmospheric.

Besiktas had temporarily decamped to the far western outskirts of the city after their Inonu Stadium was demolished to make way for the plush, new Vodafone Arena. Having had issues trying to entice fans to make the 14-mile hike through gridlocked traffic from the centre of Istanbul, prices had been slashed for Liverpool's eagerly anticipated visit.

What a contrast it was to that balmy evening of 25 May 2005 when the Ataturk was a sea of red and the chins of Rafa Benitez's players were lifted off the floor at the start of the second half by that defiant rendition of 'You'll Never Walk Alone' from the travelling Kop.

This time there was no mass exodus from Merseyside. The stakes were considerably lower. UEFA can rebrand it all they want. They can give the Europa League its own fancy anthem and match ball. They can even give the winners a golden ticket to Europe's elite, but it will always be the poor relation of the Champions League. Playing on Thursday nights is rubbish. Always has been, always will be. The 1,000 or so Liverpool fans who made the 1,700-mile pilgrimage back to the banks of the Bosphorus were in a minority – their vocal backing drowned out by the din around them.

Earlier in the day, Taksim Square – the scene of such joyous celebrations a decade earlier – had been surprisingly quiet. I'd been asked by the office to send back some video of expectant Kopites looking ahead to the clash with Slaven Bilic's side. The only ones wearing colours in the square were Russian and they didn't speak a word of English between them.

I ended up having to loiter for an hour, taking on the impromptu role of photographer for a hundred Japanese couples who wanted their picture taken in front of the statue. Eventually I got what I needed outside the nearby Maccies. Where else? Like Scouse bees around a honey pot. Fries were being generously donated to the steady stream of begging gypsies.

Every fan seemed to have a stack of spares. With tickets in the away end on sale for just £10, many had snapped them up but had no intention of travelling as they simply wanted to get the credit on their buying history for more significant trips in the future.

A spare ticket to watch Liverpool at the Ataturk. The thought brought back some painful memories for me.

I was at work on the sports desk at the *Bath Chronicle* on 23 May 2005 when the phone went. It was my good mate Peter Clarkson, a devoted Kopite who I'd been to countless matches with over the years. He bore an unfortunate resemblance to William Hague but I'd never held that against him.

We were at the University of Liverpool together from 1996 to 1999 and we used to take it in turns to press redial for hours in the hope of getting through on the booking line when tickets went on general sale 18 days before each home game. Usually perseverance paid off. There were times when his late father's best mate, who worked away, gave him his two season tickets just above the directors' box in the Main Stand to use. We barely missed a home game and went to as many aways as we could.

This was why I had opted to study history and politics in Liverpool. To fulfil my lifelong ambition of going to watch the Reds on a regular basis. Finally, I was living the dream.

From the age of six or seven, I'd been obsessed with Liverpool.

Why? I'd love to say it was because of some long-standing emotional tie between my family and the Kop that had been passed down from generation to generation. But in truth it just happened. I don't remember life ever being any different. Looking back now, the fact that Liverpool were the dominant force in English football undoubtedly contributed to my allegiances.

At my primary school in the mid-1980s, if you were obsessed with the beautiful game like I was, you were either a Red or a Blue. That might sound strange considering we were 200 miles from Merseyside, but Bath is a rugby city with a small non-league football team. The nearest top-flight club, Southampton, is 70 miles away and there's no affinity with either City or Rovers in nearby Bristol.

It was always Liverpool for me. I can vividly remember watching Bruce Grobbelaar's spaghetti legs in Rome in 1984 and Kenny Dalglish's winner to clinch the title at Stamford Bridge two years later. I marvelled at the brilliance of Rush, Beardsley, Barnes and Aldridge. I used to cut the match reports out of my parents' newspapers and stick them in my scrapbooks. Ask me what I had for my tea yesterday and I'd be struggling, ask me about the all-Merseyside cup finals of 1986 and 89 and I'll give you the answers instantly. They are ingrained in my mind.

You never forget the highs or the crushing lows. That pain in the pit of my stomach when Lawrie Sanchez scored for Wimbledon in 1988 or the torrent of tears when Michael Thomas struck in the dying seconds for Arsenal at Anfield a year later. When you are a kid the highs are so much higher and the lows are so much lower. Perspective doesn't exist.

I'd seen Liverpool play away against Aston Villa and Coventry City before I convinced my dad to take me to Anfield for the first time ahead of my 13th birthday. It was 27 October 1990 when I finally saw the Kop in all its splendour. It didn't disappoint. Ian Rush and Steve Nicol both netted inside 20 minutes and Liverpool beat Chelsea 2-0.

While waiting outside the ground afterwards, I filled my autograph book and picked up a copy of the *Pink* – the *Echo*'s now-defunct Saturday evening paper with all the results and reports in – before heading back to the car. I remember on the long journey home rueing the fact that I'd bought a scarf which under 'Liverpool FC' read '18 times champions of England'. It would be out of date within months, I thought. It hurts that a quarter of a century on it's still factually correct.

After university, I returned to Bath in search of work. When I landed my first job in journalism as a trainee on the local paper, the number of Reds games I went to dwindled, but I still made the 400-mile round trip to Anfield whenever I could. And in 2001, Pete and I embarked on our first European trips – a glorious 2-0 win over Roma at the Stadio Olimpico, when Michael Owen scored twice, and then the gutsy/dour stalemate with Barcelona at the Nou Camp.

That UEFA Cup run reached a thrilling conclusion with the 5-4 win over Alaves in the final courtesy of a golden goal deep into extra time. I'd got a ticket off a tout outside Dortmund's Westfalenstadion an hour before kick-off and ended up sat a row in front of the Liverpool players who hadn't been named in the matchday squad, like Jamie Redknapp and Jari Litmanen. When Delfi Geli's own goal flew in, I shared a bear hug with Ronnie Moran. What a night that was.

I was there in Dortmund in 2001 and I was there in Athens in 2007. But 2005? That's a sore point.

I had long since given up hope of getting a ticket for Istanbul when Peter called two days before the final to say he'd got hold of an extra one. If I could get travel sorted it was mine. I needed to get back to him within an hour.

There were two problems. Firstly, every Red wanted to be there for Liverpool's first European Cup Final for 20 years and flights to Turkey were jam-packed. Secondly, I was skint. I was serving my notice at the *Bath Chronicle* after landing a job as a sports reporter at the *Echo*. In the middle of June my wife and I were moving to Liverpool. I'd been away six years and couldn't wait to get back.

Louise had only been to the city once before and that was when I took her to watch England v Paraguay at Anfield. Lucky girl. She knew how much I craved the chance to get my foot in the door at the *Echo* and agreed to quit her job as a mortgage advisor in Bristol and head north. Her support even extended to the fact that I'd be starting at the bottom at the *Echo* and would be taking a £4,000-per-year pay cut.

When I made some calls and looked online for flights to Istanbul, my worst fears were confirmed. The cheapest – via Germany – was £1,900. Chuck in the price of the ticket, food, drink and taxis, and I was looking at the best part of £2,500. I'd be gone less than 36 hours.

Peter needed an answer and it was with a heavy heart that I phoned him back to say thanks but no thanks. I couldn't justify that kind of outlay just weeks before the big move. Anyway, Liverpool were only just embarking on a glorious adventure under Rafa Benitez and there would be other nights like this. How wrong I was.

I ended up watching the final with mates in a packed pub in Bristol – the Clifton Wine Bar. Carlo Ancelotti's AC Milan were overwhelming favourites. They boasted the brilliance of Maldini, Nesta, Pirlo, Seedorf, Crespo, Kaka and Shevchenko. The Reds had made a habit of upsetting the odds, with Juventus and Chelsea vanquished en route to Istanbul. But this was a step up in class.

For 45 minutes it was the mother of all nightmares as the Italians ran riot. I remember being sat there as an assortment of Cockneys and Mancs in the corner gloated at Liverpool's embarrassment. Sorrows were increasingly drowned and the only positive I could cling to at half-time was the fact I hadn't paid £2,500 to be at the scene of such a public humiliation. I genuinely feared records would be smashed and Milan would end up scoring half a dozen.

What followed is of course the stuff of legend. Ten years on it still seems scarcely believable. Three goals in six minutes. From the depths of despair to the dizzy heights of ecstasy.

After Xabi Alonso tucked away the rebound from the penalty to make it 3-3, my glasses got trampled beneath a sea of feet amid the manic celebrations. It was a small price to pay. When Jerzy Dudek saved from Andriy Shevchenko in the shootout and Carra broke the land speed record with his victory charge, it was pure joy.

Never in my life have I experienced both ends of the emotional spectrum in such quick succession. After that initial rush came a pang of regret. I could have been there. I could have witnessed 'The Miracle of Istanbul'. At half-time I'd been counting my blessings. By the end I would have happily paid treble just to be able to say, 'I was there.'

A decade later I had finally made it to the Ataturk Stadium. The drive up to the stadium felt strangely familiar. It was like visiting a place of huge historical significance you've seen and studied from afar so often in the past.

If someone told me all those years earlier that I'd be here one day as the *Echo*'s Liverpool FC reporter I'd have asked for a pint of whatever they had been drinking. That privileged position was only a pipedream when I started at the paper in June 2005. I was a writer/sub-editor who was initially tasked with producing copy for the junior sport section. I bagged every opportunity to take on more responsibility and was soon doing the athletics, rugby, basketball and cricket.

Eventually I started to be sent to matches. Usually I'd be the 'second man', writing up the manager's post-match quotes for either Liverpool or Everton games. I worked my way up and learned a huge amount from the likes of Chris Bascombe, Tony Barrett and Dominic King – all now successful Merseyside reporters on national papers.

There were plenty of knocks along the way. Some warned me that they'd never give that job to a non-Scouser, and there were times when I wondered whether I'd ever get to where I wanted to be. When I was appointed Liverpool FC reporter in March 2011, it was a case of fourth time lucky.

Being taken down to Melwood by my boss to be properly introduced to manager Dalglish was both a proud and surreal day. I now had my boyhood hero's mobile phone number and he would be expecting a call after training the following afternoon. Nervous? I was petrified.

Liverpool is my home now and I wouldn't want to live anywhere else. My two children, Holly and Max, were born there and I love the fact that no one will ever question why they support the Reds. 'I'm a proper Scouser, not like you,' my daughter regularly informs me.

People often tell me that I've got a dream job, and in many ways it is. I get paid to follow the Reds home and away. My passion has become my career. I also get on well with the vast majority of the players and each week I get to interview Brendan Rodgers in his office. I never lose sight of how lucky I am.

But I'd be lying if I said it was all a bed of roses. It's always a challenging balancing act between maintaining key relationships with people at the club and doing your job properly. You want good access but without sacrificing your principles about saying and writing what you really think. And it's crazy when the success or failure of my day hinges on whether a footballer earning more in a week than I earn in a year agrees to stop to offer up a few soundbites in a short interview. I once waited four hours to get six minutes with Dirk Kuyt. He's one of the nicest men in football but a betting firm had messed up the time slots.

I waste hundreds of hours every season standing around in press rooms, car parks and corridors. I frequently occupy service stations in the early hours – desperately trying to take on board enough caffeine to stay awake for the long journeys home. The demands of the job have changed massively with the shift in emphasis from print to digital. Where once it was all about ensuring you had a decent story for tomorrow's back page, now it's all about constantly feeding the bottomless pit of the internet.

Clicks are now the overriding priority. You don't get the time you once had to construct a story. It's all about getting it out there.

There's constant pressure to deliver breaking news, transfer stories and concise, informed analysis of the big issues the fans are talking about. Being both a supporter and a reporter is a double-edged sword. When you are writing comment pieces it helps because whether it's positive or negative it comes from the heart. You are able to convey what fans are feeling because you're one yourself.

But I do sometimes miss the buzz of watching a game as a fan. It's easy to become cynical in this profession. The job can become all-consuming. It's all about meeting deadlines. There are times when you don't crave a late fightback from the Reds because you are thinking about the repercussions that would have in terms of a hefty rewrite.

A late rewrite was exactly what was required at the end of the first leg with Besiktas at Anfield. With five minutes to go, an air of frustration was lifted when Ibe was chopped down in the penalty box. What followed was the unedifying spectacle of Mario Balotelli grabbing the ball from the hands of Henderson, who was ready to take responsibility in the absence of the injured Steven Gerrard.

Balotelli shrugged off the complaints and showed remarkable composure as he dispatched it into the bottom corner. Why always him? At least he had given everyone something to write about after a largely forgettable contest.

Rodgers's side had a lead to take to Istanbul but it wasn't enough. By the time that Arslan made it 1-1 on aggregate, Liverpool had run out of both gas and ideas. They were fortunate to make it to extra time with Demba Ba hammering against the bar late on.

The Reds went the distance at the Ataturk, just like they did in 2005. There were echoes of that night with Liverpool's number 23 once again going down stricken with cramp. Even the penalties were taken at the same end where Dudek thwarted Shevchenko. The scenario was so gloriously familiar but the outcome was so painfully different.

Roma 84, Milan 05 and Chelsea 07 – penalties have been good to Liverpool in Europe, but not this time. Lambert, Adam Lallana, Emre Can and Joe Allen all found the net amid the crescendo of jeers and whistles after Ba, Gokhan Tore, Veli Kavlak and Atiba Hutchinson had scored for the Turks.

When Arslan beat Mignolet to make it 5-4 the pressure was all on Dejan Lovren and the £20m centre-back crumbled as he blazed high into the night sky. The Croatian stood shell-shocked, wishing the ground would swallow him up. This time a long night at the Ataturk ended in despair.

Liverpool's underwhelming European campaign was over and as the home supporters went wild, I noticed a large dollop of Turkish phlegm dangling off my right shoulder.

1 March 2015, Liverpool 2 Manchester City 1

'The real Mr Tueart was always thwarted by the real Mr Clemence'

By Simon Curtis

Alec Lindsay, Brian Hall, Alan Waddle. Perhaps not the very first words you'd expect from a Manchester City supporter when asked about Liverpool, but there you go.

Richard Money, Colin Irwin, Bob Bolder. Ah, Bob Bolder.

Liverpool have always fascinated me, troubled me, lingered in my worst nightmares and, to wit, spoiled many a good matchday rumble. But they have also made me wonder. Particularly those names mentioned. Just how did they stick with it? How did they concentrate, stuck in the reserves waiting for Phil Thompson to pull a hamstring or Peter Cormack to finally bang his head on the door frame? Liverpool dominated everything about my football upbringing. If the end of the season did not feature Emlyn bloody Hughes with his melon grin and a selection of pots and trophies adorned with fluttering red ribbons, there was something badly skewed with life as we knew and recognised it.

We had Marmite butties. We had Scooby Doo. We had the Double Deckers and we had Kevin Keegan scoring in front of the Kop. These were the staples, the fabric of life, the very pillars of growing up in the 1970s.

A little later, Anfield took on shadowy proportions away from the playing field, too. For City fans heading into enemy territory, it was well worth 'minding your backs'. In the late 1970s and early 80s, under the blood red sky of Thatcherite Britain, a trip to Liverpool, that trudge out of Lime Street, wading through the rain and litter on the Scotty Road, meant anything might happen. Liverpool the city, a fine upstanding place that had become downtrodden and beaten, looked to its football clubs to help keep the chins of the locals off the ground. A weekly trip to Anfield or – to a lesser extent apart from a blip in the mid-80s – to Goodison, helped put a spring in the step of a local population taken to task by the Tories and their anti-northern, anti-football philosophies.

The boarded-up shops. The discarded shopping trollies. The upturned hopes of a whole generation, lay bare for all to see. Even the football brought troubles in those terrible late 80s days, when politicians lied and Old England was dying. Crowds sunk to the late 20,000s at Anfield and into the teens at Goodison. At City, times were rough, too. Maine Road, sat plum in the middle of Moss Side, a war zone to rival anything Toxteth could muster, was falling apart at the seams. A putrid atmosphere of decay and simmering violence lay everywhere.

In Thatcher's Britain you needed distractions or you would have gone mad. We had our music in these two great cities. We had our clobber. And we had our football. For all the hatred, the bridge of these three cultural elements brought the youth of Merseyside and Manchester into close proximity, whether you were red or blue, Bunnymen aficionados or Oasis fans, Adidas followers or wearers of off-the-back-of-a-lorry Tacchini. It was pure escapism from the daily flow of factory closures and miners' strikes.

But most of all we had our football, and football in the 1970s and in those dreaded 80s meant Liverpool.

For City fans it was worse than for most others. A caning always awaited us at Anfield and the same thrashing was more often than not delivered at Maine Road, too. I even stopped going to Anfield for a bit as it had become just too predictable, too painful. While Alan Ball, in his dubious capacity as City's 1995/96 relegation mastermind coach, could say he had 'enjoyed watching Liverpool' as they beat us 6-0 and 4-0 within three totally inglorious days, I could not. I hated it with a passion and I'd had enough of Anfield, with its songs raining down from the Kop, its misty Saturday afternoons and its spicy Irish Sea gales flying in off the Mersey to play havoc with Stevie Kinsey's quiff and Andy May's shorts.

But it was not the 1990s that invented Liverpool drubbings of City. These things have existed since I was a scruffily-dressed kid fresh off the school field, where I had been a mud-spattered mini-version of Dennis Tueart, firing nerveless winners past chubby, rosy-cheeked Ray Clemence all afternoon. In off a tree stump, rebound from the bicycles, it mattered little if you had a chance to pop one past the mini Ray in his stolen Sondico gloves.

Come the end of the week, however, the real Mr Tueart was always thwarted by the real, lithe, athletic Mr Clemence.

City had some decent sides in the 70s, trailing in second in 1977 and fourth the season after. Guess who scooped the main prize as we struggled over the finishing line? Doesn't need answering, does it? Liverpool were omnipotent. The aforementioned Clemence safe and agile, a back four that was strong and unforgiving, an ultra-mobile, ultra-competitive midfield four and two excellent goal-hungry frontmen. Phil Neal. Alan Kennedy. Alan Hansen. Mark Lawrenson. Steve Heighway. Graeme Souness. Terry Mac. Kenny Dalglish. Keegan and Toshack. John Barnes. Ian Rush. Ray Houghton. The names roll off the tongue one after another.

Rush was supposed to be coming to City from Chester but Malcolm Allison stopped for a cigar and a sausage roll at Warrington services and John Smith got in ahead of him. What a difference that single issue would have made to this correspondent's life. Rush went on to become an even bigger thorn in City's sides than either Keegan or Dalglish.

One of the great football topics: what might have been. Instead of watching Wayne Biggins, Tony Cunningham and Trevor Christie mash up the striker's role before our disbelieving eyes on the Kippax, it could have been the languid and deadly Rush. Instead he wore red. And indeed he did score regularly at Maine Road. Much too regularly, in fact, and in totally the wrong coloured kit. With deadly accuracy, with speed and punch, displaying the inimitable goalscorer's ability to be in the right place at the right time, season after season after season. Such is life.

In those innocent days of growing up, when Liverpool hit the European trail, you would follow avidly. If you were English you supported all the home sides in European combat. I don't even think I made an exception for United, such was the naivety of youth. I certainly remember being an enthusiastic follower of Liverpool's progress through the old European and UEFA Cups, with glorious dismantlings of Aberdeen, FC Zurich, Benfica, St Etienne, Borussia Monchengladbach and others readily springing to mind. Unlike United's dominance of the 1990s – which made me sick to the pit of my stomach – I watched Liverpool's 70s sides in a state of shock and awe. This was a young lad's first view of what powerful, successful football looked like.

The *Kick Off* match would bring us a weekly blast of red goals every Sunday. Gerald Sinstadt, with his queer little moustache and his clipped southern accent, would be there to show us a 7-0 beating of Spurs or a 5-0 demolition job on Derby, five past Forest or nine past Palace. Everyone, it seemed, was ripe for an Anfield hammering. Not just City, after all.

Yet it still felt like we came off worse. When we did win in Liverpool, an occurrence as rare as hen's teeth, we got our comeuppance in no uncertain terms. 1980/81 season: Liverpool struggling towards Christmas in a right old state. Wallowing down in tenth as City visit. Bruce Grobbelaar has one of his days and lets in three goals. City winning 3-1 – at Anfield! I can still feel the elation to this day. The Kop celebrated by flinging a wine bottle that hit big Joe Corrigan on the head. Such an unusual act of unsportsmanship from that famous end. Straight away a thousand arms are pointing out the culprit and Corrigan, England's number three goalkeeper in those days, is serenaded with a raucous burst of 'England's number one' by the home support. A great day all round, unless you happened to be Corrigan.

Come April, City and Liverpool have swapped places. City mid-table, marooned and hopeless. Liverpool back at the top after a surge of unbeaten games. The Reds arrive at Maine Road for a sunny Easter fixture and carry off a 5-0 win that puts City right back in their basket after the December victory at Anfield. Even Sammy Lee, wearing his shorts like a nappy, belts one in from 30 yards. It is, once again, total ignominy to add to the list of mishaps, failures and thrashings.

And on and on it went.

By the time Liverpool were beginning to tire of all those trophies, City had headed south and were bathing their wounds in the Second Division against the likes of Carlisle and Cambridge. The good times rolled again in 1988 in the FA Cup as Mel Machin's young marauders carried the team into the FA Cup fifth round. A homegrown side featuring Ian Brightwell, Paul Lake, Paul Moulden and Andy Hinchcliffe came up against the last great Liverpool side before the present day.

A soaking wet, mud-up-to-your-eyeballs pitch greeted a full house at Maine Road. There was hope again and a chance to measure ourselves against the best in preparation for a return to the big time. At least the four-goal thrashing dealt out on that afternoon, beamed live to a hungry television audience across the country, would prepare us for more ignominy at the hands of Liverpool when we did return.

Strangely, the early 1990s brought little of this traditional sour-tasting football disaster. Suddenly, and quite out of the blue, City became good at playing at Anfield. For a short while at the beginning of the decade it looked a little like we had worked out what we were doing. Admittedly, the mighty Reds were slightly diminished by a set of traffic cones with names like Harkness and Burrows, but two consecutive 2-2 draws at Anfield, one featuring a last-minute Niall Quinn header at the Annie Road end and the other a spectacular double from David White, made us believe for a while that the hoodoo might just have passed.

Then came Ball and his odd ideas stored away under a flat cap. As Liverpool slipped off the pace, City slipped off the back end of Planet Football and disappeared towards the third tier. Liverpool no longer occupied City minds, even if humiliation readily did. Now the thrashings were from lower life forms, and that really stung. Getting tanned at Anfield drifts to the back of your mind when you are trying to locate the away entrances at Northampton or at Darlington in the first round of the FA Cup. Oh for a Kenny Dalglish back heel or a Ray Kennedy ghosted strike then.

The long haul back reunited the clubs in league action at the start of the new century and an Anelka and Fowler-inspired win at Anfield in 2003 was hailed as the first such miracle since the wind-assisted Kinsey affair of 1980. It had been a long time coming and the celebrations in the cramped confines of the away section were loud and long. With bruised shins and scuffed trainers, we howled with delight.

It's a good thing that we made the most of it because since then, City have failed to repeat the feat. Two wins at Anfield in my City supporting lifetime, a mere 40 years or so, stands comparison with the worst record of any teams on any grounds on these green and pleasant islands of ours. Mind-numbingly, irrevocably awful is another way of putting it.

Although City now have a decent record against Liverpool in Manchester, turning our away stats sheet into something legible and acceptable is proving a little more taxing. Anfield still feels much like the immovable object it always was, still creates an atmosphere that makes our boys turn into mice, and still reeks of the old days of thunder and lightning. Even if the players change and the reputations dwindle, that old ground still strikes fear into each new generation of City players and supporters.

Whereas everyone else seems to have moved on and can play decently without fear and, sometimes, come away with a point or two, City stubbornly stick to the age-old script, exiting with absolutely nothing. When we manage a draw, as we did in the League Cup semi second leg in 2012, it was when we needed to win.

Mention of League Cup semis takes me straight to Alf Grey, who may not register on any Liverpool fan's radar but is a prominent piece of furniture in the cluttered memory of any City fan over 45. It was he who reffed the 1981 League Cup semi-final first leg at Maine Road between the two sides, disallowing a perfectly good Kevin Reeves headed goal after just three minutes for – according to the hapless whistler – a push on Hansen. There had been no contact whatsoever.

Liverpool regrouped and Ray Kennedy did what Ray Kennedy always did, sliding in undetected at the far post on one of his stealth raids and to knock all the stuffing out of the Blues. A hard-fought second leg at Anfield finished 2-2 and Liverpool progressed to a final they won against West Ham. It was, if memory serves, their first League Cup win.

On this opening day of March 2015, when Liverpool beat City at Anfield with two stunning goals, most of the City support looked at each other, shrugged and headed for the exits. Even Edin Dzeko's excellently-worked equaliser had felt like putting your finger in the dyke and having to wait for the water to begin seeping out again. City played competently, within themselves, rather like quite a few of their performances in a deeply disappointing defence of that 2013/14 title. But, as ever, it was not to be. Philippe Coutinho's rasper was added to Jordan Henderson's rocket shot and City, once more, were buried. If the inevitability never quite finishes you off, the misplaced hope certainly does.

The year before, at the same stage of the season, Liverpool had won a cracking game 3-2 and seemed on the very brink of winning the title for the first time since the glory years. The atmosphere that day was raucous, celebratory and, it has to be said, slightly premature. City fans were as low as an armadillo's belly that afternoon, estimating their own side's chance had gone. Once more we had been beaten at Anfield, on this occasion after a stirring fightback that had led to such a reversal of the game's original flow it seemed there could be only one winner. In a way there could, and we should have known who that one winner was and seemingly will always be.

That crestfallen feeling came over the away end like a huge wet blanket. The slow trudge to the exits, the half-hearted farewells to mates, the walk to the buses and cars, the slow departure from the grey, windswept landscape of Stanley Park and its precincts to hit the clogged roads east.

It is a well worn path trodden many times over the years, each time with shoulders hunched and the gleeful shouts of a thousand Scousers ringing in our ears. Even in their fine new clothes, Manchester City at Anfield continues to be a disaster waiting to happen.

4 March 2015, Liverpool 2 Burnley 0

'The saunter forward, the sideways duck, the fizzing banana-shot'

By Alex Hess

anny Blanchflower famously said that football is about glory, but it hasn't been very glorious being a Liverpool fan for the past two decades. There have been a couple of ephemeral exceptions of course, but generally speaking, during the time I've followed Liverpool, the club's quest to claim silverware and recover its stature has mostly involved falling short and falling behind.

Glory – which is to say trophies – has been rare. Instead, my 20 years of fandom has witnessed rivals emerge, a power gap open up and Liverpool's ambitions being downsized accordingly. It reached the point where our holy grail became simply to qualify for the Champions League. The assumption became set in stone that finishing fourth was first on the club's list of priorities. It's what marks each season a success or a failure; the purported first rung on the ladder back to greatness.

We'd long come to accept that the teams who jostle for first place are untouchable. Liverpool might be able to beat a Manchester United, a Manchester City or a Chelsea on their day, but anyone who truly believed it possible to compete with those moneyed superclubs over 38 games was some combination of drunk, delusional and living in the red-tinted past.

But then last season happened.

Last season changed everything. It was like the final five minutes of *Usual Suspects*; it came out of nowhere, showed up everything we knew to be a work of utter fiction, and dashed back out the door before we had the chance to snap out of our wide-eyed, slack-jawed daze.

In those whirlwind months between January and May, the very idea of Champions League qualification was reduced to a footnote, a folly and an irrelevance by that free-scoring Liverpool side that came within a whisker of freely scoring themselves to the title.

If the greatest trick the devil ever pulled was convincing the world he doesn't exist, then the supreme achievement of Abramovich, Mansour and the rest has been to convince the world you can't compete with them. Last season, Steven Gerrard's pen at Fulham, Luis Suarez's volley against Arsenal, and a 3-0 win at Old Trafford that should have been five or six, smashed that truism into a thousand pieces. It was, to say the least, enlightening.

So on to this year – and on to a major problem. Last season's joyous chaos, instead of picking up where it left off, had been replaced by slow-paced stodge. For a good half-season, Liverpool were unrecognisable. The magic feet of Daniel Sturridge were nowhere to be seen, Simon Mignolet suddenly seemed two foot shorter, Gerrard's legs two tonnes heavier. Worst of all, every Kopite's summer-long fear turned out to be perfectly well-founded: with Suarez gone, madness had become mundanity. Having scrambled up a towering ladder to the brink of glory, Liverpool had slid right back down a snake.

Deflating, sure. But the season is still here to be enjoyed, right? Except that with football as with anything, enjoyment is defined by context. For example: strip away all context and *The Godfather Part III* is a perfectly functional crime drama, and very probably a wholly entertaining watch. But in reality the film's a hideous disappointment. Andy Garcia, while a thoroughly decent late-90s slickster in his own right, is nothing on the Robert De Niro character we met in Part II. Francis Ford Coppola's direction goes from subtle to self-indulgent. Al Pacino's raucously overcooked acting functions not as a source of throwaway fun but as a tarnish upon the legacy of one of cinema's greatest ever performances.

Last season was my *Godfather Part II*. Seeing the Reds go on that 11-game winning run was like watch Vito Corleone work his way up from penniless Italian immigrant to New York's Mafia don supreme. The win against City – seven points clear with four games left – was as thrilling and as terrifying as watching Michael administer the kiss of death in Havana. And when Jose Mourinho rolled up to Anfield in April it was the equivalent of seeing Fredo slinking off to accompany a shady henchman on a fishing trip on Lake Tahoe.

Basically, the whole saga was electrifying, magnificent and ultimately heartbreaking – but never was there a point when my emotions were not ramped up to 11.

So I hope you'll forgive me if I'm finding it hard to really get behind the idea – that old, stale familiar idea – that our target this year is top four. Top four, in and of itself, is no bad thing. It's even quite a good thing. But top four is functional. Top four is Andy Garcia.

And so to a cold March afternoon in Crewe, where I'm waiting on the platform at Crewe and thinking about Philippe Coutinho. I'm en route to Anfield and with a notable absence of tangible targets to focus my season on, my attention is increasingly honing on individuals. And of all of Liverpool's individuals, Coutinho is increasingly the one that causes your heart to pound and breath, tracksuited and unshaven, vengeance the only thing to catch.

More and more, Coutinho receiving the ball at Anfield is soundtracked by that low rumble you only ever hear in football grounds: the sound of thousands of plastic seats folding up on themselves as the home fans rise in instinctive anticipation, craning their necks to get the best view they can of Phil's dancing feet.

In a team containing the high-end razzle-dazzle of Sturridge and Raheem Sterling, the timeless, gladiatorial heroism of Gerrard, and the sheer drop-dead gorgeousness of Emre Can, Coutinho is, more and more, the one who quickens the pulse. He's the one who takes your imagination for a wander, who stirs your loins, who convinces you that a 13-hour round trip from London to watch a routine win over Burnley is a Wednesday well spent.

McManaman, Fowler, Alonso, Gerrard. Four bona fide personal heroes so far in 20-odd years of semi-rabid fandom. Will Coutinho be the fifth? Maybe.

I'm loath to get my hopes up just yet, and I'm not one to commit to this sort of a relationship until I'm 100 per cent certain. But certainly, of late, my taste in footballers seems to be moving from the emphatic players to the elegant. This probably has a lot to do with my own swelling snobbery. And, actually, the increasing snobbery of football fandom in general – five years ago, Andrea Pirlo sounded like something you might order with your latte while Scott Parker was being crowned player of the year. Now one is chuckled about as a bygone relic of dinosaur-ball and the other worshipped as football's answer to James Dean. But the changing face of this Liverpool team has played its part too.

In the Gerard Houllier years, there was very little elegance to be seen – Gary Mac and Jari Litmanen only played cameo roles and it was all about Gerrard and Michael Owen: power and pace. Under Rafa Benitez things changed a bit and subtlety took some precedence – thanks largely to the irresistible man-god that was Xabi Alonso. But the enduring memories of the Benitez era – Istanbul 05, Cardiff 06, Old Trafford

09 – were still brought about by old-fashioned means: sinewy power, eye-bulging desire, a rugged refusal to lose.

These traits were largely demonstrated by and through Gerrard, and having grown up watching Stevie thundering around Anfield, confiscating the ball from Salif Diao and Igor Biscan and amassing Liverpool's points pretty much on his own, his was the style I most appreciated.

Under Brendan Rodgers, though, with delicacy of touch having suddenly become compulsory for a Liverpool first-teamer and the team starting to master the sport's slightly shrewder arts, I've found myself more able to embrace the game's more understated pleasures. Coutinho, all dropped shoulders and caressed passes, has been at the forefront of this shift.

Coutinho goes into tonight's game in the form of his life. Three days ago at Anfield he spanked in a remarkable winner against Man City. A deftly dropped shoulder, a half-yard of space jinked into, and a shot struck into the side-netting with perfection. A genuinely marvellous goal and one that, in a split-second, turned a respectable draw against the esteemed champions into a gleeful victory against nouveau riche evildoers.

The game before, he'd walloped one in off the bar against Southampton with staggering effortlessness. A couple of weeks before that, Bolton had fallen victim to the same trick: the saunter forward, the sideways duck, the fizzing banana-shot.

It's the first part of that trick that I've grown to enjoy the most. Not the finish but the way he engineers the space beforehand. Suarez, who's by some distance the most gifted footballer I've seen play for Liverpool, had the bizarre gift for dribbling past defenders while all the time seeming as if he barely had the ball under his control. It took me a good year or so to figure out that this was simply an illusion, that the sheer proportion of Suarez's forays that concluded with the striker looming down on goal while his marker blundered around, red-faced, like a city-centre tourist who's just realised his wallet has disappeared, was proof that I was watching not an act of incredible luck but in fact an act of incredible skill.

I mention this because Coutinho exists at the exact other end of the spectrum. To watch Coutinho dribble is to witness one man's quite remarkable capacity to retain absolute mastery of a football. Even when he's tackled – a rarity these days – you suspect the defender's gotten lucky. The way he forages towards the heart of a defence is hypnotic, not only because it appears that the grass beneath him barely registers his footsteps but because the ball comes with him every inch of the way.

His ability to shimmy into space on the edge of a crowded penalty box is unparalleled. As one of the editors of this very book has pointed out to me (Sachin, in case you're wondering), the way he creates the extra room by not touching the ball, by waiting that extra half-second for his marker to plant his weight before shifting the ball, is mesmerising.

Coutinho's recent displays have been such that Liverpool fans are truly starting to suspect that they might, in time, have another Steve McManaman or Peter Beardsley on their hands. And why not? When he was Phil's age, Beardsley was still playing for Carlisle United. The words 'Kenny' and 'Digger' aren't quite being whispered yet, but you get the sense that we're not far off.

I'm far too young to have seen Kenny Dalglish in the flesh, but his hip-swivels are the stuff of legend. I imagine Kenny watches Coutinho's signature move – collecting the ball on the half-turn, spinning away from his marker and zigzagging his way towards goal – and allows himself a quiet nod of approval. Likewise, I'm sure, does a certain former colleague of Coutinho's.

I have largely come to accept that Suarez was a complete one-off. He was, I think, genuinely unmatchable. Perhaps there's only the very remotest possibility that Liverpool will ever again find themselves with a player who exhibits both thn frothing rage and the swaggering, staggering finesse of the Uruguayan. Coutinho, though, has plenty of the latter, and that certainly helps softens the blow.

Inevitably the moment of what turns out to be a rather cagey and unremarkable game comes from the man himself. By happy coincidence, it occurs right out on the wing, a matter of feet away from me (it turns out the Centenary Stand has its benefits after all), and it precedes the opening goal by a few seconds.

Collecting a pass on the halfway line, with back to goal, Coutinho whisks the ball away from the touchline, twirls 180 degrees, and scoots off goalwards.

When put in those terms, it sounds like nothing special. It could even be mistaken, albeit by a fool, for not looking like anything special. But that's the magic of it; the control, the redirecting of the ball and the pivoting of his own course of movement is all part of one fluid motion, and it happens in the blink of an eye. It's exactly the sort of thing that would look neat and tidy on TV, but when seen in real life is an astonishing act of silky dexterity from the dainty Brazilian, and one that leaves a pair of Burnley midfielders in his wake (although you'd think he'd never noticed them there to begin with).

A couple of seconds later, once Phil has feinted his way past a couple more defenders and rattled away a shot (blocked), Jordan Henderson pounces on a loose ball to rifle a thoroughly adequate finish into the side-netting from the edge of the box; 1-0.

Aahh, Jordan. Heir apparent to Steven Gerrard; Liverpool's captain-to-be – and Liverpool's captain tonight. Forever doomed by his own groundedness.

Don't get me wrong, I really like Henderson, and given someone has to wear the armband once Gerrard's gone, there's no better candidate. He's mature, he works hard, he organises. And, as a Sunderland boy, he's often been compared to the current captain in his old-fashioned, salt-of-the-earth persona; the humble product of an industrial town who grafted his way to the Anfield turf. But simply being relatable doesn't make you ripe for hero status.

It's often said that the key ingredient shared by Robbie Fowler and Gerrard – Kop icons the pair of them – was that they were relatable. That they were lads for Toxteth and Huyton who'd have been paying their way through Anfield's turnstiles if they weren't playing under its floodlights. This is true, of course, but it's only half of it – the other half lay in their absurd talent, their God-given footballing genius.

Fowler may have concretised his legend by publicising his support for Merseyside's dockers, but he also did so when he Cruyff-turned Steve Staunton and picked out the top corner from 30 yards. Gerrard's story, meanwhile, might begin with a no-frills upbringing but it only becomes mythical after his antics in Istanbul.

To be a real hero you need a large sprinkling of fantasy to go with all that gritty realism, to be simultaneously relatable and utterly incomprehensible. Our Jordan, lovely lad as I'm sure he is, has plenty of the former but just not enough of the latter, and I suspect he never quite will.

The first time I set foot inside Anfield, Fowler scored a hat-trick against Arsenal, each one rattled definitively past the moustachioed colossus that was David Seaman. It was Fowler's finishes (so many of them, in the mind's eye at least, dinked over a prone, humiliated keeper) and McManaman's nomadic dribbles, all elbows, knees and flailing defenders, that formed the basis for my love of football as a kid, watching season review videotapes on an endless cycle and replicating the feats of those two in my back garden with a plastic flyaway ball, a fence panel the makeshift goal frame.

In those days it didn't register that Liverpool Football Club was an institution in decline and that any hope of a league title was fast becoming a lost cause – I was just hypnotised by the football itself, the stripped-down purity of 22 men trying to outscore and out-skill each other. Coutinho, at his best, can restore that mindset, if only momentarily.

In the later years, it's been Gerrard and Alonso who've stolen the heart. Gerrard, brow constantly scrunched, all thundering tackles and 30-yard screamers, catastrophic back-passes and cup final own goals, has basically been the on-pitch manifestation of every fan's most extreme anxieties and fantasies. Dismembering United at Old Trafford, slipping against Chelsea; trophy-gathering majesty and Hodgson-led mediocrity – he's lived the lot, he's been the one constant and it's comforting to think that he's lived it in the same way we, watching on from the stands, have done.

Alonso, in contrast, existed on another plane, swanning in from San Sebastian and introducing Britain's unrefined masses to the lost art of the ten-yard pass, the side-footed finish, the immaculately trimmed beard. When he did one to Real Madrid it hurt, but it also didn't seem like a surprise. They're a club that occupy the same suits-and-cigars universe that Xabi does. They're a club who make a point of employing the world's costliest players; Liverpool is a club that, not so long ago, employed Neil Ruddock and Phil Babb in defence.

If Gerrard was both extreme fantasy and extreme anxiety, Alonso was pure fantasy. Coutinho, I suppose, is a lot more Alonso than he is Gerrard or Fowler. His enticement lies purely in his exoticism and his honey-laden close control.

Having arrived in Liverpool from Rio de Janeiro via Milan and Barcelona, he may not be particularly relatable. But as Xabi taught me, a silky first touch will render all of that secondary.

Sturridge adds a second later on and he and Henderson are tonight's standout players. Coutinho, in truth, has been fairly peripheral. But peripheral can still be magical. In the flesh it is blindingly obvious that he is the side's most gifted player, and by a distance the most exhilarating to watch.

Last season may have been a game-changer but it didn't change the fact that glory has become a desperately precious commodity. There will always be the odd exception (one might even arrive as soon as May), but silverware and stature nowadays tend only to be properly, consistently accessible to a small contingent of moneyed superclubs, a contingent which Liverpool, at the moment, exists just outside of. Instead top four is our holy grail; our Rosebud.

I know this. So why, given all this knowledge, do I still make the conscious decision that a day off work (unpaid), an afternoon, evening and night of my time and the best part of £150 are a perfectly worthwhile sacrifice in order to travel the length of the country, on my own, to witness Liverpool register a run-of-the-mill 2-0 win over Burnley? The answer is that glory and trophies are not actually what football is about.

What football is really about is escapism – it's about heroes. It's about going to a match and drinking in the joys of the players who quicken the pulse, who take your imagination for a wander, who can leave two markers eating dust with a quick twizzle of the hips.

The notion of a league title might once again be cordoned off, Liverpool's ambitions may once again have been downsized, but with Coutinho in the side every week, playing as he is, the element of fantasy is still there.

A worthy heir to the crown of McManaman, Fowler, Alonso and Gerrard? Like I said, we'll see. But things are looking promising.

16 March 2015, Swansea 0 Liverpool 1

'He's 18 years old, he has no right to do that'

By James Dutton

My name is James and I am a late-to-the-party Liverpool supporter, born in 1991. A year after the Reds' last title triumph, and only weeks after Kenny Dalglish's shock resignation, I entered the world. Am I a jinx? Certainly the experience of growing up as a Liverpool fan from the late 1990s and into the 2000s has shaped my outlook on the club in a remarkably different way to older generations.

Football did not immediately enter my life – and by association, neither did Liverpool. My earliest memories of Liverpool are of being indoctrinated by my dad and oldest sister. Dad grew up in the same town I did – Wrexham in north Wales, and his adolescence was spent on the terraces at the Racecourse Ground. His attachment to Liverpool Football Club, as far as I'm aware, is one of attraction to the glory days of the 1970s and 80s.

My first memory of football came in the shape of the 1998 World Cup. They always say that your first World Cup is the best, and it just so happens that France 98 is the greatest World Cup of all time. I remember that Dennis Bergkamp goal against Argentina, being awestruck by Ronaldo (the Brazilian one) and then let down by his performance in the final, where Zinedine Zidane – probably the greatest player of my childhood – etched his name into eternity. I fell for football, hook, line and sinker, because of that tournament.

But something else grabbed me in that World Cup, or more specifically, someone else. I had no idea at the time but he played for Liverpool. His name? Michael Owen. He came on as a substitute in

England's opening game against Tunisia and my family pointed out that he played for the Reds. He'd scored loads of goals the season before and he was really young. But the most important fact was that he played for Liverpool. Immediately I warmed to him. He looked like a kid in a man's world. Maybe I identified with him.

There was the late equaliser against Romania, but then there was Argentina. You cannot underestimate the effect a game like that second-round clash in St Etienne has on an impressionable seven-year-old. The battle lines were drawn in the long-standing rivalry between the two nations, but the game went beyond all that. Goals from Gabriel Batistuta and Alan Shearer. David Beckham's red card. Sol Campbell's disallowed goal. David Batty's missed penalty.

But Owen and his goal surpassed all of that. It remains one of the greatest things I've ever seen on a football pitch. How can he do that? He's 18 years old, he has no right to do that. It brought me pure and unconfined joy.

That game has stayed with me and forever will. I was heartbroken by England's defeat (the first and last time that's happened) but I was hooked, I wanted more. The night ended in broken dreams, but I had football. I had found this wonderful, wonderful thing and a poster boy for it.

Michael Owen was my childhood hero. Over the next six years he *was* Liverpool and Liverpool *was* Michael Owen. As soon as the 1998/99 season began I was a Red. I remember sitting in a car park in Calais on the way back from a family holiday listening to Owen's hat-trick against Newcastle in the 4-1 win, when he rubbed his hands together with Paul Ince. I was overjoyed. Is it always this good? Is it always this easy being a football supporter?

That season proved it was anything but. Liverpool lost often and barely beat anyone worth beating. It was a miserable season, but Owen still scored 23 goals. His searing pace and dead-eye finishing were a sight to behold even if the team weren't. Your first experiences as a football supporter shape the prism within which you view football for years to come.

That season Liverpool lost 14 league games and finished seventh, while Manchester United won the treble. It's as harrowing as debut seasons get. I grew up accepting United's dominance. I grew up to accept Sir Alex Ferguson winning football trophies. I came to expect it. That was the environment that the current young generation of Liverpool supporters have grown up in. Too used to mediocrity and too used to them from Manchester winning everything. Too used to false hope – 2002, 2009, 2014.

Owen was the shining beacon in the darkness. He was the name on the back of my first replica shirt and the player I yearned to see on my first visit to Anfield in October 2000, a 1-0 win over Leicester City with a goal from Emile Heskey. I was too young for the best of Robbie Fowler – sure, he was great during the treble year of 2001 but knee injuries had restricted him. The full-throttled, precocious, peroxide blond-haired lad from Toxteth was one I only saw in highlight reels on old season-review VHS tapes.

Owen swept all before him, and his crowning glory came in 2001. Winning the Ballon d'Or as a culmination of being the fulcrum of a successful Liverpool side – the first glorious incarnation of LFC that I came across. His goals in Rome, his partnership with Heskey and the daylight robbery that was the FA Cup Final against Arsenal. What a moment, what a feeling.

Four days later came Alaves. The tension got the better of me that evening and I could barely watch in extra time, hidden instead behind the sofa. A 5-4 scoreline? Football matches don't finish 5-4, let alone cup finals. But that was it, the treble. The Reds were on the up. The next step was inevitable...wasn't it?

Gerard Houllier had built a genuinely good Liverpool side inside two years. This was now the time to dream. Ten games from greatness, the Frenchman claimed in 2002, but that title push fell short. El-Hadji Diouf, Bruno Cheyrou and Salif Diao arrived, Liverpool fell away and the Houllier empire crumbled at the seams. False dawn number one.

The summer of 2004 broke my heart. Owen departed to Real Madrid and everything I had believed in and invested in as a child was shattered. The romanticism died; it flickered again when a floppy haired Spaniard arrived to wear the number nine shirt three years later and until he slashed apart what remained of it in January 2011. By the time Luis Suarez left in 2014 I had long accepted that nothing lasts forever, not even footballing love affairs.

Owen was the first, and it's a shame that now, as a cynical adult, I feel embarrassed to admit this. And that's before you get into the anodyne punditry and sterile personality. His departure was hard to take, yet I could still hold on to the memories of his goals. But he ruined it all when he joined United. I still struggle to make sense of why he did it. It left an indelible stain on his legacy and it's tainted memories of his time at Liverpool. He was a phenomenon, he was my hero, and it's a shame that his achievements are largely overlooked now.

Another whose time at Liverpool has now been shrouded by acrimony and pettiness is Rafa Benitez. Oh Rafa. I'd have gone to war for that man. A lot is said and written about Benitez; for right or wrong he distorts opinion, but the man brought me my best night in football. Istanbul. Nothing will take that away from my estimation of him, not just as a football manager but as a man. When the older generations speak with reverence of Dalglish, Rush, Barnes, Paisley, Shankly – the list goes on – it's difficult to identify with. The burden of the club's history is easier to understand when you haven't seen it or lived through it. It exists not only within the bowels of the Anfield museum but in the stories you hear everywhere you follow the Reds. History.

Whether my heroes shape up to the examples of those luminaries is immaterial – they have given me the joy and the memories that the legends of the 1970s and 80s did for others. Owen, Torres, Suarez; the holy triumvirate. Benitez and Houllier; the wise men. Litmanen, Garcia, Alonso and Maxi; the icons and cult heroes. Dirk Kuyt holding it all together. Working hard.

Above all of them, though, stands Steven Gerrard. The top, the pinnacle. He doesn't need to be King or God. He is just Steven Gerrard. The unassuming lad from Huyton with greatness thrust on him and the history of Liverpool Football Club weighing on his shoulders for an eternity. Gerrard came through in that first season of mine, 1998/99, and Liverpool Football Club makes no sense without him.

I remember where I was on 29 November 1998. It's rare for days and dates from your childhood to stick with you so readily, and there's only one thing I remember of that day. I was sitting in the back of the car, with 5 Live on the radio. Liverpool were cruising to a 2-0 win over Blackburn Rovers, but exact details of the game don't spring to mind, neither the goalscorers nor the general pattern of play. Did Liverpool deserve to win? Did they ride their luck? Was Roy Hodgson still in charge of Blackburn at that point? No idea. All I remember is one name. Steven Gerrard.

He was making his debut as a late substitute at right-back. Impressions from those at the game recall a scrawny, lanky and gormless 18-year-old entering the fray, evidently wracked by nerves. I had little idea that this kid would become the embodiment of Liverpool through my journey from childhood into early adulthood.

Growing up with a footballer brings a special affinity. I'm part of the Harry Potter generation too, not only around the same age as the actors but also the characters in the book, and that brings a unique appreciation for following the development of a story. From being a child at the start to a teenager by the end, you can identify with the narrative and character development so readily. In footballing terms, this is Gerrard to me.

While Owen is the childhood hero, his story had already begun. I watched Gerrard's growth as I grew to love the club. He's not just any footballer either. His longevity, his achievements and his ability have given him an outstanding career, but his personality remains fascinating. So deeply complex, layered in insecurities and anxieties that have dictated his greatest and worst moments on the football pitch. A deeply flawed character defined by moments on a football pitch.

The announcement of his departure at the start of the year brought me profound sadness. For 17 years I have followed Liverpool and for 17 years I have watched Gerrard don either number 28, number 17 or number eight. It has yet to sink in that these are his final death throes, that by the start of 2015/16 he will no longer be around.

His decline this season has laid bare the ravages of time. All good things must come to an end. Knowing they're coming doesn't make you any more ready. Not really. The concept of mortality is one you can't understand as a child, but now I'm 23 and I appreciate it more than ever.

I lost my mother to cancer last year, the culmination of a five-long-battle that she had been losing for the final 18 months. She always retained her dignity as she stared the end in the face. It's the most that you can do in that situation. The end diminishes nothing that came before and how you embrace it speaks volumes about you.

Gerrard has been acutely aware of his own mortality as a footballer this year and it's weighed him down. As Liverpool travel to Swansea on a Monday night in mid-March the captain is back after an injury lay-off. But he's deemed fit enough only for the bench. He's getting used to this.

It's a Monday night – the graveyard slot for Liverpool matches and so often where dreams go to die. One of those games where you feel the time plays a big role in the flow of the game. It's a leveller and the Reds are not at the races at all.

For the first time since the switch to Brendan Rodgers's 3-4-2-1, Liverpool are found wanting all over the park. Not in control, not penetrating in attack and losing the midfield battle resoundingly. Emre Can is far from the German-Turkish prince he has portrayed himself as since Christmas.

Swansea have our number. Should that be any surprise? They're a clever club with a young manager in Garry Monk who has not been overawed by his premature elevation to the role. This is, after all, the model FSG bought into in the summer of 2012. The arrival of Rodgers, the signing of Joe Allen and the rhetoric of 'Death by Football' was a recognition of the great work that the Welsh club have done.

Swansea were Third Division in 1998, and Wrexham were a level above. One is now in the Premier League and the other has been rooted in the Conference since 2007. Textbook case studies in how to run and how not to run a football club.

The home side lack a cutting edge but they have out-thought the Reds. Rodgers has been here before, when a formation becomes unstuck and teams find ways to target its weak spots. The second half is where he shows his mettle, though, where he shows the intuition the owners invested in when he put forward his 180-page dossier.

From being out-numbered in the middle, Rodgers switches it round – a return of last season's messianic midfield diamond. It's a subtle switch at first but Swansea's midfielders are unable to close the passing angles as readily and the Reds gain a footing in the game, albeit without looking incisive enough going forward.

An hour gone and the first change beckons. It's Stevie, of course it is. The haircut is still the same but his jawline is more chiselled, the brows on his forehead ever more furrowed. The armband returns to its owner and the midfield shores up. Gerrard sits deep, allowing the passive Jordan Henderson to surge forward more and it leads directly to the winning goal, one of stunning simplicity executed to comic perfection.

The 20-yard forward pass from Martin Skrtel, the flick-on from Daniel Sturridge and Henderson's running gait. The vice-captain bears down on goal but not before a Swansea defender slides to the rescue. Fortune smiles on Jordan, though, as the ball cannons off his leg and balloons over Lukasz Fabianski before nestling in the back of the net. Liverpool do not deserve this luck, second best for much of the game, but when your luck's in, it's in. Things like this didn't happen in the autumn.

The final 25 minutes is textbook in how to defend a lead. Calm, authoritative and intelligent. Gerrard at the centre of it all. You can get behind this, you can get behind Gerrard being this figure for these young players. You can always get behind Gerrard, the last 17 years has taught me that.

Watching his decline has been distressing, an absolute wrench. The super-human figure, the man I could always rely on to be there, shrunk down to size by age. No one is immune to it. After years of fearing the loss of Gerrard, fearing life without him, we're in a strange situation where it can be embraced. A springboard for the future. But I'm still not ready for it. Give me one more moment, Stevie. After Owen, now this. Liverpool Football Club doesn't make sense without you.

22 March 2015, Liverpool 1 Manchester United 2

'Devon Loch job, as someone once said'

By Steve Kelly

For my dad it was Everton. It was always Everton. There was just something about those eight years in the Second Division, between 1954 and 1962, when he was in his 20s, which absolutely scarred him for life. In the portable TV age he would be banished to the bedroom while mum watched *Dallas* or some such rubbish, and you could hear him laughing at an Everton defeat upstairs. I mean, even I wasn't that bitter. These were full, raucous yucks.

He told me years later that his life had been made an absolute misery by Bluenoses, even though their team was hardly in the ascendancy except by locality. When Bill Shankly came along and blew all that nonsense out of the water, my dad had his one and only religious confirmation, with room enough for just the one nemesis. He passed it on to me. Man, that shit at Kiev was funny. Full, raucous yucks.

Manchester United? Yeah, he couldn't really stand them either. But being a grown man in the 1950s, I suppose he couldn't help but admire what they'd done with ex-Liverpool captain Matt Busby at the helm. The tragedy at Munich was a national one. When I was small I once heard my dad rip somebody to shreds for the usual '58' nonsense. 'We cried that day,' he said. Whether he actually did or not I've never asked him. He might just have been embroidering his point, but a genuine distaste for the merciless mockery of a plane crash and that senseless waste of all that talent was also part of my inheritance, at an age when what your dad says goes.

There was ambivalence, of course. We both watched a documentary on the disaster once, part of the anniversary 'celebrations' Granada TV often did, and one of the journalists that had also been killed got a mention. 'That twat,' came the mutter from the other end of the couch. This was new. 'They had the team to end all teams and we had nothing, but he never put the whip down once that bastard.' So this wasn't a modern phenomenon, then. Those of us who at the time were tired of reading about what Bryan Robson had had for breakfast and needed a looking glass to find out who Liverpool had been drawn against in yet another European Cup quarter-final, weren't the first to get tetchy.

This was also around the year of my first trip to Old Trafford. I'd been to Manchester lots of times before, to sell second-hand records on Oxford Road and shuffle cautiously through the concrete nightmare that was Hulme to a curiously-decorated art-house cinema before going home at night. It was dark, moody, the sort of place you knew Joy Division were born to make the soundtrack for, but nothing ever happened to me.

Both cities loved their music, loved their art – or 'aaaarrrrrrrt' as we both seemed to call it – and yet football was the dividing line. A jagged, glass-shard line that could not be crossed.

The special train pulled into the cricket ground's station and we all stood around in a dishevelled horde, waiting to be frogmarched up to the ground. It was thrilling, once you knew no one was actually daring to push through our large, truncheoned overcoat. In the ground there was the usual back and forth between the fans, with Munich at the fore and sharpened coins raining down from behind. You soon learned not to turn around.

There was also a new ditty now – 'Shankly 81' – and the match passed off almost as an irrelevance. We won, luckily, but there was more danger in the overcrowded underpass at Warwick Road waiting to go home.

In 1983 I returned and heard just what it meant to the Mancs whenever they put one over on us. Arnie Muhren scored and it was like a bomb went off. Impressive, despite the pain of the scoreline. Kenny equalised four minutes later. The songs, and the atmosphere, continued to nosedive for years after that.

I struggled a bit with all of this. You knew full well that others found it as tacky as you did but stayed silent and let everyone else spew out their bile. How could you stop it except with violence of your own? People on the outside never knew just how unpleasant it got. One 'indie' magazine about LFC once showed its readers how to make the perfect paper aeroplane. This is true, I swear. It stood alongside a cartoon about the adventures of Kop Kat. People were oblivious. Like Manchester City's inflatable bananas, they just thought paper aeroplanes were a cute addendum. Oh, you wacky football fans.

So it had always seemed a bit rotten. It meant trying to keep your distance from the sheer hatred of United despite their team doing virtually nothing while we were winning virtually everything in sight. It's almost like it's come full circle because they're like us now and we're like them; bemused and resentful.

Hillsborough had something to do with it, our own disaster and a brutal realisation of what we'd been doing to them before. United then started to win stuff too, while we began to struggle. It was all going horribly, horribly wrong.

'They' could always have their own moments of course. 'Where's your famous Munich song?' was code for you-know-what, no one ever really thought otherwise. I saw one lad dragged out by a steward once for making an 'H' sign with his hands. I suppose it's not that impressive a feat for somebody with six fingers (oooo look, I'm getting just as bad as everyone else now). I'll bet as he was being arrested outside he told them he meant Heysel, not Hillsborough, that tiresome cop-out which fools nobody but which they still cling to like a life raft.

United won loads and it began to get nasty again. Munich songs returned, at Old Trafford anyway, along with a new tilt about Harold Shipman. A mass murderer of vulnerable pensioners in Cheshire? I mean, *really*? I was getting on a bit now anyway and going to Man U games now felt like we needed that stuff Jodie Foster puts under her nose to blot out the corpse's stench in *The Silence Of The Lambs*.

What the hell? It was usually just twice a year. In a way, as Kevin Sampson explained in his excellent *Extra Time* back in the 1990s, it was invigorating to find an event that cut through the post-Sky 'Football's Coming Home' gentility and which actually mattered to people despite its physical menace and moral vacuity.

United were always winning stuff now, including a treble which we tried to dismantle twice (in the league and the cup) and failed miserably. We once sat watching an utterly dismal home game against Leicester and there were delirious cheers for Juventus going ahead against United in a Champions League semi-final, the loudest noise of the night. The three United goals after that passed in silence, and Leicester won – also in silence. This club had seen better days but it's doubtful it's seen many that were worse, purely in football terms obviously.

There were rare occasions when it all mattered on a football level as well as a tribal one. Gerard Houllier got the better of them quite a few times in such a guarded, sucker-punch manner that it began to feel genuinely hilarious. It didn't really matter, though. In fact, when you sat down and thought about it Liverpool have never really got the better of them.

In an era of Scouse plenty, Liverpool couldn't beat United at home for eight years. Eight! They, of course, had already scuppered our own 'proper' treble way back in 1977, and also destroyed what would have been our first double in 1979. We'd won a couple of League Cup finals, but even that competition started to seriously decline as a major achievement, so that almost didn't count.

FA Cup finals? Forget it. League deciders? Well, we did sort of win one in 2009 that dragged us back into the race, but they still won the thing at the end to make it 18 titles each. Liverpool's best ever league performance and we came second. To them.

For all of my rationalised too-cool-for-school demeanour, there was no denying they were becoming incredibly irritating. The Reds still rose above petty rivalry by beating Blackburn for them in 1995 and got no thanks for it. By 2010 such niceties were done away with as Liverpool feebly collapsed at home to Chelsea. No favours that day; Steven Gerrard even made the gruesome mistake that put a Chelsea striker clean through on goal to make it 1-0. Remember that, because it becomes important later on.

For the last three league challenges Liverpool have managed to muster in these not-so-halcyon days, they coincidentally managed to beat United home and away. A fat lot of good it did us. In the last one the big bad wolf had retired and they'd put Little Red Riding Hood in charge instead – on Fergie's strict instructions, no less. Comedy gold. David Moyes was awful and, unsurprisingly, way out of his depth. Liverpool won at their place 3-0, with penalties and a red card. The away end was bumptious and triumphant. This was all coming to an end, finally.

No, it wasn't. Gerrard made a gruesome mistake that put a Chelsea striker clean through on goal a month later and that was all she wrote. It didn't even matter that it helped give the title to City. United were now so contemptuously arrogant, so assured of their own neighbours' lack of substance and consequence. The mere fact that the unelected leader of the Scouse gang had fucked it all up made it another United triumph over Liverpool.

Just as United's title collapse had made them a national laughing stock in 1992, when even a calamitous dud like Mark Walters could still be a hero and bang the final nail in the coffin, Liverpool had fucked up in the final strait. Devon Loch job, as someone once said.

OK, so now they were beginning to annoy me a little. This was Evertonian behaviour they were indulging in. When City strolled out of Goodison with three points and barely a whimper from the Blues, with the Oasis record 'The Masterplan' blaring through the tannoy at half-time, that was only to be expected. A photo of grinning gimp Howard Kendall (Everton's greatest manager, snigger) emerged of him holding up a T-shirt with Tony Book and Mike Summerbee which read 'It's not the winning; it's the taking part that counts'. Teams, date, venue, everything.

This was the kind of company United were now keeping after all those years of glory and one poor season. They were welcome to each other. Moyes couldn't last obviously, we lost Luis Suarez to Barcelona and Daniel Sturridge got nobbled by The Hodge again. The times they weren't a-changing after all, and that feeling was authenticated by an easy United victory at Old Trafford just before Christmas.

Liverpool fans were relatively nonchalant. There was a brand new system in place and Brad Jones was in goal, the football equivalent of doing the three-legged race with Stephen Hawking. Better results eventually followed and now both clubs were vying for the fabled Champions League spot. Wonderful. I wonder if we can get bounced out by Basel and humiliated by Real Madrid next year as well.

This was the time to revive the old Borges quote about the Falklands War: two bald men fighting over a comb. Still, it had the semblance of a fight for something vaguely significant and it *was* Liverpool versus Manchester United. We had a good record at home against them as well, so what could possibly go wrong?

As it turned out, everything. Even my becalmed hackles rose before the game. I got stitched up by a combined project at work involving me and a United fan. I wrote the usual guff about both sides being as bad as each other while the Manc went full pelt about Munich songs and cups of shit being thrown. I felt like a right old Colonel Blimp – 'Wars start at midnight don'tcha know?' and all that.

OK, calm down. Hardly anyone will read it anyway and you can't help it if the other lad is a prize gobshite. Let them have their petty triumph; the Reds are going to win the one that actually matters.

And then the game started.

Oh dear, we do not look bothered at all. Brendan Rodgers had done a little bit of crowing after the previous game against Swansea – how they were messing with us in the first half but he had got it sorted out in the dressing room at half-time and that's how we won. If managers blowing their own trumpets can ever be converted to actual jazz, Brendan certainly has a Kind Of Blue in him for sure.

So what does he do, the great innovator? He starts the United game exactly as he started the Swansea game. What, did he think that clueless novice Louis Van Gaal wasn't capable of coming up with anything complex to outfox us?

Actually he was right on that score. United's main trick was to stifle the midfield, cut off Liverpool's supply to the forwards, get Juan Mata chasing after the hopeless Alberto Moreno and Marouane Fellaini launching himself into Emre Can. And it was working, too. Perhaps too many of us have gone too-cool-for-school as there is little of the intensity this fixture absolutely demands. When we lost Suarez we didn't just say farewell to one of the most gifted footballers of his generation, we lost a man who could cause a bloodbath in a convent.

United go in front, and there's a muffled mutiny on the Kop now. They've come into our place, our home, doing exactly as they please. Taking the piss, actually. This is not on. Time for some loud bellowing, with coherent words merely optional. There are a few tackles flying in now and United aren't backing down. The referee, Martin Atkinson, books Joe Allen, and then talks to Fellaini. And talks. And talks. Jesus, get his phone number and have done with it.

The away end is in its element and any idea of blotting them out has evaporated. It's time for the greatest hits, 'The Sun was right, you're murderers'. Christ. Even Kelvin bastard Mackenzie isn't clinging to that one any more.

It's pure incitement. 'Murderers' and 'Justice for the 39', it's all seeping out now. Anfield hasn't indulged in this sort of crap since the 1980s, and what's more the Mancs know it and they just get worse and worse.

They never ever get called on this shit. Mention it to anyone and they've got one for that too, 'always the victim'. You get more and more pissed off, wriggling in a web they've created and every 'neutral' bootlicker panders to them. Back and forth it goes, proving Darwin wrong with every utterance.

All that's left now is to win the game, turn it around, ram it right back down their throats – but Adam Lallana misses a sitter. He's also launched into the air by Phil Jones and this challenge doesn't even merit the lecture. This is starting to stink a bit now, but it's not as if we deserve any better the way we're playing.

Half-time and a chance for Brendan to work some of that 180-page dossier magic of his. There's another saddening event on the pitch as the great Pele is in town. Not because it's Anfield, not even because it's Liverpool v United. He's here to flog butties for some corporate monstrosity. The interview on the pitch is tedious, embarrassing and interminable. There are numerous comments on the Kop about a legend's indignity, happening as it does at the same time Raheem Sterling is holding out for over £150,000 a week. I found out later that Pele was wearing a yellow and green tie, Subway's colours.

The second half starts and this looks like something. Gerrard is ready to come on and the first thing he does is an excellent 40-yard pass. The second thing he does is go crunching into a tackle. The third thing he does is stand on Ander Herrera. The fourth is to walk forlornly off the pitch. It's a red card.

The Kop is now at boiling point. In days of old it would have stayed that way but everyone has a smartphone now. Texts from friends, vines on Twitter, it all happens in the blink of an eye. It was blatant. He had to go. The atmosphere is suitably solemn again. He walked in and walked out again like Grandpa Simpson. More Manc hilarity ensues as Liverpool's talisman continues the worst football farewell of all time.

Now there's shock and not a little dread. United had already made 11 versus 11 look easy, what's the rest of this going to be like? They get a second – not a bad goal, actually – and we're starting to watch this through our fingers while Atkinson starts taking some serious piss. Every United dive is a foul while Jones just assassinates Jordan Henderson. There's no other word for it. There's also no apology and he doesn't even look back. He knows full well what colour the card will be. Yellow, like the streak down the referee's back. It's bordering on comical now.

Sturridge gets one goal back but it never looks like another will come. We were relying on Mario Balotelli, that's how desperate it got.

Simon Mignolet saves a Wayne Rooney penalty, Martin Skrtel stands on David de Gea, the referee blows for time and the Mancs are making an almighty meal of the last incident. The werewolf-faced rat goes down belatedly in a farcical, fraudulent heap. They can't even win with a slither of grace.

So that's that then. It's now time to practise all those 'I wasn't bothered about the Champions League, it's just a gravy train and we're shit in it anyway' diatribes that aren't going to fool anybody. Even for Liverpool v United, this is a real red-letter day for them. The spoils, the laughs and the eventual 'triumph' at the end of the season, with one, probably two bans for us. They even got to sing their tiresome venom safe in the knowledge that no one will ever corner them on it. How can this keep on happening?

You can paraphrase Doctor Johnson here and say that when a man is tired of Liverpool versus Manchester United, he is tired of life. Well, book my flight to Switzerland and get a room at Dignitas ready.

There's a United fan that e-mails me sometimes and he nearly always calls me 'comrade'. He knows what he can do with that today. The Hillsborough shite they come out with is the worst kind of class treachery and they're deluded if they think it's in any way warranted.

Some Reds will read that and just say, 'For God's sake man, stop your bloody whimpering and just hit them back harder.' At one point in the afternoon I actually wished some of the little rats who hang around Anfield's street corners, one of whom had given me grief (an accent test, most likely), really did manage to make his way through the police cordon and catch one of them with a knockout blow. Chances are they just stood on the tips of their toes, bounced around for a couple of minutes and eschewed the usual tasteless jibes about lethally-injected pensioners. That'll learn 'em.

If we lose to Arsenal in a fortnight's time that'll probably be it. The Great Dream, over. Lost another chance to play six tedious group matches, shown on TV because people will stare at absolutely anything as long as there's 22 blokes kicking a ball about. We'd have only spent the precious wedge on three new players no one had heard of, but guess what? There's a video on YouTube and he looked absolutely boss in the French league.

When I did a fanzine years ago I often got called 'Victor Meldrew' because I was a miserable old get who got annoyed with anything and everything as it honestly felt like the world was leaving me behind. Even when things were at their finest for us we could never really get the better of United, and now there's been a reversal in overall fortunes we still can't. Where's the fairness in that?

So yeah, OK, they probably do bother me a little.

4 April 2015, Arsenal 4 Liverpool 1

We're nearly at the end of this book so this feels like the appropriate time for me to make a confession – I used to support Arsenal.

Now before you all march to my house and shove turds through my letterbox, let me explain how this came about. Firstly, I was very young at the time, around nine or ten. Secondly, I was press-ganged into it by my older cousin, Amit, a Gooner from birth who as a youngster (and even a little bit now) loved telling anyone and everyone possible how great Arsenal were while not being able to believe there were actual people who didn't share his passion. He nudge and nudged until, finally, I gave in.

Thirdly…well actually, there is no thirdly. But you'll be glad to know this madness didn't last long, less than a day in fact, and as soon as my dad found out and told me to behave.

In general Arsenal have been a big part of my football life – along with Amit, quite a few of my other relatives are Gooners (see the Real Madrid versus Barcelona chapter for more), and the first Liverpool match I can properly remember involved them.

It took place on Friday 26 May 1989. You may remember it.

We gathered as one massive extended family to watch the mother of title deciders and by the end of the evening I was in tears and taking out my despair on a desk. Or was it a wardrobe? Anyway, whatever it was, it got it. Hard and violently.

In the subsequent years I've got to know quite a few Arsenal fans, and almost to a man and woman I like them. Among them there's Jerry, who I worked with at the *Harrow Observer*, and more recently, Toby, Paul, Katy and Rob, who I work with at the *Guardian*. All great people.

So I have something of a soft spot for the team that broke my heart as a child and who I briefly (and it was brief Reds, honest) supported. And yes, I always want us to beat them, but it's never the most painful of defeats.

Which brings me on to Saturday. Fuck me, that was bad.

I thought we would get beat, what with us coming into the match on the back of losing to United, lacking the suspended Martin Skrtel and Steven Gerrard, and having had to deal with all the shit around Raheem Sterling's contract. But I didn't see a tonking coming. We were terrible, truly, truly terrible, and any hopes of qualifying for the Champions League have pretty much evaporated.

What hasn't evaporated is Reds losing their minds, as one glance of Twitter in the 24 hours after the match would testify to. Christ, people were angry about this loss – some called the team spineless, others demanded Brendan Rodgers be sacked immediately – and reading it all you'd think Liverpool's recent run of 13 league games without defeat was a trick of the mind. Seriously, some of these keyboard wailers should've been around when Tom and George were in the boardroom and Roy was in the dugout. Now that was a crisis.

Anyway, I'm not massively upset. Instead my attention is on Wednesday and the FA Cup replay against Blackburn. Win that and we're one game away from the final, where we'd probably face Arsenal again. A chance for revenge.

See you at Wembley family and friends.

SN

8 April 2015,

Blackburn 0 Liverpool 1 (replay; 0-0 in original tie)

'We trade the pints in for caffeine and polo shirts'

By Andrew Gargett

Blackburn. In the FA Cup. And it's stupid o'clock – 3am on Monday. Monday at three-bloody-am is never a suitable time to watch football. Anyway I've just rolled out of bed, bleary eyed and half asleep…up the Pool!

I grew up in Blackburn. Not the Blackburn 20 miles north-west of Manchester with a park named Ewood. My Blackburn is in Australian suburbia, about 20km east of Melbourne.

At 3am on a school night, a Monday no less; there is no way to dress this up as a good thing. It would have to be the worst of all the kick-off times we suffer through here in Australia. The game finishes at 5am so it's not like you're going to stay up for it, and it starts at three, so unless you can nod off at nine-ish the night before you've got to try to sneak in a few more hours before work. Either way it's not fun.

Anyway, it's the quarter-final of the FA Cup and Liverpool have a mid-table Championship side to contend with. It is a fantastic opportunity for another trip to Wembley.

The Blackburn team – I'm none the wiser once I see it, although the commentators advise that the big lad up top, Rudy Gestede, is a handful. And big lads up top always seem to cause us grief. For the Reds, Lazar Markovic and Glen Johnson come in for Alberto Moreno and Joe Allen. Emre Can is pushed into midfield. We are in good form and I expect us to win this comfortably.

I have an affinity with the FA Cup. It has left an indelible mark on my now 26-year love affair with the men of Shankly's best. My first and unforgettable Liverpool Football Club experience was the 1989 FA Cup Final. I was eight and my parents allowed me to stay up to watch this showpiece occasion in the English football calender for the first time. I had no understanding of the tragic context that engulfed the game. For me in the pre-Sky (or in Australia, pre-Foxtel) era, it was simply the first full game of top-level football I'd watched. I'd already fallen in love with the game, playing junior football, so watching this felt like the big time.

That sight of Kenny Dalglish in his big manager's jacket leading the team out is burnt on to my retinas. In that instant my world changed. Four minutes in, John Aldridge did what he did best and Liverpool subsequently coasted, until Stuart McCall equalised late on. Fortunately my new favourite player, Ian Rush, bagged a brace in extra time. I was hooked.

The 1989 final was replayed over and over again in our backyard. Unfortunately for my older brother Ben, who also supported Liverpool but wasn't as passionate about it or as stubborn, I was always Liverpool. This made him Everton. It also meant I always won. Before each epic battle we'd mimic Kenny and co and get into tracksuit jackets before entering our little stadium.

Over the next few years my passion for Liverpool grew. Every Monday morning I'd wake up, run down and collect the paper. Liverpool's results and the First Division table were catalogued in the 'Other Sports' section of the paper. It comprised of the score, the goalscorers in brackets and the table. No review, no detail. At that age of innocence it was more than enough. Looking back it was pitiful.

My fading memory tells me that a season later the Monday morning score-collection exercise was supplemented by a one-hour highlights package that same evening. For some reason Leeds 4 Liverpool 5 acts as the archetype for this period in my mind. Mike Hooper was in goal, John Barnes was brilliant and Lee Chapman kept scoring against us. I had no idea this was the beginning of the end of Liverpool's era of dominance.

Two minutes in and Gestede collides with Martin Skrtel, who is taken off on a stretcher with a head injury and replaced by Kolo Toure. Gestede then wins a header which goes wide, but not before clattering into Simon Mignolet. This could be ominous. Liverpool are looking slow, the game is turgid. It's 3am…why am I watching this?

On 32 minutes Kolo jolts me out of sleep and/or boredom by scoring following a Daniel Sturridge flick-on. Unfortunately the linesman's flag is raised – offside. The half peters out, Liverpool have enjoyed enough possession but don't look likely to score and Gestede continues to cause us trouble.

It wasn't long before my football world changed. Formative glimpses were replaced with constant coverage and total immersion became possible. My brothers and I pestered our parents into becoming early subscribers to pay-TV. The consequent result was that we could now frequently watch football live. Live! And so my teenage years became as much about watching Liverpool play at stupid hours as anything else. It became the new norm.

In those days Blackburn Rovers were flying. With Shearer and Sutton – the SAS – Stuart Ripley, Tim Sherwood and Colin Hendry, and under the stewardship of King Kenny, they were on their way to win the title. Which they achieved 20 years ago this May.

It's a Blackburn corner following a(nother) Dejan Lovren mistake and Mignolet saves superbly from a Baptiste header that was definitely going in. The big Belgian's turnaround in form has been something to behold. He still can't kick the ball but he's currently excelling at his primary function – saving it.

The game continues to drag on but Liverpool cannot drag themselves above their inferior opponents. On 55 minutes Sturridge has a shout for a penalty that was never going to be given. Amid the monotony, Kolo hits the post with a header from three yards. He should have scored. This has goalless draw written all over it.

Liverpool never exert the kind of pressure that makes a goal an inevitability. It is 4.55am, the game drifts off into a replay as the referee blows for full time. I think I've already drifted back to much-needed sleep.

It's not 3am but, let's be clear, 4.45am is not a sane time to watch football either. Then again, insanity is probably the best way to describe a dedication to Liverpool Football Club when you live on the other side of the planet. My wife certainly files it under insane, and I think of all of the friendships I've made watching Liverpool at times such as 4.45am, and of some of the insane times we've had together, and the most logical conclusion is we are all just the slightest bit, well…insane.

I try to watch as many games as I can at Cheers Bar on George Street in Sydney, which is the home of the Liverpool Supporters' Club of New South Wales. When Liverpool play, this bar is a sea of vibrant red, covered in handmade banners swaying back and forth. During last year's title run, the place regularly reached its 300-person capacity three hours before kick-off, with about the same amount of people stuck outside. For a feel of the atmosphere back then simply Google 'Liverpool v Man City Cheers Bar'.

Unfortunately this replay is not one for Cheers due to new laws which prevent pubs based in the Sydney CBD opening before 5am. Going to Cheers would mean me missing the first 15 minutes of the game, so home it is.

Along with a few other Liverpool-supporting mates I work in the city, so midweek and European fixtures that start between 5am and 7am are ideal for watching at Cheers. We trade the pints in for caffeine and polo shirts, and mayhem for suits and seating, but it's good fun and getting 50 or so people in for a midweek kick-off is the norm.

My good mate Matt was also contemplating watching the game at Cheers. He lives miles away; Cheers attendance would require him getting a train at 3.30am. Fortunately sanity – or a version of it – kicked in and he, like me, is watching from home. Another mate, Nick, did catch a train, although he had the luxury of a relative sleep-in, catching a 4.28am service to watch the game round at John's.

Insanity, it's never far away, especially with Nick and John. They are two of the leaders of the fun at Cheers. Like me they are young(ish) professionals, but in Cheers they, along with Macca, are a sight to behold. John, arms in the air leading the fray; Nick singing about a right-back called Steve Finnan, or leading his infamous rendition of the Gary Mac song; and Macca is a Kop season ticket holder who arrived in Sydney about the same time as me. You will find him standing near the bar singing the most distinctive of Liverpool songs.

The beginning of the game is reminiscent of the Anfield fixture – monotony. We look blunt but I'm hoping that an early change of boots for Sturridge is the tonic to snap us out of it. Unfortunately on 19 minutes he curls a shot over from outside the box following a period of sustained pressure. Despite a decent goal return, his form following a return from injury is concerning – he just doesn't look confident in himself.

I moved to Sydney from Melbourne in early 2010, during Rafa's unhappy final season. On our first night in Sydney, I convinced my wife Alex to come watch the Liverpool game with me. I checked the internet; Cheers was the destination.

We sat down in the corner and quickly spotted a loud group singing all manner of Liverpool songs. John, then as now, had his arms in the air and was belting out the songs. Alex leant over and said with a knowing smile, 'I bet these become your mates up here.' She was right, and almost six years later these guys are some of my best mates. We form a nucleolus of the LFC NSW and have shared some unforgettable times.

On 25 minutes Rhodes misses a free(ish) header inside the box. Mamadou Sakho, who failed to challenge the Blackburn striker, soon goes off having injured his hamstring. Kolo is coming on following his nightmare against Arsenal. It's now Lovren and Toure at CB. Somehow I'm still confident.

I cannot say I've ever seen Liverpool win the league. Yes, I began supporting the club in 1989, but age, technology and access meant it was done so at a distance and I cannot in good faith 'claim' our last title win as mine.

Saying that, Liverpool's 1990/91 team photo adorned my wall for years, meaning the 1990 league trophy and those glorious Candy kits were a big part of my early years as a Red.

I have, like many Liverpool fans, witnessed a few title challenges. Stoke away in 2008/09, when Steven Gerrard's goal was disallowed and which I watched on our honeymoon on the Vietnamese island of Phu Quoc, still sticks in the craw. Later that season when Liverpool schooled Manchester United at Old Trafford, I spent what seemed an age jumping on a bar stool in a crowded bar in Melbourne full of Liverpool fans, waving my shirt over my head. The best of times and we were the best team in the league that season; except we weren't because of Federico bloody Macheda, United's brilliant backline and the very fact they accrued more points than us.

Nothing, however, compares to last year's ride. Especially for us fans Down Under. Liverpool's pre-season tour of Australia was an unforgettable collective experience for the countless passionate Reds that live here. For many it was going to be the first time they'd see Liverpool in the flesh; that it was a friendly and counted for nothing was irrelevant.

I'd seen Liverpool live once, the 1-0 loss to United at Anfield courtesy of a Carlos Tevez goal and the game when Gerrard squared up to Anderson. In the absence of a ticket and desperate, I arrived at Anfield early and ended up in an alleyway forking out an astronomical amount of cash for a ticket. At the time I wasn't sure when I'd be back to England next, or if Anfield would still be standing, so it was a no-brainier...probably in more ways than one.

Almost immediately after half-time, Tom Cairney hits one from outside the box. Thankfully we've got Mignolet. But Blackburn are coming for us and I'm nervous.

Liverpool's trip to Australia really was unforgettable. On the Saturday night before the Wednesday game we had The Anfield Wrap guys do a great live show in Sydney in front of 300 or so punters. This was followed by a mass migration south for four days of chaos. I crashed at my good mate Tom's place. He joined the LFC NSW on what felt like a European away – hours upon hours in pubs with your mates and not a care in the world.

During this whirlwind week I made numerous friendships with those who had travelled across from Liverpool. Our supporting experience is vastly different yet it is amazing how much we have in common – the feeling that we are supporting an idea as much as a club, the culture, an affinity with the city, and of course solidarity around Hillsborough.

LFC NSW secured 170 tickets in the 'Kop End' at the MCG. Our mates from the Melbourne Supporters' Club were in the bay next door. Forget the quality of the game, turning a city half a world away, a city I grew up in, into a wall of red was something to behold.

The MCG is one of the most amazing stadiums in the world and you could argue the heart of Melbourne resides in its hallowed turf, bricks and mortar. And it was covered by us, with our banners, flags and scarves. It was spectacular.

For me the most special thing of all was standing in that great colosseum, looking left and right and nodding knowingly to the same friends I watch the game with at stupid hours in at Cheers, or in the comfort of our home. This would be a rare time when all of us, the collective 'we', would stand shoulder by shoulder and watch the team we love. That feeling will stay with me forever, and to say it set the tone for an amazing season would be an understatement.

Twenty minutes left and Philippe Coutinho scores. I shout at the top of my voice and wake up our seven-month little legend, Annie Hope. Watching the replay, the goal is better than I first thought. He is a gem, is Phil Coutinho.

Annie's connections to Liverpool go beyond her father's obsession. We were on a six-week trip to Europe in December and January 2013/14, and to my wife Alex's ever-patient 'surprise' our time in Liverpool coincided with a busy festive fixture list for the Reds. We had Man City away, Chelsea away and Hull at home. Thanks to some of the aforementioned friendships, I was lucky enough to secure tickets to all three games.

Alex went to City away and sat in the home end with a good friend who harks from Manchester and now resides in Sydney. He was back home visiting his family and was kind enough to sort Alex out with a ticket.

On returning from London following a second successive defeat but a second successive brilliant day out, Alex informed me that we might need to visit the doctor. The next day we went to the NHS and the lovely nurse informed us that Alex's persistent jet-lag was in fact our little Annie on her way.

As we left the hospital, the receptionist shouted, 'Are you? Are you?' When we responded in the affirmative she grinned from ear to ear, gave us two thumbs up and bellowed with joy, 'Discovered in Liverpool and a little Scouser!'

That interaction with a stranger was a microcosm of our time in Liverpool. We were welcomed by strangers and friends and consistently enjoyed hospitality that went above and beyond. It was a special time and the kindness of many will stay with us forever.

The last few minutes are eventful. Sturridge should have scored and killed the game, Allen has a nailed-on penalty not given and then Mignolet saves a good effort from the Blackburn keeper. Yes, keeper!

An FA Cup semi-final it is, then. Liverpool are heading south again and I for one am tired but absolutely delighted.

13 April 2015, Liverpool 2 Newcastle 0

'Beware. Whimsical Knobhead Below'

By Neil Poole

'Build it and they will come, Neil'

There is every chance that I had significant levels of carbon monoxide in my bloodstream when the voices in my head told me to put together a new Liverpool fanzine, choosing as I did to ignore the fact people don't buy fanzines anymore.

One year on from the voices and it's 13 April 2015, one hour before we kick off against Newcastle. There's no misleading toxin in my bloodstream today. I look down to the heavy rucksack of unsold fanzines at my feet. If I was cynical, soul destroyed, a mere husk of a man, I'd say it resembled a ball and chain tethered to my ankle.

As I stand with my back to the Paisley Gates, the chirpy yellow sign mounted on the wall of Christ Church in my eyeline thrusts forward heavy black words across Walton Breck Road, 'Free Debt Advice'.

I look back down at my ball and chain and start memorising the phone number on the church sign.

A man stops in front of me, takes out his wallet and starts fiddling around inside for £1.50. I ready myself with excitement to sell a singular issue seven of *We Are Liverpool*, the fanzine I had conceived and piloted at the end of the 2013/14 season full of hope.

I hadn't planned to be selling this issue at this game. However, like a Red who knows that a win tonight drags us within four points of Manchester City and equates that to a chance of a top-four finish, I'd had a similarly inexplicable rush of blood to the head. Based entirely on the flimsy premise that I'd sell more than usual, I went and had extra copies printed.

Hope can be a wicked mistress.

But, no, we're on here! Jesus is over the road providing fiscal support and he's got my back tonight. The miniature Daniel Sturridge in my tiny mind has stepped over the touchline, crossed himself and is all pointed fingers to the sky in gratitude at this prospective sale.

Back to the real world and my new best friend finishes fishing around for my shimmering bounty and reveals his hand to display… the ticket he'd been looking for.

Ahh for fuck's sake!

He stares blankly at my fixed grimace and carries on about his way. One arm still aloft, I hold a clutch of fanzines above my head. It has a nice picture of Jordon Ibe with the caption 'Flash Jordon' on the cover; it may as well have an arrow pointing downwards and the accompanying caption, 'Beware. Whimsical Knobhead Below.'

The early spring sun makes its apologies for having to leave early and sneaks down behind the roof of The Park. The throngs of crowds dressed in red dissolve in front of my eyes and the clocks turn back to a time 12 months earlier.

'Fanzines are dying on their arse, mate. I wouldn't bother.'

That was the entirely factual and correct advice I was given when I aired my new fanzine venture to Dave Usher, the creator and editor of *The Liverpool Way*. I believed Dave. He'd already stated he was going to finish up once he reached 100 issues at the end of the 2014/15 season because it wasn't worth his while anymore. At that time, however, I was desperately seeking a distraction, any distraction.

During the 1970s and 80s, Liverpool Football Club afforded the people of our city something positive at a time when a government thought it was entirely reasonable to toy with the idea of allowing a city and its people to exist in a state of 'managed decline'. At the turn of 2014, Liverpool had dusted itself down and was back on the way up but unfortunately, after a series of building calamities leading to disastrous events, the four walls of my house were in a serious case of decline I only wished to God somebody would manage for me.

I'm not entirely sure when it was that I snapped. It may have been when I had to smash one of the super-expensive new windows installed only days earlier after we'd locked ourselves out of the house and could find no other way in due to the super-secure new front and back doors. We don't have blame culture in our house, but I didn't lock us out and the kids didn't lock us out. My wife is the only other person who lives in the house. As I say, no blame.

It may have been when we ran out of money and had to send the builders away. That left the house a bloodied carcass and it dawned on me I would be paying the loan off for another five years with all the privilege of living in a bomb site and with no prospect of rectifying the problems.

In truth, though, it was probably when we lashed the irreplaceable fire away that sat in front of the back boiler, leaving it exposed in the chimney breast. We were told afterward this creates something called a double flue. Essentially this means gas escapes back into the house and there is a good chance your entire family will be killed by carbon monoxide while they're sleeping. Boss.

Yes. I think that was it. Sitting alone in the dark staring at a back boiler in a jagged hole as the intermittent green light of four – yes four – carbon monoxide detectors sinisterly winked at me in my peripheral vision at the rate of a slowing heartbeat.

Emergency escapism was required so I did what generations of Scouse men have done and turned to the one constant: Liverpool Football Club. However, I was already going to every home match, so a stronger and more time-consuming footballing drug was needed. I'm a Liverpool fan. I'm well into my history. Going out of my way to create something as anachronistic as a fanzine seemed like an entirely reasonable idea.

I'm not the first to want to preserve relics of the past. In 1914 French troops hot-footed it into the first battles of the First World War fitted out in the same blue coats, bright red trousers and white gloves of the Napoleonic Wars 100 years earlier. Suggestions that such get-up may not be conducive to the camouflage needs of modern warfare fell on deaf ears. The counter argument went something along the lines of, 'But we've always worn red trousers. Don't you understand? We proper love our red trousers. I don't give a shit if the Germans are wearing field grey and are all but invisible in the Belgian mud and we may as well have neon signs on our heads. I am wearing my fucking red trousers!'

The French, having failed to move with the times, were mowed down in the early parts of the war in the face of modern German technology and tactics. A hundred years later and under far less duress, I'd argue that my decision to enter into the fray of the aggressive digital age by waving a paper football fanzine above my head was as frivolous folly as refusing to bin off bright red trousers just because they'd been around a long time.

Fanzines have nowhere near the audience range of the modern digital medium. Football content is fired through the ether right into the palm of supporters' hands via smart phones, tablets and laptops. Neither do fanzines satisfy the modern demands for immediacy and up-to-date news. In this new era of screeching, fast-paced bedlam in which we've convinced ourselves there's no time for anything, fan-produced football podcasts mean you can get your fix of fan opinion when on your way to work, school or sitting on the shitter. Don't get me wrong, I love a bit of brown-loading as much as the next 21st-century man or woman. However, I do like to remind people they don't need to insure a copy of *We Are Liverpool* to protect against dropping it in the bog. I'll send you a free one, I've got plenty left.

I like to think my fanzine is the Benjamin Button of modern football media; instantly old and knackered at the point of birth. But ultimately very huggable. Come on. Give me a hug. Please hug me.

Much is said about the burden of history connected with Liverpool Football Club, and how the shirt weighs heavy on the back of new players. This translates very much to fanzines. I live in a permanent state of disagreement with myself over the tone of *We Are Liverpool*. I feel instinctively compelled to try and replicate the edgy, original independent feel of bygone fanzines from 25 years earlier. On the other hand, I'm fully aware that trying to recreate 1989 when both the club and football are very different is in no way edgy, original or independent.

If the last 25 years of Liverpool has taught us anything it's that even if you dress Dean Saunders, Nigel Clough and Harry Kewell in a thousand number seven shirts and brand their arses with white-hot number seven irons, they're still not going to play like Kenny Dalglish. Simply put, it's futile trying to recreate the past exactly as it was.

So I've focused on the complex principle of making sure *We Are Liverpool* is not complete shit. But the inherent curse of all Liverpool fans is an inability to acquiesce to mediocrity. Some people call this being deluded. I call it not being a shithouse. What starts as not wanting to embarrass yourself very quickly becomes wanting to be the dog's bollocks. It's vitally important to me that the dog's bollocks are well structured and grammatically sound.

Luckily my brother counters my concerns about missing apostrophes and typos by reminding me that fanzines are punk and no one cares if there are mistakes in there. I can't help but think that trying to fill a fanzine with good writing, even-handed arguments and pleasing use of semicolons makes it less Sex Pistols and more Crowded House. But what can I say? I like Crowded House.

But it's not all doom and gloom. I do manage to sell a few hundred of each issue and it's well received. But more than this, the seemingly tired old fanzine has a sprinkle of magic dust left in its creases which brings alive the age-old joy of spending time with good people because of football.

I'll never recapture the days of standing as a kid during my first season in 1987 with my dad and brother and meeting my granddad and uncle in exactly the same part of the Kop. But the creation of *We Are Liverpool* has reinforced old relationships and brought about new ones, and it tips its flat cap to the sense of football community that many of us think has been lost.

The search for content has meant that I've come across loads of sound people from Liverpool and further afield. And whether it be the contributors, other fanzine owners, lads running websites, podcasts or YouTube channels, there's a lot of talented Liverpool supporters out there all doing their own thing but helping out with each other's ventures. I'm sure this exists at other clubs too, but I doubt whether it's to the same scale.

In regards to the fanzine itself, the romantic side of me likes the idea of a collective group of Liverpool supporters working together to create something. I'm so God damn socialist that I list all contributors' names in alphabetical order so that my name isn't singled out. However, I also despair that no one notices my grandiose gesture and raises me above their heads and parades me round Anfield just so I can show everyone just how bloody equal I am.

Although selling the fanzine can be a gloomy affair if it's a slow day, people who buy it do love a chat. My God do people love a chat, and it's great. To those who think football has become gentrified and lacks characters, try selling a fanzine outside Anfield for two and a half hours and you'll realise you've stopped looking properly.

My dad and my mate Browny help me sell the fanzine at the games. Browny will be the first to admit he's little more than an armchair Liverpool supporter. However, our 23-year friendship was founded on his pursuit of me across the school field in a bid to rip my head off after he'd accidentally nearly snapped a lad's neck by carrying out the wrestling move commonly known as a piledriver. All I said was it was a bit arlarse.

Since that day Browny's Catholic guilt has compelled him to provide me with a lifetime of favours, and it's only recently I've found out he has turned up to Anfield every time with three pounds on him in case of emergency. Such is the real risk of literally selling no copies of the fanzine, he's instantly been poised to buy two copies himself under the pretence of having sold them.

Apparently this is preferable to the awkward moment when he has to tell me he hasn't sold any and I look at him with a sad, forgiving smile and a single tear slips down my cheek. In true Rafa Benitez speak, I admire Browny's attention to detail with his friendly fraudulent action. He explained to me that, akin to the way that taking two days off when throwing a sickie at work makes it look more authentic, he felt faking two sales rather than one was more likely to throw me off the scent.

My dad retired a few years ago and loves Liverpool. I think he hates them as well. But from what I can gather this will happen to most of us by the time we're 68. Last season, his teeth fell out while celebrating Phil Coutinho's winner against Manchester City and it looked like we might go on to win the title. I can't help but admire a man who cares so much about Liverpool that in his sixties he'll celebrate with such violence that he dislodges his false teeth. I've asked him if he can pull a similar trick when selling fanzines to get attention and improve sales. He's not having it.

A surprise figure in the life of the fanzine has been my mate John, who I work with. Sound lad but hates footy. Actually, I think he only pretends to hate footy, much in the same way he pretends to like jazz to make himself appear sophisticated. John's interest in *We Are Liverpool* ultimately amounts to someone rubber-necking as they pass a car crash, but he has proved useful. He bought a book called *Freakonomics* which looks at the hidden reasons behind why things happen. I'm reliably informed it's all about incentives. He takes to imposing the theory of *Freakonomics* on any decision I make regarding the fanzine. Sometimes you need someone to ask you the difficult questions and help you to see the wood from the trees. Often, it's just one difficult question, 'Yeah, but why are you doing that?' The *We Are Liverpool* experience has changed him, though, and his diabolical and incorrect approach to the beautiful game has softened. I received this e-mail from him just the other day:

'I've modified my views on the jingoism of football fanaticism somewhat. Whilst I maintain that football fanaticism is nothing more than a form of crass micro-nationalistic jingoism, I've now developed the view that it does at least provide a relatively benign outlet for the jingoistic tendencies of the English male. Without having a match to shout at every weekend, Christ knows what you animals would do with your spare time!'

I wish the 'animals' read fanzines in their spare time. At the Newcastle game I'm slowly encouraged there are still people who do as I slowly sell about two-thirds of my remaining copies. I give one last loud, tuneful shout of, '*We Are Liverpool*. Only £1.50' and in the distance hear someone echo the next line of the song with a 'tra la la la la' and then laugh. I laughed the first time I heard it, too. Now if I'm having a slow day, I have to restrain myself from jumping on them and ripping their throat out.

Not tonight, though. Maybe it is the absense of pressure to sell what I need, or just the fact that the outcome of the game doesn't really matter that much. I decide I'll take the handful of remaining copies into the ground and leave them around and about for people to pick up on the off chance they read it, like it and buy the next one. It's the first generous act of the night.

The atmosphere is politely restrained in a game in which Newcastle politely decline to turn up. It's very good of them. Such is the current malaise after back-to-back league defeats against Manchester United and Arsenal that we struggle to get out of first gear. Thankfully we don't need to. I struggle to remember an easier and less eventful game at Anfield this season. A sublime curling effort from Raheem Sterling after just nine minutes and a rare but well-taken Joe Allen goal in the second half are pleasing if not euphorically celebrated. The referee kindly ignores a nailed-on foul by Dejan Lovren which should have resulted in a penalty. It was the only football action of real note.

However, similar to the subtler pleasures of fanzine production, sound people are the real stars. A couple of days before the 26th anniversary of Hillsborough, the minute's silence is impeccably observed by both sets of fans. The thought enters my head as I stand there that these days it nearly always is. The penny, it appears, has finally dropped.

The arrival of Newcastle substitute Jonas Gutierrez prompts the Anfield crowd into a standing ovation in recognition of his fight with cancer and in respect of his return. As a crowd we pat ourselves on the back too much, and sometimes our response seems a little choreographed. For example I'd argue we clap the returning player who doesn't celebrate his goal because we believe that's what is expected of us. However, I also know the difference and this is genuinely spontaneous and kind hearted. I don't want to hear us bragging about it but it does instil the faith that as Liverpool supporters we can be a class apart.

After the game I scoot around inside Block 208 of the Kop to see if any of the fanzines have been taken. I see one left and feel slightly deflated. About to turn away to descend the stairs, a late straggler passes by and it catches her eye. She stops, picks it up and flicks through. Something in it catches her attention and she starts reading. I pop into the bog for a slash. When I come out she's still there, absorbed. I lean against the wall with my hands in my pockets trying to look casual while I enjoy the voyeuristic pleasure of observing someone enjoying something I worked so hard to create.

I then realise coming out of the bogs and staring at a woman while smiling with my hands in my pockets just looks like I'm feeling my balls. So I leave her to it.

Back at home it comes out that Sterling will be in the papers tomorrow because he's been inhaling nitrous oxide, commonly known as laughing gas. It's entirely legal but like most of these things no one really seems to know the long-term ramifications or effects.

Don't be surprised if you see Sterling standing outside Anfield trying to flog his new fanzine idea in the coming months and quoting *Field of Dreams*. Join the party Raheem.

19 April 2015, Aston Villa 2 Liverpool 1

'One of the lads put a melted Mars bar on the roof'

By Karl Coppack

Ah, Wembley. Most of our first memories are taken from Wembley. Growing up in the 1970s and 80s, the FA Cup Final was a big day. Not only was the match live on terrestrial telly at 3pm on a Saturday, it was on both BBC and ITV. Younger readers are advised to rub their eyes at that sentence and read it back. Live football. Terrestrial TV. Saturday, 3pm. Both channels.

Those were the days, my friends.

My first football memory was taken from a maisonette in Bond Street, Liverpool 3. It was July 1974 and I was sat with my uncle Tony, who was talking me through how important this match was. We had a colour set which was apt to wobble when you least needed it to, but I took a limited interest. He said that both teams had scored already. I wasn't the least bit arsed. Five years old, I blinked at the screen, looked back at him, then back at the screen. I wondered just why he wasn't massively into Action Man.

Mine was sat at my feet, next to his Action Man tent. I began to tell Tony about the adventures he'd been on and how he'd (hint, hint) like another Action Man mate, ideally in the new camouflage kit for when he was trapped in the desert or tundra, but he seemed to prefer watching men in white play against men in orange. I had important views about the Six Million Dollar Man too and was anxious to get them across, but, sat in his Rod Stewart haircut, he wasn't overly arsed.

'That's West Germany and that's Holland. They're trying to put the ball between those two white posts, Karl. They've both done it already so far.'

Yeah, OK. That made sense. I could handle that. Was onboard with it, even. It's just that this man could see miles and run faster than a train and…

'And this is the World Cup Final.'

…he solved crimes and…hold on. Did he say World Cup Final? World?

Life is strange at that age. Nothing is small. The champions of England? Nah. The European champions? Fair enough, but WORLD CHAMPIONS? He might as well have told me that Steve Austin was coming to Liverpool and wanted my help sorting out those terrorist twats.

I stared at him intently. My next question, and I swear this is the truth, was a logical one.

'Who do the winners get to play?'

I wanted to hear the word 'Galactic'. I wanted talk of Venus sending a team over and getting ready for the match on the Moon. I wanted, wanted, wanted.

Instead he shook his head and went back to the game. I went back to my Action Man and thought about galactic armies coming over and taking on the lads in orange (nicer shirts).

My first proper match was the 1976 FA Cup Final. Up until that point, my new interests (dinosaurs and chess, in that order) couldn't allow football into the room. I knew Southampton couldn't win. They weren't supposed to. I knew United were the enemy, but I liked Steve Coppell as the first four letters of his surname were the same as mine. Things like that matter when you're a kid, but Southampton had nicer kits. Nicer kits always win when you're not that bothered.

My dad celebrated Southampton's goal like it was an Everton winner. That is – raucously. Football had begun to seep into me by now. I knew my dad supported Everton and my uncle Dave was a Red. They didn't discuss football, but I knew that rivalries were a big thing and, at some point, I'd have to pick a side. I was a neutral in 1976.

But it was all about Wembley. The two TV channels. The coach leaving the hotel. One player talking about his team-mates. It was a whole day. It was like the Home Internationals, but with proper teams.

Younger and overseas readers, bear with me again while I explain this. In the 1970s, the home nations would play a round-robin tournament. England, Scotland, Wales and Northern Ireland. Wales tended to play Northern Ireland on Friday nights, which I suspected was due to no one being arsed. The big game was England v Scotland. Kevin Keegan v Kenny Dalglish – the classic transference of love. By 1977 I was pretty much obsessed by Keegan and by the end of it, Kenny had taken the baton. My dad never liked Keegan, he found the aftershave commercials to be a betrayal and a flimsy annoyance. I've just realised that this is why I can no longer feel anything like admiration for Nivea Henderson.

But it was about Wembley. I loved Wembley immediately. The reasons for this were manifold. Firstly, no one played there! The greatest non-Anfield ground in the land and no one played there. How mad was that? It was that special. Secondly, the Queen would go to the match. Even the Queen. The woman who looked rich enough to live in Southport. Then there was a brass band. They got to go on the pitch. Then there was a helicopter. A helicopter would hover over the pitch and show the team coach crawl up Wembley Way to the greatest cathedral in the land. This meant something and I was buying.

That magic has never left me. I still love Wembley and even now as a curmudgeonly 46-year-old man I have to admire its elegance. The towers may have gone but it's a beautiful stadium. Not a bad seat in the house. Being there means something. Liverpool could win something. Liverpool should win something.

I was last here at the 2012 League Cup Final, high up in the gods and with a particularly virulent strain of food poisoning contracted in a Camden seafood place the night before. I shook and shivered and wanted desperately to feel the magic as I did in 1976, but modern football had crept in. Now there were music, announcers and poems. All three are very, very loud and all three are bloody awful.

I don't want fireworks. I don't want a show. I want football. Sit back, Wembley, and let us sing. We'll do the singing, the entertaining. Have this one on us. All we want is the bricks and mortar and we'll provide the backing band. Nah. Not happening.

But the view is great. Mind you, it wasn't always this good.

My view at the 1988 FA Cup Final wasn't the best. No. It was very, very hot. An old man in front of me collapsed. One minute he was standing there, the next he was sprawled across the two rows in front of him. The stewards – minimum-wage kids – looked at each other and shrugged their shoulders. The lad woke up and held on to a crash barrier. I was never comfortable from that minute and every time the crowd lurched I found myself holding the scruff of his jacket. As a consequence, I couldn't see a thing as I was just happy that he was upright in front of me.

When we won the penalty every single person around me said, 'He'll miss this.' No doubt about it. He hadn't missed a pen all season and this was one that he absolutely had to score. Ordinarily when someone says that they get shouted down, but on this occasion people nodded. It was written in the stars. It'd been one of those days. We'd had a goal chalked off and people were talking about fairytale cup wins for the plucky underdogs. A reminder here that Wimbledon had finished seventh in the league that season. Hardly Blyth Spartans.

The end of that match was odd, too. When the final whistle went, Wimbledon players sunk to their knees or hugged each other. There was no cheer from the stands. Not really. There were so many Liverpool fans in the ground that the small pocket of Dons were drowned out by Reds harrumphing and moodily making their way to the exits.

Back on the coach we found that a box of Mars bars (other chocolate-based products are available) had melted due to the heat of the sun and the lack of a window being left open. Everything was hot about the coach. I couldn't touch the window. The plastic arm rest was practically on fire. The Mars bars had melted into their wrapper, and were fit for nothing.

As we crept out of the car park we noticed how miserable the Wimbledon fans looked. They'd just won the cup against the best team in the universe (just to keep my 1974 self happy) and they looked like they'd missed the game. What was the matter with them? A few people knocked on the windows and pulled up their lips into a rictus grin to encourage at least a scintilla of joy, but they were happy to be sad.

One of the lads opened up the sunroof, put a melted Mars bar on the roof and pushed/slid it on to the adjacent car. He'd hoped to have hit the windscreen, but by an astonishing piece of luck/skill he managed to find a trajectory which allowed it to fly across the gap between coach and car, squeeze through the sunroof of the Dons car and on to the lap of a very surprised Cockney. The driver didn't even look up when everyone cheered and laughed. I'm not entirely sure that he knew we were next to him. One minute he was looking for a way out of the car park, the next it was raining Mars bars.

That was the highlight of my day. Well, that and the no alcohol rule on the coach and the confused driver who couldn't work out why people appeared pissed from drinking water from an old man's flask. It wasn't water, mate.

I've been back to Wembley many times since and not always for Liverpool games. In 1996 I was working for the *Guardian* selling recruitment advertising space. One of my mates had a language school as a regular client and one day they told him they had Euro 96 tickets that they couldn't use. I went to the England v Scotland and England v Holland games. I paid £50 for Holland and told myself that paying such a sum for one game was a one-off. The Dutch side were great so it would be worth it. Imagine paying £50 for one football match.

I loved Euro 96. Got dead into it, in fact. I supported England as I quite liked Terry Venables and there were plenty of Liverpool players there. I went to cheer those lads first and foremost but gradually became embroiled in the drama. It was still partisan support, though. I booed Nick Barmby when he came on and was asked to sit down when I delivered an invective at Bryan Robson whenever he stood up.

But the main reason I couldn't get totally involved with it was the support. I can't sing the national anthem. I won't even put it in capital letters. I couldn't get behind cheering on Gary Neville. I've been told that you put club allegiances aside when England are playing as it's the country that comes first, but that just isn't true. See, Liverpool *is* my country. Sorry, lads, but England is someone else's side and, as much as I enjoyed both games and was gutted when England went out, I couldn't take it any further. I think that Dutch game was my last England match.

I've also been to Wembley for the big one. The behemoth. The *capi di tutti capi* of all sporting trophies: the 2011 FA Trophy Final between Darlington and Mansfield.

Think of Real Madrid v Eintracht Frankfurt. Think of Liverpool v Alaves. Think of Reading 5 Arsenal 7. Now think of the opposite. Think of the slowest, quietest, skill-lacking snooze-fest of any game in the history of anything anywhere. Welcome to Darlington v Mansfield Town.

My mate supports Darlo and follows them everywhere. He's seen grounds that I haven't, and I've been around a bit. He supported England too and saved up about £5,000 for Euro 92. He watched every second of their games save for the moment they scored their only goal. He'd gone for a piss then. Talk about being cursed.

He asked me to come along and meet a few mates from North Yorkshire. It was cheap, you could drink and I'd seen neither Darlington nor Mansfield in the flesh before, so I was up for it. I got a bit of a tan if memory serves. That was the only plus point. The ground was two-thirds empty and was just about the worst two hours in the footballing calendar. Darlo won in the last minute of injury time and we all celebrated like Marco Tardelli. For them it was a trophy under the Wembley arch. For me it was because I didn't have to sit through penalties and could get home quicker. Ruth was cooking Thai prawn curry.

But today it's Aston Villa. I've read the papers, listened to the podcasts, taken in this season as a whole and come up with one truth. Liverpool beat Aston Villa. Yes, they've beaten us at Anfield and are resurgent under Tim Sherwood but, ultimately, Liverpool beat Aston Villa. Arsenal took extra time and an unlucky keeper to beat Reading but we play Arsenal next month, not Villa. That's how this ends.

And then came the teams. Good Lord

Goalkeeper
Midfielder Centre Back Centre Back
Midfielder Midfielder Midfielder Full-Back
Midfielder Midfielder Midfielder.

Mario Balotelli's on the bench with the other strikers. Daniel Sturridge is out, but this came as no surprise (my laptop auto completes 'is out' whenever I type his name). Liverpool are going to try to win this without a recognised striker.

I'm watching this with a throng of journalists. A Villa fan sees me staring intensely at the teamsheet and comes over.

'You're not worried, are you? You'll still beat us.'

I stare open-mouthed at him. 'Where is Gerrard playing?' I beg, almost pleading. He laughs, pats me on the shoulder and wanders off. I'm still in the same pose when he returns five minutes later.

We take our seats. I'm sat next to Tony Evans. He asks me what I think about the midfield shape. I'm tempted to give him the Gandhi gag about Western civilisation and tell him that it would be a good idea, but it's not quite a question. It's rhetorical at best but we're of the same mind.

Everything was there today. The occasion, a side we could beat and a sizeable support baying for blood, but it just didn't happen. Rodgers (note how he's 'Rodgers' when I'm unhappy with him and 'Brendan' when I think he's all right) changed the formation halfway through the first half but failed to make the key change.

I'll laud Steven Gerrard until my voice gives in but he was being overrun time and again. He can't do it on this pitch and we have to take him off and stop Fabian Delph and Tom Cleverley from playing in and around us. Everyone can see that. The manager takes Lazar Markovic off instead. A quick half-time straw poll ranks him as the eighth worst player of the first half, but off he trots.

Rickie Lambert is brought on with about 90 seconds left to help but it's to no avail. We surrender at 2-1 and, some late pressure aside, we lose. Pre-season starts at the final whistle. There's a battle for fourth place but this side looks all washed out. Nothing to do now but wait for next year.

Two semi-finals this season. Lost semi-finals don't count.

The next day I hear Alyson Rudd compare Rodgers's in-game tactics to an overbearing mother readying her child for a beauty pageant. Brendan just couldn't decide what dress to wear so wore all of them and hoped one fitted.

As I trundle back to the Tube I call Sachin and give him a stream-of-consciousness rant about everything from the eight midfielders team ('and Ibe was cup-tied!') to the rather surreal sight of Villa fans celebrating their reaching Wembley while being at Wembley. I've a vague recollection of him, also making his way back from the match, talking me off a ledge and asking if I 'have someone who could sit with me?'

Earlier I'd walked to the Tube with Rory Smith. I'd told him how surprised I was at the effect of this defeat. When Kenny Dalglish was dismissed I swore Liverpool couldn't hurt me anymore and that I would withhold a complete commitment. But those are just words. Wembley hurt. Wembley really hurt.

I'm reminded of an episode of *Family Guy* where Peter, Joe, Quagmire and Cleveland perform some fairly awful karaoke. They're so drunk that they're convinced they can start a proper band. They do so, get a gig and take the stage amidst high fives. Then, as the lights come up, they freeze. They stand in silence. They can't sing or play their instruments. It was just an act of bravado that wasn't thought through. That's how Liverpool were today. We called for Gerrard to get to Wembley. He got there but the lads couldn't play.

I go back to a darkened flat. It was a while before I put the lights on.

25 April 2015, West Brom 0 Liverpool 0

'Get in, kill Bin Laden, get out'

By Rob Gutmann

'Six o' clock in the morning and I'm the last person in this plane still awake.' That's from The The's seminal 1980s over-produced-but-still-decent tune 'Sweet Bird Of Truth'. The The was actually just a lad called Matt Johnson and that track's lyric was a first-person stream of consciousness thing about being in a US military plane about to crash somewhere in the Middle East. It now seems an ominously prescient little ditty. It's been in my head all season.

I set myself a challenge in August that for the first time ever I'd watch every LFC league fixture. I've been close before. I'm 48 and I don't miss home games (I'd quite like a version of that to be my epitaph, *'Here lies Robert Gutmann. 1967–2071 – he didn't miss home games')*. I also get to most of the aways. I must have nearly done the 38 or the 42 before, but I can't really remember now. Certain seasons gained such momentum that games were simply not going to be missed. The 1987/88 one – Barnes and Beardsley and all that jazz. The treble season of 2000/01. And last year, where we nearly won the title and were the most exciting Liverpool team in, like, forever.

Think I only missed three or four last season. I should check (I won't check).

After the giddy wondrousness of the last campaign I vowed to myself that I would not be not attending any Liverpool FC games in the near future. I'd say to people that it was about completing one season, for the first time, but really it's about forever. It may be part of my mid-life crisis, which is going on for an interminably long time. What no one warns you – about the mid-life crisis – is that it isn't a temporary state. I know what it is now, and I know it'll only end when I die.

The main thing I'm getting is the crushing realisation that *this* is it. No more dress rehearsals. That notion you have when you're younger – that you'll improve at certain things, or eventually get round to doing postponed tasks, that you've got time to fulfil ambitions, to mend relationships, to be a better person, is entirely a delusion. None of those things will happen. Well, they could, but you need to start doing them today. FFS.

For a naturally impatient person this came as an extra burden. I didn't think I could be any more impatient. I was very wrong about that. So I now look at every Liverpool game as maybe my last. When I was a kid, I couldn't go to that many games, and there was mainly only access to live football via the radio. I used to tolerate the frustration and anxiety induced by having to rely only on the one sense for information knowing that soon would come the day when I'd actually *be there*. At a game. In the flesh. In a stadium. Taking everything in. Senses working overtime.

Later, there was more football on TV. It was miles better than listening to a game on the radio. Oldens will get misty eyed about listening to the vocally ripped and toned Peters, Jones and Brackley on Radio 2, but the reality is that radio was and remains a shit way to follow your team. I always felt the radio commentators were deliberately getting a thrill out of winding me up. They'd contrive a near certain goal every two minutes, with their quickening tempos and falsettoing registers. 'Oh my word how did he miss that?!' You later found out exactly how he missed it when you watched it back on the telly. He missed it because he was 35 yards out or was shooting from a ridiculously acute angle with five bodies between him and the goal.

Video killed the radio star. Thank fuck. TV was much more like real football. For a while it may even – whisper it – have felt slightly better than actually going to a real game. Legend has it that the 1966 World Cup Final didn't sell out because it was a live football game on TV for the first time and people couldn't resist the lure of the new.

After enduring the actual experience of attending aways throughout the 1980s the respite of the living room or the pub in the 90s was not to be underestimated. Standing for hours in the wind and rain was not enjoyable. Travelling the length and breadth of the country on trains that got stopped outside Nuneaton for a gratuitous hour and a half because there were leaves on a line, or because it was somebody's birthday bash the night before meaning the signalman hadn't turned in, wasn't fun. Wasn't a laff. Worrying about turning the wrong corner and getting ambushed by recreational violence merchants wasn't *Boys Own* stuff. Inedible burgers topped with onions made out of leaves and snot, and washed down with bloody Bovril, isn't something to get nostalgic about. Bovril was, is and shall remain a terrible drink. Bad gravy but without the meat or potato required to at least give it some purpose.

Live football got better, though, and the lure of the box waned. There were seats for starters. They were nice. Most had legroom too. There was transport that you could count on. Sustenance that could be enjoyed other than when totally paralytic. And there was no aggro. No more potential kickings to be had. There were still dreams and songs to sing. The atmosphere was still there. Or at least it was no more or less inconsistent than it had ever been. Don't let anyone tell you Anfield was a cauldron of noise for every home game in the 1980s. It wasn't. More often than not the Kop was bored shitless with all the endless winning and it took a lot to get the crowd really going.

The other thing that changed in the 90s and beyond was that people started really talking about tactics. I was always into a bit of a tactical chat. I put it down to an enduring relationship with Subbuteo. You couldn't enjoy that perfect birds-eye plan view of the game and not want to play chess with it. Not want to play God. The TV folks also loved a bit of tactics. They had trucks for it, and screens that they could touch and make circles and arrows come to life. They made the fan tactically literate, those Sky TV pioneers (and Alan Hansen).

Ironically for me, it made their medium seem increasingly inadequate. On TV you could see the action, but not the game. They were all about the handball incidents, the multiple angles for showing a goal, the offsides, the two-footed tackles. It was engaging but it wasn't Subbuteo.

To get that thing I wanted – the whole game, the eagle's view – you had to go to the game. OK, sometimes you were planted on the first row behind the goal, but you still got to see the width of the pitch (if not its depth). There was still a geometry on show that you never got from TV. Increasingly then I made it my mission to physically go to as many games as finances and fate would permit.

'Six o'clock in the morning and I'm the last person in this plane still awake.'

When we go on away trips these days, I'm always first out my crib. The excitement overwhelms me. We could be playing on Mars and need to make a 4am start to beat the inter-galactic traffic, but I'd still be awake before everyone else. I barely sleep the night before an away mission. I rarely do anything the day before that doesn't involve preparation for the journey and for the day. I love the planning. Love the anticipation.

My comrades, in life and on football away trips, think the way I approach watching Liverpool away is typical of my horrific impatience and control-freaky personality. They mock it, and me, but they like it too. Because it, me, I, get the job done. I get the tickets, organise the ride, plan pit stops, select the food venue, locate the boozer. I get us to the church on time. Ungrateful motherfuckers.

So it's 8am and I've been up for three hours. Paul, Neil and Andy will be at mine soon. I'm in the car with my Danny. He's 16 now and has been a home and away stalwart since he was six. There's little he hasn't seen on a football pitch, or in the back of a car full of drunken grown boy-men who should know better. On some days – and this is one of them – the alcoholic revelry starts too soon. Neil piles into the back of my sweet ride, all smiles and says, 'Don't know 'bout yoose but I'm ready to get on it straight away.' I sigh the good sigh. The sigh that knows that he won't be denied and that he's already the enabler-in-chief for the rest of us. Today, my Danny won't just be my son, footy aways partner-in-crime and best friend, he'll also have to be my seeing-eye dog.

I'm a firm believer that planning gives you the freedom to be spontaneous and enjoy yourself properly. It creates a framework for fun. Others would say this take on football and life makes me an anal, OCD-ed up weirdo. I disagree. You don't want to have what should be a perfectly enjoyable away day with the lads ruined because you missed the game by not doing the math(s) on how long it takes to get from A to B. You don't need to be desperately looking for an away-friendly boozer that's within walking distance of the ground but also sells some basic scran simply because you failed to give this day any thought until you woke up to it. Do you?

You think ahead. My BFF, brother-in-arms and oldest away trip cohort, Giulio, and I always talked about the quest for the textbook away trip. We first started going to aways together when we were 13 (in 1980). We evolved our tastes and our corporal-needs schedule – from our away experiences – together. Although Giulio wasn't on this West Brom trip, I will credit him with the co-authorship of the 'Englishman's quintessential guide to the perfect LFC away day'. It's still not been written but when it finally is, it will be a hefty tome. The gist of it follows…

I like to leave stupidly early for away trips. Some lads won't do my missions anymore because they can't take the early rise. For me the away day is exactly what it says it is – a day. Not an afternoon. Not an evening. A day. It begins from when you first open your eyes. I think it must be like this for the players, too. They don't think, 'Better get the shopping in, or do some DIY, or have a lie in 'til midday,' before the game. They think only of the task in hand. Of the challenge it poses. Of the anxieties it presents. Of the glories it may bring.

They also don't have to worry about which services on the M6 has a McDonald's and will we get to it before they stop selling sausage and egg McMuffins at 10.30am. They also don't have to worry about finding a boozer that is both near enough to the ground that it's walkable but that can also be arrived at in time so that getting served food and ale isn't a fucking nightmare.

Today is a sunny day. It's crisp, but crisp is good. Who wants to be sweating this early. Paul is driving. He's the jockey-in-chief these days. He has a firm hand and a steady eye. He'll tell you a joke, or light up your smoke. He can't follow a sat-nav for fuck though and I have to interpret for him for the entire journey.

'What's it saying here Rob?'

'Its saying turn off left here, Paul. You can tell that by the arrow pointing to the left.'

'Oh yeah. I'll do a left then.' Good lad.

I'm co-pilot. It's my motor and I want the leg room. Gotta be a few privileges. Co-pilot's got responsibilities. I tend to mind the pile of tinnies and small wines by my feet for starters. Naturally I've been to Tesco the day before to purchase our booze picnic for the journey. Also, I like to 'smoke' the odd one on an away trip.

Generally I've given up all terribly unhealthy habits, but the away seems a reasonable occasion for allowing lapses. 'Smoking' requires leg room. You need maximum lap space, and a hard surface to facilitate the full, stress-free skin-up.

'This is your captain calling with an urgent warning/We're above the Gulf of Arabia, our altitude is falling/An' I can't hold her up, there's no time for thinking/All hands on deck, this bird is sinking.'

For an early start getting a good breakfast in is essential. I always caution co-journeyers not to make the schoolboy error of having a bowl of Weetabix and slice of toast before we meet up. Eating before the meet just spoils the appetite for one of the day's many main events – the first being that visit to a motorway McDonald's for a 'Maccies brekky'.

There's usually one freak on a trip who will eschew the obvious and go instead for a fucking cake and a latte at the adjacent Costa. Those guys don't get invited back readily.

The key component of the pre-game preparation and ritual is the main eating/drinking venue of choice. I'm not one who looks for away supporter pubs. I like to have the option of a sit down and a scran. I think being able to actually access the bar and, later on, the bog is desirable. I've paid my dues at the coalface of doing real men's aways. Ones where you travel only by coach or 'special', and drink only at the gaffs within two minutes of the ground that will only serve you beer in plastic glasses. The ones where you stand outside the boozer, even in winter, visibly supping and singing. Showing them that you're in town.

Me, I'm after a gastropub or a Nando's, or an Indian or Chinese restaurant. At Man City I can always be found in that really smart-looking place called Vermillion that does an all-day pan-Asian buffet for about £13.95 a head. If you go to the Midlands it's curry pubs or Indian restaurants. In the North East it's usually a Wetherspoons. Actually on any trip where the kick-off is midday-ish and you have to arrive before sane pub opening times, *Weathies* is the only bar in Britain that will serve you both beer and wine and a full 1,400 calorie belly-buster breakfast before 11am.

The road to The Hawthorns is a fairly smooth one with no great incidents expected, other than sitting haplessly in M6 traffic. Incident free is always a marker of a decent away. There's lads I know who have a list of away-day stories as long as your arm that to my mind are interchangeable with stag night tales. They're usually about people being hurt, humiliated, arrested, lost or ending up naked somewhere. You're going to be half-cut on an away. That's a given. The imperative, as far as I'm concerned, is to therefore control your environment sufficiently so that you don't come to any great harm. In my head I'm a Navy seal – get in, kill Bin Laden, get out. Or more – get to the ground, get fed, have a drink, watch the Reds win, get home safely.

West Brom is one of those rare aways where my tastes for the finer things and normal fans' away merge. For this trip, all comers in the Liverpool-following fraternity make a beeline to a curry pub called The Vine. It's a lovely place and it majors in kebabs. In a pub. Such a thing we could only ever have dreamed of when I was a child. Good kebabs, too, with proper naan bread.

We get there as they're turning the key to open the place up for 11.30am. We're virtually first in. We've got the pick of the tables. We're sauntering to toilets and bars. No rushing around like panic-stricken fowl for us. My plan is working like clockwork.

We kitty up, 20 notes in each. Neil's going to the bar. Andy's going to the kebab counter. Danny and Paul are off for a piss. I'm minding the specs and sitting pretty. Faces start to stream in. First it's Mike Nev and Chris. Then Phil B. The Suttons are here. Nico too. John Mackin's bedding in. Martin Fitz will be here soon. Backs are getting slapped, rounds are being got in. It's all good. The Reds are gathering. We're going to win here.

The football, I've barely mentioned it thus far. This isn't because it's in anyway secondary. Its omnipresent. We've talked little else but formations, transfers, the manager and Mario Balotelli all the way down, between slurps from cans, tokes from smokes, and mouthfuls of McMuffins. I'm telling the throng that the internet rumour is of a rare start for Mario B. I'm excited. He'll supposedly be paired with Raheem Sterling and Jordon Ibe. We'll put on a show today.

There are some lads – good lads – who love their team with a passion, but the day overwhelms them. The crack, the bonhomie, becomes the biggest thing. I wish I was a bit more like that. I am until kick-off. Then it's all business. Hazy drunken, bloated business, but business nonetheless. I want the win. The result. All else pales.

This is the reason why we're here and the event that will make or break the status of this trip. A defeat really bursts the balloon and ruins the day, and the weekend. There's no hiding from that reality. This is where all the planning in the world goes right out of the window. Please Jesus, let the Reds win today. Let the long, traffic-static ride home be filled with mirth and tears of joy. Let the breakdown on the hard shoulder with a flat before Stafford be rendered a mere hiccup in the wider scheme.

We don't win. But we don't lose either. It's a confusing one. We played quite well – 72 per cent possession, we later learn, bears out our unreliable testimony. The result is a bad one though, and we know that Champions League qualification is almost certainly beyond us. The truth is we should be more gutted, but maybe, subconsciously, we already knew our fate and that this season was already being run down.

The occasion doesn't pass without incident, though. Fondly remembered aways always have some bolt-on anecdote that can be seamlessly applied as an aide-memoire. A week ago at Wembley I fell off my seat. I don't know how it happened. I just slipped off it and landed cramped semi-under it, on my arse, in minor pain and discomfort. How my mate John Riles laughed. And laughed. We can now refer to that game as 'the Aston Villa semi, 2015, remember, the one where you fell on your arse'. Sort of like the way *Friends* episodes got labelled.

Today I manage to nearly get in a fight with a fellow fan. This does happen to me a tad too often for my liking. Maybe once a season. By day I'm quite a calm reflective sort of guy, but in a football ground I can be a bit accident prone.

Anyway, at West Brom there was this lad – he was berating Mario from first whistle to last. Relentlessly so. It was almost getting funny. Except it wasn't really. It felt nasty and just an all round shit thing for a supporter to be doing towards one of his own. Obviously he felt no sympatico with Mario, but still, he had a duty to the cause to keep it shut.

I politely but firmly advised him that he really should cease with his endless misgivings, and unsurprisingly he didn't take my advice that well. It could have all got very out of hand but he must have thought I had menacingly stared him out as he actually backed down pretty quickly. How I'd achieved this staring contest win despite not being able to see straight is something to take away from the day. It may also have been that I had four lads with me and he was a lonesome Billy No Mates.

Coming out of the ground we manage to lose each other. Fuck knows where Paul and Neil went. We've been together all day and sat together for two hours, but now we manage to all get separated. Football crowds are always conducive to people losing sight of loved ones. We all practise that which we learned as children and stay close when we come out of grounds. We all but hold hands. Not today, though.

No panic. The car was parked up by The Vine and no one is forgetting where we left it. We reconvene soon enough, whinge about the 0-0 scoreline and the manager, and it being the end of days. We get in the car and head north, initially with little left to say to each other. No one's in a party mood. Andy has a brainwave. 'Tin anyone? Small wine?' Yeah, why not. Good idea. Can't do any harm to get back on it. So we do.

Fast forward 30 minutes and the party has restarted. No footy talk now, that's consigned to the dustbin of 'it'll keep for another day'. Now we're all about the tunes. Andy's iPod gets plugged in and he's bashing out the bangers. He even has the soundtrack to *Frozen*. We're all word perfect to 'Let It Go'.

Paul's been doing all the driving – the hero – so he's not touched a drop all day, but he still has a song in him. Especially when it comes to Disney anthems. I take Andy's sounds off and put my playlist on, and take the whole thing to another level. By the time we're getting to the end of the M62, two hours later, there are hands in the air to 'Heads Will Roll' by the Yeah Yeah Yeahs. The death of our Champions League qualification dream is a distant memory.

At 8pm-ish we arrive back at mine in south Liverpool. We're parting company here like soldiers, like men, who've been through a tour of duty, an experience together. We embrace, drunkenly. Often we've overdone the physicality earlier in the act of celebrating goals – I've ended up rolling around a few stadium floors with Neil this season – but today we were scoreless, goalless and no one has got felt up.

It's all good. Bye. See ya lids. Gimme that £20 you owe me next week. No rush. You going to Chelsea? Might do, I'll call yer. No worries man. Adios amigos. They slip off into the night, 'And I'm the last person in this plane still awake.'

28 April 2015, Hull 1 Liverpool 0

'When Casey has a plan he's a relentless bastard'

By Trevor Downey

Leave it to us Irish to have a delicate tendril of connection wrapped around whatever's happening at any given time in the world. In the most ironic of fashions, given Saint Patrick's sterling efforts at eradicating the scourge of the Hibernian snake, there was a serpentine coil of Irishness wending its way through the laudable supporter-action that took place when Liverpool visited Humberside. Many of our fans, led by the Spirit Of Shankly group, decided to make an admirable stand against inequitable pricing, and their method of protest took the form of a boycott.

This practice was invented in 1880 when my countrymen, inherently political creatures that they were, systematically shunned the agent of an absentee English landlord following his attempts to evict tenants who would not pay extortionate rent. You'll never guess what the land agent's name was.

The match itself was the drabbest of affairs. Breaking with a lifetime of superstitious tradition, I watched it pan out in the company of some gents who shall feature later. The pathetic nature of the Redmen's efforts was hardly befitting of the occasion. If only the conviction shown by the fans had been matched by the players at the KC Stadium then the central framing device of this piece might have been an altogether more prominent and edifying feature. It didn't, however, and Steve Bruce's lot inflicted a spirit-sapping 1-0 defeat just when the door to Champions League football had been left ajar. It was wretched stuff to behold and the Hull manager, yet again, walked away giggling his magnificently large and misshapen head off.

Once news broke of the fans' protest, Reds over here were quick to educate themselves on what was going on and, unsurprisingly, they were equally prompt about contributing their tuppence worth on the subject. It's a national trait, you see, this desire to know, or rather, to be in the know, followed briskly by a brashly unambiguous declaration of what we think. We love it, being in the thick of the contretemps. Having a fervid debate, but calling it a chat. Engaging in fraught argument that's always on the verge of breaking into a laugh. When we greet each other around my neck of the woods, it is often with the revealing enquiry of, 'What's the craic?' There's an insatiable national hunger for information and stories that is matched only by the urgent need to pass on both once they've been acquired.

The only people who can rival us for that curiosity and loquaciousness – at least in my four decades' worth of experience – are Liverpudlians, who are every bit as garrulous, spiky and humorous a tribe as the denizens of this island. It's hardly surprising, then, to see the disproportionate number of scribes and professional talkers who hail from both places.

Apart from politics (and given the rancid state of government on both sides of the Irish Sea, let's not open that particular Pandora's box) the topic that creates most talk is football. As an unadvisably frequent scribbler, tweeter and podcast host, I probably represent the worst of this modern breed of cyber-gobs, wittering endlessly on the topic of Liverpool Football Club.

An all-too-infrequent visitor to Anfield in recent years, I have found myself desperate to maintain my connection to a club and a city I feel an inexplicably strong affinity with. The reasons for my sporadic attendance at matches are the usual amalgam of geographical inconvenience, familial duty and fiscal incapacity. If I had my way I'd never miss a game, but the realities of life have bitten hard of late, and it has been with an air of frustration and mild irritation that I've noted the increasingly quiet atmosphere in the ground – a trend ironically blamed by some on 'day trippers' like myself.

Clearly these folks have never been in the company of the maniacs that often share a cheap Ryanair flight with me. Quiet, they are not.

One always fancies being able to influence the mood inside Anfield with a well-timed exhortation or the initiation of a chant. Alas, in my rural Irish home, the only things feeling the impact of my expletive-heavy vocal support have been the delicate ears of my poor daughter when she inadvertently strays into the fraught scenario of the matchday living room, where her father is alone, pacing and prowling throughout the 90 minutes.

Eyes wild beneath the hood of what was once a lucky top, with the remote controls arranged just-so on the couch and the volume set at 90 (in a very loud nod to the last time we won the league), I am the very epitome of unhinged obsession and she is, unsurprisingly, always quick to exit. Ain't superstition grand?

Being an absent but absurdly passionate fan is a peculiar kind of agony. Until recently it had also been a solitary one. Then things changed in a seismic fashion when the good folk at The Liverpool Offside – which had been my go-to site for a couple of years and remains, to my mind, the finest source of online LFC writing – offered me the chance to contribute as a staff writer. Over three seasons I've churned out some 370 pieces, each and every one of which I've poured my metaphorical guts into. I quickly discovered that I can't do short and newsy, and each piece is happy hours in the crafting.

The whole process has been rewarding on so many levels. Working with a massively talented team of various nationalities is in itself an honour, but the real strength of the collective is the shared belief in eschewing the sensationalistic, clickbait nonsense that pollutes so many sites. We just tell the stories, look for the humour and avoid the agendas.

Folk have been incessantly kind about the stuff I've inflicted upon them three or four times a week, and that is immensely gratifying if a little awkward for a fellow with the residual traces of self-loathing only a rural Irish Catholic upbringing can imbue. If I'm honest I'd do this scribbling lark for free, if only for the oddly therapeutic catharsis I have found in writing down the nonsense that had previously been rattling around in my battered brain-pan, tormenting only me. A problem shared, and all that. Hey, it saves on shrink bills.

Two seasons ago the solipsistic nature of my support faded even more. Shameless ex-thespian that I am I never tire of my own obnoxious voice, and I'd floated the idea of a podcast with the aforementioned TLO crew across the Atlantic. But they were entirely too modest and decorous for such a venture. That was when I met Mr Phil Casey, a model of immodest indecorousness.

Phil had been thinking of a similar project and set about recruiting a team of Irish-based Liverpool fans. When Casey has a plan he's a relentless bastard, and before you knew it we'd formed The Daytrippers and began recording on a device belonging to my film director brother.

The gear has improved over time and the podcast has become so much more successful than either of us had dared to hope initially. Most of the credit for that goes to Phil, who does the heavy lifting of production and editing, as well as performing the arduous task of sabotaging my attempts at calmly hosting as often as he possibly can. It's my fault really as I can't resist poking at the chap's latent megalomaniacal tendencies just to see what will happen. I mean, we're talking about a man who possesses an ornate vaping pipe that Stalin would have looked comfortable puffing on.

As mentioned earlier, the Irish are an irreverent and raucous bunch, and that blithe spirit is what we try to capture in all our weekly shows. Certainly, we've tackled serious topics and we're fiercely proud of that work. We've also talked to the likes of John Barnes, Ian Rush, Rob Jones and former Irish international Jason McAteer, who duly took the piss out of my 'dead posh' voice the second we went live. As abusing the hapless host seems to have become a proper 'tripper rite of passage enjoyed by all our contributors at some point, Jason's now an honorary member.

We do take our football very seriously and the analysis is never less than earnest but, inevitably, the mask of solemnity will eventually slip and the glorified broom cupboard in which we record, affectionately dubbed 'The Bunker', will rock with the kind of cacophonous and often libellous abandon that ensures Herr Editor will have a job of work on his hands when he gets home.

The most gratifying thing about the whole enterprise has been the response of listeners. Whether based in Malaysia or Huyton, it's genuinely humbling to think we've enhanced their experience as a supporter in some small way, even if it's only been to make them chuckle incongruously on their commute in the wake of a crushing defeat. Indeed we've found that the recordings after the Redmen have been beaten are often the most uproarious, as passions are running high and my tenuous grip on the rein is often lost in the sheer chaos created by some of the most brilliantly funny characters I've ever met.

All of which self-indulgent rambling brings us back to the events of this match. Huddled around the less-than-ample screen of my shiny new Macbook, Phil, Paul Brennan, Stevo Daly, mellifluous Welsh 'tripper Dave Thomas and myself yawned, groaned and cackled bitterly as the Redmen spurned another Manc-given opportunity to close the gap to the top four.

Let's be clear, it was turgid stuff. A plethora of tame shots, blocked attempts, intercepted passes and lifeless interplay hardly demanding of one's attention. After an early warning on seven minutes, when Dame N'Doye headed too close to Simon Mignolet, Philippe Coutinho had a decent half-volley well stopped by Billy Mitchell lookalike Steve Harper, before Michael Dawson headed in the game's only goal.

To be honest, none of us expected Liverpool to get back into the match, despite the fact that over half of it remained. It was one of those evenings and we had one of those feelings. You know the one. The sick hollow sensation in your gut that makes you feel sure you have wasted your evening, and a goodly portion of your life, obsessing over a bunch of twonks who simply don't have the decency to do what they're supposed to do and make you feel better.

On a night when Liverpool fans were drawing attention to the fact that Hull were demanding £50 from travelling Reds, having asked just £16 from their Stoke counterparts, the notion of value was to the fore of many minds. In 'The Bunker', as we wrestled with our quiet rage in the immediate aftermath of another underwhelming performance, it was pointed out that even the £10 fans had paid to secure a child's seat and retain their participation in the loyalty scheme, was too much to shell out for the Redmen's insipid efforts.

The rage subsided – what are you going to do? We had a show to get on with, and it wasn't long before the laughs returned. I woke up the next day with a column to write and conjured up a piece about Brendan Rodgers's similarities to *Taxi Driver*'s Wizard. Don't ask. This is how one survives obsession on this level.

The wheel keeps turning – this is a lifelong infatuation and one cannot just tune it out. If anything, the paucity of my visits in recent years has added a further significance to each pilgrimage. I will simply never tire of the joy that going to the game gives me. The routine is well established now. The early flight to Liverpool on match day. The wander around town and pre-game pints with some of the very sound locals I'm pleased to call friends. The excited walk up the steps before emerging on to the Kop for that first look at the Anfield turf. The feeling of expectation and hope that never fails to fill my heart before the whistle blows, when everything is still possible, no matter what the opposition or the standard of our side. Magic is not uncommon in this place.

Years ago, on my first visit, my brother and I were drawn back to the ground the day after a European game. Someone had left a gate open and we walked freely and cheekily through the stand and down to the pitch. We stood there in awe of the verdant magnificence of the surface and simultaneously crouched to simply lay a reverent palm on the grass we'd only previously seen through the filter of television, grass which had played host to the mastery of our heroes, men like Kenny Dalglish, Barnes and Rush. By then a permanently lapsed Catholic, that was a more powerfully spiritual moment than any religious experience from my youth.

The solemn exaltation of the interlude didn't last and our reverie was somewhat shattered by an understandably annoyed groundsman wondering why there were two jokers apparently attempting a Vulcan mind meld with his precious surface. We were politely but irritably escorted from the immediate vicinity of the pitch and pointed in the direction of the tour guide. Giddy still, we preferred a pint. Consumed in a haze of gratification arising from our small adventure, we couldn't shake the regret that we hadn't brought a ball, to have rolled just one side-footed pass on that pitch.

I'll be in Liverpool for Steven Gerrard's final game at Anfield, the first time the stars have aligned and allowed me to watch my beloved club in 2015. It'll be all the more special for that. Try telling someone like me that the enforced infrequency of their trips to L4 makes them somehow less of a supporter. That'll be a short and rather curt conversation.

Beforehand, in the city, the old routine will be observed with as much ritual and ceremony as ever and, once inside, I'll cajole and roar, sing and cheer from the Kop, as I always do. If I'm honest, I'll likely have a moan with a few of the usual suspects at half-time, too. I'm old now. It's allowed. Hell, it's de rigueur.

Sentimentality will no doubt enhance the poignancy of the occasion to almost unbearable levels. Grown men will probably claim the ground is full of dust from the builders' work on the stand. I won't. A great player will move on, yes, but I will simply continue to love Liverpool. Everything will change and yet everything will stay the same. One does not simply get off this bus. One rides it to the terminus. Maybe, if we're lucky, we'll stop soon to take on board a trophy or two.

2 May 2015, Liverpool 2 QPR 1

'Bag of chips'

By David John Jaggs

I t's getting to be a rare thing, this. Far too rare a thing. The triple-whammy of being rooted OOT in deepest Lancashire thanks to my better half, the ever spiralling cost of everything football and being faced full on with the age-old decision of the match versus the music, means trips to Anfield, in fact trips anywhere, have become the exception rather than the weekend rule that you long them to be as kick-off looms.

That fluttering, stomach-churning feeling doesn't really leave you, and if anything having to make do with listening on the radio or fumbling to refresh a smartphone screen to get a fix of how the tricky Reds are getting on feels much worse. You're helpless. Without sounding like some platitude-filled Barclays advert, when you're there you can be an actual tiny part of it. Every song started. Every 'man on!' shout.

I had sleepless nights after missing last year's Chelsea game. That open-throated, head-back bellowing of someone in red's name to draw others in might have inspired something, one moment of brilliance, a fraction more composure to smash a hole through that blue bus window. Chaos theory in action. Me, the butterfly on the other side of the world, trying to help Phil Coutinho flap his wings and start a hurricane in front of my eyes.

If my car insurance company got wind of the over-exuberant goal celebrations that punctuate every occasion I've had to tolerate waves of Alan Green's insufferable negativity towards us on BBC Radio 5 Live, an army of meerkats and talking robots couldn't get me a low enough quote to stay on the road. You're not meant to beep your horn on the motorway. You're definitely not meant to beep your horn driving through heavy Manchester traffic to a gig when Rickie Lambert has just equalised away against Ludogorets. The fume in the cars around me. Oh, the fume.

So, QPR then, and a game that doesn't really mean a lot now. After West Brom and the Hull debacle, the Mancs look home and dry for fourth. Equally there's been surprisingly little coverage in the build-up of how it's almost exactly 25 years since we played the same fixture (and, ultimately, with the same scoreline), and came away with our last league title to date.

I've always had something of a soft spot for QPR. Even with Neil Warnock at the helm, when Harry Redknapp was there moaning about their 'bare bones' having outspent Borussia Dortmund's Champions League finalists, or after that phenomenal Sebastian Coates overhead kick was denied the place in history it deserved by a Reds capitulation, this didn't really wane. It stems partially from my mate Mooro, a huge Red and veteran of many a triumph and tribulation, being appointed their club doctor a few years back. I wanted to see them in the big time so they'd get to play us and he'd get to live out one of those childhood fantasies we all have; walking on the hallowed Anfield turf, or sitting on the bench just along from those lads in red.

It started a bit before that though, in the mid-to-late 2000s to be precise. I'd ended up wandering into one of the pubs around Loftus Road while on a meandering little jaunt around west London. It'd been a particularly shit week. I'd lost my job on the Monday and after heading down to London to meet my then girlfriend, we split up after she announced she was moving abroad for the year. It was August Carnival weekend and after a few searching texts and phone calls to people I knew who might be about, I was off to meet James, my mate from university on Tyneside. Freshly arrived in the capital, he was at a loose end that Sunday afternoon and, for some reason, willing to listen to my whining in exchange for a few pints of Red Stripe and some jerk chicken.

The only downside was a complete lack of knowledge of where we were going, but like the best adventures, we made it up as we went along.

After spending an age getting into the centre of London, we realised neither of us were in the mood for a steel drum-soundtracked street party and needed to find somewhere a little quieter to bevy and put the world to rights, so we tried to find the nearest station. After what seemed like another age on a myriad of aimless Tube journeys we walked out into the beckoning August dusk and continued, fuelled by a few cans of Jamaica's finest acquired from the corner shops we'd ambled past on foot. Somehow we missed the small yet not inconsiderable sight of Loftus Road, and it was only on finding somewhere to drink and spotting that the frosted glass on the door to the gents was embellished with the Queens Park Rangers crest that I finally stumbled across my bearings.

James was waiting at the bar, balanced precariously half on/half off his stool and occasionally leaning across the beer taps to gesticulate wildly. He had, in my absence, been laying my woe-filled recent situation on pretty thick to the lone, doting, raven-haired barmaid who walked round to embrace me in sympathy. Some free Jack Daniel's was duly served up, along with a silver promotional hip flask (which forever comes in useful to get around the outrageous cost of booze at Academy venues) and accompanied by a couple of pints from locals who'd been listening and trying, in vain, to pinpoint where James's Middlesbrough twang was from.

It was pointed out how blind we must have been to miss the football ground we'd just sauntered past. What wasn't missed, however, was that I'd been cheered up considerably by Queens Park Rangers. As such, they've occupied a soft spot in my heart ever since.

Today's journey is a hell of a lot more focused than that one was, but the lingering, rumbling legacy of what seems to be our captain's anti-fairytale ending is evident early on at our Saturday morning six-a-side game. Every slip across the drenched east Lancashire astroturf is greeted with the now customary 'Steven Gerrard!' or 'Demba Ba!' shouts by some wool bell-end or other (how I talk about my friends, ladies and gentlemen). No more the acknowledgement of the postage-stamp screamer, the raking 50-yard pass or the gritted-teeth, driven run into the box. Nope, the calling card moment of one of the greatest players of his generation now revolves around his poorly chosen footwear on an April afternoon.

Still, there's a keenly fought game to be had pre-Anfield on this rain-soaked May morning, followed by an enforced post-match drive to play an acoustic gig in Stockport. The complete absence of beer transforms the matchday experience into something akin to being in your mid-teens again, with that joyous union of a freezing cold can of Coke and a bag of chips upon landing back in Liverpool straight after a kickabout with your mates. If that's not what football's about, momentarily being transported to a place you thought you'd never go to again, I don't know what is.

With a few errands to run in town, I leave the car on Upper Parliament Street outside my mate and former Ragamuffins keyboard player Jonas's house for safe keeping. And after a quick trip to Dawson's to stock up on strings and restock a dwindling supply of plectrums, I head up to the Lobster Pot on Renshaw for the aforementioned chips. Incredible. I didn't write a song about this just for the metaphor about throwaway news items you know.

The spiralling financial aspect of going to the match has hit me hard. In part it's more fool me for choosing a career where 'job satisfaction' is, unless you reach the pinnacle, always going to be compensatory for making less money than mates of mine that I did better than at school. In this context, it's been great seeing ticket prices all over the news this week thanks to the Hull boycott. Similarly, I've seen many barbed social media posts about 'Scousers getting their own house in order first' in relation to the cost of today's match ticket, which misses the point and shows what a long way there is to go.

Saying that, I can't get my head around this fixture costing £45 or £47 for the QPR fans, and leaving the debate on tiered ticket prices aside, how can a game against a relatively newly-promoted team be deemed a Category B fixture when games against Swansea, Hull and Stoke, all cup finalists in recent years, are considered a tier below them?

But as pointed out by many articles designed to confront the worsening atmosphere at the match, the idea of lowering ticket prices in order to bring in a new generation of younger fans with more vociferous vocal support, especially in our unique case, probably won't help as much as you'd think, and might just mean more older fans going more often rather than allowing younger fans to get a foothold in supporting the club.

As I say, in my case the music versus football conflict resulted in me siding with the former, and not just because of time and expense. When your income becomes solely dependent on being able to sing with reasonable proficiency (insert your own joke here, folks), you can't go blowing your voice every week singing songs about Henderson, Can and Coutinho, especially when you're aiming vocally for Brian Wilson or Marvin Gaye and consistently waking up the morning after European games sounding like the illegitimate son of Tom Waits and Captain Beefheart. This came to a head when the constant wear and tear led to me needing a throat operation in 2011, and in truth I've had to go to the match far, far less since then.

Cost is sort of taken out of the equation today as, quite brilliantly, our trumpet player Flo has sorted the pair of us out with complimentary tickets courtesy of a mysterious, unnamed customer at the fashion shop he works at in town. I tried pressing him on the identity of said person a few times but he was insistent on keeping firmly schtum, so I dropped it. After all, a freebie is a freebie.

This is his very first trip to Anfield so I get to be a tour guide in the taxi up there, with the occasional shout from the fella behind the wheel. It's at this point that we find out the incredibly tragic news about Rio Ferdinand's wife, Rebecca, passing away after battling breast cancer. I was genuinely speechless and didn't even know she was sick. But then again why would I?

I'd be lying if I said I liked Rio, and some of my favourite *Schadenfreude*-laced memories of watching Manchester United's occasional toils relate to his facial expressions when struggling to get back after a defensive mix-up. I'm talking a half-fit Fernando Torres leaving him looking like a statue in 2010, Craig Bellamy turning on the afterburners past him while wearing Manchester City blue, or even his infamous own-goal mix-up with Edwin van der Sar against Portsmouth. That all means nothing now. This isn't Rio Ferdinand the one-time captain of that lot down the East Lancs. Instead it's Rio Ferdinand the young dad-of-three who's lost his wife. I'm not ashamed to say I was a bit tearful at the subsequent applause five minutes into our game.

Flo grew up a Steaua Bucharest fan in north Romania, which means I still get to mock how we stuffed his lot a few years ago when inhibited by the rigours of Hodgeball, and how even Lucas scored – an insult normally only reserved for teams likes Havant & Waterlooville and Newcastle United. He admittedly has a soft spot for Chelsea (never mind) as a result of Adrian Mutu and Dan Petrescu's playing days there, and has seen the great Gheorghe Hagi ply his trade for the national team in person. Not bad, eh?

I'm always curious to watch and witness people's first impressions of Anfield. A mate of mine, Chris, attended our FA Cup game against Bolton as a Trotters fan back in January and his first impressions were of the appalling view from the back of the Lower Annie, as well as the incredibly tight legroom compared to the almost luxurious-in-comparison Macron Stadium (his words). However, this was quickly followed by him pointing out how much he loved it.

Flo suggests Anfield has a similar sort of feel to Goodison (while casually mentioning Samuel Eto'o once sorted him with a ticket for a Europa League group game), which will no doubt enrage some of you. But I let him off, guessing that the two grounds are similar compared to the other English grounds he's been to. Steaua have a classic European running-track stadium, which probably explains a lot.

I normally head to the Twelfth Man for a pre-match pint and do my obligatory thing of getting lost in search of the toilet (as we've established – my sense of direction is diabolical), but with the weather not exactly hospitable I suggest The Albert would serve as a more appropriate watering hole, and if nothing else I can point out a Steaua scarf that adorns the wall there.

I still feel a pang of nostalgia at the way the pub stands alone now. Obviously the redevelopment is something that has to happen, but it almost strikes you as a lone bastion of a bygone age. Sigh.

Anyway, in we go. The Main Stand it is today, and the pillars aren't too problematic in restricting our view. I've got a superstitious thing that makes me panic when recalling matches I've spent in similar seats, and it was in this almost exact spot in 2008 that I watched John Arne Riise slice us out of the Champions League. This does not bode well, especially considering I'm sat next to a Chelsea sympathiser.

Still, we don't look too bad. After their bright start (that corner didn't look out by the way) we seem more comfortable. Rickie Lambert looks more at a level he's used to in competing physically with players like Richard Dunne and Clint Hill and before long he slips in Coutinho for the first goal. The little magician does the unexpected repeatedly and brilliantly and this is simultaneously what fans want to see, why they love him, and also why defenders get bamboozled by him. They literally have no idea what he's going to do either.

Adam Lallana's inconsistency in front of goal after the break is more alarming than Raheem Sterling's but it is a miss by the latter which really sticks in the mind. It's certainly not the finish of someone after a pay packet in excess of £100,000 a week. Ho hum.

That's also the feeling when Leroy Fer smashes in a bobbling ball after the first half-decent set-piece delivery QPR have mustered since the one in minute one. Ho hum. The season's been full of them hasn't it? Ho fucking hum. West Ham away. Ho hum. Going out of the Champions League after at least giving it a go with ten men, and at least looking comfortable in possession at the Bernabeu. Ho hum.

And Gerrard missing a penalty after Nedum Onuoha decides he wants Martin Skrtel's shirt ten minutes earlier than he should? Ho hum. It's one of those days. It's been one of those seasons.

But the relief after Gerrard restores the natural order of things. Oh the relief. Not for us, but for himself. Whatever we've been feeling these past 12 months must be nothing to what that fella's had to deal with in terms of professional pride. Admittedly he's looked awful at times, a fact made more painful by the heady heights Steven George Gerrard has taken us, taken himself, taken Liverpool Football Club, and even taken football to throughout his career.

Watching some plucky Brummie teenager with a terrible haircut run rings around him the other week must have smarted too, and missing a penalty when it counted will have rubbed salt into an open wound. Fortunately, Steven wasn't to be denied. A big shout (definitely audible from the Main Stand given the flat atmosphere after the penalty miss) and a big header and a big goal. Joyous.

So off we go, swiftly back into town and an even swifter one before heading over to Stockport in the lovely surroundings of Bier bar on Newington. I have to sacrilegiously avoid the Bavarian bounty they have in great store and settle for a Coke, as well as resisting tinkling the ivories on the piano stood right by the front door.

Flo's now waxing lyrical about the celebration of the winner as well as the flags. I know I've seen much better, from Gerrard and from us in the stands, but seeing that leviathan of a man wheel away to celebrate in front of the Kop couldn't help but remind me of the camera angle vantage point of that goal against Olympiakos; me smack bang in the middle of those scenes of jubilation, for some reason wearing a pair of gloves and a short-sleeve replica shirt (more sacrilege right there) and waving a flag above my head while hugging my mate Liam as if my life depended on it.

The Mancs have lost to West Brom. We would be above them now had we fared better against Albion ourselves and Hull. Ah well. Ho hum.

10 May 2015, Chelsea 1 Liverpool 1

'I love a bit of quality defending'

By Rebecca Knight

Chelsea versus Liverpool is a modern rivalry. It has to be given the Blues have no history.

The rivalry isn't as long-running as Liverpool versus Manchester United, or as well known as Real Madrid versus Barcelona, but that doesn't mean it is any less bitter. For a club that only started in 2003, Chelsea have had a remarkable number of incidents with the Reds that have added a tick to their supporters' 'reasons to dislike' box. And Liverpool supporters probably feel the same way. It all started with that Luis Garcia goal, with our lot feeling the Demba Ba incident was cosmic payback for 2005.

Jose Mourinho has made no secret of his distaste for the atmosphere at Stamford Bridge and, make no mistake, he would cut off his right arm and give you Rui Faria to get a 12th man like Liverpool have. You lot are the best in the league when it comes to noise and passion – and that accolade is coming from a staunch Blue.

But it's what happens on the pitch that really matters and the way this season has played out for our respective teams is not really a surprise given Brendan Rodgers's decision to go on a manager's version of a supermarket sweep down on the south coast last summer while Mourinho sold average players for huge prices and purchased the missing pieces of the puzzle. After that, anyone who thought the Special One would finish this term without at least one honour was as delusional as a post-match Rodgers interview.

A visit from Liverpool is always something I look forward to, particularly given my first football memory is of just that. It was the day I fell in love – 11 May 2003.

Jesper Gronkjaer (there's a blast from the past for you) scored what was dubbed the '£1bn goal' to give Chelsea a win over Liverpool that secured Champions League football for the club and, crucially, attracted Roman Abramovich. The rest, as they say, is history.

Everything changed for Chelsea, everything changed for me. I became football obsessed, I wouldn't miss a game, I got to know everything there is to know about Chelsea players and their rivals both at home and abroad. More than falling in love with Chelsea, I also fell in love with football, something that has changed the direction of my life, both personally and professionally.

My parents' dreams of me becoming a lawyer went out the window. I wanted to write about sport for a living, and now I do. Aside from that, the amount of football I watch is truly shocking. A former housemate of mine said the low point of living with me came when I wanted to watch Russian cup football. So you get the picture.

To clarify – I'm 25, live in Manchester and have a Manchester United-supporting father, so I'm no glory hunter. If I was then, given my location, it would make more sense for me to have dyed my shirt a lighter shade of blue last season and honed my birthday cake-making skills for Yaya.

Liverpool have been a huge part of my footballing life (they were, after all, one half of the match that made me fall in love with the game) and while I thank God I was drawn to Chelsea, I have a grudging respect for the men in Red. While I may not like them, their result is the one I look for straight after Chelsea's game is done and dusted. Not because they're a rival (obviously) but because, as some Liverpool fans claim, I am a little bit obsessed with them. And given the venomous level of banter directed from Liverpool fans to those of a Chelsea persuasion, it seems to work both ways.

As a Chelsea fan there are games against Liverpool I will never forget, for a multitude of reasons. Winning the first trophy of the Mourinho era in Cardiff is one. A 4-1 win at Anfield during the defence of our Premier League title back in October 2005 is another.

And then there were the Champions League games. That Frank Lampard penalty in 2008 goes down in history as dramatically as John Terry's slip in the final as far as I am concerned. The quarter-final the year after also makes the list, with Branislav Ivanovic starting what has been a fruitful goal-scoring career against Liverpool to send Chelsea through to the one game I will never forget – the 'Scandal of Stamford Bridge' against Barcelona.

I thought that Garcia 'ghost goal' of 2005 would be the one that killed me as a Chelsea fan, and it still hurts – I can't watch that game without getting frustrated (to put it in a printable way), and to this day it still irks Chelsea and Mourinho. But that goal pales in comparison to the last-gasp one Andres Iniesta got for Barcelona at the Bridge in 2009, and for that reason they are the club who I genuinely hate with an unbridled passion. I dislike Liverpool, yes, and it's more than three points when the clubs meet, but when it comes to Barcelona it's just out-and-out hatred – for Mourinho as much as the fans and players.

Speaking of players, we can't possibly go through a Chelsea/Liverpool discussion without talking about Steven Gerrard. The player who has given so much for Liverpool and Chelsea over the years and who, even if Chelsea and Liverpool did not have their rivalry, would still be intertwined with Chelsea simply because of Frank Lampard and the seeming inability of fans and the media to talk about one without bringing up the other.

It was fitting that what looks like being Gerrard's final goal in a Liverpool shirt came against Chelsea. A club who have given him so much stick down the years and one he very nearly joined. While it's probably best to gloss over the burning shirts in a bin on Merseyside, it's safe to say moving to west London would have made Gerrard a very successful player in terms of trophies. But for adoration and testimonial purposes, he was better off sticking where he was. Something Robin van Persie is learning quickly.

Mourinho is a huge fan of Gerrard and has admitted trying to buy him on no less than three occasions – with Chelsea, Inter Milan and Real Madrid – and while Mourinho (and deep down Gerrard, one suspects) may lament that never quite working out, as a Chelsea fan I don't.

I never wanted to sign Gerrard, not once. That is not a slight on someone who has been one of the best midfielders the league has ever seen, but we didn't need him. At one time Chelsea had the best midfield in the world, with Claude Makelele, Michael Essien and Lampard. And it is Lampard who, despite moving to Manchester City and scoring a goal against us this season, remains the best. No questions asked. He did it for Chelsea time and time again, and I know Gerrard was similar but the argument that he carried Liverpool whereas Lampard was surrounded by top talent and did not have to do the same job holds no weight with me.

Lampard popped up with goals on the biggest occasions and on the not so big. He never did a John Terry and managed to get himself sent off when we needed him most – he stood up and was counted, as Liverpool fans will remember only too well. After his beloved mother died, he begged Avram Grant to feature in the Champions League semi-final against your team and scored *that* penalty. Lampard never let Chelsea down...until he saved it all for the nuclear explosion of his loan-which-isn't-actually-a-loan to City.

But back to the point in hand. Gerrard and Lampard shouldn't be pitted against each other. As is the case every time Lionel Messi and Cristiano Ronaldo are compared to each other whenever one or both of them does anything decent (so twice weekly). Why can't we just admire Gerrard and Lampard for what they bring to the table? Each are brilliant in their own right. Lampard and Gerrard are of the same breed. Don't diminish one to bolster the other. It's not needed.

While I don't really buy into the whole comparison thing (bar for a bit of banter on Twitter), one thing I believe in is that they didn't bring out the best in each other when playing together for England. That is why I never wanted Gerrard at Chelsea – and was also the reason I didn't really subscribe to Michael Ballack joining us, either. Of course Andriy Shevchenko rocked up at the same time, so you know, priorities when it comes to moaning and all that.

As Gerrard left the field during this match, Mourinho applauded and asked Chelsea fans to do the same – and like the sheep some of them are, they complied. Steven Gerrard managed to get a standing ovation as he walked off the pitch at Stamford Bridge for the final time. Frank Lampard did not. Imagine what that must do to Chelsea fans and Lampard in particular when they think that through. It is devastating, but, in fairness, entirely of Lampard's own making. Say what you want about Gerrard and his lack of Premier League titles, but he has been loyal.

And when asked about the Chelsea fans and their ovation at the end of the game, the response from your captain was so good it should have been laminated. He made the age-old dig at the Chelsea crowd that even Mourinho has made reference to at times this season. Not that you can blame the Chelsea manager, or Gerrard, with the Demba Ba song now one of our fans' top three staples in football-supporter life.

Before you Reds get worked up, take a minute to note this. Chelsea fans don't have the biggest back catalogue of songs, and considering the Diego Costa chant basically just goes 'Diego, Diego, Diego', it's safe to say we're not the most inventive bunch. Hence the promotion of the Demba Ba song – it's all we really have.

In all seriousness, Gerrard has been abused by Blues fans as much as he has United ones, so what did people expect him to say after this game? While I nearly fell off my chair in fury at the time, I can laugh now. The Liverpool fan I watched the match with certainly did.

Gerrard is a legend, no question, and deep down Chelsea fans will be sad to see him go because, let's face it, when the chips are down against the Reds a Chelsea player will now have to step up and do the business instead of waiting for Stevie to make his seasonal contribution to our cause.

Sorry, I couldn't resist.

I have to say, legend or not, the furore around Gerrard's departure is a bit much, as, let me say, was the guard of honour the Chelsea team received from your players. While I found it mildly humorous, the boys in blue just looked embarrassed. And when John Terry is embarrassed, you know you've crossed a line.

Speaking of Terry, Gerrard and Liverpool legends, the three combined lead me to one man. The man I actually think is a real Liverpool legend – Jamie Carragher.

I love a bit of quality defending (it's the Mourinho in me) and Carra, for me, is the player Liverpool fans should adore above all others. In my eyes he was your leader on the field, armband or not, and someone I think is criminally underrated when people talk about the best Premier League defenders over the last decade or so.

JT, Ricardo Carvalho, Rio Ferdinand and Nemanja Vidic (bar, ironically, when he faced Fernando Torres in a Liverpool shirt) are the names mentioned the most, but Carra was just as good as any of them at his peak, and someone who gave every single thing he had in every single game.

As much as I love Carragher, it seems he feels the same way about Terry, who he called the best centre-back of the Premier League era. And it was Terry who scored the opening goal of this most recent encounter with Liverpool to become the highest-scoring Premier League defender of all time.

Terry has arguably had his best season to date in a Chelsea shirt, managing to play in every single game, with his performances off the chart. And all after being told by one man Liverpool fans know very well that he couldn't play twice in a week, let alone 38 games in a single domestic season.

Terry managed to get a dig in at Rafa Benitez when Chelsea were officially crowned champions, but his on-the-field performances have said everything he's needed to say. Meanwhile, Chelsea fans hate The Interim One as much as Liverpool fans love him, and quite why anyone thought it would be a good idea for him to rock up at Chelsea bemuses me to this day, as well as providing an intriguing sidebar to the Chelsea/Liverpool relationship. He got more love from Liverpool fans while he was Chelsea manager than he did from Chelsea fans. Football, eh?

Terry and Gerrard have been skippers of their teams for so long and have given so much for so long, that it was fitting to see both on the scoresheet come full time. In truth, the result of this match did not matter. The season is all but over for both clubs and it says a huge amount that Chelsea actually managed to get a draw given their abject showing against West Brom the week after – the players are clearly on the beach.

But the Chelsea/Liverpool carousel never stops turning and, despite Gerrard's departure, next season's matches between both sides will be as spicy as ever, I'm sure. And if it's extra spice you're after, how about bringing back Benitez? Now that really would get the songs flowing.

'He didn't tell me his name. He never has'

By Sachin Nakrani

A red hat with a green bobble. That's what he wanted more than anything else. Oh and it had to have a Liverbird on it. Yes, a red hat with a green bobble, and a Liverbird.

And it *had* to be from the official club shop. Not from a stall outside the ground, or from some random bloke he met on the way to the ground. No – the official club shop. A red hat with a green bobble, and a Liverbird, from the official club shop. That's what he wanted.

Children are strange. The way on one hand they are utterly mesmerised by everything around them, full of curiosity and wonder, desperate to explore the outreaches of their street, city, world and galaxy. Yet on the other they obsess about the small things, like a hat. That's what this 11-year-old boy I once knew was obsessed about ahead of his first trip to Anfield. He was going to watch the team he adored at the greatest stadium in the world, for the very first time, and all he cared about was a hat.

The fucking idiot.

And who was that 11-year-old boy?

It was me. Obviously.

It started as soon as my uncle Babu said he'd got tickets for me, him and his son (my cousin) Ricky to go to the match. I vividly remember telling him from the off that we had to get to Anfield early so I could go to the club shop and buy a hat.

'What type of hat do you want?' he asked.

'A red one with a green bo–' …you know the rest.

And we got it, the exact one I wanted. I saw it as soon as we entered the club shop, which back then if memory serves me right, was a hut. A tiny thing with probably a 16th of the quantity and variety of merchandise the current club shop/megastore sells. But there it was, the hat I wanted, hanging above the shoulder of one of the guys behind the counter.

And I wore it straight away. Partly through excitement and partly because it was freezing. An icy cold afternoon in December – 13 December 1992, to be precise. It was a Sunday and I had a brand new hat.

I was excited about the football, too, and once the hat was sorted that's all I could think about. Finally, I was going to see the Reds play in the flesh. Barnes, Rush, Nicol and McManaman, all in front of me. And then there was Piechnik. He was really tall and fierce-looking, like Ivan Drago in footy boots. He was going to be brilliant for us, no doubt. Absolutely none. Great signing, Souey.

The game was a big deal – Liverpool versus Blackburn and the return of the King. Yes, Kenny Dalglish was back at Anfield 22 months after resigning as manager. I'll be honest, I wasn't massively fussed. I was fully aware Kenny was a huge figure in Liverpool's history but I'd never seen him play and was only nine when he left the club. I had affection for him but he had essentially passed through my Liverpool-supporting life quickly and almost instantly. So while those around me applauded ferociously when Kenny emerged from the tunnel to take his seat in the opposition dugout, I clapped only politely before turning my gaze towards the pitch.

And then there was the Kop. Jesus Almighty, the Kop.

It's a regret of mine that I never got to go in there pre-1994. I'd hoped our tickets for this match were Kop tickets but instead we were in the Anfield Road end. Area AC, Row 24, to be precise. Sat there (in Seat 183), I looked on jealously as it swayed in those minutes before kick-off, moving like a starving leopard crawling through wild grass, searching for prey, scaring the shit out of Bobby Mimms. I was gutted not to be in there but took appreciation from being able to watch it in its full, famous glory. At least I'd always have that.

I don't remember much about the game, to be honest. Reading back old reports that's largely because nothing happened until Mark Walters gave us the lead on 77 minutes and kick-started a frantic finale. Alan Shearer equalised for Blackburn soon after with a volley right below us before Walters got the winner five minutes from time.

And that was it; the sights, the sounds, the goals – I was hooked on going to the match. I lived miles away, had no regular income and homework to do, but somehow I was getting back here as soon as possible. With my hat.

As it turned out I didn't return to Anfield for another two and a bit years, for that Coca-Cola Cup tie against Arsenal. Babu mama (mama means mother's brother in Gujarati – go on, impress your friends) and Ricky were there for that one, too.

Looking back, it was pretty remarkable that my uncle got three together for Blackburn. As said, the game was a big deal and so demand for tickets must have been high. Also, my uncle wasn't an Anfield regular. I think he got the tickets from a friend who was a season ticket holder who knew another season ticket holder. But still, three together for Kenny's return. That's pretty good going.

I'd love to ask Babu mama how he got the tickets but sadly I can't. I can't because he died from a brain tumour in 2006.

He was 54.

Now I could say I think about him every time I go to the match, but I don't. Occasionally, but not every time. I think about him more often at other times, like whenever I pass his photo on the landing at my parents' house, or whenever my mum says 'brother', or whenever I remember the darkest, most difficult time of my life, because when he got sick, in late 2000, our respective families suffered a major falling out.

It got really ugly, with fists thrown in hospital car parks and unforgivingly harsh words exchanged in all manner of other places. To this day I don't really know how it all started, but I do know it's had a lasting, bitter effect on the people I love and used to love. Ricky and I haven't spoken for 15 years while his older brother, Raaj, and I have only started communicating in the past 12 months.

And in the middle of it all remains the memory of the man who took me to Anfield for the first time. A man I miss deeply.

But I don't think about him every time I go to the match. Instead I think about my life in general and how this club, Liverpool Football Club, has been part of it for so long. And I've thought about that more than ever during the past nine months, because the 2014/15 campaign has been my first with a season ticket. Poignantly, it's in the Annie Road.

Being able to call myself a Liverpool season-ticket holder is great but without sounding too much like an *X Factor* knobhead, it's the journey rather than the destination that matters here. I first went to Anfield in 1992, struggled to get tickets and so, in the summer of 1999, applied for a season ticket, knowing that if and when I got one, I'd never have to experience the frustration of not being able get into Anfield again. There'd always be a seat for me. My seat.

I knew when I applied that my patience would be tested. There were thousands of people on the waiting list and it would take years for me to move up it. So it was a case of sitting tight and, in the meantime, continuing to scrounge around for tickets, asking mates if they knew of any spares and keeping an eye on the club's website to see if there was a general sale or any late returns.

Occasionally I got lucky. There was another home game against Blackburn (again with Babu mama and Ricky) in September 1995 and Roma home and away during the UEFA Cup run of 2000/01. I was also able to take Shanil to Chelsea home in March 2002 (the 'Scaaasers' and 'Yids' game) and to Leeds home in October 2003. I also went to a couple of games with my mate Mark while we were at journalism college; Blackburn home (them again) and West Ham away. But otherwise that was it. That season ticket couldn't come quickly enough, but quickly it wasn't coming.

And then something brilliant happened in November 2003. Fate intervened.

I had recently joined the *Harrow Observer* and was on one of my first reporting gigs – a woman was celebrating her 100th birthday at a local care home and my editor wanted me to go down and do a feel-good story. Speak to her family about her life, get the photographer to take some snaps of the cake and make note of any other interesting tit-bits. All pretty standard stuff.

As I waited to speak to someone or other, the manager of the care home wandered over and struck up a conversation. He asked me how long I'd been at the paper and what I did there.

'Since August, and I'm a news reporter. But I'd like to do sports. Football mainly.'

'Which team do you support?'

'Liverpool.'

'So do I!'

This didn't come as a surprise given he was Asian and we were in London – frankly you can't move for brown-faced Kopites in the capital. So I nodded and subtly rolled my eyes, presuming that, unlike me, he wasn't a proper Red. He didn't go the match, or at least try really, really hard to.

As it turned out he was a season ticket holder and had barely missed a game since the mid-1980s. He also ran a supporters' club. His name was Riyaz and he could sort me out with tickets and transport for every home game and quite a few away ones, too.

It was an utterly coincidental, life-changing moment.

I immediately joined the supporters' club and immediately started going to as many games as possible, with the 2006/07 season my peak year – I barely missed a game. And it's because of Riyaz (as well as Anil and Munir, the two other regulars who help sort tickets and transport for members), that I have experienced some of the best, most heart-soaring, earth-moving moments of my life; Juventus and Chelsea in 2005, Barcelona and Chelsea, again, in 2007, Inter Milan in 2008, Real Madrid home and away in 2009, Manchester United home and away last season, Everton so many times I've lost count, and numerous other games in this country and abroad.

And while the supporters' club didn't sort me out with a ticket for Istanbul, I know for a fact I wouldn't have gone had it not been for the firm sense of 'absolutely needing to be there' that being a member instilled in me (they did sort me out with a ticket for Athens, but the less said about that shambles of an evening the better).

Being part of the supporters' club has also meant the desperate desire to get hold of a season ticket has receded over the years. Nonetheless, it was a pretty special moment when the lady from the ticket office called last summer to say I was finally eligible for one.

She sounded surprised when I told her that I'd have to think about it. But as I explained, a lot had happened since I applied. Then I was 18, carefree, single and about to head off to university. Now I was 33, constantly anxious, married and trying to get my daughter into primary school. Priorities had changed and, as said, because of the supporters' club I was no longer desperate for tickets.

But then I remembered the journey. I remembered walking into Anfield for the first time as an 11-year-old with a new red hat and an immediate sense of wonder. I remembered getting back into Babu mama's Nissan Sunny and telling myself, as well as him and Ricky, that I wanted to be at the match as often as possible, that I wanted to be a season ticket holder. And I remembered writing a letter to the club asking them to put me on the waiting list, and waiting, and waiting, and waiting…

I remembered all that and, the following day, I called the lady back and told her I'd take the season ticket, that I owed it to my 11-year-old self. Her subsequent tone was that of a person who wanted to get the nutter off the phone as quickly as possible.

As it's transpired, I've barely used my ticket this season. I went to Southampton on the opening day and subsequently to Aston Villa, Stoke, West Ham, Manchester City and Manchester United. I also went to Real Madrid and Basel in the Champions League but was in the Kop for those.

In fact Shanil (who's also a supporters' club member) has used my seat (Block 125, Row 14, Seat 126, to be precise) more than I have, while a host of strangers have also sat there on the back of me returning the ticket to the club whenever my brother or I haven't been able to use it.

It's a great spec; almost dead centre and just above the goal. I've also been lucky with the people around me. There are the lovely twin brothers to my right, (one of them couldn't make Stoke, hence the crazy woman in the white coat), a couple of properly funny lads just behind me and then a young fella and his dad to my left.

It was the young fella who I got to know first. He's next to me and we got talking during the Southampton game. In between patting each other on the back when Raheem Sterling scored and embracing wildly when Daniel Sturridge got the winner, I told him this was my seat and, in turn, he told me he'd been coming to the match with his dad for over ten years.

I liked his story and liked him. We're going to be mates, I thought leaving the ground that day. No doubt.

Come Villa, the next home game, we spoke again and this was the moment to introduce myself properly.

'Forgot to say the other week, mate...my name's Sachin.'

'Nice to meet you Sachin,' he replied.

Any minute now he'll tell me his name...any minute...oh he's about to speak...here it comes...

'You seen the team? Balo's starting.'

He didn't tell me his name. He never has.

It's a bit weird and I'm now convinced he's completely forgotten that we spoke at length on the opening day and that I told him my name a few weeks later. To be fair, you can hardly blame him given the few and far between times I've actually sat in my seat. To the young fella (that's literally all I know him by), I'm just a bloke from London who occasionally shares a space he's been occupying with his dad for over a decade (and won't be there at all next season given I've recently switched my seat to the Kop).

Why have I been to Anfield so rarely this season? For much the same reasons I haven't been going regularly for a little while now – work, expense and, as painful as it is to admit, because I just don't enjoy it as much as I used to.

Don't get me wrong, the buzz of going to the match is still there. But as I've got older and felt less overwhelmed by a place I used to find so overwhelming, it thrums at a lower level. Whereas once I was desperate to go to every game possible, now I can survive on half a dozen home games and a decent number of aways per season.

I could blame my downturn in enthusiasm on a downturn in the atmosphere at Anfield. Certainly when I've been there this season it's generally bounced between flat and furious with nothing in between. And don't even get me started on the half-and-half scarves.

But to echo what Rob Gutmann wrote in his chapter, we often see these things though red-tinted spectacles. For instance, I remember plenty of games during the 2004/05 season when Anfield wasn't rocking. Ear-splitting on European nights, you could hear a Josemi drop during countless league fixtures. And I'll never forget our home game against West Ham the following season when the two fellas in front of me in the Kop spent most of the first half talking about the best way to pave your front drive. They were watching the champions of Europe for fuck's sake!

No, it's just a consequence of life. Things you once found incredibly exciting lose some of their magic over the years. Still magical but less so. Like Christmas, and going to the match.

But health and finances permitting, I'll never stop going completely. It's too ingrained, too much part of who I am – jumping on the coach with my mates, having a pre-match pint with my brother, and stepping into the light and seeing the green grass of Anfield. The place I love, the most beautiful place on earth.

And it was a place I simply had to be on the Saturday just gone. Our last home game of the season. Steven Gerrard's last home game ever.

I was definitely going to be in *my* seat when *my* captain played at *my* ground for the final time. And when he walked around to *my* end during the lap of honour I was going to give him *my* thanks, for everything. Except that didn't happen because I wasn't in *my* seat. Shanil was. *Again*.

About a week before this game our football editor, Marcus Christenson, asked if I wanted to cover it for the paper. I was torn but ultimately this was a chance to write about Steven Gerrard's final Anfield appearance, an opportunity that a Liverpool-supporting journalist like myself simply couldn't turn down.

So there I was on Saturday evening, in the Anfield press box, watching Gerrard's farewell. And as has been typical of his last 12 months, it was a disaster.

Adam Lallana's goal aside, there was nothing positive to take from the game. We were gutless and clueless, and while some of that could be blamed on the distraction of the occasion, the truth is this side has completely lost its way. I've never been as furious with them as the most furious of our fans, but post-FA Cup semi-final my level of annoyance has definitely gone up a notch or three. Quite frankly, they all need a massive kick up the arse; the players, manager and owners. Some also need to be shown the door in the summer.

Gerrard deserved better and my overriding feeling upon watching him during this game was of the hole in leadership and inspiration he is going to leave at the club. In truth, I'd been contemplating that a couple of hours before kick-off and while flicking through the programme in the press room. Unsurprisingly it was a Gerrard-fest, from the one-off cover to the photo of him as a kid on the back page, wearing our home shirt from the 1992/93 season while cleaning a pair of Adidas boots.

I stared at that photo and realised the Gerrard looking back at me couldn't have been much older than I was when I went to Anfield for the first time, indeed the shirt he had on was the very one Liverpool wore on that December day when I got my red hat and truly fell for the Red Men.

We're about the same age and his career has spanned the most significant period of my life – from boy to man, from falling in love to losing loved ones, from desperately wanting to be here every other week to, well, something a little less than that. In that sense it feels wholly appropriate that I should finally get my season ticket for Gerrard's final season at the club – the completion of the journey, for both him and I.

I shed tears when he departed down the players' tunnel for the final time, because I wasn't just saying goodbye to the captain, I was also saying goodbye to a huge chunk of my life. No longer will I watch a Liverpool player, at Anfield or elsewhere, who instantly reminds me of my youth, who *is* my youth.

I'll miss Steven Gerrard. I'll miss everything he represents.

24 May 2015, Stoke 6 Liverpool 1

'Maybe we could build a new country'

By Karl Coppack

I t's an hour to kick-off and I've got a bad feeling about this. The season ends at Stoke and no one wants to play Stoke. Ever. Stoke is the place where fancydan prima donnas can't play. Stoke is the place where the sun cannot heat. Stoke is the place where we send our cast-offs only for them to be reborn for the 90 minutes we share with them. I don't like playing Stoke.

It's a natural graveyard. It sits atop a hill, it's usually cold and the best thing about it is the journey home.

I've been there twice and that was enough. One was for a 0-0 draw under Rafa, days after his supposed 'rant', and the other the League Cup win with Kenny when Luis Suarez scored two ridiculous goals as we marched to our last trophy. That's about as good a return as most Reds will get there. I'm declaring on one draw and one win. Don't judge me.

I'm writing this on my phone on the Northern Line. I'm in work at 3pm. It's not as bad as it sounds. I may be in work but work, on Sundays, is football.

My mobile signal collapses as we go underground at Golders Green but I've seen the side. It's a side without Raheem Sterling. We've let him off.

I said this in the introduction but it still stands today. You have the advantage over me. By the time you've read this you know the score, the performance and how the whole Sterling saga plays out.

At this moment I'm disappointed that we've let him off the hook by putting him on the bench. I don't want him there. I want him scoring for Liverpool. That comes first. But I suppose he deserves some punishment. Yes it's his agent acting the goat, but it's under the player's

306

instructions. If anything I'd like him to get on just so my mates can shout at/ignore him.

I say graveyard as it's at grounds like the Britannia that managers lose their jobs. Rafa's last game was in Hull – and what is Hull but an east coast version of Stoke?

I've got a bad feeling about Brendan, too. No amount of hyperbole can cover the mess of this season, despite the PR machine rolling out anniversaries and partnerships. I'm still not sure about Brendan either. I haven't met him so can only judge on second-hand info, but I can look at his record and even that's not easy. I mean, which is the typical Rodgers season? This one or the last? I consider myself a football man and I just don't know. The owners are not football men so Christ knows how they're getting on. Anyway, it's a big day for him. Fifth or seventh. Bad or terrible.

Earlier I took to Twitter to voice a few concerns about the direction of the club. Many agreed with my worries but some are still buying the 'everything is fine' line as stated by Steven Gerrard on the pitch last Saturday. It's not, lads. Fifth isn't fine, lads. Fifth isn't par. Fifth is the best of the teams who aren't good enough.

But, I'm off to work so should plan the day ahead. I work for *The Times*. Since November I've done the odd lower-league match report. It's interesting as I write about clubs other than my own and I have to interview managers. It's a fascinating practice – finding the story, writing the story, cramming it into a word count while all the time making contacts at clubs and with other journalists. So far I'm on nodding terms with two or three. There's a great camaraderie in the press rooms. You'd think that it would all be jackal-like, but we swap information.

My favourite moment this season was during a goalless draw between Charlton and Middlesbrough at The Valley. The man to my right had been silent for the entire game but with ten minutes left he nervously poked my arm.

'Sorry, mate. Just wondered…have you seen a shot today?'

I laughed. 'One, mate. Off target. The left-back.'

'You're counting that, are you? Go on then. I'll do the same. I've got to write 1,200 words about that shot.'

Pity the poor journalist. It's not as easy as you'd think.

That said, for the last few months I've given up the games. Instead I've been helping out in the office, doing a bit of late news writing and learning, learning, learning.

Newspaper offices are great places to work. People genuinely dislike quiet times. Everyone is busy all the time. Even just watching the game is work as we record notes, look for angles, possible pictures and find the story that will engage the reader.

We all have our roles. My boss, Tony Evans, often tweets about his average day in the office. He has a million decisions to make, be it pictures or the page layout. He also has a column to write and an editorial team to organise. He has no idea how his day will pan out. My role is much simpler.

Firstly I have to watch an awful lot of football. Terrible, isn't it? Then I ring a few people and write objective prose about anything from European football to domestic bans – sometimes these words appear below my name, sometimes not.

Today I've got no idea what I'll be writing about. I never know and I love that the most. It could be about something I know or it could be the back story of Ivory Coast's goalkeeper, Boubacar Barry. That's what I do. I do stuff that no one else has time to do and I love it.

It's my last day here (it's back to match reports from August) so I'm expecting a full guard of honour and a mosaic.

I get in at 3pm. Ordinarily this means I catch the last part of the 1.30pm game, but thanks to it being the last day of the season everything kicks off at 3pm. I'm hoping that this makes for an exciting day as stories change within minutes.

Sky are showing the Hull–Man United game so I put that on one of the double monitors I have. The other shows the page layout along with my Twitter feed. My plan is to watch the game and have Twitter relay news from the Britannia.

Nice plan.

I've barely got my coat off before Tony tells me that he needs a run-down from the top seven European leagues. He needs to know who has Champions League qualification, who has Europa League and who has been relegated. Sounds easy, doesn't it? I reckon it will take ten minutes. Tops.

Forty minutes later I'm poring through pages of complicated information about the Eredivisie play-offs. It seems that relegation is decided between two teams in the top tier entering into a play-off with eight clubs from the lower division. I have to write this up in a manner which allows the casual reader to understand it perfectly, which isn't easy as I'm still not convinced myself. Add to this the amount of clubs who have won their domestic cups but have already qualified for the Champions League, meaning that the place is either offered to another club or not at all.

I was so engrossed in reams of UEFA co-efficient stats that the Liverpool game completely left my mind.

A nudge from my right. 'Stoke are one up,' Tony tells me. I grimace accordingly and get back to making sense of the Portuguese Primeira Liga. Don't get me started.

'Stoke are three up.'

I put the Portuguese on hold and check the BBC website. 3-0 to Stoke? What happened to 2-0?

The Times has an app which allows you to watch any Premier League goals seconds after they go in. I watch all three of them on Tony's phone. I issue several views on Emre Can which I express in coarse language. Then I remember that he's being played out of position so continue my invective benchwards.

Back to work and to…

'Four.'

Oh, for fu–

I don't even look up but I'm furiously stabbing my keyboard, trying to extract reason from the structure of Dutch football.

Four nil!

Four? But it's Steven Gerrard's last game and…

'Karl, it's five.'

My shoulders shudder like Sideshow Bob. I've forgotten all about Raheem Sterling, I've forgotten all about Peter McDowall's Pravdaesque question and I've almost forgotten that Holland has a four-team play-off to decide its last Europa League place and that I can't spell 'Heerenveen'. No. My mind is elsewhere and in another time. I'm at Highfield Road, Coventry, in December 1992. The scene of Coventry 5 Liverpool 1 – the biggest defeat in my lifetime, and we have to score to just match it. And we have no strikers.

I post my research through to Tony. It's in seven little blocks and I'm glad it's over. I go back to the half-time scores and stare at ours, imploring it to change.

Stoke 5 Liverpool 0

I've been on the other side of this score a few times. I was at both 5-0s against Coventry and Birmingham in the latter stages of the 1985/86 season. I have a vague recollection of a 5-0 against Crystal Palace, too. I've seen us score six against Norwich, Cardiff and Leicester City. I've seen nine against Palace and ten against Fulham. Call it luck or judgement but the worst defeat I've seen in the flesh was our first game at the Emirates when we gave Arsenal a 3-0 win where even William Gallas scored. But 5-0 though. At half-time. Against Stoke.

I'm released from this reverie when Tony taps me on the shoulder.

'I want it written, soft lad. Not as a table.'

Ah.

I thought he wanted a straight research box but he wants me to write it in paragraph form. I hold my hands up in apology and, as it's still early, we're OK. I retrieve the piece and try to think of new ways to say the word 'qualify' and 'relegated'. The piece will be subbed but I'd like to think that I'm a friend to the sub and don't make life too difficult for them.

5-1.

I barely lift my head until someone tells me it's Gerrard. I allow a small smile to form. Good lad. I'm glad it was him and that he could claw back the smallest crumb of comfort. He'll finish our top goalscorer, too. Only right and proper.

6-1.

The anger's gone now and is replaced with an intense sadness of what this means.

I watch the remains of the Hull game but my interest is waning. I don't care about Newcastle versus West Ham either. Sky do their best to tease the drama out but it's left me. 6-1 at Stoke. That it's come to this. To go so close last season and fall so far this.

Later I have to call Tony Cascarino, the former Republic of Ireland striker. He has a column in the paper called The Tony Awards where he discusses five things he's noticed in the week. He knows of my football leanings and tells me (with no glee, I should say) that Stoke spent just £3m last summer. We spent £113m and finished just eight points above them.

6-1.

Meanwhile, Big Sam™ has left West Ham in what has become football's worst kept secret. We re-jig a few pages accordingly. Newcastle staying up is a bigger story than Hull going down. Then we hear of Brendan's press conference.

It's the first time he speaks openly about the possibility of his departure. 'If the owners say I go, I go.' This is far removed from the bullish Brendan who spoke of the 150 per cent certainty of keeping his job only a few days earlier. He didn't factor in a 6-1 defeat at a ground where we scored five last season, but who the hell expected that. A defeat, maybe, but not by that margin.

The day ends and I catch up on my Twitter feed. People are angry, people are gleeful, but come midnight the humour has become gallows-based. The first team are now on a plane to Dubai. I joke that they're off to play the opening qualification round tomorrow morning.

Now I'm home via three pints and a night bus. It's very difficult to put this mood into words. I don't feel angry. I should be. I should be screaming up the M6 on my way up to the training ground to shout at the fence, but that's gone now. It's been replaced by sadness. An intense sadness. Sadness that the Liverpool I stand for has been humiliated.

I've put up with a lot. I've seen our new captain advertise male grooming products, I've seen our goalkeeper advertise doughnuts while posing in a Christmas jumper, I've seen the worst start to a season since the 1950s, I've seen us go out of Europe twice, I've seen a Wembley performance which should give the men responsible sleepless nights and I've heard things. Oh, I've heard things.

I've heard the captain practically being ordered to tell the world that the club is in safe hands, I've heard the manager say that the occasion of Wembley was a bit too much for a team crammed with internationals, I've heard fans say that I'm no fan if I criticise the ownership and direction of the club. One man told me that I should be grateful – grateful! – for letting the doughnut people give us money. I've heard excuses, arguments, counter-arguments, agendas, counter-agendas, vitriol, barbs and slanders. But never in my life have I seen Liverpool battered. Oh, I've seen Liverpool lose heavily at the Emirates, at Anfield, and a dozen other places in my time, but I've never seen us concede six goals. I've never seen us lose five goals in 45 minutes. I never thought I'd see that.

I've never been an outright fan of the manager. Nothing personal but I don't react well to that sort of personality. I have no anger for him as others do. The problem is the club. It's everything. We have major issues to address all over the place. From transfer committee to manager to players. We have to look at ourselves as fans, too. For too long we hide our weaknesses behind the blanket bluster of our difference to other fans. Yes, we may be the lowest end of a top-six side but we have Istanbul, we have generations of glory and a new way of doing thing. That's great. I'm really proud of that. I'm also really lucky. I had all of this on my doorstep. I was born one mile away from the centre circle at Anfield. But there's a downside to it. If we fall behind we look away from the real reasons and bring out the banners again. This is where music comes in.

This week Martin Fitzgerald has been writing about an R.E.M album for his site ramalbumclub.com. The site is based on an ingenious idea: he asks special guests to listen to an album of his choosing three times. They write why they don't like the band/artist, give it a listen and then give it a score. This week it's *Lifes Rich Pageant* (no apostrophe). It's one of my favourite albums and contains possibly my favourite songs in Cuyahoga.

The song is about the Cuyahoga river in northern Ohio and around which the city of Cleveland was built. The opening line is, 'Let's put our heads together and start a new country up.' Those words have been in my head all week. Isn't that what we need to do? Start a new country up?

311

At some point we have to realise that the past, no matter how glorious, has to be confined to history and kept there. It's akin to a village of stonemen living in the modern day world, talking about the glory of the flint. Yeah, great lads. Where's that getting you?

The middle eight of the song gives us this:

'Rewrite the book and rule the pages/Saving face, secured in faith/ Bury, burn the waste behind you.'

If this is the lowest ebb then maybe we could build a new country. We had Year Zero three years ago but how about one where the fans stop its ludicrous and attritional civil war? One where owners take direct day-to-day control of the club rather than sitting in overseas boardrooms. One where the manager buys his players rather than by committee so no blame can be avoided. One where the club spends every single second of every day concentrating on another league title.

This may be a bit 'I Have A Dream' but we've adopted similar strategies in the past. This season just looks like mush with targets not met, players being played out of position and absolutely no passion once things go wrong. I want a new Liverpool. I want a Liverpool which is infuriated when it goes behind. I want a Liverpool which shrugs off criticism and is unharmed by troublesome squabbles with wantaway players. I want a Liverpool which won't settle for the top four and wants to be the top of everything. Then have the urge, the passion, to do it again the year after. I don't want to be party to sponsorship deals sold as news, to nice PR pieces about the players or excuses, excuses, fucking excuses.

It's 2am now and I'm not sure what comes next. Brendan may well have gone. As I said, I've never warmed to him but I owe him for last year. Last year was ridiculous. Is he lucky or unlucky? Which is it? Do we risk waiting around to find out?

Yes, we had Year Zero three years ago but we can't keep plodding along with the same strategy hoping for a different outcome. Suffering 6-1 defeats is rare but there has to be consequences for them. Absolutely has to be. Again, you have the advantage on me here as you know what we've done and whether it's a good thing.

Anyway, the football is over and I for one am grateful. The whole club could do with a rest. But before too long it will be back to transfer gossip and the early rounds of the Europa League. I only hope we can confine this season to the bin and use it as an example of how poor seasons can be followed by better ones.

Most of all I want change. As President Bartlett in *The West Wing* says, 'The old formulas don't work anymore.' Time to write some news ones, then.

Up the Reds.

Conclusion
by Sachin Nakrani

He was leaning against the steel railings and playing with his phone. I can't remember if he was texting, but he was definitely playing with his phone. And he smiled when he saw me. And I smiled back, at him, outside Charing Cross station. My date for the evening. Karl Coppack.

It was warm, gloriously so, and we had quite the event to attend – canapés at the Brazilian Embassy, where we'd also be served free alcohol and watch Brazil's opening game of their very own World Cup. Imagine that, free food and drink while watching Brazil play at the Brazilian Embassy. And not a friendly – the World bloody Cup. Karl couldn't believe his luck. He mentioned something about leaving Ruth and us running away together…

In all seriousness it was a great night, albeit one that came about in odd circumstances. About a week earlier, I'd got an e-mail from a bloke at ESPN inviting me to watch Brazil versus Croatia at the Embassy. The way he worded the message suggested we'd met before but I honestly had no idea who he was. Nevertheless, I wasn't going to turn down this brilliant opportunity so pretended we were mates and said I'd be there, and that I'd definitely take the plus one. A load of people turned me down, so I asked Karl if he wanted to come (only kidding mate).

The Embassy's located on Cockspur Street, a short walk from Charing Cross, in the direction of St James's Square, and it was absolutely heaving when we got there on that June evening. A great atmosphere but shame about the beers, which were lukewarm. Karl and I still had a decent few and then positioned ourselves to watch the game on one of the specially set-up large screens. Brazil won 3-1, leaving the majority of those in attendance absolutely delighted. The ambassador even did a little samba (he didn't really).

313

A memorable occasion, then, but as Karl and I departed into the darkness and went our separate ways, it wasn't the food, booze or footy that was at the forefront of my mind. Instead I was mainly thinking about the chat we'd had a short while after arriving at our destination – one that has led to this, every word and page you've just read.

By the summer of 2014 I was ready to write a book. Like anyone who's even half into writing, I'd wanted to do one for ages and about ten years ago did write the first draft of a novel. It was OK, but a long way from being good and my intention was to eventually get back into it. But I never did. Life moved on.

But here I was again and this time there was to be no half-arsed measures. All in. Total commitment. And it wasn't going to be fiction, instead it was going to be about Liverpool, or Liverpool-related, or at least have Liverpool in the title. Yes, that was what I was going to do. But not on my own. No, I needed someone to do this with me, to make certain I stuck with it and ensure this thing was as good as it possibly could be.

Enter Coppack.

I first got to know Karl in early 2008. I was in my trainee year at the *Guardian* and, one quiet afternoon, was hunting around for a news story. Liverpool were playing Arsenal in the league that April and I read somewhere on the internet that money would be collected before the game for Ray Kennedy. The fundraising was being organised by The Ray of Hope Appeal and to find out more, the internet also told me, I should speak to some fella called Karl. So I did.

He seemed nice enough, provided the info I needed and even a number for Ray so I could speak to him, too. Karl warned me that Ray struggled on the phone so I had to be patient with him. And I was, while utterly in awe of the fact I was having a natter with a Reds legend.

Anyway, after our conversation Karl and I lost touch and it wasn't until I spotted him knocking about on Twitter a few years later that we started communicating again. During this time I also noticed through his contributions for various sites that Karl could write.

The thought grew that if I was ever going to produce a Liverpool book I'd like to do it with him, and so, come summer 2014, it was he who I turned to. I'm not afraid to say I was a little nervous when we met at Charing Cross because if Karl said no to my proposition, I was stuck.

I raised the topic inside the Embassy and thankfully Karl was up for it. The only question was what we were going to do. A diary of the upcoming season seemed the obvious answer and quickly and naturally we came up with a firm idea of how it should look. I honestly can't remember who suggested what, but by the time the canapés trays were heading our way again, we had a plan:

- The book would be diary of Liverpool's 2014/15 season.

- We'd write a few chapters ourselves but we'd also get a load of people we liked and/or rated, from this country and abroad, to contribute.

- The chapters would not be about the football. There'd be a decent amount of football, obviously, but they'd mainly be personal stories (as we stated to all the writers – WE'RE NOT LOOKING FOR A MATCH REPORT).

- The chapters would be long, around 3,000 words. This was going to be about varied and high-quality writing. Serious in substance if not always in tone.

There were concerns, primarily would anyone contribute given we didn't have a publisher? The plan was to self-publish, which Karl and I were happy with, but would those we wanted involved do so on that basis? Karl was pretty confident most would. He also suggested we should aim high.

'I reckon I can get Kevin Sampson to do a chapter.'

I nearly spat out my tepid Brahma.

'Kevin Sampson?! He'll never do a chapter for this.'

'I reckon he will. I'll ask him.'

'OK mate, but I can't see it. He's a proper writer, he won't want to get involved in this.'

Karl got Kevin Sampson. The author of *Extra Time*, the greatest Liverpool-related diary ever, was going to do a piece for our book. This shit was suddenly real.

And it wasn't just Kevin who said yes. Practically every person we asked to do a chapter gave us the thumbs up. It then became a case of organising who did which game (a fluid process given cup ties, personal circumstances etc) and waiting for the contributions to come through.

The joy Karl and I felt reading each and everyone's chapter. Brilliant pieces of work, week after week, month after month, and it didn't take long for the pair of us to realise we had something very special on our hands. I felt it as soon as Karl sent me his piece for the opening game against Southampton, and by the time Martin Cloake sent his for the Tottenham game in late August I was close to combusting with excitement. I remember reading both for the first time on the train into work. Fellow passengers looked at me and wondered if I was doing an impression of Meg Ryan from *When Harry Met Sally*.

This book is exactly what I visualised post-Embassy, a collection of pieces which offer a window into the heart, mind and soul of Liverpool supporters. It's been this which has always interested me most. I love a bit of tactics talk, and the odd transfer rumour will get my tail up, too, but since the day I fell in love with football, and with Liverpool FC in particular, it's been the people who feel the same as I do that have occupied the largest share of my curiosity. I've stared at them at Anfield and elsewhere, wondering what their story is, how watching 22 men kick a ball about for 90 minutes makes them feel, think and behave. How it fits into their life. What they see as the point of all this. And here in these pages are some explanations, some insight, some context.

And it doesn't just focus on the experiences of Reds, either. In that regard a special mention must be given to Martin Cloake, David Downie, Sam Long, Simon Curtis and Rebecca Knight, who all agreed to take part in a book about Liverpool despite none of them supporting the club. I can't remember when Karl and I decided we wanted to get opposition fans involved, but it was early and the reasoning was obvious – wouldn't it be brilliant to see what non-Reds thought about us and our club? That five of them, including a Bluenose, agreed to take part was and remains incredibly heartwarming. Honorary Kopites one and all, whether they like it or not.

A special mention, too, for John Barnes for agreeing to do the foreword. Yes, I know John Barnes. We've spoken on the phone. He called me 'mate' in an e-mail once. But you know, whatever.

It was in October, and on the same day I put my foot through the attic floor (don't ask), that Karl and I discovered we had a book deal. I'd make contact with Paul and Jane Camillin from Pitch Publishing a couple of months previously and pitched our idea, said how convinced I was that, all going well, it would be an incredible piece of work and stressed that Karl and I were willing to meet with them to discuss it further. Paul and Jane were interested but an invite for a coffee and a chat didn't come, leaving me fearing the worst. But then on that fraught autumn day (it was a Friday, we'd just returned from New York and the last thing I needed was having to call a plasterer out) an e-mail dropped from Jane. They wanted to publish our book and contracts were on their way.

This shit was even more real.

The proceeding months saw me, as the person managing this process, become near-obsessed with the book, as Karl can no doubt testify to. E-mail after e-mail came his way from me mentioning the book, fretting about the book, praising the book, fretting again, praising again, over and over to the point where I often found myself viewing the 2014/15 season not in terms of what it meant to me as a Liverpool supporter or to Liverpool as a club, but to the book.

I remember meeting Karl for a pint the evening before the home game against Stoke in November. Liverpool were in the midst of a properly horrible run and we naturally talked about the team, the manager, who needed to come in January. But I had something more pressing to discuss and, as quickly as possible, raised it with my drinking partner:

'We might need to change the title of the book, mate. How about calling it *Through The Wind And The Pain*?'

Karl wasn't keen, and not only because it was him who'd come up with *We're Everywhere, Us*. Stick with the original plan, was his message, as it was when I e-mailed him during half-time of 'the 6-1'. Liverpool were getting properly battered, the most battered I could ever remember, and again it was the book that was on my mind.

'We may have to reconsider the cover,' I wrote. 'It's brilliant but hardly reflective of the season anymore.'

On both occasions Karl was correct in telling me to hold firm because, as we decided at the Embassy on that hot June evening, this book isn't about the football so the title and cover should not be affected by the football. Win, lose, draw, get hammered 6-1 and fuck up at Wembley, the title works because this book is and remains about 'us', the fans, and the cover works because it captures a moment in the season when 'us', the fans again, came to the fore. No one more so than Mike Nevin. Look at him there. Legend.

Speaking of legends – Steven Gerrard. There's a lot of him in this book isn't there? The original plan was to box him off in one chapter on the basis this was likely to be his last season at the club and he came into it on the back of that horrific moment against Chelsea. Kevin Sammo was chosen to do the piece and, as I'm sure you'll agree, he did a stunning job.

But then in January Gerrard announced he was leaving at the end of the season and it was perhaps inevitable that subsequent pieces would reflect heavily on him. Hopefully this book provides a full and rich take on a man who dominated the second half of the season and has dominated the narrative of the club for even longer.

There's not much more I can, and perhaps should, add here in regards to Stevie. All I'll say is that it was really difficult watching him during those final, few months, partly because of the horrible abuse he got from dickhead opposition fans and partly because he deserved a better send-off. Those final couple of games were a disgrace to his legacy. But history will be kind to him, I feel sure of that. Karl and I may even write a book about it.

And if we do, we'll get the band back together – the 34-piece football-funk collective that have brought you *We're Everywhere, Us* (Barnes on saxophone, obviously). Seriously, I cannot put into words how grateful Karl and I are to every person who wrote for us, each showing a level of kindness, intelligence, wit, wisdom and honesty that blew our socks off and will never be forgotten. These are our lifelong friends and we thank them all.

Karl and I would also like to thank Paul, Jane and the entire team at Pitch for giving us their backing. We'd also like to thank Duncan Olner for producing the utterly brilliant cover. And yes, it is a coincidence Nevin features so prominently. A wonderful coincidence, but a coincidence nonetheless.

Finally, we'd like to thank you for reading. I'll be stunned if you haven't enjoyed this book and been moved to tears and laughter. You may also have been left a little wiser, or perhaps a little more unsure. It doesn't matter, because this book isn't about right and wrong answers. When it comes to football fans, and Liverpool fans in particular, there are none.

We're a complex and varied bunch brought together by a club. Our club. During the 2014/15 season that experience was a dire one – Liverpool lost loads of games and, in the process, lost a little bit of its soul. But the one constant remained the fans. Angry and frustrated we may have become but we stayed this course and will continue to do so, because this is what we do. This is our life.

We're going nowhere.

We're everywhere.

We're everywhere, us.